Behavioral Approaches
to Brain Research

Behavioral Approaches to Brain Research

Edited by
TERRY E. ROBINSON
Department of Psychology and Neuroscience Laboratory
University of Michigan

New York   Oxford
OXFORD UNIVERSITY PRESS
1983

Copyright © 1983 by Oxford University Press, Inc.

Library of Congress Cataloging in Publication Data
Main entry under title:

Behavioral approaches to brain research.

   Bibliography: p.
   Includes index.
   Contents: Why study behavior in brain research? :
The influence of psychological concepts on brain
-behavior research / C.H. Vanderwolf—Why measure
behavior? / S.J. Hutt and Corinne Hutt—Neurol-
ogy and the mind-brain problem (an excerpt) / R.W.
Sperry—[etc.]
   1. Neuropsychology. 2. Brain—Research—
Methodology. I. Robinson, Terry E. [DNLM: 1. Be-
havior—Physiology. 2. Brain—Physiology.
3. Psychophysiology. WL 103 B418]
QP360.B427   1983   599′.0188   82–12588
ISBN 0–19–503258–6

Printing (last digit): 9 8 7 6 5 4 3 2 1

Printed in the United States of America

Preface

The ultimate goal of most research in the neurosciences is the unraveling of functions of the many different neural systems that comprise the nervous system. A knowledge of normal function will lead to a better understanding of dysfunction, and it is hoped, to the development of effective medical approaches for treating nervous system disorders. Although we are still a long way from this goal, recent advances in the neurosciences have been tremendous. Much progress is due to the development of new methodologies. The advance in cellular and molecular neurobiology has been particularly dramatic. For example, the number of neurotransmitter and "neuromodulator" candidates seems to grow proportionately with the number of methods available for demonstrating neurochemicals. Although cellular and molecular approaches in the neurosciences obviously deserve support, we must keep in mind that the ultimate function of the nervous system is to initiate behavior (see Sperry, Chapter 3, this volume). Therefore, to ever achieve any real understanding of the brain, we must ask questions about function. To answer these questions, behavioral approaches to brain research are required.

In recent years, many people interested in behavioral brain research have expressed concern that support for behavioral approaches in brain research has suffered disproportionately, relative to support for more "molecular" approaches. The reasons why this might be the case are not clear. Perhaps advances in behavioral brain research are not considered as dramatic as methodological developments in cellular and molecular neurobiology. Controversies over the "function" of various neural systems or specific brain regions are very much in evidence. Maybe the level of controversy is mistaken for a lack of progress. Questions of function are by far the most complex and difficult to answer, and therefore do lead to differing opinions. However, only a balanced program of support for research on both the "molecular" and behavioral levels will result in any real understanding of the nervous system. The purpose of this book is to illustrate and argue the necessity and value of behavioral approaches in brain research. Although this may seem self-evident to some, it was thought it would be useful to bring together various people to discuss this thesis from different perspectives.

In the neurosciences, behavioral research usually involves one or two types of experiments. In one type of experiment, behavior is used solely as an index of activity in a neural system of interest. For example, a widely used "behavioral index" of activity in the nigrostriatal dopamine system is the rotational (circling) behavior elicited by dopamine-mimetic drugs in animals with unilateral 6-hydroxydopamine lesions of the substantia nigra (Ungerstedt & Arbuthnott, 1970). The amount of stereotyped behavior induced by large doses of dopamine-mimetic drugs or the amount of hypoactivity produced by neuroleptic drugs are other examples of behavioral indices of activity in brain catecholamine systems. The limb flicking behavior produced by LSD has been used to study hallucinogens that depress central serotonin-containing neurons (Jacobs, Trulson, & Stern, 1977). In such studies, the experimenter is usually not interested in the functional significance of rotational behavior or limb flicking per se. The nigrostriatal dopamine system did not evolve so that rats will turn in circles when they are given amphetamine by neuroscientists. However, if a behavior can be shown to be a valid and reliable indicator of activity, or inactivity, in a neural system, it may be an invaluable tool for studying that system. For example, it may be the only way to determine if an experimental treatment has functional significance. Most behaviors used in learning experiments have been of this type. The learned response is often chosen arbitrarily. Neuroscientists who study the ability of animals to press a lever, poke their nose through a photocell beam, or blink are not interested primarily in the specific learned behavior, but rather in what the performance of the behavior shows about the changes in neural systems involved in learning.

In the other type of behavioral brain research, behavior is not just a convenient "assay," but rather the analysis of behavior itself is of primary interest. The goal here is to determine how neural systems or regions function and how they interact with other neural systems to initiate or influence observed behavioral patterns. This type of behavioral brain research tends to be the most controversial type probably because the questions asked are very complex ones and the variables that influence behavior are very numerous. This type of behavioral brain research is the topic of the present volume.

The book is divided into three parts. Part I deals with the general question, Why Study Behavior in Brain Research? The fact that two of the three chapters in this section were originally published over 10 years ago underscores the fact that this question is not a new one. The first chapter, by C.H. Vanderwolf, deals with a philosophical issue of great importance in behavioral brain research and sets the tone for the rest of the book. Vanderwolf specifically asks, What kind of an approach is needed in studies of brain-behavior relations? He reviews two major approaches. One, a "psychological approach," involves the study of inferred processes. The other, a "behavioral approach," involves monitoring moment-to-moment changes in an animal's actual motor behavior. Vanderwolf very effectively argues that a behavioral approach is absolutely necessary in many areas of psychobiology today. In fact, much of the confusion and controversy that surround questions of function may be attributable to a failure of psychobiologists to study what an animal actually does. Behavior is often viewed as secondary to some inferred process, which is of primary interest. Tinbergen has suggested, "In its haste to step into the twentieth century and become a respectable science, Psychology skipped the preliminary descriptive stage that the other natural sciences had gone through, and so was soon losing touch with the natural phenomena" (cited in Hutt and Hutt, this volume, p. 15). This is probably true of much behavioral brain research.

Although different terms are often used to describe the behavioral approach advocated by Vanderwolf, one commonly used term is "neuroethological." As Vanderwolf points out, it is really more of "a combination of American behaviorism and European ethology" (p. 11). The need for a neuroethological approach in the present state of brain-behavior research has been convincingly argued by O'Keefe and Nadel (1978, p. 194). They point out that, although what they call the neuropsychological approach (Vanderwolf's psychological approach) allows greater control over the experimental situation, it is also far too limiting. They say, "When we first venture into the unknown, we need not the incisive beam of the proud penetrating laser, but the gentle diffuse illumination of the humble torch. There will be plenty of time later for detailed investigation of the nooks and crannies; first we must find the mountains. The neuropsychological approach is too myopic for the job." The point that a relatively nonstructured, observational approach is necessary to pose appropriate questions before designing highly structured, paradigmatic experiments is made in a number of other chapters in this book (e.g., see Ranck et al., Chapter 5; Whishaw et al., Chapter 8).

Chapter 2, "Why Measure Behavior?," is reprinted from the book, *Direct Observation and Measurement of Behavior*, by S.J. Hutt and C. Hutt (1970). This book is well known to many people interested in the measurement of behavior, but probably not to many neuroscientists. Although most of the book deals with techniques for measuring behavior, its first chapter seemed especially relevant to the aims of the present volume, providing excellent answers to the question above. Hutt and Hutt point out that, frequently, when attempts are made to relate brain activity and behavior, the methods used to analyze brain activity (neurochemical, electrophysiological, etc.) are explained in great detail, whereas the meth-

ods used for behavioral analyses are often crude, and dealt with superficially. In one of my favorite quotations they say, "To correlate behavioral
measurements of the crudity of better-worse, more-less with physiological variables measured to two decimal placements in micrograms is, to say
the least, faintly ridiculous" (p. 24).

This raises an important question concerning behavioral approaches to
brain research, and that is that the measurement of behavior is often considered the "easy" part of an experiment. It is relatively easy to measure
the latency of an animal jumping on a pole, the latency to step down from
a pedestal, the number of grams of food eaten, or the number of errors
made in a maze. The ease in making this kind of "behavioral measure" is
misleading because (1) it is exceedingly difficult to interpret these kinds of
measures, (2) it is difficult to know if you are measuring the appropriate
behavior(s) and (3) it is difficult to design an experiment with the appropriate behavioral controls. These issues are discussed in a number of chapters later in the book.

The last chapter in Part I was written by R.W. Sperry in 1952. It is an
excerpt from an article, "Neurology and the Mind-Brain Problem," and it
is reprinted here because it provides one of the earliest and most direct
answers to the above question. The article is now a classic, one of the best
presentations of the rationale for a behavioral approach in brain research.
In essence, Sperry argues that the brain is "a mechanism for governing
motor activity." Therefore, only by an analysis at the level of motor output will we ever understand the organization of the brain. Sperry's chapter should be required reading for all new students in neuroscience, and
older "students" would do well to reread it.

It is one thing to argue for a behavioral approach to brain research, and
quite another to design experiments in your area of interest. The chapters
in Part II of this book, "Behavioral Approaches to Brain Research," show,
by example, how the approach discussed in Part I can be used in designing experiments. The more theoretical issues raised in Part I are discussed
further in Part II.

Part I concludes with Sperry's arguments on experimental approaches
in the analysis of sensory systems and perceptual processes. He concludes
that in order to understand the neural basis of perceptual phenomena researchers must focus more on the motor output than on the dimensions
of stimulus input. It is, therefore, no accident that Chapter 4, "Vision as
a Sensorimotor System," by M.A. Goodale, follows Sperry's chapter.
Goodale has taken Sperry's advice and studied the neural basis of visual
processing using a behavioral approach. Goodale briefly reviews some of
the history and assumptions of the neuropsychological tradition in vision
research and contrasts this with what he calls a neuroethological tradition.

In the neuropsychological approach, "providing an integrated and unitary perception of the external world" (Goodale, p. 43) is considered to be the primary function of the visual system. Studies in this tradition pay little attention to the behavior of experimental animals, and in fact, immobilized or anaesthetized animals are often the preferred preparation. In the neuroethological approach, visuomotor behavior is emphasized. As Goodale shows, the picture of how the visual system is organized emerges as very different from that emerging from the neuropsychological tradition.

After reading Goodale's chapter, one wonders whether the picture, which has emerged from studies on the receptive field characteristics of cells in the lateral geniculate and visual cortex, is an accurate representation of cellular activity in animals moving freely through their environment. All of the studies by Hubel and Wiesel (e.g., Hubel & Wiesel, 1979), and many others in this field, were conducted on immobilized animals. Yet we know from other studies that the electrophysiology of both the lateral geniculate and visual cortex is dramatically different when an animal is immobile than when it is moving. For example, multi-unit activity in the lateral geniculate shows phasic relations to motor behavior; it increases during behaviors like walking and decreases during immobility or such behaviors as facewashing or lapping (Schwartzbaum, 1975). The amplitude of both visual evoked potentials and transcallosal evoked potentials recorded from the visual cortex are also related to moment-to-moment changes in motor behavior (Pond & Schwartzbaum, 1972; Schwartzbaum & Kreinick, 1973; Vanderwolf, personal communication). In other brain regions, single unit activity has been shown to be radically different depending on whether recordings are taken from immobilized or freely moving animals. For example, in a series of experiments using immobilized animals, Groves, Rebec, and their colleagues have studied the effects of various drugs on unit activity in the striatum (Groves, Rebec, & Segal, 1974; Rebec & Groves, 1975). They found that amphetamine initially enhanced neural firing in the striatum, for a short time; this was followed by a longer inhibition of activity. However, when Hansen and McKenzie (1979) performed similar experiments in freely moving rats, the firing rate of 90% of the striatal neurons was enhanced for a long period of time by amphetamine.

The major point here is that since the goal of neuroscience is to understand how the nervous system functions in normal, freely moving animals, and not just in immobilized animals, it would be wise to study freely moving animals whenever possible. The use of immobilized animals is often more convenient, especially for single unit recording studies, but the results obtained may not be generalizable to the normal animal. This point is made most elegantly in Chapter 5 by J.B. Ranck et al. and in Chapter 6 by J.M. Siegel. In the chapter "Single Neuron Recording in Behaving Mammals: Bridging the Gap between Neuronal Events and Sensory-Behavioral Variables," J.B. Ranck, Jr., J.L. Kubie, S.E. Fox, S. Wolfson, and R.U. Muller present a very thoughtful and thorough analysis of the conceptual issues involved in relating single unit activity to behavior in freely moving animals. The terminology proposed and issues raised should serve as a standard reference for those interested in relating electrophysiological events to behavior.

The critical importance of recording moment-to-moment changes in motor activity when relating electrophysiological events to behavior is also very clearly illustrated in the chapter by J.M. Siegel, "A Behavioral Approach to the Analysis of Reticular-Formation Unit Activity." Experiments involving mostly immobilized animals have related unit activity in the reticular formation to a wide variety of processes, including pain, arousal, habituation, and active (REM) sleep. Siegel shows that most reticular formation units actually fire in relation to motor activity. Siegel's chapter also highlights the importance of monitoring many different behaviors when relating brain activity to behavior. The studies by Hobson and McCarley (Hobson et al., 1974; McCarley & Hobson, 1971) relating reticular formation unit activity to stages of the sleep-waking cycle are an excellent example of how one may draw an erroneous conclusion when the range of behaviors examined has been restricted. Hobson et al. (1974) reported that units in the gigantocellular field of the reticular formation are quiescent during waking and synchronized (quiet; slow wave) sleep, but that they dramatically and *selectively* increase their rate of firing during desynchronized (active; REM) sleep. These results led to a rather sophisticated theory as to how this neural region is involved in the generation of active sleep (Hobson, McCarley, & Wyzinski, 1975; McCarley & Hobson, 1975). However, the data were obtained from restrained animals, and the behavioral states studied consisted of only "waking (W) and synchronized (S) and desynchronized (D) sleep" (Hobson et al., 1974, p. 498). Later studies by Siegel (e.g., Siegel & McGinty, 1977; Siegel, McGinty, & Breedlove, 1977) and Vertes (1977, 1979) showed that these units also fire vigorously during waking behaviors. Obviously such behaviors could not be monitored in restrained animals. Whether information obtained in studies on immobilized or anaesthetized animals can be generalized to normal behaving animals is a very serious question. It is emphasized throughout this volume that if the technology is available, studies in freely moving animals are highly desirable, since studies in immobilized animals may be misleading.

Another way of relating behavior to electrophysiological and anatomical variables, especially during development, is presented in Chapter 7,

"Behavioral Insights into Neural Changes Accompanying Visual Development and Deprivation," by D.C. Smith. Smith shows how the establishment of "brain-behavior isomorphisms" can demonstrate which physiological and anatomical factors have functional significance. Also, by using quantitative behavioral techniques, one can determine the consequences of subtle changes in cell populations that occur during development or that are induced by experimental manipulations, such as deprivation.

It is often difficult to predict which behaviors may be altered by a manipulation of brain regions. If one's focus is too narrow, the effects of an experimental procedure may be attributed to changes in one type of behavior, when in fact many types of behavior have changed. For example, from highly structured, paradigmatic experiments, it was often concluded that lateral hypothalamic lesions produced a purely motivational deficit because rats with these lesions did not eat. Later studies involving more observational approaches in which many different behavioral abilities were examined revealed a wide variety of behavioral deficits following lateral hypothalamic lesions, many of which directly or indirectly contributed to aphagia. In Chapter 8, I.Q. Whishaw, B. Kolb, and R.J. Sutherland examine the issues involved in "The Analysis of Behavior in the Laboratory Rat," in a comprehensive manner. They address many practical questions concerning what behaviors should be examined in laboratory rats following brain manipulations. The importance of studying some of the behaviors discussed is not always immediately obvious, but Whishaw et al. do an admirable job in explaining why the examination of many behaviors is relevant to determine the nature of behavioral changes.

Studies on the neural basis of learning and memory represent one area of neuroscience in which the analysis of behavioral change is used extensively as an index of an inferred process (learning or memory being the inferred process). A variety of behavioral tasks have become almost standard in such experiments; they include such tasks as one-way or two-way active avoidance, passive avoidance, and T-maze learning. However, the problems in determining what behavior(s) to study are possibly the most complex, and the most ignored, when the experimental aim is to identify neural regions involved in learning and memory. The literature on constraints on learning makes it abundantly clear that an arbitrary behavioral response cannot be used as an index of learning or memory. In Chapter 9, "The Conditioned Defensive Burying Paradigm and Behavioral Neuroscience," J.P.J. Pinel and D. Treit discuss some of the assumptions that underlie some standard learning tasks and draw interesting conclusions as to the importance of using "species-relevant" tasks.

One major goal of brain-behavior research conducted in animals other than man is to learn something about human brain-behavior relations. It is hoped that principles of brain-behavior relations will generalize from non-human animals to humans. However, the problems involved in such generalizations are often heatedly debated. It is therefore appropriate that Part III addresses these problems. In Chapter 10, "Problems and Principles Underlying Inter-Species Comparisons," B. Kolb and I.Q. Whishaw use examples from the literature to illustrate that when a sufficient number of both "class-common" and "species-specific" behaviors are studied, such generalizations can be reasonably made.

The present volume by no means addresses all the issues relevant to research on brain-behavior relations. Examples similar to those discussed can be obtained from many other areas of psychobiology. However, the goal here is really to make two major points: (1) To understand the functional organization of the brain, we must make a greater effort to integrate the rapidly developing cellular and molecular approaches in neuroscience with a more careful analysis of brain-behavior relations; and (2) we need to examine a much wider variety of behavioral situations than has been the case in the past. If the reader is convinced of the validity of these two points, the book can be considered a success.

Ann Arbor
June 1982

T.E.R.

Contributors

Steven E. Fox, Department of Physiology, Downstate Medical Center, 450 Clarkson Ave., Brooklyn, NY 11203

M.A. Goodale, Department of Psychology, University of Western Ontario, London, Ontario, Canada N6A 5C2

Corinne Hutt*, Human Development Research Unit, Park Hospital for Children, Oxford, England

S.J. Hutt,** Department of Psychology, University of Keele, Staffordshire ST5 5BG, United Kingdom

Bryan Kolb, Department of Psychology, University of Lethbridge, Lethbridge, Alberta, Canada T1K 3M4

John L. Kubie, Department of Physiology, Downstate Medical Center, 450 Clarkson Ave., Brooklyn, NY 11203

Robert U. Muller, Department of Physiology, Downstate Medical Center, 450 Clarkson Ave., Brooklyn, NY 11203

John P.J. Pinel, Department of Psychology, University of British Columbia, Vancouver, British Columbia, V6T 1W5, Canada

James B. Ranck, Jr., Department of Physiology, Downstate Medical Center, 450 Clarkson Ave., Brooklyn, NY 11203

Jerome M. Siegel, Neurobiology Research, Sepulveda Veteran's Administration Medical Center and Department of Psychiatry, School of Medicine, UCLA, Los Angeles, CA 90024

Douglas C. Smith, Department of Psychology, Southern Illinois University, Carbondale, IL 62901

R.W. Sperry,† Division of Biology, California Institute of Technology, Pasadena, CA 91125

Robert J. Sutherland, Department of Psychology, University of Lethbridge, Lethbridge, Alberta, Canada T1K 3M4

Dallas Treit, Department of Psychology, University of British Columbia, Vancouver, British Columbia, Canada V6T 1W5

*Deceased
**Present address. The article was written while Dr. Hutt was with the Human Development Research Unit, Park Hospital for Children, Fellow of St. Catherine's College, Oxford.
† Present address. The article was written while Dr. Sperry was at the Hull Anatomical Laboratory, University of Chicago.

C.H. Vanderwolf, Department of Psychology, University of Western Ontario, London, Ontario, Canada N6A 5C2

Ian Q. Whishaw, Department of Psychology, University of Lethbridge, Lethbridge, Alberta, Canada T1K 3M4

Sloane Wolfson, Department of Physiology, Downstate Medical Center, 450 Clarkson Ave., Brooklyn, NY 11203

Contents

I | Why Study Behavior in Brain Research?

1 | The Influence of Psychological Concepts on Brain-Behavior Research

C.H. VANDERWOLF

A. INTRODUCTION

In earlier times, it was generally believed that human behavior was directed by the mind or soul, a mysterious entity capable of existence independent of the material body. As knowledge of the structure and function of the human body developed, it became increasingly apparent that the central nervous system had a special role in behavior. Hippocrates, for example, knew that brain damage could result in aphasia (Esper, 1964, p. 126). Such knowledge lead to the various theories of brain-mind relations known to us as monism (materialism, idealism) and dualism (interactionism, parallelism, epiphenomenalism). In recent times, there has been a widespread acceptance of the idea that mind is closely associated with some aspect of brain activity, or even that mind is synonymous with the brain activity that controls behavior (Hebb, 1980).

Such ideas lead naturally to attempts to explain behavior and mental phenomena in neurological terms. As a result, neurological theories have had a strong influence on philosophical and psychological thought. Hebb (1980) shows how the early speculative hypotheses of Descartes gradually became a part of "commonsense knowledge" and continue to have a strong (though often unrealized) effect even at the present time. Thus, the idea that the conscious human self is something imprisoned in the brain, unable to achieve direct contact with the outside world, appears to be a direct descendant of the neurological theories of Descartes.

Neurological ideas and psychological ideas have often influenced one another. Psychological theories have had, and continue to have, an important influence on brain research. One way in which this influence is exerted is in the application of psychological concepts to brain function. According to a commonsense point of view, simple introspection tells us that we are capable of experiencing a great variety of states of consciousness or feelings, such as sensation, thought, various emotions, or volition. If mental phenomena are related to brain activity in some lawful way, it

3

is natural to assume that these traditional subdivisions of the mind will apply to the brain. Thus, there might be distinct brain processes corresponding to conventional psychological concepts. This assumption is basic to attempts to relate one or another aspect of brain structure or function to such psychological concepts as consciousness, attention, memory, affect, or emotion (e.g., Buser & Rougeul-Buser, 1978; Popper & Eccles, 1977).

Is the assumption correct? To what extent do the familiar terms of commonsense psychology really correspond to division of function in the brain? There are a large number of possible psychological processes. Skinner has compiled a list of 68 such processes. These are "sensations, habits, intelligence, opinions, dreams, personalities, moods, decisions, fantasies, skills, percepts, thoughts, virtues, intentions, abilities, instincts, daydreams, incentives, acts of will, joy, compassion, perceptual defenses, beliefs, complexes, expectancies, urges, choice, drives, ideas, responsibilities, elation, memories, needs, wisdom, wants, a death instinct, a sense of duty, sublimation, impulses, capacities, purposes, wishes, an id, repressed fears, a sense of shame, extraversion, images, knowledge, interests, information, a superego, propositions, experiences, attitudes, conflicts, meanings, reaction formations, a will to live, consciousness, anxiety, depression, fear, reason, libido, psychic energy, reminiscences, inhibitions, and mental illnesses" (Skinner, 1974, pp. 207–208). If an investigator assumes that brain function is naturally divisible into distinctive processes corresponding to psychological concepts, he must take such a list seriously (even though Skinner regards the list as an absurdity). How many mental processes are there, and how can they be defined and measured in a laboratory setting? Naively, one might assume that such questions could be resolved by careful introspection. Unfortunately when this method was tried (roughly in the period 1880–1910), it was found that mental activity is largely or entirely inaccessible to direct examination. Consequently, statements about mental activity are necessarily inferential (Hebb, 1980). This conclusion is of fundamental importance. If it is correct, then statements to the effect that behavior is determined by inner activities (presumably located in the brain) of the type in Skinner's list are hypotheses rather than the obvious truths they might at first appear to be. One must examine the factual basis of these hypotheses and consider other possible alternatives.

B. A PSYCHOLOGICAL APPROACH
TO BRAIN-BEHAVIOR RESEARCH

The program of much brain-behavior research appears to be somewhat as follows. Since psychological processes cannot be observed directly, they must be studied indirectly, inferred from objective measures of behavior or autonomic activity. If quantitative objective tests can be devised to measure specific psychological processes, then the use of such tests in combination with the techniques of experimental physiology should reveal how mental processes are organized. For example, removal of a given part of the brain should lead to a specific impairment or loss of a psychological process associated with it. This loss should result in a change in overt behavior. Alternatively, it might be possible to alter behavior through activation or depression of specific psychological processes by pharmacological or electrical stimulation of specific brain regions. It should also be possible to measure the electrical or chemical activity of specific brain regions during tests that activate specific psychological processes, thus revealing the regions where these processes occur. Some of these methods (especially unit recording and pharmacological and chemical methods) should be successful even if neurons subserving a different psychological function are intermingled with neurons subserving the function under study in the same general brain region.

An example of the psychological approach is found in research on the delayed response test, a technique devised by H. Carr and W.S. Hunter to demonstrate symbolic processes (ideation) in animals or young children (Woodworth & Schlosberg, 1960). One form of the test consists of allowing a caged monkey, for example, to watch while a raisin is hidden under one of two small cups. The cups are then concealed by an opaque screen for a few seconds or minutes (delay period) before being pushed forward to a point where the monkey can reach them. Initial correct choice of the cup concealing the raisin can be regarded as evidence of a symbolic process or memory indicating the location of the raisin. When Jacobsen (1935) later discovered that lesions of frontal association cortex in monkeys produce a profound deficit on this test, it appeared possible to conclude that symbolic processes (Morgan & Wood, 1943) or some aspect of memory (Jacobsen, 1935) were, somehow, associated with the frontal lobes.

Other psychological processes have been assessed indirectly in a similar way. Defecation, urination, and the tendency to walk about in a large open field have been used as measures of emotionality (Hall, 1934). The conditioned emotional response (Estes & Skinner, 1941) and various types of shock avoidance tasks have provided measures of fear (Miller, 1951) or of learning and memory. Tests of exploratory behavior have provided mea-

sures of curiosity (Berlyne, 1955). Strength of motivation has been assessed by measuring quantities eaten or drunk or by using an obstruction
box (Bureš, Burešová, & Huston, 1976; Miller, 1956). Various types of
autonomic measures have been used as indices of arousal or emotion
(Lindsley, 1951; Malmo and Bélanger, 1967). Performances in various types
of mazes or in lever boxes or the Wisconsin General Test apparatus have
been used as measures of learning, memory, or motivation (Kreezer, 1949;
Mackintosh, 1974).

It is important to note that in much of the research in which these tests
were used, the behavioral or autonomic phenomena actually observed have
been regarded as instruments, only, gauges to indicate hidden inner activities. Thus, the psychologist who counted the droppings deposited by a
rat in a box did so, not out of any interest in feces or in the act of defecation, but rather because the number of fecal pellets produced was regarded as an index of the level of fear or arousal. Similarly, the long preoccupation of physiological psychologists with the delayed response test (and
the related alternation tests) was not an attempt to elucidate the neurology
of a monkey's trick of finding raisins hidden under little cups. The appeal
of the test arises from its promise as a means of investigating memory or
ideation (Hebb, 1980).

Despite its initial promise, the psychological approach to brain function has been disappointing. It is far more difficult to locate and study
psychological processes in the brain than one might have imagined 50
years ago. For example, the initial conclusion of Jacobsen (1935) that frontal lesions impair memory has been challenged by a variety of rival interpretations. It has been suggested that frontal lesions impair (1) concentration or attention (Grossman, 1973, p. 402; Milner, 1970, p. 415); (2)
inhibitory functions (Rosvold & Mishkin, 1961), especially those inhibit-
ing appetitive drives and motor activity (Konorski, 1961); (3) "problem
solving whenever a process that corresponds to a flexible noticing order is
demanded" (Pribram, Ahumada, Hartog, & Roos, 1964, p. 51); or (4)
"memory specific for spatial information" (Goldman & Rosvold, 1970, p.
303). It has also been suggested that frontal lesions "increase the reflexo-
genic strength of the external stimuli" (Konorski & Lawicka, 1964,
p. 286).

It seems fair to conclude that investigators have not agreed on an interpretation of the poor performance of monkeys with frontal cortex damage
on delayed response tests in terms of impairment of any specific psychological process.

Many similar examples can be cited. For example, attempts to define a
psychological correlate of hippocampal rhythmical slow activity (RSA)
resulted in a number of rival theories variously claiming a relation to at-

tention, arousal, motivation, frustration, recall, memory, and learning (Black, 1975). Thus, single brain areas or single patterns of brain activity have been related to a variety of psychological processes. Further, individual psychological processes have been related to a great variety of brain areas or patterns of brain activity. For example, attention has been related to (1) the ascending brainstem reticular formation (Lindsley, 1961); (2) nonspecific medial thalamic nuclei (Jasper, 1958); (3) the cingulate gyrus (Kaada, Jansen, & Andersen, 1953); (4) the hippocampus (Bennett, 1975); (5) the parietal cortex (Mountcastle, 1978); (6) the superior colliculus (Wurtz, Goldberg, & Robinson, 1980); (7) the globus pallidus (Hassler, 1978); (8) efferent fibers that suppress sensory input at a peripheral level (Hernandez-Peon, Scherrer, & Jouvet, 1956); and (9) the dorsal noradrenergic bundle (Mason & Iverson, 1979). None of these hypotheses is widely accepted; none has been decisively refuted.

As Newell (1973) put it in a commentary on the state of experimental psychology, "clarity is never achieved. Matters simply become muddier and muddier as we go down through time. Thus, far from providing the rungs of a ladder by which psychology gradually climbs to clarity, this form of conceptual structure leads rather to an ever increasing pile of issues, which we weary of or become diverted from, but never really settle."

In order to understand this state of affairs, we must examine more closely some of the assumptions implicit in the psychological approach to brain-behavior research.

1. One of the functions of scientific theories is the designation of certain phenomena as important and worthy of serious study, whereas other phenomena are designated as "trivial." For example, detailed knowledge of the interconnections of neurons is currently held to be of great importance, whereas minor irregularities in the shape of the skull are trivial. At one time, phrenological theory made the appearance of small bumps on the skull seem very important. In the psychological approach, the implicit assumption appears to be made that most of what is important in the brain-mind-behavior field can be discovered by putting animals in boxes or seating humans at tables and recording their success in solving various problems. (This criticism can also be made of American behaviorism—see below.) It is assumed that the basic processes revealed in such tests will apply straightforwardly to more complex situations. As a result of these assumptions, many important problems have received little or no study. For example, although lesions of the frontal lobes lead to remarkable changes in social behavior (Myers, 1975; Myers, Swett, & Miller, 1973), this effect was ignored for many decades by physiological psychologists interested in frontal lobe function. This is unfortunate, since a thorough study of monkey social behavior and the effects of frontal lesions on

it might elucidate the basis of the "personality" changes seen in humans
following damage to the frontal lobe.

2. One major effect of this preoccupation with psychological concepts
has been a failure to observe, describe, and analyze behavior adequately,
as Skinner (1950, 1966, 1974) has pointed out repeatedly. Failure to describe the details of overt behavior may be due to the fact that, in humans,
a given psychological state can apparently be manifested by a variety of
different behaviors. Thus, when a man feels cold he may respond by putting on a sweater, turning up the thermostat, building a fire, etc. Such
observations may suggest that the details of overt behavior are of little
importance in understanding why behavior occurs. A variety of different
behaviors can be regarded as indicators or "measures" of a given psychological process and a broad range of different behaviors need not be studied.

However, other considerations (see below) suggest that detailed study
of a broad range of behavior is essential in the brain-behavior field. The
neglect of such study has impeded research seriously. For example, the
neglect of overt behavior has resulted in a situation in which, despite many
decades of brain lesion and behavior studies, we still lack adequate descriptions of the effect of most types of brain lesions on animal behavior.
Currently this situation is being rectified with respect to hypothalamic
and cortical lesions (Golani, Wolgin, & Teitelbaum, 1979; Levitt & Teitelbaum 1975; Robinson & Whishaw, 1974; Schallert & Whishaw, 1978;
Vanderwolf, Kolb, & Cooley, 1978), but a great deal remains to be done.

3. At a methodological level, the preoccupation with inferred psychological processes has had the effect of diverting researchers from a thorough analysis and description of the behavioral tests used in experiments.
For example, although there is evidence that such factors as the dimensions of the test apparatus have an effect on rat behavior (Denny & Thomas,
1960), there does not appear to have been any serious attempt to study
the effect of varying test conditions with a view to developing optimal
standardized apparatus. Carried over into the brain-behavior field, lack of
standardization of tests may be partially responsible for the conflicting
results that are often reported. For example, O'Keefe and Nadel (1978)
have tabulated the results of various tests in animals with hippocampal
lesions. A remarkable feature of their tables is the variability in the data
they summarize. Thus, their Table A19 reveals that in non-spatial discrimination reversal tests, six studies showed no deficit after hippocampal
lesions, whereas eight studies showed deficits. In one-way active avoidance (Table A21), eight studies showed no deficits after hippocampal lesions, four showed deficits, and three showed mixed results. One can only
express the hope that if the controlling stimuli were identified and if the
test procedures were more carefully standardized than they are at present,

at least one source of variability in this field would be eliminated.

4. Psychological concepts do not appear to be susceptable to prec.ᴜᴄ definition. It is commonly assumed that this problem can be circumvented by providing clear "operational" definitions. Thus, "attention" might be defined in terms of performance in a signal detection task; "fear" might be defined in terms of heart rate or of a psychometric scale to be checked off by a human subject. However, such procedures do not solve the original problem of definition, since it is always possible to provide alternative operational definitions and the different definitions may not agree. It is an empirical fact that different measures that, intuitively, may seem to reflect the activity of a single psychological process frequently do not correlate with one another (Anderson, 1938; Bindra & Thompson, 1953; Bolles, 1959; Hall & Kobrick, 1952; Miller, 1956). For example, the amount of work an animal will do to get food and the amount it will eat might be regarded equally as measures of hunger. However, these measures fail to correlate in many situations, suggesting, perhaps, that the assumption of an underlying unitary hunger state is inadequate. Similarly, one must question the implicit assumption of some learning theorists (Hull, 1943; Rescorla & Wagner, 1972) that different behaviors can be used interchangeably to measure the same basic learning processes. The mere fact that our language includes a particular psychological term is not a sufficient basis for assuming the existence of a unitary neural process corresponding to that term.

Hebb (1980, pp. 44–45) offers a defense of the use of psychological concepts in the brain-behavior field on the grounds that we need concepts for complex as well as for simple levels of organization. Thus, "anxiety" stands in relation to "firing of neurons" much as the structure of a bridge stands in relation to the molecular structure of steel. In both cases, concepts at different levels of organization are equally valid as descriptions of reality. There can be no question that we require concepts for complex levels of brain organization and behavior. However, there are many possible sets of concepts from which to choose. Conventional psychology offers one set; psychoanalytic theory another. Behaviorists and ethologists are frequently content to describe the movements and postures visible to an observer without troubling themselves with inferred psychological processes at all. Consequently, although Hebb's argument is a good defense of the necessity of general concepts of *some* sort, it is not a defense of any *particular* set of concepts.

The use of psychological concepts in brain-behavior research encourages the belief that we already understand the broad outlines of cerebral organization. However, as we have seen, it is possible that the categories suggested by conventional psychological theory are misleading or nonexistent. Perhaps we do not yet possess the broad concepts ultimately needed to understand how the nervous system generates the phenomena we call behavior.

C. A BEHAVIORAL APPROACH TO BRAIN FUNCTION

The view that the brain is primarily a device for regulating motor output was expressed clearly by Sechenov well over a century ago. According to Sechenov (reprinted 1965, p. 3) "The infinite diversity of external manifestations of cerebral activity can be reduced ultimately to a single phenomenon—muscular movement. Whether it's the child laughing at the sight of a toy, or Garibaldi smiling when persecuted for excessive love of his native land, or a girl trembling at the first thought of love, or Newton creating universal laws and inscribing them on paper—the ultimate fact in all cases is muscular movement." If movement is the ultimate outcome of all cerebral activity (disregarding autonomic and endocrine effects, for the moment), then it might be advisable to study motor activity, or behavior, as a phenomenon in its own right and not merely as an index of hypothetical mental states. Such an approach has been advocated by American behaviorists, particularly J.B. Watson (1913) and B.F. Skinner (1938, 1974). According to Watson (1913, p. 176), "What we need is to start work upon psychology, making *behavior*, not *consciousness*, the objective point of our attack" (italics in original).

However, despite their emphasis on behavior as an independent field of study, American behaviorists have been content to analyze a rather restricted range of behaviors, focusing particularly on learning as displayed in various contrived situations such as lever boxes. This choice of research topics may have been dictated by the wish (emphasized by Watson) to work in fields in which a direct contribution to human welfare might be made. Since learning plays an immense role in human behavior, the study of learning in animals was seen as useful and was strongly emphasized. An interesting short history of behaviorism is provided by Ratliff (1962).

K. Lorenz and N. Tinbergen, and their fellow ethologists, have favored a broader approach to behavior (Lorenz, 1950; Tinbergen, 1951, 1963, 1972, 1973). Their initial aim has been to describe *all* the behaviors that occur in a given species under natural conditions. It is noteworthy that particular behaviors were not selected for study on an *a priori* basis. Even behaviors that at first might appear inconsequential were carefully observed and described. This emphasis on an inductive empirical approach does not mean that the study of behavior was carried on in an "atheoretical" manner. Theory was provided by a consideration of the significance of behavior for such broad biological problems as adaptation and evolution. The early descriptive phase of investigation of behavior has been followed by more analytical studies of selected behaviors with a view to discovering causal mechanisms. This has lead to neuroethology, a discipline that attempts to account for the naturally occurring behaviors of animals in terms of the activity of the central nervous system.

It is not widely appreciated among neuroscientists that, despite many superficial differences (e.g., heredity vs. learning; laboratory studies vs. naturalistic observation), American behaviorism and European ethology have a strong fundamental resemblance. Tinbergen (1963, p. 411) defined ethology as the "biological study of behavior." However, he asks in a later publication (Tinbergen, 1965, p. 10), "What exactly *is* animal behavior?" The answer he provides is "on the whole—we tend to call 'behavior' movement or a change of movement, including the change from motion to absolute nonmotion or 'freezing'—in short, what one can directly observe."

It appears that a combination of American behaviorism and European ethology offers the neuroscientist a broad scientific basis for studies of nervous system function. In opposition to this conclusion, it is often said that "behaviorism" in any form is an inappropriate starting point for neuroscience research, since it appears to ignore the internal determinants of behavior. If we attempt to understand the neural basis of behavior, we must, so the argument runs, take into account such internal processes as attention, motivation, emotion, and memory. The difficulty with this argument is that it takes for granted the rather questionable proposition that the brain is organized in accordance with psychological categories. An alternative view, which is compatible with behavioristic or ethological approaches, is that the brain is organized extensively in terms of its output, i.e. motor activity. It can be argued that the brain evolved largely as a result of selection pressures on behavior. In higher animals, survival and reproductive success are heavily contingent on behavioral performance, regardless of how it is achieved. According to this view, elaborate sensory systems and complex central processing capacities are useful only insofar as they contribute to a motor output, the consequences of which promote survival and reproduction. If this is so, the prime function of the central nervous system must be one of controlling efferent output (including the output that governs endocrine and autonomic activity). Consequently, one might expect the brain to be organized extensively in terms of its outputs, especially that of behavior.

As Sperry (1952, p. 298–299; Chapter 3, this volume) put it: "all brain excitation has ultimately but one end, to aid in the regulation of motor

coordination. Its patterning is determined throughout on this principle."
Sperry continues: "Instead of regarding motor activity as being subsidiary, that is, something to carry out, serve, and satisfy the demands of the
higher centres, we reverse this tendency and look upon the mental activity
as only a means to an end, where the end is the better regulation of overt
response."

Discussion of ways in which this general approach can be translated
from the level of a rather vague theory to realistic experiments form the
subject matter of a number of chapters in this book (e.g., Goodale, Chapter 4; Siegel, Chapter 6; Whishaw et al., Chapter 8). Thus, if one studies
"vision", as Goodale does, the ultimate aim is to explain, not "visual perception," but rather how visual stimuli control particular behaviors. Visual stimuli may control posture, head and eye movement, individual limb
movement, locomotion, "freezing" (cessation of all movement), and circadian activity cycles, as well as a variety of autonomic and endocrine
phenomena that vary considerably from one species to another. In the
traditional approach to vision, little emphasis has been placed on the output that ultimately results from a visual input. However, when output is
considered, it appears that a large number of input-output channels are
distinct in a neurological sense. Thus, circadian activity cycles are probably controlled by a direct retinal input to the hypothalamus (Rusak &
Zucker, 1975), whereas visual control of head and eye movement involves
neurons of the superior colliculus (Goodale, 1983; Wurtz et al., 1980).
Visual influences on reproductive functions depend on the accessory optic
tract (Hoffman, 1973). Visually elicited cessation of licking or face-washing movements in a rat are not associated with activation of ascending
reticular inputs to the hippocampus, although such activation regularly
accompanies visually elicited head movements or locomotion (Vanderwolf, 1969). This suggests a different involvement of the ascending reticular formation and hippocampus in the two types of behavior.

A degree of separateness of different input-output channels undoubtedly extends to complex learned behaviors. A number of years ago,
McCleary (1961) showed that shock avoidance behavior involving locomotion depended on different brain areas than shock avoidance involving
non-locomotion (passive avoidance). Other studies showed that different
conditioned responses in situations involving electric shock (locomotion,
"freezing," vocalization, defecation) were abolished selectively by various
brain lesions (Maher & McIntire, 1960; Vanderwolf, 1962, 1963). Conditioned eye blink responses to light or sound develop quite normally in
hemispherectomized cats (Norman, Villablanca, Brown, Schwafel, &
Buchwald, 1974) although, as we know from other work (Pinto-Hamuy,
1961), locomotor conditioned responses develop poorly or not at all in

animals whose cerebral hemispheres are extensively damaged. Such data suggest that it may be necessary to modify the popular view that there is a common repository for engrams which is accessible to many different inputs and has the ability to control many different outputs. Instead, it is possible that many individual sensorimotor channels include synaptic linkages that are capable of modification (plasticity), independent of other channels. Thus, "learning" may occur at many points in the nervous system depending on the nature of the controlling stimuli and the response required. At a minimum, one can conclude that the nature of the motor response, as well as the nature of the sensory input, is important in the investigation of the modifiability of behavior and should be studied much more carefully than it usually is.

The extent to which brain activity is organized in terms of overt behavior remains an open question. The beginning of the answer may be provided by recent studies on reticulocortical activity. For several decades, the ascending reticular activating system has figured prominently in discussions of the cerebral basis of such psychological processes as consciousness, attention, emotion, and motivation. However, critical examination shows that psychological theories of reticulocortical activity do not account for the known facts. It appears that ascending reticular activating pathways comprise at least two subsystems. One of these subsystems is responsible for any cerebral activation that may be present during behavioral immobility and reflexive behavior; the other ensures the occurrence of cerebral activation during such voluntary movements as locomotion (Vanderwolf & Robinson, 1981). In this volume, Siegel (Chapter 6) reviews studies in which reticular unit activity is reported to be closely related to motor activity.

An important implication of recent behavioral studies of the function of the reticular formation is suggested by the well-known fact (French, 1960) that the reticular formation controls the activity of virtually the entire nervous system. Thus, if the activity of the reticular formation is organized in terms of motor output to a high degree, it seems to follow that much of the remainder of the nervous system will also be active in relation to motor activity. Therefore, a behavioristic or ethological approach is likely to be an important avenue to further advances in our understanding of central nervous system function.

2 | Why Measure Behavior?

S.J. HUTT and CORINNE HUTT

A. INTRODUCTION

One aim of this book is to show how recent thinking in ethology, the biological study of animal behavior, may contribute significantly to an objective, quantitative and descriptive science of behavior. The conjunction of *descriptive* and *science* will be an anathema to many experimental psychologists, but we maintain that for certain problems (and for the study of certain subjects) direct observation of the free behavior of the organism is the method par excellence. Some workers, notably clinicians, have correctly identified some of the problems for which observational methods are the appropriate tool, but they have been careless in their application. What is required in observational studies, but is seldom applied, is a degree of rigor in measurement commensurate with that expected of experimental studies.

Techniques of systematic observation are not themselves new: they have been used scientifically, at least since the time of Darwin (1872), in studying the behavior of men and of other animals. The heyday of observational studies of behavior was the 1920's and early 1930's. Zoologists and psychologists each concerned themselves with the "systematic recording in objective terms of behaviour in the process of occurring, in a manner that [would] yield quantitative individual scores" (Jersild & Meigs, 1939). Zoology, while giving increasing prominence to controlled experiments, has continued to be sustained by a core of field studies; coherent and comprehensive principles of animal behavior (see, for example, Hinde, 1966, and Marler & Hamilton, 1966) have been induced as much from observational as from experimental studies. Psychology on the other hand has witnessed a gradual decline of observational studies. Very little is now heard of the early observational work on humans; even in child development, where such studies have always been more popular then in other

Reprinted with minor editing from S.J. Hutt and Corinne Hutt, *Direct Observation and the Measurement of Behavior*, Springfield, Ill.: Charles C Thomas, 1970, pp. 3–14 (with permission).

areas of investigation, estimates of recent studies employing exclusively observational techniques have been as low as 8 percent (Wright, 1960).

Several reasons have been given for this decline of interest in direct observation: "Experimentally-oriented workers soon decreased their interest because of the degree to which the method (that is, observation) permitted and perhaps even encouraged absence of manipulative control over the situation in which the behaviour occurred" (Nowlis, 1960). Systematic observation "also lacks the clean, decisive flavour of an experiment" (Gellert, 1955). Probably the overwhelming reason for this decline of interest in direct observation was the psychologist's need for scientific respectability. Tinbergen (1963) puts the case thus: "It has been said that, in its haste to step into the twentieth century and to become a respectable science, Psychology skipped the preliminary descriptive stage that other natural sciences had gone through, and so was soon losing touch with the natural phenomena." Hence by 1960, in a review of studies of child development, Mussen was able to comment that "There are proportionately fewer purely descriptive, normative studies, and more studies geared to the 'whys' of children's behavior." Mussen's preceding sentence shows clearly that he regards this as one of the "signs of scientific maturating." A decrease in descriptive, normative studies however is not evidence *eo ipso* of scientific maturation. Astronomy, which ranks as an important scientific discipline in its own right, is based entirely upon observation. In this chapter we wish to restate the case for using observational techniques as an essential part of behavioral studies. We shall first consider some of the areas in which such techniques may be applied.

B.   BEHAVIORAL REPERTOIRE

Many psychologists might wish to take issue with the statement quoted above from Tinbergen (1963); we regard the statement as essentially true. Present-day psychology is essentially an analytical science, concerned with the whys of behavior, and as such its method is experimental. It is often forgotten that an animal in an experimental procedure already has a well-established behavioral repertoire and that knowledge of this repertoire may be essential to understanding the results of an experiment. In other words, before attempting to modify behavior, we need to know what behavior there is to modify. A detailed knowledge of the natural history of behavior is necessary from several points of view.

The animal under study may have an endogenous cycle of activity in which the periodic waxing and waning could be erroneously attributed to the experimental conditions. Such periodicities have been described in the behavior of a wide variety of animals from lizards (Hoffman, 1960) through rodents (Richter, 1965) to man (Thomae, 1957; Aschoff, 1965). The sleep states are an obvious manifestation of periodicity in human activities. Since responsiveness to stimuli is a function of the state of the organism, we might expect that a stimulus repeatedly presented would elicit periodic responses. If the underlying endogenous periodicities are not adequately documented, it may be tempting to interpret the changes in responsiveness as evidence of (say) habituation and dishabituation.

A detailed analysis of the motor patterns recruited by an animal may give a much more precise indication of what motivational changes may be taking place within the animal's central nervous system than a single measure, such as bar pressing, chosen on the basis of its ease of instrumentation.

An almost allegorical example of the importance of detailed behavioral observation is provided by a study of memory-interference effects in rats (S. Zinkin, personal communication). If a rat is placed on a stand above the floor of a cage, its normal response is to step down fairly rapidly to the floor. If the floor is electrified so that the rat receives a shock as it steps down, it is likely to do so less rapidly the next time it is placed in the apparatus. This situation has been used to test the effect of ECS (electroconvulsive shock) on memory. It has generally been thought (e.g., Chorover & Schiller, 1965) that ECS, if administered soon enough after a learning trial, will disrupt the consolidation process believed to be necessary to establish a long-term memory trace. In the step-down situation, this effect appears to be demonstrated if animals who have received the treatment after a shock to the feet show no retention of the learning trial when tested 24 hours later. However, retention is always assessed in terms of the animal's step-down latency, no other aspect of its behavior being studied. Zinkin suspected that other components of the animal's behavior might indicate retention. She therefore carried out an experiment in which not only was the step-down latency measured before and after various treatments, but also several other aspects of the animal's behavior were recorded after stepping down. The results were somewhat surprising. There were many animals who, after treatment, stepped down from the platform just as rapidly as before treatment (often in less than one second). However, their behavior after they had stepped down changed dramatically compared with that before treatment. Animals who previously had stepped down and then spent the next 30 seconds exploring the apparatus, were now likely to freeze on the grid floor for the whole 30-second observation period. Others, after a delay of perhaps 10 seconds, attempted to jump out of the apparatus. This type of behavioral change was found as frequently in the animals who had received ECS one-half second after the learning trial as in those who had received only the punishing foot-shock. These changes were not seen in animals who had had no treatment.

If only latency had been recorded (and this could have been done automatically without even looking at the animal) the interpretation would have been that foot-shocked animals had remembered the learning trial but the others had not. By studying what the animal was actually doing, it was apparent that at least some retention was present in both experimental groups. The theoretical importance of this and of subsequent studies by Zinkin is considerable. The fact that, as a result of observation of the animals rather than the timing device, studies with an accepted interpretation for over two decades should have been thrown into theoretical disarray is a salutary lesson.

Lack of knowledge of the behavioral repertoire of experimental animals can often lead to experiments that are quite unsuitable to answer the question for which they were conceived. Riess's experiment (1954) to test the innateness of nest building in rats is such a case. From shortly after birth female rats were reared in isolation in wire mesh cages that did not provide them with any opportunity to handle objects. Later, they were allowed to mate and were then placed with their young in a test box containing only strips of paper. The mother rats neither built nests nor retrieved their young. Instead they scattered both the paper and their young around the cage with the result that many of the nestlings died from lack of care. Riess concluded that during ontogeny the rat learns to build nests and retrieve young through experience in handling objects.

Eibl-Eibesfeldt (1961) carried out an experiment that was identical with that of Riess except that he used virgin females who were experienced in nest building. When placed in the test box, none of them began building, and only three out of ten animals had built within five hours. The explanation for Riess's results was, according to Eibl-Eibesfeldt, that when placed in a novel environment, rats first freeze and then show escape and exploratory behavior. These behaviors inhibit all others, and it does not require much biological sophistication to recognize that such a hierarchy of behavior patterns would have survival value. It is only when the environment has become fully familiar that nest building begins. If, on the other hand, isolation-reared rats were tested in their home cage, eight out of thirty-seven animals began building immediately, and all had built within five hours. In contrast with Riess, Eibl-Eibesfeldt also made detailed observations of the motor patterns used by the animals in nest building. The behavioral sequence could be subdivided into 11 discrete elements, e.g., collecting, grasping, and depositing. The morphology of these elements was identical in the experienced and isolation-reared animals; only the sequence was different. Inexperienced animals would often employ an element too early or too late in the sequence for it to be optimally useful.

Clearly Eibl-Eibesfeldt's results did not support Riess's interpretation that rats learn to build nests through experience in handling objects. The behavior patterns of nest building are available, given an appropriate material, as tools ready to be used. Only the optimal ordering of the elements has to be learned.

Eibl-Eibesfeldt's study has many interesting implications that are amplified by a number of complementary studies not mentioned here. For our purposes the lesson to be drawn is clear. Without a detailed knowledge of the behavior patterns normally exhibited by animals, inept experiments may be set up which in turn lead to misleading conclusions. In Riess's investigation the main independent variable, rearing in isolation, was of little relevance in understanding the ensuing behavior of failing to build nests, since a crucial fact about the normal everyday behavior of rats was not known to the experimenter.

It may be hazardous to treat any behavior as biologically irrelevant. Some activities are derived, that is they contain elements from sequences of behavior that occur in other situations. So-called displacement activities are of this kind. Displacement activities are behavior patterns that appear to be inappropriate in the environmental context: They may appear as an unexpected discontinuity with respect to antecedent behaviors, they may have components of motivationally contrary behavior patterns (e.g., approach and avoidance), or they may occur in the absence of their usual causal antecedents. Fidgeting, nailbiting, nose picking in humans, rocking in higher primates, twirling in dogs, and staring down in gulls are all of this kind. In recent years evidence has accrued suggesting that displacement activities may have an arousal-reducing function (Stone, 1964; Delius, 1967; Hutt & Hutt, 1968). It is difficult to see how the notion of displacement activity could have arisen without the 'displaced' activity having been seen in its original functional context.

Again in some animals, and indeed in some humans (as we shall see below), certain behavior patterns seen in the laboratory may have no counterpart in the animal's natural habitat, and vice versa. Thus Lehrman (1962) warns: "Analyses of behavior based solely on the behavior of captive animals may represent important distortions of the actual ways in which the animals relate to their natural environment." This leads us to the second main area in which direct observation is required.

C. ADJUSTMENT TO PHYSICAL AND SOCIAL ENVIRONMENT

There are certain major areas of human and animal behavior the very concern of which is how the subject relates to his natural environment, both physical and social. Adjustment to the physical environment comprises the group of behaviors of particular importance in the development of the young of the species: exploration and play. Exploration has been described as that behavior that "brings the organism into contact with certain selected parts of the environment rather than others . . . any behavior, motor or perceptual, which has as its end-state contact between organism and selected portions of its environment" (Dember & Earl, 1957). It has been pointed out that most early learning in children comes about through exploration of their environment:

> To a great extent learning comes about through the motility, exploratory behaviour, or curiosity of the child. It occurs in response to environmental changes produced by the manipulations of the individual himself or of other persons. In his "search for novelty" as Piaget terms it, the child explores the actions of doors, drawers, stairs and light switches, learns to produce the effects which intrigue him and learns to avoid the hazards they impose (Strauss & Kephart, 1955, p. 166).

There is little possibility of obtaining real-life records of the development of exploration and learning in this sense except where the life history of individual children are completely known (see Hutt, 1967b). The monumental work of Piaget has been very largely the result of intensive behavioral observations of a limited number of children; *The Origins of Intelligence in the Child* is a model of painstaking observations made on his own children.

Exploratory behavior can be studied by simulation of a real-life situation to which children are first familiarized and in which they are then introduced to standard novel objects. Since part of the interest of such studies is in the range of behaviors displayed by the child, only direct observation by an observer is both sufficiently flexible and sensitive to record the nuances that ultimately may prove important.

The social environment of an animal comprises the contacts between individuals we might call communication, cooperation, aggression, and territoriality. In animals and young children, such transactions are largely carried on by means of nonverbal signals, and it is only by virtue of detailed observational analysis that the morphological vocabulary can be ascertained. A spate of books in aggression (Carthy & Ebling, 1964; Lorenz, 1966; Morris, 1967; Storr, 1968; Russell & Russell, 1968), which have freely homologized from subhuman to human mechanisms, has served to emphasize the need for an adequate analysis of the components and organization of human aggressive behavior.

Even where a relatively sophisticated level of verbal analysis of a problem is possible, it is doubtful whether a questionnaire study of how subjects *say* they behave is a suitable substitute for a real-life situational analysis of how they actually behave. The kind of discrepancy that may arise between report and fact is shown by the classic series of studies by Hartshorne et al. (1928, 1929).

The aim of these studies was to "apply the objective methods of the laboratory to the measurement of conduct under controlled conditions" (Hartshorne & May, 1928). Children were given written ethical judgment tests and were then observed in real-life situations involving ethical behaviors, such as cooperation and honesty. Cooperation was studied by observing the children in real-life situations offering the child the opportunity of doing work for, or giving away things to, other children or of taking and retaining things for himself. To test honesty, party games, athletic contests, classroom and everyday situations were arranged with inherent opportunities for cheating and (apparently) little likelihood of detection. In fact, the tests were devised so that the observer not merely could detect cheating but could measure its magnitude. For example, the children were sent on standard errands with excess change, so that the amount appropriated could be measured. The correlations between ethical judgment scores and scores on the tests of actual ethical behavior were around + .25. (It is of interest that the correlation between the scores on the ethical judgment tests and intelligence was + .70, suggesting that good intelligence confers some fluency in telling lies.) As Rosenweig (1948) comments: "What the subject says about his behavior and personality is a very unsafe guide for prediction about his actual performance in real-life situations." This brings to mind Gellert's (1955) complaint of the time-consuming and cumbersome nature of direct observation studies. Regrettably, if we are to find out how people actually behave when they are not being tested by psychologists, there seems to be no substitute for detailed and painstaking observation. Ethologists apparently have never felt the need to spare themselves this drudgery, in the knowledge that there are no shortcuts to scientific postulates. In the following sections we shall consider a number of areas in which research workers have been particularly determined to find such shortcuts.

D.   UNCOOPERATIVE SUBJECTS

Professional psychologists have become so used to finding a constant supply of eager volunteers, ready to play almost any game, that psychology, the scientific study of human behavior, has become virtually synonymous with performing mental tests and working laboratory gadgets. Indeed, it probably would be no exaggeration to say that over 95 percent of our total information about how human beings behave is based upon studies in which the subject's total behavior repertoire is reduced to one or two responses to a carefully regulated stimulus constellation.

When faced with the problem of finding out how a hitherto neglected subgroup of *Homo sapiens* behaves, the natural tendency of the psychologist is to reach for his handbook of psychometric tests or manual of laboratory methods. It therefore comes as a shock to find that the subjects under study are neither willing nor able to answer conundrums, to fill up questionnaires, or to work laboratory models. There are two main subgroups of *Homo sapiens* who are particularly perverse in these respects: preschool children and psychiatric patients. In general, the younger the child, the less likely he is to cooperate in investigations involving traditional psychological paraphenalia; should he be both young and psychiatrically disabled, he ceases to be a viable object of scientific psychological inquiry.

One of the aims of direct observation studies is to bring within the purview of objective analysis the behavior of subjects who might otherwise be excluded by virtue of their unsuitability, for psychometric or laboratory study. The main reason for looking toward ethology for guidance is that its subjects of inquiry too have been free ranging and hence relatively uncooperative. The ethologist learns to work with the behavioral data the animal provides in his natural habitat. While fundamentally more complex, the behavior of *Homo sapiens* can in principle be treated in the same way as that of any other animal studied in his natural habitat.

E.   CLINICAL ADJUSTMENT

While interesting questions can be, and have been asked about the perceptual and learning abilities of schizophrenics in laboratory situations, the questions usually asked about a patient by doctors and medical ancillaries are ones about his aggressive and impulsive behavior, his eating habits and personal hygiene, his working and social relations. These behaviors are usually subsumed under the umbrella term of *adjustment*. Since important (and expensive) decisions depend upon the correct evaluation of this ill-defined concept, it is not surprising that those entrusted with such decisions are impatient if all the psychologist has to offer are measurements of reaction time, susceptibility to illusions, and so on. Granted that such measurements are relevant—and we are not arguing for or against—their validity must still be established against criteria of adjustment derived from real-life situations outside the laboratory or testing room.

Whatever meaning we attach to the term adjustment, which consists of an amalgam of behaviors, all of which are necessary but none sufficient to define it, it has to be assessed in the patient's own habitat. Most of the behaviors that would have to be included in an estimate of personal adjustment are directly observable; they are therefore in principle quantifiable. Here however, a curious phenomenon is encountered. Although almost all the physical and physiological data about a patient are measured to at least one decimal point on parametric scales, the behaviors of the patient, with the exception of the small proportion measurable on psychometric tests, are given only ordinal ratings. The rating may be as rudimentary as good–poor, better–worse, or it may contain odd numbers of items up to seven arranged on an ordinal scale. Often the midpoint of such a scale is treated as an optimal or neutral condition from which the variable in question may deviate in either direction.

In general, ratings of adaptive behavior have been of three kinds: (1) A single, easily observed variable is chosen as representative of behavior as a whole. For example, an assessment of locomotion may serve as an indicator of the overall behavior of a hyperkinetic child or of a catatonic schizophrenic patient, since aberrant motor behavior is such an obvious feature of each disorder. This we shall call the *representative* model. (2) Assessments are made, again on ordinal scales, of several different areas of behavior, the scores from each assessment being added to give an overall measurement of behavior adjustment (the *additive* model). (3) A single gross assessment is made which purports to characterize behavior as a whole (the *global* model). It seems to us that each of these approaches has an inherent weakness.

The representative model comes to grief because it ignores the fact that behavior has a structure. The word structure is used about behavior in much the same sense as it is used in building. If a building has to fill a certain space we have a restriction upon the total amount of material which can be used in its construction. If we assume that the building will be comprised of certain elements, say mortar, bricks, wood, glass, nails, we may juggle with the amounts of each which will be used; but for every increase in one element, there will have to be a corresponding decrease in one or more of the others. In behavior, we again have a finite number of elements which can be displayed with a temporal restriction, not all behaviors can be manifested in unit time. If one element of behavior increases, it must be at the expense of others. Thus if we restrict our attention to one variable, we must not assume that other variables bear a monotonic relationship to it. For example, a drug administered to reduce or increase the prevalence of one behavior may have no effect upon, or even an adverse effect upon, an equally undesirable behavior. A drug such as Ospolot, which produces the greatest reduction in the aggressive behavior of an hyperkinetic child (Hutt et al., 1966) may actually increase his locomotion. Changes may therefore be best assessed in terms of shifts in the structure of behavior.

A particularly unfortunate example of the practice of adding ordinal assessments of several behavioral variables is provided by a study of the effects of changes of occupational regime upon the behavior of chronic psychotic patients (Hutt et al., 1964). Assessments were made on five-point scales of the patient's locomotory, eating, and toilet behaviors, speech retardation, and delusional utterances. The scores on each five-point scale were then added to provide an overall measure of adjustment. This practice is to be deplored on at least three grounds. In the first place, most of the 20 variables could have been measured objectively without resort to the crudity of ordinal guesswork. Degree of speech retardation can easily be assessed by recording speech samples and counting their rate of generation (Hutt & Coxon, 1965); number of delusional utterances per unit time can be counted (Rickard et al., 1960); and amount of food eaten, frequency of spilling can all be counted (Ayllon & Michael, 1959). Where a variable actually can be measured, there is no justification for ordinal assessment. In the second place, it is manifestly absurd to add ordinal scores for delusions, for cleanliness, and for cooperativeness to obtain a gross score for adjustment. Qualitatively, these are different subsystems with their own appropriate units of measurement. To add them is as indefensible as adding together watts, decibels, and centimeters to give a measure of bigness. In the third place, the practice is indefensible on statistical grounds. Each scale is highly correlated with the others, since all are a function of the underlying physiological process illness called schizophrenia or depression. To add measures that are themselves intercorrelated is to produce spuriously large changes in scaled scores for minimal changes in the underlying physiological process.

Whether a single global measure can legitimately be used to characterize behavior as a whole is a matter of considerable doubt. The intelligence quotient is probably the only measure that even approaches such a role. However, just as the contributions of the subitems of an intelligence test to the global IQ measure are unequal, so are the weightings given to different behaviors in assessing (say) social adjustment. This is seen clearly in the study already referred to (Hutt et al., 1966) of the effects of drugs upon hyperkinetic behavior in an epileptic child. When nurses and other medical staff were asked to say which drug regime improved her behavior most, they unanimously selected the one that had increased attention span most even though it was less effective than other drugs in reducing destructive activity. It is thus clear that the global assessments attached greater weight to attention span than to other variables. The nurses themselves were quite unaware of this bias. We might thus argue that the notion of a global assessment is illusory.

F.   CORRELATIONS OF BEHAVIORAL AND PHYSIOLOGICAL MEASURES

Even if an assessment were truly global, it would be open to one conceptual criticism that it shares with both the representative approach and the additive approach above. Behavior may be treated as either the dependent or as the independent variable of an investigation. In the first case, changes in behavior are measured in response to specific stimuli, to prevailing environmental conditions, or to alterations in the subject's internal milieu effected by drugs, brain disease, epileptogenic lesions, etc. In the second case, changes in the subject's behavior are observed while records are collected of electrocerebral activity, of metabolic changes, skin temperature, and so on. In almost every case, behavior is being correlated with variables that can be specified with great precision on a parametric scale. A sound stimulus can be quantified in terms of its frequency, band width, sound pressure level, rise time, and other characteristics; a drug may be specified in terms of its concentration, its dosage, its blood plasma level. The concentration of sodium and potassium ions in a blood sample may be precisely determined, the power-density spectrum of an electroencephalogram epoch may be measured, and so on. To correlate behavioral measurements of the crudity of better–worse, more–less with physiological variables measured to two decimal places in micrograms is, to say the least, faintly ridiculous. In physics such a situation would be treated with derision. Yet this is the situation which obtains in psychology.

Let us take for a typical example a correlative study of the "behavior" of psychiatric patients and catecholamine metabolite excretion (Nelson et al., 1966). Six psychotic patients (two schizophrenic, one manic-depressive, and three depressed) were studied over periods varying from 20 to 74 days. At the same time each day the patients were observed and interviewed, following which a sample of urine was taken. The trouble taken over the biochemical analysis of the urine and of the analysis of behavior contrast markedly:

> The urine was refrigerated; after collection, aliquots of all samples were frozen until processed. The samples were analyzed for creatinine, metadrenaline (MA), and normetadrenaline (NMA). The analysis for MA and NMA involved ion exchange resin purification, bidimensional paper chromatographic separation, and photometric quantitation. All samples were tested in duplicate. The coefficient of variation of duplicate measures was 8% for MA and 11% for NMA. Mean recoveries of NMA and MA were 71% ($\pm$9) and 84% ($\pm$9), respectively (p. 217).

The presence of metadrenaline and normetadrenaline was determined in nanograms per milligram creatinine. An attempt was then made to correlate the metabolite excretion with behavior during the previous 24 hours.

> When possible, direct quotations of the patient regarding expressions of emotional states and attitudes were recorded. In addition, the notes of continuous observation by the ward staff were obtained from the hospital record. Both sets of behavioural observations were organized and recorded before the urinary levels of catecholamines were determined and were presented to two psychiatrists, neither of whom was acquainted with the patients involved. These judges were asked to evaluate independently the patient's course and to identify periods of relatively homogeneous behaviour. Gross changes in physical activity, eating and sleeping patterns, social interaction, and emotional content of speech were used as major indicators of behavior (p. 217).

Although three references are given to technical papers showing precisely how the biochemical assays are made, no information is given as to the circumstances and form in which the behavioral information was recorded or for how long. Except by later inference from the diagrams in the paper, we have no idea what kind of information was given to the two judges whose task it was to provide a perfunctory quantification of the material. What, for example, are periods of homogeneous behavior? It was found that the course of each patient's illness could be divided into three stages: an initial period of "psychotic turmoil," a period of "relative equilibrium," and finally a period of "anticipation and mild anxiety during the terminal part of hospitalization as a patient began to prepare for adjustment outside the hospital." The judges' task was to decide whether the notes on the patient's behavior suggested primarily a state of psychotic turmoil (given a numerical value of 3), a state of relative equilibrium (value of 1), or a state of mild anxiety and anticipation (value of 2).

It is not surprising perhaps that the results of the study are somewhat equivocal. In some subjects there appears to be a positive relationship between phase of illness and metabolite excretion, and in others, a negative relationship. The overall trend is slightly positive. Had a detailed quantitative analysis been made of the behavior, it would have been possible to apply a powerful parametric statistical test to the data. As it is, we are left with at least one doubt: the role of increased motor activity in determining the metabolic excretion. We are told categorically that the results could not have been explained on these grounds: "The changes observed are greater than those produced by mild exertion and none of the patients engaged in more than moderate amounts of activity." What meaning are we to attach to the terms mild and moderate? In the preceding two sentences we are told: "Exercise even in moderate amounts, increases the secretion of NA and A. The increase in these hormones is roughly parallel to the amount of *physical* activity, so that mild exercise, as in everyday experience, is sufficient only to produce moderate elevations in NA and A." Are we to assume that psychotic excitement and agitation are not in quantity sufficient to account for the elevated metabolite excretion at behavioral rating 3?

One of the main features of so-called psychotic excitement is increased physical activity. It is interesting therefore that the only significant differences found in the study were between rating 3 and the others for the total creatinine and normetadrenaline determinations. We presumably have to accept the authors' contention that physical activity was not the operative factor, but the point could have been settled beyond dispute had they made time-sampling observations each day of what in practice is quite the simplest behavioral variable to quantify, locomotion. Moreover, had a more systematic quantification of behavior been undertaken, we would have been in a much stronger position to evaluate whether we were dealing with a statistically reliable association, a suggestive trend, or a procedural artifact.

If we appear to have been overbelligerent to this study, it is because the study illustrates a general feature to which we take exception in the correlation of physiological and behavioral findings: the hidden assumption that either it is too difficult or too much trouble to quantity behavior with anything like the precision of the physiological data.

3 | Neurology and the Mind-Brain Problem

R.W. SPERRY

A. INTRODUCTION

The discrepancy between physiological processes in the brain and the correlated psychic experiences to which they give rise in consciousness has ever posed a baffling puzzle to students of psychology, neurology, and the related sciences. Despite steady advancement in our knowledge of the brain, the intrinsic nature of mind and its relation to cerebral excitation remains as much an enigma today as it was over one hundred years ago.

Interest in the problem of the mind-brain relationship extends far beyond the immediate concerns of neurology and psychology. Inability to comprehend the essence of mind has been a major obstacle to the progress of philosophy throughout its history. Questions such as those concerning scientific truth, the nature of reality, and the place of man in the cosmos require for their study some knowledge of the constitution, quality, capacities, and limitations of the human mind, through which medium all such problems must be handled. Much of man's religious dogma and his moral and even legal codes is deeply influenced in the final analysis by mind-matter concepts. In fact, all the ultimate aims and values of mankind could be profoundly affected by a thoroughgoing rational insight into the mind-body relationship. It was the broad significance of the problem as much as the difficulty of reaching a solution that prompted William James (1890) to declare that the attainment of a genuine glimpse into the mind-brain relation would constitute "*the* scientific achievement before which all past achievements would pale."

The struggles of philosophy with psychophysical problems, although carried on over centuries and by some of the greatest thinkers in history, have as yet failed to produce anything of much satisfaction to the tough-minded scientist. Further progress from philosophical synthesis can be

Excerpt reprinted with minor editing from *American Scientist*, 1952, *40*, 291–312 (with permission).

expected only after science has succeeded in furnishing philosophy additional data with which to work. For example, we shall be in a much better position to study mind-brain relations after we have attained some conception of the neural patterning involved even in such simple mental activities as the perception of color, time, pattern, size, and the like. Eventually it should be possible to list the special features that distinguish those brain excitations that are accompanied by consciousness from those that are not. Once this latter objective is achieved, it may be feasible, at last, to attack the mind-body problem with some effectiveness.

It is really the "brain" part of the mind-brain relation that most urgently needs clarification. Neurological science thus far has been quite unable to furnish an adequate description of the neural processes involved in even the very simplest forms of mental activity. Once the unknown neural events become sufficiently understood, it may be found that the mind-brain problem will tend to resolve itself. In any case, hope for progress now seems to lie entirely in this direction.

Accordingly we may by-pass many blind alleys of philosophical controversy, and turn immediately to the neural correlates of conscious experience. In the following discussion we shall be concerned principally with the nature of the neural processes themselves, keeping in mind questions such as the following: How do the brain patterns of visual sensation, for example, differ essentially from those of auditory or other modes of sensation? How does the pattern of brain excitation in the visual perception of a triangle differ from the excitation involved in perceiving a square or a circle? And so on. Thus, we propose to deal primarily with definite scientific questions subject to objective scientific answers in neurological terms.

B. CURRENT STATUS OF THE PSYCHONEURAL DILEMMA

Any immediate attempt to relate brain processes to psychic experience appears rather discouraging. To provide the colorful richness and infinite variation of quality and meaning in mental experience we find only a mass of brain tissue consisting essentially of closely packed nerve fibers and cell units roughly similar to one another in constitution, in structure, and in physiological function. Such variation in size, shape, chemistry, conduction speed, excitation threshold, and the like, as has been demonstrated in nerve cells, remains negligible in significance for any possible correlation with the manifold dimensions of mental experience.

Near the turn of the century it was suggested by Hering (1913) that different qualities of sensation, such as pain, taste, and color, along with other mental attributes, might be correlated with the discharge of specific modes of nervous energy. Electronic methods of recording and analyzing nerve potentials, developed subsequently, have however failed to reveal any such qualitative diversity. A refined constitutional specificity among neuron types was demonstrated by other methods (Sperry, 1951; Weiss, 1950). However, proof is lacking that this specificity influences in any manner the quality of impulse conduction. It seems rather to be operative primarily in the developmental patterning of the neural circuits. Although qualitative variance among nerve energies has never been rigidly disproved, the doctrine has been generally abandoned on a number of grounds in favor of the opposing view, namely, that nerve impulses are essentially homogeneous in quality and are transmitted as "common currency" throughout the nervous system.

Impulses traveling in the optic, auditory, proprioceptive, and other sensory pathways are, accordingly, believed to be similar in nature. "It is not the quality of the sensory nerve impulses that determines their diverse conscious properties but rather the different areas of the brain into which they discharge." This is the current point of view, and it seems to be warranted. When an electric stimulus is applied to a given sensory field of the cerebral cortex in a conscious human subject, it produces a sensation of the appropriate modality for that particular locus, that is, a visual sensation from the visual cortex, an auditory sensation from the auditory cortex, and so on (Penfield, 1938). When one looks for intrinsic differences in the matrix of these sensory fields that might account for qualitative psychic differences, there is disappointingly little to be found. Slight variations in the size, number, arrangement, and interconnections of the nerve cells have been demonstrated, but as far as psychoneural correlations are concerned, the more obvious similarities of these sensory fields to each other and to all other cortical fields, including the association and motor areas, seem much more remarkable than are any of the minute differences. Furthermore, sensations as diverse as those of red, black, green, and white, or of touch, cold, warmth, movement, pain, posture, and pressure, apparently may arise through activation of the same cortical areas. For these and other reasons the reference of subjective quality to cortical locus, in itself, has little explanatory value. What seems to remain is some kind of differential patterning effects in the brain excitation. We may state, rather vaguely, that it is the difference in the central distribution of impulses that counts.

In short, this brain theory encouraged us to try to correlate our subjective psychic experience with the activity of relatively homogeneous nerve-cell units conducting essentially homogeneous impulses through roughly homogeneous cerebral tissue. To match the multiple dimensions of mental experience we can only point to a limitless variation in the spatiotemporal patterning of nerve impulses. The difference between one mental state and another is accordingly believed to depend upon variance in the timing and distribution of nerve excitations, not upon differences in quality among the individual impulses.

On the foregoing points there is comparative agreement (Adrian, 1946; Boring, 1942; Clark, 1947). When we proceed to the question of exactly how conscious meaning is related to the spatiotemporal patterning of brain excitation, all certainty is lost and we enter an area of free speculation. The oldest, simplest, and very common notion on this matter holds that brain patterns resemble in form, and in a sense copy in miniature, outside objects and those of consciousness. For example, in the visual perception of a simple geometric figure like a triangle, the brain pattern is considered to be, at least roughly and with certain qualifications, triangular in form. This doctrine, formally called *psychoneural isomorphism* (Kohler, 1929), has been extended to correlations in intensity, and in temporal organization as well as in spatial patterning. It appears to receive some direct support in the anatomical evidence that the sensory surfaces, such as the retina, skin, cochlea, and so on, are in fact projected onto the brain centers according to an orderly topographic plan.

In a corollary of this hypothesis adopted particularly by the Gestalt school of psychology (Kohler, 1929; Koffka, 1955; Kohler & Wallach, 1944; Kohler & Held, 1949) it was contended that subjective experience is not correlated with the orthodox neural excitations traveling along fiber pathways, as commonly supposed, but rather with secondary electrical fields and currents that these excitations create in the brain tissue. The secondary electrical patterns, with their "field forces," are conceived to be massive and to spread through and between the nerve cells and fibers, pervading the cerebral tissue as a volume conductor. Unlike the scattered array of separated impulses from which they are generated, these mass patterns are unified and continuous in nature and therefore more like the patterns of subjective experience. This added correspondence in continuity and unity, along with the postulated similarities in form, intensity, and temporal patterning already mentioned, is believed to alleviate the discrepancy between neural and psychic processes.

Isomorphism, as has been stated by Boring (1942), represents the most natural and naive way of dealing with mind-brain relations. It is implied unintentionally in a great deal of scientific as well as lay thinking about brain function, especially where perception, imagery, or memory is involved. For example, the neuroanatomist unwittingly works on this premise when he searches the brain for fiber pathways to unite the two halves of the visual field, which—inconveniently for the concept of isomorphism—are projected separately to opposite hemispheres of the cerebral cortex.

When the philosophical and logical basis of isomorphism is examined, its seeming metaphysical solace tends to dissolve, and it becomes difficult to see how anything is gained by having the neural processes copy the contents of consciousness. Furthermore, experiments designed specifically to test the importance of the postulated field forces in cerebral organization failed to disclose any significant influence of such factors (Lashley, Chow, & Semmes, 1951; Sperry, 1947). Finally, it seems to me that our general knowledge of brain structure and physiology has for many years been quite sufficient to rule out any possibility that cerebral processes duplicate, even remotely, the patterns of subjective experience. This point is amplified in some detail below.

Other theories of perception based more closely on the classical concepts of brain physiology ignore or deny any need for psychoneural isomorphism. In an effort to account for the retention of perceptual habits following destruction of major portions of the brain areas involved in learning, Lashley (1942) suggested that incoming sensory excitations may spread outwardly in waves that travel along the homogeneous fiber feltwork of the cortex. These spreading waves are presumed to set up widespread interference patterns such that any visual figure—a triangle, for example—becomes translated in the brain into a multi-reduplicated "scotch-plaid" type of pattern extending over the entire cortical area. All correspondence in shape with the original figure is lost in the reduplicated brain patterns.

Another hypothesis proposed to account for our knowledge of universals and the perception of auditory and visual forms (Pitts & McCulloch, 1947) postulated a scanning function to the alpha brain rhythm, which, as it passes up and down through the successive layers of the cortex, is supposed to bring about an enlargement and reduction inversely of the incoming sensory patterns. The authors of this theory expressly denied that the spatiotemporal distribution of brain excitations representing a given figure need resemble the actual figure in any simple way.

A third, rather different picture of the perceptual process was proposed by Hebb (1949). Convinced that visual perception occurs beyond the sensory receiving area of the cortex, he attempted to follow the sensory pattern deeper into the brain. The type of excitation process arrived at, although vague in actual detail, retains even less resemblance to the original stimulus pattern than in the two foregoing theories.

In these and other hypotheses of perception it was assumed in opposition to the tenets of isomorphism, that sensory stimuli become transformed in the brain into patterns of excitation that need not resemble in any way either the original stimulus or the contents of consciousness. The brain is presumed to work with a kind of code of its own, in which the symbols bear no direct correspondence to the mental experiences they represent.

With the doctrine of psychoneural isomorphism rejected along with that of specific nerve energies, some such codal scheme has seemed to be the only remaining alternative. The problem is thereby reduced to that of discovering the correct nature of a brain code based on the patterning of homogeneous nerve impulses. Even these restrictions have continued to leave a wide range for speculation. Advancements in neurology and psychology tended progressively to limit this range, but its boundaries were again widened by contributions from the field of computing-machine and signal engineering. Again one can find estimations of the contents of consciousness based on the total number of possible combinations and permutations of neuron elements. Other writers would code mental information into individual neurons, and still others into their protein molecules. The scope and diversity of opinion to be found in the current literature reflect our general confusion and almost complete lack of guiding principles.

Whereas the doctrine of psychoneural isomorphism purported to bridge the mind-brain gap through principles of similarity and correspondence, the various "coding" schemes left one with no basis whatever for resolving the problem. Even the most neurologically sophisticated of these latter hypotheses, as now stated, seemed only to exaggerate rather than to minimize the mind-brain dichotomy. Perhaps as a hang-over from early behaviorism, many investigators continued to pride themselves on a deliberate policy of ignoring entirely any questions that touch upon the relation of subjective experience and neural activity.

The following comment of Charles Sherrington (1933) remains as valid today as when he wrote it 50 years ago: "We have to regard the relation of mind to brain as still not merely unsolved, but still devoid of a basis for its very beginning." It is not a solution we aspire to but only a basis on which to begin.

C. A DIFFERENT APPROACH TO THE PROBLEM

A tentative attempt is made in the following discussion to point out and to justify another approach to the interpretation and understanding of mental activity. So far, only the vague outlines of the scheme are discernible. Even these outlines, however, if they could be verified, would help considerably to orient our efforts and would automatically eliminate much misguided speculation.

The proposed scheme rests on a view of brain function that was most nearly approximated in the old motor theory of thought, now largely abandoned. Despite its recognized shortcomings and errors, this forsaken offspring of behaviorism taken in combination with the pragmatism of C.S. Pierce (1878) possibly holds the key to a comprehension of brain function far advanced beyond anything developed subsequently. An analysis of our current thinking will show that it tends to suffer generally from a failure to view mental activities in their proper relation, or even in any relation, to motor behavior. The remedy lies in further insight into the relationship between the sensori-associative functions of the brain on the one hand and its motor activity on the other. In order to achieve this insight, one-sided preoccupation with the sensory avenues to the study of mental processes will need to be supplemented by increased attention to the motor patterns, and especially to what can be inferred from these regarding the nature of the associative and sensory functions [see Goodale, Chapter 4, this volume]. In a machine, the output is usually more revealing of the internal organization than is the input. Similarly in the case of our thinking apparatus, an examination of its terminal operations and finished products may be more enlightening than any amount of analysis of the transport of raw materials into it.

Only after we have attained some understanding of the way in which the sensory and thought processes become transformed into motor activity, can we hope to comprehend their meaning and plan of organization. Only then can valid working principles be found to curb and to guide future theorizing [see Vanderwolf, Chapter 1, this volume.]

Utilization of this motor approach immediately helps us to view the brain objectively for what it is, namely, a mechanism for governing motor activity. Its primary function is essentially the transforming of sensory patterns into patterns of motor coordination. Herein lies a fundamental basis for the interpretation, direct or indirect, of all higher brain processes including the mental functions. At first thought such statements will probably seem most short-sighted and unsatisfactory. Nevertheless, for purposes of scientific analysis, a perspective of this kind seems necessary, and we may turn now to an attempt to justify it.

Partial support is found in phylogenetic considerations, which indicate that the vertebrate brain was designed primitively for the regulation of overt behavior rather than for mental performance. As one descends the vertebrate scale, purely mental activity becomes increasingly insignificant compared with overt response. Among the salamanders and lower fishes, where thought processes are presumably negligible, the bulk of the nervous apparatus is clearly concerned with the management of motor activity. To the extent that sensation and perception are evident, these would appear to serve directly for the guidance of response. From the fishes to man there is apparent only a gradual refinement and elaboration of brain mechanisms with nowhere any radical alteration of the fundamental operating principles. In man as in the salamander the primary business of the brain continues to be the governing, directly or indirectly, of overt behavior.

Overt behavior, upon analysis, we find to be constituted almost entirely of patterns of muscular contraction. It follows that the principal function of the nervous system is the coordinated innervation of the musculature. Its fundamental anatomical plan and working principles are understandable only on these terms.

Further support for this point of view may be found in the study of brain architecture. One searches the cerebrum in vain for any structures that seem to be designed for the purpose of forming, cataloguing, storing, or emanating copies or representations of the outside world. If any scheme or plan at all is evident in the complicated fiber associations and nuclear interconnections of the brain, it is a design patterned throughout for governing excitation of the "final common (motor) pathways." Such information as is now available regarding physiological functions of the various brain centers correlates with the anatomical data to support the same thesis.

To the neurologist, regarding the brain from an objective, analytical standpoint, it is readily apparent that the sole product of brain function is motor coordination. To repeat: *the entire output of our thinking machine consists of nothing but patterns of motor coordination.* The neurohumoral and glandular components may be disregarded in this discussion. We may also disregard the various by-products of brain activity such as heat, electric potentials, carbon dioxide, and other metabolites released into the bloodstream, cerebrospinal fluid, and surrounding tissues.

This classification of the electric potentials as an irrelevant by-product rather than an important end product of brain activity requires some comment, inasmuch as certain authors have considered these to be the essential correlates of consciousness. It is well established that brain activity generates electrical currents and potential changes which vary greatly in rate and amplitude. These phenomena extend well beyond the confines of the brain and may be recorded readily at the surface of the scalp. It would be difficult or impossible at this point to furnish irrefutable proof that the manufacture of these electrical changes is not a major object of cerebral activity. However, many reasons for doubting it, both direct and implied, will be found throughout the present discussion.

In our scheme these stray mass potentials have no more special function or meaning than have the similar electrical currents that pervade the entire body whenever the heart beats, muscles contract, and so on. There is no evidence that they react back upon the processes that produce them or otherwise influence these processes in any significant fashion. Brain organization, we suspect, is maintained in spite of these secondary electrical effects, not because of them. In a conscious patient with brain exposed under local anaesthesia it should not be difficult to pass electric currents through a sensory field of the cortex during perceptual tests. We would anticipate no functional disturbance provided the currents were maintained within the normal physiological limits. Insofar as electrical changes do operate directly in the conduction of nerve impulses, synaptic transmission, maintenance of excitatory thresholds, and so forth, they constitute an essential part of the brain function itself and are not to be classed as one of its end products.

The layman naturally assumes the major work of the brain to be the manufacture of ideas, sensations, images, and feelings, the storage of memories, and the like, and often expects the physical correlates of these to be some kind of aural end product phosphorescing within the cortex or emanating from its convolutions. These subjective phenomena may, however, be regarded as phases of brain function itself, not products of it. Scientific analysis has failed to disclose any output at the cerebral level other than the miscellaneous by-products mentioned above. Excepting these, the entire activity of the brain, so far as science can determine, yields nothing but motor adjustment. The only significant energy outlet and the only means of expression are over the motor pathways.

Thus, whether accompanied by consciousness or not, all brain excitation has ultimately but one end, to aid in the regulation of motor coordination. Its patterning is determined throughout on this principle. It follows that efforts to discover the neural correlates of consciousness will be more successful when directed on this basis than when guided by arbitrary correlations with psychic experience, stimulus patterns, or outside reality, or by analogies with various types of thinking machines.

The above approach to mental functions may require some shift in our customary perspective on the interrelation of cerebral and motor processes. Instead of regarding motor activity as being subsidiary, that is, something to carry out, serve, and satisfy the demands of the higher centers, we reverse this tendency and look upon the mental activity as only a means to an end, where the end is better regulation of overt response. Cerebration, essentially, serves to bring into motor behavior additional refinement, increased direction toward distant, future goals, and greater overall adaptiveness and survival value. The evolutionary increase in man's capacity for perception, feeling, ideation, imagination, and the like, may be regarded, not so much as an end in itself, as something that has enabled us to behave, to act, more wisely and efficiently.

Perceptions and ideas are found, upon analysis, to have their factual significance and meaning in terms ultimately of overt operation. Their meaning derives from the potential effect, that is, the difference they make or may make in behavior. In both its phylogenetic and ontogenetic histories, mental activity develops out of, and in reference to, overt action.

Actually the interrelation of motor and mental activity is one of cyclic and reciprocal interdependence. However, the nature of the problem and current trends in our thinking make it necessary at this time to emphasize particularly the dependence of the mental upon motor activity.

Any separation of mental and motor processes in the brain would seem to be arbitrary and indefinite. Mental processes are intimately associated with other integrative mechanisms, which we are accustomed to recognize as serving for the regulation of motor adjustment. Sensory and associative processes, conscious and unconscious alike, are obliged to merge and interlace in the brain with the motor patterns. There are no boundary planes in the cerebrum to keep the two apart. In many or most situations overt response is guided closely and directly by the excitation patterns of thought and perception. Temporally, therefore, as well as spatially, the mental and the motor patterns must integrate, mesh, and interlock.

The same relationship is indicated in more specific anatomical and physiological observations. The great pyramidal motor pathway from the cerebral cortex is constituted of fibers that arise from many cortical areas, sensory as well as motor. Motor responses may be elicited directly by electrical stimulation of sensory areas, as, for example, the visual and the somesthetic cortex. The extrapyramidal motor outflow from the cerebral cortex likewise arises from associative and sensory cortical fields as well as from those traditionally designated as motor. Excitation patterns in the sensory and associative areas, therefore, have to integrate with patterns in the subcortical motor systems as well as with those in neighboring motor fields.

In brief, we conclude that the unknown cerebral events in psychic experience must necessarily involve excitation patterns so designed that they intermesh in intimate fashion with the motor and premotor patterns. Once this relationship is recognized as a necessary feature of the neural correlates of psychic experience, we can automatically exclude numerous forms of brain code that otherwise might seem reasonable but that fail to meet this criterion.

It follows further that the more we learn about the motor and premotor mechanisms, the more restrictions we add to our working picture of the unknown mental patterns and hence the closer our speculation will be forced to converge toward an accurate description of their true nature.

D. SUMMARY

At the core of all metaphysical problems stands the mind-brain relationship, real understanding of which could have vast influence on all the ultimate aims and values of mankind. The logical, philosophical, and semantic approaches to the question, though employed intensively by some of the greatest of human minds, have repeatedly failed to yield a satisfactory resolution of the problem. Hope for further progress is seen to lie in a scientific analysis of the neural correlates of psychic experience, and the present discussion has been restricted primarily to this essentially neurological problem.

Present-day science is quite at a loss even to begin to describe the neural events involved in the simplest forms of mental activity. Conjecture has been vague and varied, ranging from theories in which the brain patterns are supposed to parallel and to copy roughly the contents of consciousness, to a series of codal schemes in which psychic experience is represented by implication in various brain codes with no other meaningful psychoneural relation indicated.

An approach to the interpretation of higher brain functions is here suggested in which motor adjustment, rather than stimulus patterns or the contents of subjective experience, figures predominantly as a proper frame of reference for understanding the organization, meaning, and significance of brain excitation. Such an approach would seem to guarantee at least a better understanding of the brain processes themselves. Whether this in turn may help to resolve the baffling mind-brain enigma remains to be seen.

ACKNOWLEDGMENT

For the basic concept developed in this discussion concerning the relation of mental processes to motor adjustment the author is indebted to the unpublished lectures and informal teachings of the late Professor R.H. Stetson, chairman of the department of psychology at Oberlin College, 1909–1939.

II | Behavioral Approaches to Brain Research

4 | Vision as a Sensorimotor System

M.A. GOODALE

A. INTRODUCTION

Few students of perception today believe, as Kepler and Descartes did in the Seventeenth Century, that the inverted image falling on the retina provides our internal representation of the external world. Instead, most would agree with Neisser (1968), who has argued that although "light enables us to see . . . optical images on the retina are only the starting point of the complex activities of visual perception and visual memory." In modern theories of perception, the retinal image provides only the raw material for the constructive activity of the visual system. Visual perception is regarded as an active, not a passive process, in which our visual world is constructed from information provided by these rapidly changing retinal images as our eyes move about, as well as from information retrieved from our memories of past visual input. Nevertheless, most contemporary theories of perception share with Descartes the view that the function of the visual system is to provide us with an internal representation of the outside world and the objects and events within it.

Most accounts of the neural organization of the visual pathways have tended to reflect and reinforce this view of visual perception. Although single-unit analyses of the pathway from retina to primary visual cortex and beyond have emphasized the specificity of individual cells in terms of their receptive field properties and degree of binocularity, the multiple inputs and their cortical transformations have been considered as part of a single (albeit complex) perceptual system. Cells sensitive to particular spatial frequencies, orientation, or retinal disparities and others sensitive to different rates and direction of movement or to different intensities and wavelengths of light are assumed to be part of the highly integrated mechanism underlying visual perception (Hubel & Weisel, 1979). Information arriving over these different channels is thought by many to be organized by higher-level models or schemata (Ginsberg, 1975; Gregory, 1970; Roberts, 1965). Thus, perception is not simply a process of pattern classification, a separation of incoming sensory information into different categories, but instead is an active inferential process in which incoming information is organized and enhanced by higher level "hypotheses" about the world outside (Oatley, 1978). Indeed, the process of perception has often been likened to a computer-assisted system for identifying patterns or objects (Marr, 1975, 1976; Oatley, 1978; Roberts, 1965; Shirai, 1975). Debates within this literature tend to focus on how much of the process develops from the "bottom-up" (from the retinal image) and how much is imposed from the "top-down" (from higher-level models or schemata). Theorists with a strong physiological orientation, like Marr (1975, 1976) or Dodwell (1982), have emphasized a bottom-up analysis in which early visual processing is thought to play a major role in the development of the percept. More cognitively oriented theorists, like Gregory (1968), have favored a top-down model in which "the retinal image does little more than select the relevant stored data." Most theories of perception, however, incorporate both bottom-up and top-down operations within a formal structure the organization of which could be described as "heterarchical" rather than hierarchical in nature (Oatley, 1978). But whether the accounts of visual perception are bottom-up or top-down, physiological or cognitive, they all agree that the end result is an integrated representation of the external world. It is true that, within cognitive psychology, there has been considerable debate over the nature of a visual image (Pylyshyn, 1981)—Is it continuous or discrete, concrete or abstract, pictorial or discursive, holistic or articulated, or indeed is it functional or simply epiphenomenal? But whatever the formal rules of visual imagery might be, models of perception that postulate a unified visual percept are extremely compelling, since they coincide so well with our own phenomenological experience. Our visual world is not a whirling kaleidoscope of independent sensory events, but rather it is most definitely a unitary experience with continuity in time and space.

In most people's minds, including the minds of most physiological psychologists and other neuroscientists, vision has become identified with visual perception. For them, the function of the visual system is to provide a representation of the external world. Thus, in his introductory textbook on physiological psychology, Thompson (1975) suggests that the visual receptors and pathways are involved in "delivering a representation of the external visual world, and particularly movements in that world, to the brain" (p. 197). No other functions for the visual system are suggested. Similarly, Kuffler and Nicholls (1976) argue that "much progress has been made in determining how the activity of an individual neuron is related to specific features of visual perception," and go on to suggest that "receptive fields are the building blocks for the synthesis and perception of the complex visual world" (p. 16). Again, the function of the visual system is described entirely in terms of providing an integrated and unitary perception of the external world. In this chapter, I shall argue that such a point of view has resulted in a theoretical stance and a methodological tradition in physiological psychology that has limited our understanding of how the neural pathways comprising the visual system are organized. I shall argue that in trying to establish the neural basis for an inferred process such as visual perception, physiological psychologists have neglected almost entirely the neural organization of the visually guided patterns of behavior that can be directly observed. Finally, I shall present an alternative approach to the study of the visual system that emphasizes visuomotor behavior, rather than visual perception, and direct observations, rather than inferential measures. The visual system, it will be argued, evolved in vertebrates and other organisms as a network of independent sensorimotor channels. Thus, it can be fully understood only by studying the organization of its motor outputs as well as its sensory inputs.

B. THE NEUROPSYCHOLOGICAL TRADITION IN VISION RESEARCH

By the latter half of the Nineteenth Century, neurologists knew that damage to different parts of the cerebrum in human beings would often result in blindness or some other form of visual disturbance. The precise localization of visual functions within these cerebral areas, however, depended on experiments with animals. Neurologists began to explore the cerebral cortex of monkeys, dogs, and other animals with stimulating electrodes attached to galvanic batteries and generators, producing eye movements, head turns, and other apparently visually related behaviors. They also removed or cauterized parts of the brain to see how different lesions affected the visual abilities of an animal. Much of this early work was characterized by rather crude and idiosyncratic behavioral tests of visual performance. For example, in the second edition of his highly influential text, *Functions of the Brain*, published in 1886, the British neurologist David Ferrier described a series of experiments he conducted to determine the locus of the "visual sphere" in the cerebral cortex of the monkey. In one of these experiments, a monkey was given chloroform and the posterior portion of the cerebral cortex was exposed on both sides. The animal was then allowed to recover from the anesthetic and

the angular gyri were seared with the cautery without further narcotisation, and without the slightest sign of pain or discomfort on the part of the animal. It was at once let loose, but appeared scared, and would not stir from its place. It was therefore for some hours impossible to obtain any satisfactory information as to its powers of vision. The pupils were contractile to light, and a light flashed in the eyes caused some wincing. When a piece of apple was dropped near it, so as to come in contact with its hand, it took it up, smelt it, and ate it with signs of satisfaction. Hearing was acute, and it turned its head and replied when called to by name. With the exception of the reluctance to move from its position, arising evidently from a sense of insecurity, there was nothing to indicate decisively that the animal was blind. But I had found that this animal was very fond of sweet tea, and would run anywhere after it. I therefore brought a cup of sweet tea and placed it to its lips, when it drank eagerly. The cup was then withdrawn and placed in front of it, a little distance, but the animal, though from its gestures intensely eager to drink further, was unable to find the cup, though its eyes were looking straight into it. This test was repeated several times, and with exactly the same result. At last, on the cup being placed to its lips, it plunged its head in, and continued to drink till every drop was exhausted, while the cup was lowered and drawn half-way across the room. The next day the animal still continued blind, and paid no attention to threats, grimaces, or other means of appeal to its sense of vision (p. 278).

Although Ferrier clearly shows no hesitation here in concluding that the animal was blind, and argued on the strength of this and similar observations that the angular gyrus is an important visual center, his conclusions did not go unchallenged. The German physiologist Hermann Munk (1881, 1890) and the British anatomist and physiologist Edward Schafer (1888) both argued on the basis of their own work with dogs and monkeys that visual sensation resides in the occipital lobe and not in the angular gyrus. Although it is true that they observed their animals over longer postoperative periods than did Ferrier, their observations were no more structured than his and consisted largely of anecdotal material with no quantitative measures of visual performance. Nevertheless, Munk (1881) distinguished between what he called *Rindenblindheit* or "cortical blindness" and *Seelenblindheit* or "psychical blindness." After removing most of the cortex from the occipital region of both hemispheres in a dog, Munk observed that the animal bumped into objects and did not react to threatening movements. He concluded that the animal was cortically blind and behaved as though "all visual perceptions of all visual images have forever ceased." In contrast, a dog with a much smaller lesion centered on an area Munk (1881) called A1

moves around in the room and in the garden without ever bumping into an object or if that cannot be done he surmounts them aptly. . . . However, he remains completely cold when looking at people which he used to greet with joy; he remains just as cold in the presence of dogs with which he formerly used to play. . . . Even if one puts his food and water right in his way he frequently goes around them without paying any attention to them.

Food held before his eyes leaves him unmoved so long as he does not smell it. Finger and fire approaching the eye do not make him blink. The sight of the whip which used to drive him regularly into the corner does not frighten him any more in the least. . . . Such observations can be multiplied. There can be no doubt about their interpretation. Through the extirpation the dog has become *seelenblind*, i.e., he has lost the optical pictures which he possessed, his memory images of former optic impressions, so that he does not know or recognize anything he sees (pp. 97–98).

For Munk then, it was possible to distinguish between deficits in visual perception and deficits in visual memory, and to associate these deficits with lesions in particular parts of the cerebrum.

The two passages presented above illustrate a number of different things about the classical neurological research of the Nineteenth Century. First, the behavioral methods were non-quantitative and impressionistic. As a consequence, the findings of these early investigators were subject to a number of different interpretations. Second, the anatomical foundations of their arguments were themselves rather shaky. Not only were the lesion-making techniques crude and unreliable, but since the operations were carried out under less than aseptic conditions, the wounds were very often subject to infection. Histological verification of the locus and extent of the lesion was also quite inadequate by modern standards. Nevertheless, in interpreting their results, these early investigators used a conceptual language (visual perception, visual recognition, visual memory) that does not differ in any substantial way from the kinds of language used today to account for the effect of lesions in different parts of the visual system. The techniques may have changed over the last 100 years, but the conceptual framework within which questions about the visual system have been formulated has remained much the same.

Systematic investigations of the effect of lesions on visual performance really began in earnest with the work of Karl Lashley and Heinrich Kluver in the first half of this century. Two important features characterize their work. First, the introduction of the two-choice visual discrimination test, which provides a quantitative assessment of the visual abilities of brain-damaged animals; and second, the careful use of control procedures that eliminate the possibility that the simple passage of time or some other variable could have accounted for the results. Although Franz (1911) had used discrimination training much earlier to assess the effects of occipital lesions in monkeys, he presented his data in a piece-meal way as case histories and failed to use adequate control groups. Nevertheless, with the use of training he was able to show that the region of cortex surrounding the calcarine fissure was important for visual discrimination. But it was the work of Lashley (1930, 1935a, 1939) and Kluver (1937, 1941) on striate cortex that provided the foundation for the notion that the geniculostriate pathway is the neural substrate for pattern vision.

Using the jumping-stand, a device he invented, Lashley (1930) showed that rats with complete bilateral lesions of the striate cortex were unable to learn or relearn visual discriminations based on differences in pattern or form, discriminations that normal rats or rats with lesions in areas bordering on the striate cortex had no trouble learning. Despite their deficit in "detail vision," rats deprived of striate cortex were able to discriminate between two stimuli differing in the amount of light they emitted or reflected. In addition, Lashley showed that normal rats and rats with lesions of the striate cortex used different cues when learning to discriminate between two white squares of unequal size. By varying the size, shape, and luminous flux of the two stimuli on test trials, he demonstrated that whereas normal rats used "object" cues (size and shape) to perform the discrimination, the rats with lesions used differences in the amount of luminosity between the two stimuli. For example, the operated rats could no longer perform the discrimination when the brightness of the larger square was reduced so that the total amount of light emitted was equal to that emitted by the smaller square. On the basis of these and related experiments, Lashley concluded that the striate cortex in the rat is an essential neural substrate for pattern vision and that it might also be involved in visual memory.

Kluver (1937, 1941) made similar observations in the monkey. Normal monkeys, according to Kluver, displayed "brightness constancy," choosing the brighter of the two stimuli despite changes in the size and relative distance of the two stimuli. Removal of the occipital lobes, including the striate cortex, destroyed this constancy. For example, destriate monkeys who had learned to choose the brighter of two squares of the same size when they were presented at the same distance from the eye, would consistently choose the dimmer square when the other square was moved further from the eye. Normal monkeys, of course, would continue to choose the brighter square. Kluver concluded from these and other experimental findings that "the bilateral occipital monkey cannot respond to differences in brightness but only to differences in the density of luminous flux entering the eye" (Kluver, 1941, p. 37).

Since the pioneering work of Lashley and Kluver, many investigators have used the two-choice visual discrimination task (and variations of it) to assess the visual performance of animals with brain lesions. Psychophysical thresholds have been measured, the ability to discriminate complex visual patterns has been assessed, and the capacity to store and retrieve visual information has been examined—all by the visual discrimination task. In a recent series of experiments, for example, Sprague and his colleagues (Sprague, Levy, DiBerardino, & Berlucchi, 1977) looked at how well cats learned or relearned flux and pattern discriminations following lesions of areas 17 and 18 or areas 19, 20, 21, 7 and lateral supra-Sylvian cortex, and like Lashley and Kluver had done a half century earlier, they trained their animals on a two-choice visual discrimination task. Mishkin and his collaborators (Butter, Mishkin, & Rosvold, 1965; Mishkin, 1954, 1966) have used similar discrimination learning paradigms to study the function of visual areas in the inferotemporal cortex of monkeys.

The basic unit of measurement in all these studies has been the choice made by an animal on each trial of a discrimination problem. The performance of an animal has usually been calculated as an error or trial score—the number of errors or trials required to reach criterion performance. Occasionally, equivalence tests in which stimuli have been equated along some dimension (as in Lashley and Kluver's brightness-constancy experiments discussed above) have also been used. Again the animal's choice on an equivalence test has been the basic unit of measurement.

Although the metric used in all these discrimination experiments has been much the same, the nature of the stimuli and the organization of their presentation have varied enormously from experiment to experiment. By selecting certain classes of visual stimuli and by manipulating the discrimination paradigm in various ways, investigators have managed to devise visual discrimination experiments that provide reliable dissociations in the deficits that follow destruction of different areas of the brain (principally in the cerebral cortex). Yet in all these experiments, the deficits have been measured in the same way—by comparing the error scores or trials-to-criterion measures of one group of animals with another. Although the stimulus parameters have been systematically (and ingeniously) varied in these experiments, the response demands for the most part have not. The reasons for this methodological bias lie in the theoretical position most investigators have adopted with regard to vision and the visual system.

The neuropsychological tradition from Ferrier and his contemporaries to the present day has identified the function of the visual system with visual perception. This has meant that behavioral deficits resulting from damage to the system have usually been described entirely in sensory or cognitive terms. Indeed, the visual discrimination task was introduced to quantify the disturbances in sensory or cognitive processing that animals with different lesions might experience. As a consequence, investigators have focused their attention on the decision that an animal makes in a discrimination task, arguing that the nature of that decision will reveal the way in which the mechanisms underlying visual perception have been disturbed. Interpretation of the deficits is thus an inferential process, the inferences being drawn from error scores or trials-to-criterion measures on different discrimination tasks. It was in this way that Lashley (1935a) concluded that "complete destruction of the striate areas permanently abolishes detail vision in the rat." Similarly, Sprague et al. (1977) have argued that lesions in cortical areas receiving extra-geniculate projections may also "participate in some integrated fashion in form perception and discrimination in the cat" (p. 484). Work on inferotemporal cortex has emphasized even "higher-level" processing, and Butter, Mishkin, & Rosvold (1965), for example, have speculated that damage in this cortical area in monkeys might produce deficits in "learned identification of visual stimuli." More recently, Dean (1982) has suggested that "one function of inferotemporal cortex is to extract from the rich 'perceptual' representation of the visual world (provided by prestriate cortex?) a much briefer symbolic description suitable for general-purpose manipulation (e.g., in memory, thinking, etc.)." In every case, the deficits in visual discrimination performance have been interpreted as a disturbance of perception—a disturbance in the analysis or organization of information about the external world.

It is this theoretical commitment to perception and other psychological processes that has shaped the usual methodological approach to the visual system. The logic of the argument (which for the most part is only implicit in the literature) seems to go something like this: If the function of the visual system is to provide an integrated representation of the external world, then it makes good sense to concentrate on the way in which animals with specific brain lesions process and store information that might be used in the construction of that representation. By varying stimulus parameters and training conditions in a visual discrimination task, one can probe the deficits such animals might have in extracting information from the stimulus array or in coding and storing that information. In this way, one can learn how the visual system functions in normal animals. It makes little sense to look at the large range of different visually guided movements or responses that animals make, since, except for a few visual reflexes, the behavior the animal generates is always in relation to the perceptual representation or model the visual system provides. Indeed, the visual pathways with their multiple inputs and complex transformations could be likened to a highly sophisticated television system that provides the organism with an integrated "picture" or representation of the world. This television picture is based in part on current information arriving over a multiplicity of sensory channels and in part on stored information about past visual input. All motor output is organized with respect to this complex picture or central representation of the world. In other words, according to this view, the primary function of the visual system is perceptual and as such can be studied independently of motor output of the organism. There is, however, another way of looking at the organization of the visual system, one that includes motor output as well as sensory input. Experiments from this tradition have generated results that are not easily accommodated within the perceptual framework of most neuropsychological theories of vision.

C. THE NEUROETHOLOGICAL TRADITION

Investigators studying vision in lower vertebrates such as frogs and toads have been forced to rely on behavioral measures very different from those used by most investigators working with mammals. An animal like a frog cannot be trained in the kinds of discrimination apparatus commonly used with rats, cats, or monkeys. They simply fail to learn anything in traditional two-choice visual discrimination tasks.

Thus, instead of relying on learned visual discriminations, investigators working with frogs and toads have looked directly at the visually guided movements these creatures make as they catch prey, avoid obstacles, and escape from predators. Many of these behavioral sequences would be called fixed action patterns by ethologists like Lorenz (1958) or Tinbergen (1951). Such patterns of behavior are not only species-specific and highly stereotyped, but also many of them have the added advantage that they can be reliably elicited in the laboratory by relatively simple visual stimuli.

Frogs and many other lower vertebrates possess another characteristic that makes them particularly useful for studying the neural substrates of these different patterns of visually guided behavior: The projections from the retina to their brain can be transected and induced to regrow to new locations. One potentially very powerful way to dissociate components of behavior that are generated by distinct retinal projections is to selectively "rewire" one of the pathways, leaving the others projecting to their normal targets. After the cut fibers have regenerated, one might then discover that although some visually guided patterns of behavior remain normal, others show a spatial reorganization that corresponds to the way in which the rewiring occurred. Such an observation would provide strong evidence that the reorganized patterns of behavior are normally mediated by the rewired pathway.

Ingle (1973) used this technique to demonstrate that thalamic and tectal visual mechanisms can operate quite independently in the frog. After unilateral removal of the frog's optic tectum (which is homologous with the superior colliculus in mammals), he found, just as Bechterew (1884) had a century before, that the animal totally ignored prey objects (e.g., meal-worms or small moving disks) or even large looming targets presented within the monocular visual field contralateral to the lesion. Of course, when these stimuli were presented to the eye opposite the intact tectum the frogs responded vigorously, snapping at the small prey objects and jumping away or ducking when the large looming disk appeared. Gradu-ally over the next few months, there was a slow recovery and animals with unilateral tectal lesions began to turn and snap in response to prey objects presented in their formerly "blind" field opposite the lesion. The responses, however, were far from normal. Instead of snapping in the direction of the prey object, they directed their responses toward a loca-tion nearly mirror-symmetrical to the position of the stimulus, just as Sperry (1945) had described for frogs with surgically uncrossed optic nerves. Similarly, when a large "threatening" disk was introduced into the field opposite the lesion, all their jumps were now directed toward the side where the disk was, instead of away to safety. Ingle found in his later histological analysis that the optic tract, which had been cut during the unilateral tectal removal, had regenerated and the sprouting axons had crossed the midline to innervate the remaining tectum. This meant that one eye now projected to the ipsilateral and not the contralateral tectum. Moreover, electrophysiological analysis of several "rewired" frogs re-vealed that the aberrant recrossed projection distributed itself over the ipsilateral tectum in a retinotopic, but mirror-symmetrical pattern as though the fibers were distributing themselves across the normal contralateral tec-tum with fibers from the nasal portion of the retina, for example, project-ing to that part of the tectum that normally receives nasal fibers from the contralateral eye. Thus, the mirror-symmetrical behavior observed in re-wired frogs snapping at prey or jumping away from predators corre-sponds to the mirror-symmetry of the aberrant retinotectal projection, a finding that suggests that the optic tectum plays a major role in visually guided prey-catching and predator-avoidance.

However, not all visually guided behavior showed this type of reorga-nization. When the same frogs that showed mirror-symmetrical snapping were forced to escape from a noxious tactile stimulus, they always ori-ented their escape jump correctly toward the edge of a grid barrier placed at different locations in front of them, even when the barrier edge fell within their rewired visual field. (Such behavior could also be observed immediately after the unilateral tectal lesion was made, a period when visually guided prey-catching could not be elicited from the field opposite the lesion.) This finding strongly suggests that one or more of the remain-ing normal retinofugal projections (such as those to the pretectal region of the caudal thalamus) may mediate this type of visually guided escape behavior, since only the retinal pathway to the optic tectum was rewired. Since the same rewired frog can respond in opposite directions, depending on the nature of the response and the eliciting stimulus, it would appear that there are at least two independent visual systems in the frog— one mediating localization of prey stimuli or potential predators and the other mediating localization of stationary barriers. This conclusion has been reinforced by a host of separate lesion and electrophysiological experiments in both the frog (Ingle, 1977a, 1982) and the toad (Ewert, 1970, 1982). At last count, there appear to be at least five separate visual projection systems in these animals, each system mediating a different class of visuomotor behavior. Each of the larger visuomotor systems may consist of a number of different functional networks. Within the tectal complex, for example, there are separate sensorimotor networks underlying visually guided orientation of the body toward a prey-object, snapping at the prey, and ducking the head or jumping away from predators (Ingle, 1982). There is also evidence that some of the stimulus selectivity within these tectal networks may depend upon input from the pretectum, but from pretectal areas that are separate from those involved in the visual control of locomotion around stationary barriers.

The apparent organization of the frog's visual system into several separate (albeit interactive) visuomotor channels does not fit well with the sort of model that has developed within the neuropsychological tradition. Instead of a monolithic visual system dedicated to the construction of an internal representation of the external world, the frog possesses a number of different visuomotor pathways, each of which is involved in the sensory control of a different pattern of behavior. It seems that the visual system of the frog did not evolve to provide a central and integrated representation of the world in which it lives, but rather to organize the different kinds of movements it needs to make in order to survive and reproduce in that world. The frog's visual system can be best understood by looking at both the selectivity of its sensory inputs and the characteristics of the different motor outputs that sensory information controls. Even if it were possible to train rewired or lesioned frogs on two-choice visual discrimination problems, it is doubtful whether the results of such experiments would in themselves provide sufficient information about the way in which the different visuomotor pathways are organized. A full understanding of the system depends on direct observation and measurement of the spatial and temporal characteristics of the movements made by these animals in response to different kinds of visual stimuli.

D. THE TWO VISUAL SYSTEMS HYPOTHESIS

Exactly the same arguments can be put forward for the study of visually guided behavior in mammals. Just as the frog's visual system can best be understood in terms of the relations between motor outputs and sensory inputs, so can the visual system of a mammal. Indeed, the research tradition inspired by the work of J.J. Gibson (1958, 1966, 1979) has long emphasized the importance of studying the perceptual system of any organism in relation to the movements it makes within its ecological niche. The visual system of a rhesus monkey, for example, is exquisitely adapted to providing precise (and highly integrated) sensory control of the different patterns of movements this creature must make to survive and reproduce. Furthermore, the monkey's visual system evolved from a basic vertebrate plan shared by the common ancestors of primates and present-day "lower" vertebrates, such as the frog. Thus, in the monkey, as in the frog, there are likely to be relatively independent visuomotor networks mediating the different patterns of visually guided movement underlying locomotion, posture, reaching, climbing, grasping objects, catching insects, avoiding obstacles, and escaping from predators. Yet, the neural organization of most of these visually guided movements is largely unknown. The same is true for the visually guided movements of almost all mammals commonly used in visual research. The only exception is eye movements, perhaps because the movements are so striking and so clearly related to the spatial and temporal characteristics of the visual stimulus, that investigators have routinely recorded the movements directly. Thus, it has been possible to relate the activity of single cells in the visual system not only to the characteristics of the stimulus, but also to the characteristics of the motor output. Moreover it has been possible to relate systematic changes in the latency, amplitude, velocity, and acceleration of different kinds of eye movements to lesions in specific areas of the central nervous system. Although interpretation of such relationships has often been difficult, real progress has been made in describing the neural networks underlying a number of different oculomotor movements (see Carpenter, 1977, for a review). The same is not true for most other visuomotor behaviors, principally because almost no one has bothered to look at them systematically. For most neuropsychologists, the visual discrimination task has remained the basic tool for studying the neural organization of vision, a situation that does not lend itself to the detailed recording of visually guided movement.

Nevertheless, as was outlined earlier in the chapter, the discrimination learning paradigm has been used to great effect in the development of the classical description of the geniculate field of neocortex as the primary site for pattern or form vision in mammals. But despite the obvious successes of this approach, there have been certain difficulties.

For one thing, the use of the visual discrimination paradigm with animals that have sustained lesions outside the geniculostriate network, such as lesions of the superior colliculus, has often produced ambiguous findings. The literature abounds with contradictory results. Some investigators have found acquisition or retention deficits in flux and/or pattern discrimination tasks in animals with collicular lesions (Anderson & Williams, 1971; Berlucchi, Sprague, Levy, & DiBerardino, 1972; Blake, 1959; Casagrande, Harting, Hall, Diamond, & Martin, 1972; Freeman & Papez, 1930; Milner, Goodale, & Morton, 1979). Others have found that collicular lesions had no effect or produced only slight impairments on similar discrimination tasks (Anderson & Symmes, 1969; Fischman & Meikle, 1965; Ghiselli, 1937; Horel, 1968; Keating, 1976; Layman, 1936; Myers, 1964; Rosvold, Mishkin, & Szwarzbart, 1958; Thompson, 1969; Urbaitis & Meikle, 1968).

Some years ago, in a much-cited article, Schneider (1969) attempted to resolve these contradictory findings by making a sharp distinction between the role of the superior colliculus and the role of visual neocortex in mammalian vision. According to his influential "two visual systems" hypothesis, the phylogenetically older pathway from retina to superior colliculus is directly involved in the control of "orientation behavior," enabling an animal to localize a stimulus in visual space; the more recently evolved geniculostriate system participates in the "identification" of that stimulus. This distinction was an important one to make, since it implies that visual pathways are not a unitary system, but are instead a network of relatively independent channels. Nevertheless, the two functional categories proposed, orientation behavior and identification, were still described in relatively vague terms and were not always derived from direct observation of an animal's movements. Even the concept of orientation behavior, which certainly sounds as though it ought to be related to specific movements, refers to "localizing" a stimulus in such a way that the mechanism of spatial orientation of the head and body seems to be independent of the nature of the eliciting stimulus and the particular sequence of movements that are involved in producing the orientation. Thus, Schneider's (1967, 1969) original formulation of the concept of orientation behavior not only incorporated the earlier idea of the "visual grasp reflex" (Hess, Burgi, & Bucher, 1946), whereby objects in the peripheral visual fields are relocated on the central field by movements of the head and eyes, but also the orientation of locomotor movements made by animals as they approach different alleyways or stimuli in a discrimination apparatus. Schneider reported that hamsters with collicular lesions could not guide themselves accurately toward visual stimuli in a two-choice discrimination apparatus even though they could discriminate the correct door from the incorrect door as indicated by their door-pushing behavior. It was this observation, in particular, that led to the suggestion that the apparent contradictions in the earlier literature could be resolved by examining the response demands of the visual discrimination tasks employed by different investigators (Schneider, 1969). According to this suggestion, discrimination tasks that require locomotor responses to be differentially oriented toward the discriminanda will reveal deficits in colliculectomized animals, whereas tasks that do not require orientation will not. Schneider (1969) also suggested that the visually guided reaching demonstrated by destriate monkeys (Denny-Brown & Chambers, 1955; Humphrey & Weiskrantz, 1967) might be part of the same localization mechanism.

Within the framework of the two visual systems model, the concept of orientation includes a variety of different patterns of behavior, all of which might be involved in localizing a visual stimulus. Orientation was thus envisaged as some sort of mechanism or process involving the superior colliculus and underlying several different sequences of movements, each of which might be controlled by a specific class of visual stimuli. For example, "orienting" to a food object and "orienting" to the the edge of a barrier would be treated as part of the same collicular orientation mechanism, whereas, in the frog at least, they clearly involve two very different visuomotor networks of which only one requires the participation of the optic tectum (or superior colliculus).

The two visual systems model was an important first step toward a visuomotor analysis of vision and the visual system, but it did not go far enough in that it failed to specify in any detail the visuomotor movements constituting orientation behavior. Therefore, it did little to modify the view that the principal task of the visual system (i.e., the cortical elaboration of the geniculostriate system) is a perceptual one—that of identifying visual stimuli. In terms of the analogy discussed earlier in Section B, the role of the superior colliculus might be regarded as little more than that of a simple servomechanism that points the powerful television camera (the geniculostriate system) at objects and events within the external world. But the simple division of labor implied by the two visual systems model is not based on detailed analyses of visuomotor behavior. In fact, when, in recent years, such an analysis has been carried out in a limited number of mammalian species, a very different story has emerged, one that shows a strong relationship to the organization of visuomotor behavior in lower vertebrates such as the frog.

E. VISUOMOTOR SYSTEMS IN THE MAMMAL

If we are to understand how different patterns of visuomotor behavior are organized in a mammal (how a Mongolian gerbil, for instance, orients toward and approaches a discrete visual target), then we must record its movements as directly and in as much detail as possible. In other words, we must do for visuomotor behavior what we have done for eye movements—provide an accurate and continuous record of the spatial and temporal characteristics of the motor output so that it can be related to the characteristics of the visual stimuli eliciting and/or controlling that movement. Only then will we be able to assess the effects of lesions in different areas of the visual system in terms of motor as well as sensory deficits.

High-speed films of gerbils running toward a visual target show very clearly that this apparently simple behavior consists of a number of different visuomotor programs (Goodale, 1983; Goodale & Milner, 1982; Ingle, 1982; Ingle, Cheal, & Dizio, 1979). Upon detecting the target, the animal initiates a series of discrete head movements that vary in amplitude as function of the initial position of the target in the visual field. At the same time, or shortly thereafter, the animal begins to locomote toward the target, typically accelerating its rate of locomotion to a peak velocity, and then rapidly decelerating as it makes the final approach.

In a recent series of experiments (Goodale, 1983; Goodale & Milner, 1982) in my laboratory, we were able to show that lesions of different retinal-projection targets can affect the various components of this behavioral sequence in very different ways. Most of these experiments relied heavily on quantitative analyses of film and videotape records of visually guided movements made by animals in a number of different situations. These analyses revealed, first of all, that gerbils with complete bilateral lesions of the superior colliculus were capable of approaching targets baited with food as efficiently as normal animals if those targets were located in their central visual field within 40° from the visual midline. Beyond 40° from the midline, however, they had great difficulty in finding the target, not because they could not locomote appropriately, but because they failed to turn their heads toward the target when it first appeared in their peripheral field. Thus, collicular lesions appeared to interfere with the production of the initial head turn, but not with the control of locomotor orientation once the target had been brought into the central portion of the visual field.

Gerbils with aspiration lesions of the cortical target of the geniculostriate pathway showed no impairment in either of these components of orientation behavior, provided the target was stationary and stood out in high contrast against a homogeneous background. But such animals had great difficulty in detecting a low-contrast target, or even a high-contrast one if it was presented against a patterned background. Moreover, in a very elegant experiment, Ingle (1977b) demonstrated that gerbils with lesions in the visual cortex also were deficient in their response to moving targets. Unlike normal gerbils, they failed to make adjustments in the amplitude of their orienting head movements or in the direction of their locomotion to compensate for the movement of the target. Instead of making anticipatory overshoots, they initiated brisk and accurate head turns toward the point in space where the target first appeared. These results suggest that, although the superior colliculus may be essential to the mediation of rapid head turns toward visual stimuli in the visual periphery, the geniculostriate network (via corticofugal projections to the colliculus and possibly to other brainstem structures) modulates this basic collicular function. It may do this by providing information about the direction in which a target is moving (and perhaps its velocity as well) and may also perform the complex feature detection that must sometimes precede the orienting movements eventually mediated by the superior colliculus.

In all the experiments just described, the animals were required to run directly toward the target. What happened when some sort of barrier was placed between them and their intended goal? Normal gerbils quickly learned to avoid a grid barrier (consisting of vertical black stripes on a piece of transparent Plexiglas) interposed between their starting point and the target, as did animals with collicular lesions (provided they had detected the target and were moving toward it). Gerbils with large pretectal lesions, however, often collided with the barrier or chose the longer route around it even though they showed no difficulty in orienting and locomoting toward the target when no barrier was present (Goodale, 1983; Goodale & Milner, 1982). Thus, like Ingle's (1982) frogs with pretectal lesions, they showed brisk and accurate orientation toward small targets, but were unable to negotiate stationary barriers.

A number of conclusions can be drawn from the brief set of empirical findings outlined above. First, even the apparently simple behavior of approaching a discrete target or landmark under visual control consists of a number of distinct visuomotor outputs, each of which can vary as a function of the stimulus and the response-demands of the situation in which the stimulus occurs.

Second, neither the traditional perceptual account of visual function nor the simplistic division of labor implied by the two visual systems model is sufficient to account for the neural organization of these different patterns of behavior. The neural substrate is highly complex and involves at least three separate retinofugal targets—the superior colliculus, the lateral geniculate nucleus, and the pretectal area. Although the different sensorimotor networks in which each of these structures participates interact, it is clear that the superior colliculus is neither necessary nor sufficient for all "orientation behaviors." Thus, one retinofugal system may play a role in one kind of visually guided behavior and not in another.

Third, none of these dissociations would have been noticed had we not recorded the entire sequence of movements made by different animals in several different situations. A highly analytical and quantitative description of these movements was a necessary prerequisite to working out their underlying neural organization. In other words, the sort of analysis that has been routinely used in the study of eye movements, when it is applied to other classes of visuomotor behavior, can yield similar kinds of information not only about the dynamics of the movements themselves, but also about the systematic relationship between sensory input and motor output. None of this information could have been obtained in traditional visual discrimination experiments.

In summary, these experiments have shown that it is possible to tease apart the visuomotor pathways in a mammal in much the same way that they have been teased apart in simpler creatures, such as the frog. This is not to deny that the telencephalic contribution to visually guided behavior in higher vertebrates, such as cats, monkeys, and human beings, is enormous, and that vision in these animals plays an important role in cognitive processes that are clearly independent of fixed motor programs. This is no excuse, however, for ignoring the demonstrable and highly systematic relationship between the nature of visual stimulus and the characteristics of the particular motor output elicited and/or controlled by that stimulus.

F. HUMAN VISUOMOTOR SYSTEMS

In human beings, there is also evidence for separate visuomotor systems that are relatively independent. As long ago as 1918, the British neurologist Gordon Holmes described several patients who showed profound visuomotor deficits that could not be easily explained in terms of a general disturbance in visual perception or motor performance. One of his patients, a young soldier with a gunshot wound in the occipital lobe that spared primary visual cortex, showed intact central vision and no trace of "visual agnosia"; that is, he had no trouble recognizing and distinguishing visible objects and could read individual words with little difficulty. Nevertheless, this same patient had enormous problems making even very simple visually guided movements. As Holmes (1918) observed,

throughout the whole time he was in the hospital his most striking symptom was his inability to take hold of or touch any object with accuracy, even

when it was placed in the line of vision. When a pencil was held up in front
of him he would often project his arm in a totally wrong direction, as though
by chance rather than by deliberate decision, or more frequently he would
bring his hand to one side of it, above or below it, or would attempt to seize
the pencil before he had reached it, or after his hand had passed it. When
he failed to touch the object at once he continued groping for it until his
hand or arm came into contact with it, in a manner more or less like a man
searching for a small object in the dark. . . . His difficulty in extricating
himself and in finding his way around an obstacle in his path was extraor-
dinary; in this respect he was, though he possessed good vision, much inferior to a blind person or a blindfolded man. An equally striking phenomenon was his inability, or at least his great difficulty, in finding his way
about. . . . On one occasion he was brought about five yards from his bed,
to reach which he had only to take a single right-angle turn, but though he
indicated it correctly and recognized the patient in the adjoining bed, he
commenced to walk in a wrong direction when told to go to it (p. 213).

Despite his obvious difficulty with visually guided movement, the patient, according to Holmes, "could localize sounds fairly accurately, and
when his eyes were closed walk in a correct direction toward them."
Moreover, the patient could move his hand toward any object that touched
his face or body. Thus, the deficit could not be characterized as a simple
problem in reaching or locomotion. Nor was it a sensory deficit, either,
at least not in the usual sense of that term.

In perimetry tests, for example, the patient appeared to have full visual
fields with only some amblyopia in the lower right quadrants. He also
had fair acuity in his central fields and good color vision. It is true that he
was unable to determine correctly the relative position of different objects, and often confused left with right, and near objects with distant
ones. Yet as Holmes (1918) observed,

His stereoscopic vision was unaffected; at least he always appreciated the
depth and thickness of objects, and did not see them merely as flat bidimen-
sional forms. He even recognized at once the well-known visual illusion of
the truncated pyramid, saying "that's a box; it changes according as your
eyes catch it, sometimes I can see it open, sometimes the other way"
(p. 212).

Although it might be possible to account for this pattern of deficits in
purely "perceptual" terms, such an explanation would not reconcile the
ability of this patient to recognize and individuate objects in a complex
visual environment with his complete inability to reach for and grasp these
objects or locomote toward or around them.

A better account might be that the shrapnel that penetrated this young
soldier's brain interfered with the function of specific visuomotor channels

that are relatively independent and separate from other visual inputs. In other words, the neural circuitry underlying visually guided reaching and walking may have been interrupted or depressed in some way, leaving intact the circuitry underlying other visuomotor (and visuocognitive?) abilities. Admittedly, the deficit seems rather "higher order," since the visually guided orientation of a broad class of movements was affected. Accurate visual localization and visually guided movement depend on a complex interaction between retinal input and extra-retinal input (as well as on information derived from motor commands to the eyes, head, and limbs). For this reason, the precise nature of the deficit in this and other patients may never be fully understood. Nevertheless, the fact that accurate visual recognition and complex visual skills, such as reading, can survive an insult to the brain that completely wipes out visual control of reaching, walking and most ocular movement strongly suggests that visuomotor pathways in the human being are organized as relatively independent and parallel networks, just as they are in other vertebrates.

It is of some importance in the context of this argument that brain damage in human beings can sometimes result in the obverse of what Holmes (1918) described in his patients. That is, instead of producing profound visuomotor deficits without obvious visual agnosia, the lesion results in a complete absence of visual recognition (or even reported vision) with relatively intact visually guided movement of the eyes and limbs. Although damage to the striate cortex in human beings produces a severe loss of visual capacity in correlated regions of the visual fields (Teuber, Battersby, & Bender, 1960), in the last 10 years a surprising number of visual abilities have been shown to survive such damage. Pöppel, Held, & Frost (1973), for example, have shown that patients with striate lesions can voluntarily refixate their eyes toward visual stimuli placed in "blind" portions of their visual fields, even though they deny seeing the stimuli. Although the direction of the eye movements made by these patients was correlated with the position of the target in the blind field, the relationship was very weak. A more dramatic correlation between visually guided movement and the position of the stimulus has been demonstrated in two other laboratories (Perenin & Jeannerod, 1975; Weiskrantz, Warrington, Sanders, & Marshall, 1974). In these experiments, subjects were asked to point toward or touch a small visual stimulus presented in the hemifield contralateral to their striate lesion while maintaining fixation on a central point directly in front of them. Despite the fact that all the subjects in these studies never reported seeing the target, their reaching was surprisingly accurate and in most cases was comparable to their performance in their "good" field, where they always reported seeing the target. When asked to guess the orientation and shape of stimuli presented tachistoscopically to the blind hemifield, the subjects also performed quite well. But again they denied "seeing" anything. The most that the young man studied by Weiskrantz et al. could report was that "he perhaps had a 'feeling' that the stimulus was either this way or that way." His most common reply, when repeatedly questioned about vision in his blind hemifield, was that he saw nothing at all. The paradoxical ability of these individuals to reach out and touch stimuli that they deny perceiving has been given the rather whimsical name "blind-sight" (Weiskrantz et al., 1974).

The neural mediation of blind-sight is presumed by both Weiskrantz et al. (1974) and Perenin and Jeannerod (1975) to depend on parallel retinal input to extra-striate structures such as the superior colliculus or some other subcortical retinofugal target. The superior colliculus, for example, projects (via nuclei in the posterior thalamus) to various areas in the peristriate cortex, areas that may have been damaged in the patients, described by Holmes (1918), who could recognize objects, but who could not reach out and grasp them accurately. At present, however, it is possible to do little more than speculate about the possible neural substrates mediating the "residual" visual abilities in the two different groups of patients. Nevertheless, the observations do provide compelling evidence of separate visuomotor networks within the human visual system.

Investigations of this sort, however, are relatively rare in human neuropsychology. For example, despite the fact that reaching toward and grasping objects is a particularly important human skill, there have been very few studies of visually guided movements of the arms, hands, and fingers in patients with pathology in different parts of the visual system. Even investigations like those described above, in which reaching and pointing were studied, have concentrated on deficits arising from neocortical damage and have provided information about errors in localization rather than a detailed analysis of the spatial and temporal distribution of the different components that comprise a reaching movement toward an object. Part of the reason that human neuropsychologists have neither ventured outside the neocortex nor provided a detailed description of movement is that, within the discipline, there has been a strong tendency to interpret a deficit in terms of a disturbance in perception, cognition, or linguistic capacity, often coupled with an implicit conviction that such abilities reside only in neocortex. In some ways, neuropsychological investigations of human vision resemble the traditional visual discrimination approach to the study of visual function in other mammals. They have produced an enormous body of data about perceptual disorders in brain-damaged humans and have also devised a number of different classification schemes for these disorders (the "agnosias"), which are related in part to the locus of damage in the neocortex. At the same time, little attention has been paid to the role of vision in the control of reaching movements, locomotion, posture, and other spatially oriented behavior, and almost no attention has been paid to the deficits resulting from damage to subcortical visual pathways. Admittedly, it is not easy to find clear-cut cases of discrete damage to subcortical structures in patient populations, but only by studying the visual abilities of such individuals will it be possible to differentiate clearly the functions of different retinofugal targets in human beings.

G. CONCLUSIONS

Visual systems in mammals evolved from simpler ones already present in their vertebrate ancestors. Thus, the organization of the eight or more separate retinofugal projections in the mammal (and the elaboration of those projections after the primary synapse) are likely to reflect this evolutionary heritage. In gerbils and frogs, for example, the pretectum and optic tectum (or superior colliculus) have already been shown to play the same kinds of complementary roles in the control of visually guided behavior, suggesting some important continuities in the organization of the different visual systems throughout the vertebrate line. In humans, too, there is evidence that rather complex visually guided behavior can survive the removal of the cortical target of the retinogeniculate pathway. The preoccupation of neuropsychologists with perceptual mechanisms and their reluctance to explore pathways outside visual cortex, however, has meant that such dissociations in the neural substrates of visuomotor programs have rarely been established. By concentrating on discrimination learning scores and by interpreting any deficits they observe entirely in terms of perception or some other higher-order process, they have often failed to look carefully and analytically at the visuomotor performance of their subjects. Although it is true that the mammalian neocortex carries out high-level computations on incoming visual information, the existence of well-established reciprocal connections between the visual neocortex and the several visuomotor systems receiving independent retinofugal input suggests that the neocortex exercises control over the different visuomotor programs mediated by these pathways in very specific ways. In other words, the more recently evolved geniculostriate system may influence appropriate motor pathways in part by modulating the input/output functions of other, more ancient, retinofugal systems. The nature of this control will remain obscure until neuroscientists studying vision record and quantify visually guided behavior of an animal or a human being in the same rigorous and detailed way that they describe and manipulate the characteristics of the visual stimulus.

5 | Single Neuron Recording in Behaving Mammals: Bridging the Gap between Neuronal Events and Sensory-Behavioral Variables

JAMES B. RANCK, JR., JOHN L. KUBIE, STEVEN E. FOX, SLOANE WOLFSON, and ROBERT U. MULLER

A. INTRODUCTION

In 1957, Ricci, Doane, and Jasper (1957) and Hubel (1957) reported recording electrical activity from single neurons in behaving, partly restrained animals. In 1958, Strumwasser (1958) reported recording from single neurons in moving rats, and Hubel (1958) gave a full report of his method. This ability to record action potentials in behaving animals is clearly important, since action potentials are part of the causal processes of brain function, and we can record them with relatively little interference with normal neural function or with normal behavior. The method has been widely used, even in humans (e.g., Halgren, Babb, & Crandall, 1978), and has yielded many fascinating results. Nevertheless, after almost 25 years, the full power of the technique still has not been realized. Many studies, including some of our own, have failed to recognize the strengths and the weaknesses of recording the electrical activity of individual neurons in intact animals.

This situation is due, in part, we feel, to the remarkable lack of discussion of the problems and strategies involved in relating neuronal activity to externally observable events. Although Uttal (1978) has broached many of the issues of interest, his work focused mainly on sensory systems. Hobson (1974) has discussed many of the issues we raise in the contexts of sleep and brain centers. In this chapter we will consider neurons from all parts of the mammalian central nervous system. Although we will give examples from sensory and motor systems, many of the points we make will be illustrated by examples from the hippocampus, the structure on which we work. We believe that the principles we set forth will apply to any subsystem of interest.

The ability to record from single neurons in behaving animals allows two (not mutually exclusive) categories of experiments. The first, which we will discuss in Section B, involves the sorts of physiological and pharmacological experiments that have previously been done on anesthetized or otherwise reduced preparations. The second category of experiments, to which most of this chapter will be devoted, consists of experiments in which a search is made for correlations between sensory-behavioral variables and neural firing.

A *sensory-behavioral variable*[1] is a single, experimenter-chosen parameter that measures an aspect of an animal's relationship to the outside world. When we use the term sensory-behavioral variable, the hyphen is not meant to imply an either/or choice; the input and output aspects may not be separable. At any given moment, an adequate description of an animals relationship to its environment must include many sensory-behavioral variables. Each variable requires a description and a value. For instance, a rat may be running at 5 cm/sec. A sensory-behavioral variable may have values that are discrete or continuous (e.g., the presence or absence of REM sleep is a discrete variable; rate of locomotion is a continuous variable).

A sensory-behavioral variable may change its value rapidly (phasically), in which case we say that a *sensory-behavioral event* has occurred. If a sensory-behavioral variable is constant, we will refer to a *sensory-behavioral state*. Because a sensory-behavioral event is brief, one imagines that it would be profitable to look for correlates of neural firing by use of "peri-event" histograms; a sensory-behavioral state, by contrast, lasts so long that it would seem useless to try to relate moment-to-moment variations in a spike train to the whole state. The transition between sensory-behavioral states may be an event, as in the transition between slow wave sleep (SWS) and REM sleep. Sensory-behavioral state is used here to refer both to relatively long duration behaviors and to tonic sensory stimuli, even though in common usage, "state" is often used to mean only behavioral or internal conditions.

A *sensory-behavioral firing correlation* is a statistical relationship between some representation of neural firing and a sensory-behavioral variable, or a transform of such a variable. Only a small subset of the many sensory-behavioral variables are correlated with the firing of a given neuron, and even these variables have a high correlation with neural firing over only a part of the domain of the variable. That part of the domain of a sensory-

1. A glossary of neologisms is at the end of this chapter.

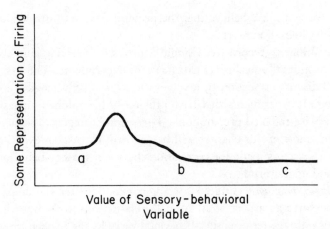

FIGURE 5.1. The sensory-behavioral correlate is the sensory-behavioral variable between a and b. Determining the exact location of a and b is a pragmatic decision for each case. The variance in firing is not represented. Note that in this example the Pearson product moment correlation would be very low. Hence, a transformation of the values of the sensory-behavioral variable would be appropriate. Note also that because there are no changes in firing for values between b and c there is no correlation between b and c, but the sensory-behavioral variable still predicts firing between b and c.

behavioral variable over which there is high correlation with firing of the neuron is the *sensory-behavioral correlate of the firing* of the neuron.[2] In other words, the sensory-behavioral correlate of firing is that part of the domain of the variable that accounts for most of the variance (Fig. 5.1). For the sake of brevity we will usually call this a *sensory-behavioral correlate*. If the sensory-behavioral correlate were excluded from the domain, then the correlation would approach zero. The decision as to what a "high correlation" is is a pragmatic one, depending on the case under study. Perhaps the simplest example of a sensory-behavioral correlate is the adequate stimulus applied to the receptive field of a primary cutaneous afferent. The sensory-behavioral variable is the stimulus as applied to the body surface, but there is only correlated firing over the area of the receptive field. (Note that in this special case, the sensory-behavioral correlate need not be studied in a behaving animal.)

Since we are interested in neural firing, we must be able to quantify it. The first problem in establishing a correlation is to decide how to describe the spike train. The best quantitative description of neural firing is the

2. There are many measures of correlation; the choice of which to use must be made in the context of the experiment.

one with the highest correlation to a sensory-behavioral variable. This best description need not be a simple average rate, but rather it may include details of the pattern of firing. The second problem is, of course, to find the sensory-behavioral variables that yield the highest correlation. We will discuss ways of finding both neural and sensory-behavioral variables in Section C.

We expect the firing of a neuron to covary with more than one sensory-behavioral variable. We also expect that sensory-behavioral correlates will interact; that is, the value of one sensory-behavioral variable will influence the correlation between another variable and neuronal firing. For example, the firing of neurons in lateral geniculate and striate cortex covary both with certain patterns of light in the environment and with the state of sleep-wakefulness. In addition, the state of sleep-wakefulness affects the firing of the neurons to patterns of light (Livingston & Hubel, 1981).

The change in a sensory-behavioral variable will often not occur simultaneously with the change in neural firing. In sensory systems, the sensory-behavioral events often precede the associated changes in firing. In motor systems, the sensory-behavioral events often follow the associated neural changes. Lead or lag times, therefore, can be introduced to find the maximum correlation.

As we accumulate data on the various sensory-behavioral correlates of a given set of neurons, describe the interactions of the sensory-behavior variables affecting the firing of single neurons of the set, and achieve better descriptions of their firing repertoires, we will be able to describe expected firing as a function of multiple sensory-behavioral variables. This description is a *sensory-behavioral firing relation*. As a group of neurons is studied, this sensory-behavioral firing relation will become more complete, in the sense that more sensory-behavioral correlates may be found, a wider range of values and combination of values of the sensory-behavioral variables will be observed, and the firing repertoire of the neurons will be better defined. Realistically, we will usually work with expressions that predict firing as a function of an intentionally limited number of sensory-behavioral variables.

Presenting the above more formally, we can define a sensory-behavioral firing relation of a neuron as an operator (R) relating any number (n) of sensory-behavioral variables $(V_i, \ldots, V_n)$ to the expectation (E) of a probability density function $[f(t)]$ describing the firing of a neuron.

$$E\{f(t)\} = R\{V_1(t + \Delta t_1), \ldots, V_n(t + \Delta t_n)\}$$

The subscripted Δt's describe the temporal relationships between the sensory-behavioral variables and their maximum correlation with the firing.

The operator R gives the expectations of neural firing for the various combinations of sensory-behavioral variables. It is unlikely that this will ever
be a linear operation. The right side of the equation is n-dimenional. The
left side may be multidimensional and becomes one-dimensional in the
case in which pattern of firing is ignored and only rate of firing is considered. In most cases, analytical expressions for $E \{f(t)\}$ will be impossible,
but a table can be constructed and rules formulated for interpolation between data points. The fact that the above relation contains only the expected value of a probability density function (for which the shape may
be unknown) emphasizes that it is useful only for predicting neuronal
firing from sensory-behavioral variables; predictions in the opposite direction are invalid. We have written the relation as an expectation rather than
as the probability density function itself, because this is a more realistic
experimental objective.

A *behavioral situation* is defined by constraints on sensory-behavioral
variables. In a given situation, some variables are constant; others are allowed to vary within certain limits. Furthermore, there may be rules governing the relationships among some of the variables. These rules may be
imposed intentionally by the experimenter, or they may simply be a property of the situation. This definition of situation conforms to everyday
usage. An animal is always in some situation or another, in the sense that
some sensory-behavioral variables are constants. These constant terms in
the sensory-behavioral firing relation represent the above-defined sensory-
behavioral states. In any situation, the expression representing the sensory-behavioral firing relation is reduced in its dimensionality (and consequently simplified) by each sensory-behavioral variable that remains
constant. The sensory-behavioral firing relation in a situation can be simplified to the following expectation function:

$$E \{f(t)\} = R_s \{V_i (t + \Delta t_i) \mid i = 1 \text{ to } m, \ m < n\}$$

where i represents the index of all the sensory-behavioral variables that
change within the situation and R_s is the operator describing the sensory-
behavioral firing relation for this situation; each different situation will
have a different R_s. If we take this simplification to the extreme and make
m equal to one, we have a single sensory-behavioral firing correlation,
where the domain of V over which $E \{f(t)\}$ changes is called a sensory-
behavioral correlate.

Some variables may be of minor importance in specific behavioral situations. For instance, it seems that SWS is similar in many different environments. Hence, SWS may be a behavioral situation largely independent of the environmental variables and neuronal firing may be independent

of most tonic sensory-behavioral variables. A subset of the variables in a behavioral situation will be relevant to the firing of a neuron and to a particular firing relation (R_s). We assume that there are rules for how the R_s functions vary as different fixed values of sensory-behavioral variables are chosen and for how the unfixed variables change. As we learn more about the full $E \{f(t)\}$ function from experiments in which only one variable is changed, we should be able to predict the function when more than one sensory-behavioral variables are changing simultaneously, as is usually the case in real life.

The strategies for discovering sensory-behavioral correlates and firing relations and the ways in which a knowledge of these can help us understand the nervous system are major aims of this chapter. Section C deals with sensory-behavioral correlates and firing relations, almost all for the steady state. The issue of sensory-behavioral firing relations that change, as may occur in learning and development, is only touched on.

The general principles of this chapter would hold if the variables we choose to correlate with neural firing were allowed to include variables inside the body. We will not use this broader definition, but rather will restrict ourselves to sensory-behavioral variables (i.e., relations of the animal to the outside world). We could also include correlations of sensory-behavioral variables with non-spiking electrical activity of neurons or release of substances by neurons. For simplicity, however, we will restrict our discussion almost entirely to correlations with action potentials. Also. when we speak of the inputs to a neuron that is not a sensory receptor, we will for simplicity discuss only the synaptic inputs, even though other inputs (e.g., hormonal) may also be important.

A *neural tag*, a notion we will use several times, is one or a group of characteristic(s) of a class of neurons that can be used experimentally to identify a neuron as a member of that class. The characteristics that can be used as tags (e.g., physiological, as in antidromic firing; pharmacological; morphological, as in dye-injected single neurons; and sensory-behavioral correlates) are important in themselves and may also allow us to know that the same class of neurons are being studied in different preparations (e.g., behaving animals, anesthetized animals, brain-slices). They also allow us to compare the firing of different neurons during similar events or states even though the neurons have been studied one at a time.

Three themes will recur throughout this chapter. First, sensory-behavioral correlates and firing relations are *only* correlations and *cannot* in themselves imply causal relations or define the function of a neuron or its neural code. Studies in this field, including many of our own, have not been sufficiently cautious in making inferences from correlations, possibly because much of the earliest work dealt with neurons so close to sensory inputs or behavioral outputs that the distinction between causality and covariation was blurred or considered trivial. We will suggest methods for the use of correlations that we feel are conservative but powerful.

Second, behavior interacts in two ways with the "cell biological" properties of neurons. Knowledge at either level may be valuable in understanding the other; for example, behaviorally defined characteristics can be used to tag neurons to help in the study of their connectivity, and cell biological characteristics can be used to sharpen the distinctions between behaviorally defined classes of neurons. We will discuss the value of holding behavior constant in order to maintain constant neuronal organization and the value of manipulating behavior in order to observe the consequences of changes in neural organization. Behavior is not only something to be explained, but can also be an important experimental parameter.

Third, the study of a wide range of sensory-behavioral variables, something which has rarely been attempted, is of value. The fragmentary data that exist indicate, however, that often a given cell has more than one sensory-behavioral correlate. For instance, as described above, the firing of neurons in lateral geniculate and striate cortex covaries with pattern of light *and* with state of sleep-wake (Livingston & Hubel, 1981). There are two rather broad explanations of how this could occur. One is that the firing of a group of the inputs of a given neuron is a similar function of multiple sensory-behavioral variables. The other is the possibility that a neuron can be fired by a small subset of its total excitatory inputs (e.g., McNaughton, Barnes, & Andersen, 1981). One sensory-behavioral correlate might arise from one subset of the input neurons, and other correlates from other subsets (i.e., there is adding of correlates). Once we admit that the firing of neurons may be a function of more than one sensory-behavioral variable due to adding of correlates at successive synaptic levels, it would seem that some neurons might have a huge number of sensory-behavioral correlates. The extent to which this is true or not true is an important empirical question for which there are few data. A related question is the relationship between different sensory-behavioral correlates of a given neuron. Thus, it is important to examine a fairly wide range of sensory-behavioral events and states for interconnecting neurons to determine both the *range* and the *limits* of sensory-behavioral correlates.

B. CELL BIOLOGY OF NEURONS IN BEHAVING ANIMALS

There are great advantages to studying the firing of neurons in normal animals; the recording itself is almost innocuous. Understanding the normal state is intrinsically important and also provides a baseline for the variations found in other states. This method allows us (1) to describe the firing repertoire of neurons, (2) to study physiological, pharmacological, and morphological characteristics of neurons for which sensory-behavioral correlates are known, (3) to determine how these characteristics change during different sensory-behavioral states, and (4) to control sensory-behavioral variables.

1. FIRING REPERTOIRE

The firing repertoire of a neuron consists of the rates and patterns of firing that occur; it also includes the shape of the action potentials. Firing repertoires differ widely from one neuron to another. Some neurons do not fire for many minutes at a time [e.g., brainstem (Siegel & McGinty, 1976) and hippocampus (Kubie & Ranck, 1982)]. Other neurons rarely fire at a rate less than 20 action potentials per second [e.g., hippocampal theta cells (Ranck, 1973)]. It is not sufficient to focus on phasic firing, as is often done, since the steady background firing of single neurons changes in both rate and pattern [e.g., during sleep (Steriade & Hobson, 1976) and in different wakeful situations (Kubie & Ranck, 1982)].

For a given neuron, certain rates and patterns of firing are never seen. When we try to explain what causes a particular neuron to fire, we must explain not only why a particular range is seen, but also why we do not see firing outside that range. Moreover, the consequences of the firing of a neuron are limited by its range of pattern and its rates.

The shape and duration of extracellular action potentials as recorded extracellularly differ among neurons. Some neurons in the hippocampus, lateral thalamus (Ranck, 1973), and cerebellum have "complex-spikes," a burst of spikes with 2- to 5-msec interspike intervals and decreasing amplitude of the spikes within each burst. There are neurons in the hippocampus and lateral thalamus that fire complex-spikes only during SWS; in other states, they only fire single spikes. Recording from neurons during sleep seems to be particularly important and is an example of the value of observing a range of sensory-behavioral states. In addition, the shape and duration of action potentials can be useful as neural tags.

2. PHYSIOLOGY, PHARMACOLOGY, AND MORPHOLOGY

Many of the classical extracellular electrophysiological measurements (e.g., conduction velocity and refractoriness) can be made on neurons in behaving animals. This is possible because, in most parts of the brain, electrical stimuli of moderate intensity do not affect the behavior of an animal unless delivered rapidly in long trains.

A knowledge of the electrophysiological characteristics of neurons in an area allows us to classify them. Whenever we read that to a given stimulus "40% of the neurons increased their firing, 40% decreased, and 20% were unchanged" we imagine that there are three different groups of neurons, which could be better defined electrophysiologically, morphologically, pharmacologically, or behaviorally. One of the most important distinctions is between projection neurons and local circuit neurons. Steriade (1978) has reviewed input-output methods for sorting neurons in this way and the usefulness of such sorting when studying sleep and wakefulness, analyzing the thalamic and neocortical interactions in sleep. In cases in which the inputs end directly on the neuron (i.e., monosynaptic response), interpretation of the results can be especially useful [e.g., perforant path inputs to dentate and CA3 inputs to CA1 (commissural and associational)]. Identification of pyramidal neurons by antidromic stimulation of the medullary pyramids is another valuable electrophysiological method.

It is also valuable to characterize neurons with known sensory-behavioral firing relations electrophysiologically. If the two methods are found to place neurons in similar sets, the electrophysiological characteristics can be used as tags so that sensory-behaviorally defined classes can be studied in simpler preparations in which other information can be obtained. For instance, in Ammon's horn, there are two major classes of neurons with clear differences in firing repertoires, sensory-behavioral correlates, and electrophysiological characteristics (Ranck, 1973). These classes are called theta cells and complex-spike cells. On the basis of their localization, number, and electrophysiological characteristics, we have suggested that complex-spike cells are pyramidal cells, whereas theta cells are mostly interneurons (Fox & Ranck, 1981). Schwartzkroin and Mathers (1978), working in hippocampal slices, have shown by dye injection that cells with the electrophysiological characteristics and firing repertoire of theta cells are in fact interneurons. An example of how extensively classical electrophysiological techniques can be applied in behaving animals are the experiments of Sakai and Woody (1980); they were able to record intracellularly and inject dyes in restrained (but awake and behaving) cats.

3. CHANGES WITH BEHAVIOR

In different sensory-behavioral events and states, there may be different distributions of rates of firing of the afferents to a neuron. Therefore, we might expect a neuron to have different electrophysiological characteristics in different sensory-behavioral situations. Steriade (see Steriade & Hobson, 1976) has shown this to be the case in electrophysiologically defined neurons in neocortex with recordings made during different states of sleep and wakefulness. Winson and Abzug (1978) have shown that summed extracellular action potentials evoked by electrical stimulation of afferents to Ammon's horn and dentate gyrus are different in different states of consciousness and vary with the presence or absence of the hippocampal theta rhythm. The fact that these are monosynaptic responses makes the results especially amenable to analysis.

Reflexes and other properties of groups of neurons are also modulated. For instance, in REM sleep there is a tonic decrease and phasic loss of the stretch reflex (Pompeiano, 1967). These differences in the state of brain are partly the cause and partly the effect of the difference in behavior. The brain is organized differently in different behaviors; aspects of these changes can be studied experimentally at the cellular level.

4. SENSORY-BEHAVIORAL CONTROL AND BEHAVIOR CLAMPING

There are two reasons for controlling certain sensory-behavioral states of an animal while studying cellular characteristics. As we said just above, there may be different cellular activities in different behaviors, so that behavior is one of many variables to be controlled. The other reason is that normal behaviors are frequently more interesting states in which to study cell biological characteristics than abnormal states, such as anesthesia or paralysis. Furthermore, the state of the animal can be controlled better in behaving animals in many ways than in animals in other states. For instance, a paralyzed animal may be awake, awake and terrified, or asleep. (There are, of course, many good scientific and humane reasons for using anesthetized animals for certain kinds of studies.) If one is not interested in behavior, behavior should, nevertheless, be controlled and not ignored.

In many studies of sensory systems, a stimulus is presented to an animal who is only described as "awake." We suspect that better definition and control of the behavioral condition would eliminate some of the variability in cell responses. In motor system studies, it is common to control behavior by overtraining an animal on a motor task. Unpredictable, sudden changes in the load may then be introduced at various phases of the task as probes of the properties of a stereotyped motion or the underlying neural events (e.g., Evarts & Tanji, 1976).

Sensory-behavioral variables need not have identical values for every repetition of an experiment, even if a behavior appears to be performed the same way. There may be changes in the internal state of the animal, such as a shift from the rat equivalent of "anxious" to that of "tranquil." To say there is no change in a specific behavior can be a relatively weak claim unless one chooses the behavior carefully. One of the most common descriptions is that of an animal who is awake (often without EEG verification) and waiting quietly. Without further detail this is not very useful, since it includes many states ranging from freezing in fear to drowsiness. The word "arousal" is often used in description of behavior with no appropriate definition of what is meant. Some behaviors are relatively stereotyped and reproducible, such as SWS and drinking; with appropriate training, these are readily obtainable. Eating and REM sleep are less homogeneous in time, but are also stereotyped and readily obtainable. We have trained rats running on a treadmill to give a constant behavior lasting up to about 30 minutes (Mitchell & Ranck, 1980; Rudell, Fox, & Ranck, 1980).

In many studies of changes associated with drugs or lesions, it is not clear whether the observed changes in neuronal firing are due to changes in behavior caused by the drug or the lesion (which, in turn, affect the neuronal firing), or whether the neuron is directly affected. In such cases, we can carry the idea of the control of behavior one step further in order to make the results clearer. The relation of neuronal firing to behavior is an example of a feedback system in which certain internal events (neuronal firing) affect the final result (behavior), but also in which the final result can, in turn, affect these internal events. In the analysis of such a system, it is common practice to hold the final result constant while manipulating the internal events that affect the final result, thereby opening the feedback loop. Curiously, this procedure has not been used in the electrophysiological analysis of behavior. By analogy with voltage clamping, let us call it "behavior clamping." Behavior clamping might be accomplished by recording from a neuron during behaviors that are *not* affected by the drug or lesion, both before and after the intervention. Behaviors that *are* affected by a drug or a lesion (and, hence, cannot be behaviorally clamped) are, of course, of great interest and are often the only ones studied. We think attention to neuronal firing and electrophysiology in behaviors that are not affected may be an additional fruitful approach.

C.   SENSORY-BEHAVIORAL FIRING RELATIONS

1.   WHY THERE MIGHT NOT BE SENSORY-BEHAVIORAL CORRELATES OR WHY THE CORRELATIONS MIGHT BE VERY LOW

When we record from a primary afferent neuron or from a motor neuron, we expect a high correlation between the firing of the neuron and sensory-behavioral events. However, when the neuron is synaptically removed from the periphery, we might expect the correlations between events in the external world and the firing of neurons to decrease or to become so complex as to be impossible to describe.

There are presumably many activities in the brain for which there is little or no simple relation to concurrent input or output. Some neuronal firing could be part of an internal timing mechanism, internal switching, or an error signal. Firing in the brain may be correlated with things often described in non-behavioristic terms (for instance, attitudes, perception, ideas, moods) that may affect behavior, but that have no simple relation to immediate behavior or to sensory input. It is possible that the neuron must be considered as part of a huge neural net and that there is no consistency in the relation of the firing of the cell to sensory-behavioral variables except when the activity of the cell is considered along with the activity of the rest of the neurons in the net. It is thus surprising that, in many cases, the firing of neurons many synapses removed from the periphery seems to have a high correlation with sensory-behavioral events.

2. DISCOVERING AND DESCRIBING SENSORY-BEHAVIORAL FIRING RELATIONSHIPS

(i) Basic Neuronal Variables

Implicit in the idea of looking for sensory-behavioral firing relations is the need to abstract some quantitative description out of the spike train. Although, by definition, abstraction entails some loss of information, presenting pictures of the actual time series of action potentials, annotated with a log of the animal's environment and activities, is too crude. Simply reporting average firing rate in many cases is also too coarse a representation of the action potential traffic. Some early studies were cruder yet in only distinguishing two states of firing—relatively fast firing and slow firing (or "off").

What is needed is more detail on the pattern of firing. The question is which features of the pattern of firing correlate best with sensory-behavioral variables. In some cases, mean rate may show the best correlation, but some efforts should be made to show that other descriptions of the pattern do not improve the correlation. Analysis of the pattern of firing has already proved important in sleep studies (Steriade & Hobson, 1976). Here the relationship is between the behavioral state and the shape of the time averaged inter-spike interval distribution, which changes in a qualitative manner as the animal goes from wakefulness to various stages of sleep. There are many important issues relating to pattern of firing, such as criteria for stationarity, randomness, periodicity, and serial correlations within the spike train (Glaser & Ruchkin, 1976).

An implicit but false assumption that is often made is that only relatively rapid rates of firing "mean something" and that slower rates do not "mean anything." As a counterexample, we note that when rats run an eight-arm radial maze, some hippocampal neurons fire faster when the rat is on certain arms, whereas other neurons decrease their rate from the mean on certain arms (Olton, Branch, & Best, 1978). There are also "pause" neurons in the oculomotor system that cease firing in association with saccadic eye movements (Keller, 1974).

Two of us (Kubie & Ranck, 1982) have recorded from single hippocampal neurons of a rat while she performed each of three different well-learned tasks in three different environments (running an elevated maze, bar pressing in a Skinner box, and retrieving pups). For many neurons, the firing rate distribution in each situation had both fast and slow modes. The slow mode of firing acted as a background discharge, the exact rate of which differed in each situation. The background firing indeed occurred most of the time, so that the total number of action potentials constituting slow firing was comparable to the number of action potentials constituting fast firing. The range over which steady background firing varied in a single neuron between situations was at least twofold and could be as much as twenty-fold. This slow firing is clearly important and, at least in the hippocampus, is related to the behavioral situation.

(ii) Basic Sensory-Behavioral Variables

An initial step in the investigation of sensory-behavioral correlates is the determination of appropriate sensory-behavioral variables. Appropriate variables are those that correlate most highly with neuronal firing patterns. In many systems, it is unwarranted to restrict oneself to binding, a priori hypotheses about the appropriate variables. Only the outcome of an experiment can be used to judge which variables are important.

An important part of the method for monitoring many variables is straightforward: *Know what the animal is doing at all times. Keep track of sensory inputs and motor outputs of the animal. Watch the animal.* There are many reported experiments in which only one or two sensory-behavioral variables are measured; in the past, this reflected the limited number of ways in which one could obtain a permanent quantitative record of the fleeting phenomena of changing behavior. Video and cinematographic methods permit both the automatic analysis of certain sensory-behavioral variables and improved human observer analysis of many others. An example of automatic analysis is the plotting of cat limb position with a TV camera (Rudell, 1979). Seigel argues persuasively in this volume that there is no substitute for the human observer. With the aid of TV tape or film, one can monitor many variables with great care. The low price and technical quality of TV methods are changing the ways we can describe behavior.

Descriptions of sensory-behavioral events and states should be in the simplest possible terms, with no implication of mechanism, either behavioral or neural; we call these *simplest effective descriptors*. Perhaps complex or abstract descriptions may be necessary to find the best correlation, but it should first be demonstrated that simpler ones will not do. It is important because one can, *post hoc*, play with the building blocks of simple descriptors and rearrange them in many conceivable ways, including the construction of complex descriptors. However, when one starts with complex descriptors, simple descriptors are often irretrievable.

In many papers, the reader is not told what the animal was actually doing, even though he might be told in considerable detail the latencies observed or the numbers of errors or bar presses made by the animal. In some papers, one cannot determine whether the animals are awake or asleep. Perhaps this was due to difficulties in collecting behavioral data without videotape technology.

Many investigators describe the correlate of neuronal firing as an abstract process, such as attention or information processing, based on recordings made while an animal performs a task for which the investigator feels he understands the behavioral process involved. Even though experimental situations, of necessity, focus on certain specific neural or behavioral mechanisms, the data can, nevertheless, be described simply and without implied mechanism. One of us has described sensory-behavioral correlates of hippocampal neurons (Ranck, 1973); however, many of the descriptive terms used (e.g., appetitive, consummatory, mismatch) unnecessarily implied psychological mechanisms.

Some problems in choosing the most appropriate descriptors are, in fact, problems in coding, an issue we will discuss later. For instance, McCarley and Hobson (1975a) find neurons in the nucleus gigantocellularis that increase their rate of firing during REM sleep. Based on this datum and other data they developed a theory of the generation of REM sleep in which these neurons play a central role. Seigel, McGinty, and Breedlove (1977) and Vertes (1977), on the other hand, find that these same neurons fire at the same high rate during movements, whether the animal is awake or asleep, and consider the firing in REM sleep to be related to the phasic movements of REM sleep. The descriptions are essentially the same. Thus, the investigators formulated their description in terms congenial with their theories. The answer as to which view is correct must be decided on the basis of how the nucleus gigantocellularis works, of the mechanisms of movement, and of REM sleep. The decision cannot be made solely on the basis of sensory-behavioral firing relations.

We do not want to imply that each experiment should be run as if it were the first of its kind and that the experimenter should have absolutely no hypotheses about relevant variables. Obviously, we look for variables that are suggested by past studies of related neurons. Similarly, when a sensory-behavioral correlate is identified for a neuron in one behavioral situation, an experimenter would naturally guess that this sensory-behavioral correlate is the same or similar in a second situation. It is, in fact, important to test the constancy of sensory-behavioral correlates across a wide range of behavioral situations, since they may not be the same in different situations.

As larger numbers of sensory-behavioral correlates are described, the descriptions of some are being found to include more complex variables than simple sensory input, motor output, or state of sleep-wake. Rolls, Burton, and Mora (1976) have described neurons in the hypothalamus of monkeys that increase their rate of firing at the sight of food as long as the animal is hungry. Lynch, Mountcastle, Talbot, and Yin (1977) have described neurons in area 7 of the monkey that increase their rate of firing during visual fixation of objects associated with a strong motivational drive.

Some sensory-behavioral correlates can only be seen in freely moving animals. For instance, hippocampal neurons that increase their firing when the rat is in a particular place in his environment (O'Keefe & Dostrovsky, 1971) can only be seen if the rats are allowed to locomote throughout an apparatus. Chapin and Woodward (1981) have studied changes in transmission in the somatosensory system of the rat as a function of phase of the walking cycle.

(iii) Sensory-Behavioral Firing Relations

As defined in the introduction, each neuron has a sensory-behavioral firing relation that is a description of the correlations of rate and pattern of neuronal firing with a group of sensory-behavioral variables. For any fixed values of these sensory-behavioral variables, there will be a statistically predicted firing of the neuron.

In different behavioral situations, there may be different steady background firing of certain neurons. This has been extensively studied in many parts of brain in sleep. Individual hippocampal neurons fire at different background rates in different situations when the rat is awake, as we described above.

A common experiment is to manipulate one variable in a particular behavioral situation and determine the relation of the variable to the firing of the neuron. Often more than one sensory-behavioral variable may be systematically changed and these may interact in the firing of the neuron. For example, the firing of a retinal ganglion cell is conjointly determined by intensity of light, retinotopic location of light, and wavelength of light. We have already noted that neurons in the lateral geniculate and striate cortex change their firing with both the state of sleep-wakefulness and the pattern of light on the retina and that these two variables interact (Livingston & Hubel, 1981).

The receptive fields of neurons in the motor and somatosensory cortex in monkeys (Fetz, Finocchio, Baker, & Soso, 1980; Soso & Fetz, 1980) and the sensory-motor cortex in rats (Chapin & Woodward, 1981) have been determined in response to passively applied stimuli and also when the paws were used actively. In some cases, similar receptive fields were found, but many features of the receptive fields when the paw was used actively were not predicted by data from the experiment when touch was applied passively. Jasper (1981) has discussed other similar examples. Except for some primary afferents with no centrifugal control, we cannot assume that a sensory-behavioral correlation will be the same in different behavioral situations. Because not much data are available, it is hard to know which situations are important in particular neurons. We would think that at least the state of sleep-wake, the states of deprivation of food, water, and sleep, and motor activity should be considered for most neurons.

(iv) Temporal Relations between Neuronal Firing and Sensory-Behavioral Events

Let us assume that we have found a sensory-behavioral event that correlates with neuronal firing. A "peri-event" histogram may reveal that the event precedes, follows, or overlaps the change in firing. A sensory-behavioral event is most commonly an antecedent of neuronal firing in sensory systems. This relation may be altered by centrifugal influences, either at the primary afferent (e.g., gamma efferent effects on spindle afferents) or at synapses. These effects may be particularly evident during active use. In the case of a primary afferent axon with no peripheral control (which is thus a passive element), the sensory-behavioral correlate is the application of the adequate stimulus in the receptive field, and the onset of the sensory-behavioral correlate will always be an antecedent of change in firing. By eliminating the complicating factors of centrifugal control and active use, adequate stimuli and receptive fields can be defined in higher-order neurons. If the sensory system is used actively, there may be centrifugal control, and a sensory-behavioral correlate may follow, as well as precede, a change in neural firing (Fetz, Finocchio, Baker, & Soso, 1980; Chapin & Woodward, 1981).

In motor systems, correlates can be either antecedents or successors of neuronal firing. Some neurons in the motor cortex may fire before a movement occurs or after a cutaneous stimulus (e.g., Fetz, Finocchio, Baker, & Soso, 1980). Interest has often focused on the antecedents of movement because of the assumed flow of causal relations in the motor behavior. However, neurons signaling motor output may fire after a motor event; for instance, the firing of a neuron involved in the deceleration of a movement will follow the start of the movement and might appear to be sensing the motion. When looking at a relatively complete sensory-behavioral firing relation of a neuron, the distinction between motor and sensory systems is not always sharp. In the context of the monosynaptic reflex, an alpha motor neuron is a second-order sensory neuron. Thus, in both sensory and motor systems, as well as in other systems, we can expect to find correlates of firing that precede, follow, and are concurrent with neural firing. We can expect to find sensory-behavioral correlates that are correlated with firing on a millisecond scale and that have no tonic effects (e.g., as in a Pacinian corpuscle).

Neurons that have a tonic rate of firing associated with a sensory-behavioral state may change their tonic firing before or after transition to that state. McCarley and Hobson (1975a) find that some neurons in the gigantocellular field start increasing their tonic rate of firing one to two minutes before the animal enters REM sleep. They call this a tonic latency.

The temporal relations between neuronal firing and sensory-behavioral events are so important that sometimes experimental attention may be unduly directed toward sensory-behavioral events, which are easily timed. Many sensory stimuli are given in such a way that neural firing is sudden and synchronous. Although sudden stimuli maybe important to an animal living in a natural setting, nevertheless, many stimuli of biological significance have relatively slow onsets. Other important stimuli are tonically present. We fear that our knowledge of sensory processing is biased toward those stimuli with sudden onset, perhaps with an unknown contamination of startle.

(v) Observational and Paradigmatic Approaches

There have been major differences in experimental approaches based on the question of how broad a range of sensory-behavioral variables should be monitored while recording from one neuron. By far the most common approach has been to limit sharply the range of events observed in a well-defined paradigm and to report detailed data on those variables that are tested. A less common strategy (observational) has been to look initially at a wide range of sensory-behavioral variables for each neuron, sometimes intentionally sacrificing quantitative detail and control of the experimental situation. Of course, both breadth of observation and well-controlled quantitative experiments are necessary. The disagreement is on the order in which the experiments should be done and the degree to which conclusions can be drawn when one or the other kind of data is lacking.

The observational approach has been used in a variety of experiments. Adams (1968) recorded from neurons in the midbrain and hypothalamus during affective defensive behavior. Gross, Rocha-Miranda, and Bender (1972) studied visual stimuli affecting firing in the inferotemporal cortex. Ranck (1973, 1976) recorded from the hippocampus and septal nuclei. Vanderwolf (1969) used the observational method in his work on slow waves of the hippocampus. Even though Vanderwolf did not study single neurons, his approach has been of major influence.

Several reasons lead us to suggest that the broad observational type of study is necessary if the sensory-behavioral correlates in a given brain region are to be elucidated. One reason is that it allows us to look at the same sensory-behavioral correlate in different situations and to look for those generalities that cut across many behaviors. A second reason is that a broad approach allows us to look at multiple sensory-behavioral correlates, many of which would have been missed in a paradigmatic study. A paradigimatic study is always designed on the basis of previous data, which carries the danger that some sensory-behavioral correlate may be unintentionally designed out of consideration. For instance, the place cells of O'Keefe and Dostrovsky (1971) could not have been predicted from prior lesion studies and were not seen in earlier paradigmatic studies of hippocampal neurons. The observational approach also helps to define a more complete firing repertoire. [In many observational studies, there is a frank bias toward a point of view that favors including naturalistic observations, active freely moving animals, and ethological perspectives. We share this bias, but we will not defend the ethological point of view here. It is argued well by Hutt and Hutt (1970), and by other authors in this volume. The ethological bias does not exclude other approaches.]

We do not mean to say that a scatter gun approach is a panacea. There are some important shortcomings in the observational approach. Some observational studies are not adequately controlled and not adequately quantitative. There is opportunity for observer bias. There are too many variables, which make many correlates uncertain. The observational approach works best as a tool for generating hypotheses for further testing.

Best and Ranck (1975, 1982) tried to meet some of the problems of the broad, relatively unstructured approach. They recorded from single hippocampal neurons while the rat performed in a variety of ways. The tasks were similar to those used by Ranck (1973). The behavior of the rat was recorded on TV tape along with the firing of the neuron in such a way that the rat and the box were in the lower two-thirds of the TV screen and the oscilloscope face on the upper one-third. The firing of the neuron was also recorded on the audio channel. These TV tapes were then shown to groups of undergraduates. The students were asked to see if they could find a relation between the firing of the neuron and the rat's behavior or location. They then wrote their group conclusions. Another observer then watched only the rat activity part of the tapes. He had read the students descriptions and was instructed to press a telegraph key whenever he felt the animal was doing what the students had described. The neuron firing and telegraph key position were simultaneously fed into a computer, which determined how well the firing of the neuron was predicted by the description of the students. The student's description predicted the firing of 19 of the 20 hippocampal neurons with high significance. A majority of these neurons exhibited place-related firing, an observation not adequately noted in a previous study (Ranck, 1973). It was concluded from this that observational description of the sensory-behavioral correlates of hippocampal neurons can be reliable and predictive. The procedure used to determine sensory-behavioral correlates is rather elaborate, but similar studies may nevertheless be worthwhile to establish the reliability of other descriptions.

Clearly, well-defined experimental paradigms are necessary to determine and to analyze sensory-behavioral correlates. These studies should be designed with some knowledge of the appropriate sensory-behavioral variables. In general, observational studies should precede paradigmatic studies. Observational studies suffer from lack of control and precision. Paradigmatic studies run prematurely can ask questions about the wrong sensory-behavioral variables. Together both breadth and precision are obtainable.

(vi) Sensory-Behavioral Firing Relations that Change: Learning and Development

Everything we have said above considers the steady state in which sensory-behavioral firing relations do not change. There are reasons to imagine that during learning and development the sensory-behavioral firing relations of some neurons may change. We will not further develop this line of reasoning in this chapter. We do this because we are still working out our ideas on this difficult subject. We think that the approaches we have developed in here will be useful in defining what is meant by a sensory-behavioral firing relation that changes.

3. CLASSIFYING SENSORY-BEHAVIORAL CORRELATES

(i) Generalizing across Neurons

Once we have a good sample of the sensory-behavioral firing relations of the neurons in an area, we will want to group neurons into various types. The classification of neurons by sensory-behavioral firing relation may proceed in parallel with classification by such other criteria as location, morphology, firing repertoire, and responses to stimulation of afferents or to iontophoretically applied substances. These classifications may coincide completely, partially, or (less likely) not at all. In the case of nearly complete coincidence, information is immediately available about the mechanisms and/or connectivity that underlie the correlation. For instance, in the striate cortex most simple cells are stellate neurons and most complex cells are pyramidal neurons (Kelly & Van Essen, 1974). The fact that the agreement was not exact may mean that the criteria that distinguish simple from complex cells are not exact enough or that stellate and pyramidal cells can be confused, or most interestingly, that other cell classes have been identified. Sensory-behavioral correlates of different neurons may vary systematically with location, as is the case with topographical localization in visual and somatosensory systems and with modality in the somatosensory cortex.

The development of descriptions of sensory-behavioral correlates of a single neuron necessarily proceeds hand in hand with the classification of neurons on the basis of sensory-behavioral firing relations. High correlations between sensory-behavioral events and neural firing can, in general, be achieved with *post hoc* analyses for each neuron. By contrast, requiring a category to include a group of neurons will, in general, decrease the correlation for an individual neuron. The decision of which categories to create, and how finely to subdivide them, is one that must depend not only on the value of the correlation, but also on our ideas about the overall working of the system. There is a trade-off between precision and generality. Fetz, Finocchio, Baker, and Soso (1980), in a study of the relation of firing of precentral neurons to active and passive movement, draw the following conclusion:

> Having grouped the responses of precentral cells into a few simple categories, we must emphasize that this procedure seriously oversimplifies the diversity of response patterns actually observed. . . . Even for a simple elbow movement, the response pattern of each cell is virtually unique. To what extent such individual differences may be neglected in favor of emphasizing those features consistent with simple conceptual schemes is open to question.

(ii) Differences between Neurons: Broad and Narrow Tuning

In many cases, the differences between neurons within a group is especially significant. The differences themselves may be used to characterize the neurons further if a variable is found to predict them. For instance, in the visual and somatosensory systems, differences between the sensory-behavioral correlates of neurons reflect position in retinotopic space or body surface. A classification should include common neuronal characteristics as well as the dimensions(s) along which they differ. The need to include these determinations is one of the major reasons for recording from single neurons, rather than using multiunit recording. In multiunit recording, differences between neurons will often be averaged out. In visual, somatosensory, and motor systems, the orderly difference in sensory-behavioral correlates of neurons is also reflected in their orderly localization in brain. This is strong evidence that the observed difference is an important one. Conversely, whenever there are topographical anatomical projections from one region to another, differences in sensory-behavioral correlates should be assumed to exist and be searched for.

We have found the ideas of Erickson (1968) useful in thinking about sensory-behavioral correlates. In sensory systems, Erickson distinguishes between narrowly and broadly tuned neurons. Narrowly tuned neurons are sensitive to a small fraction of the total, biologically relevant dimension. For instance, many visual neurons are narrowly tuned with respect to retinotopic space. Broadly tuned neurons are sensitive to a large fraction of the appropriate dimension. Wavelength sensitivity of photoreceptors and temperature sensitivity of warmth receptors are examples of broad tuning. Note that a neuron may have *both* broad and narrow tuning characteristics. In the geniculostriate visual system, a neuron has sensory-behavioral correlates that include both retinotopic space (narrow) and wavelength (broad); temperature-sensitive neurons (broad) are also line-labeled for body surface (narrow).

D. BEYOND CORRELATION

In most of the above discussions, we have mainly considered one cell at a time, or made comparisons with other neurons in the same region. Any strategy should be able to do more than increase our catalog of relations between a sensory-behavioral event and an event in brain. The brain is not just a bag of neurons, with each neuron firing in certain situations. We want to understand the mechanisms involved and to determine how these mechanisms fit into the system as a whole. We want to explain both mechanism (a reductionistic approach) and to see how a neuron whose sensory-behavioral correlate is known fits into the whole system and contributes to the behavior of the animal (a synthetic approach).

Recording action potentials from a single neuron can help us go "beyond correlation" because action potentials are not epiphenomena, but rather are parts of causal sequences. Indeed, action potentials are by and large the only way information can be transmitted more than 1 mm in the brain. They are the language of neurons. There are many important and commonly measured variables that are epiphenomena (i.e., they have minimal consequences themselves), for instance the EEG or the concentration of neurotransmitter metabolites in urine. By contrast, action potentials in one neuron have consequences in other neurons. We can use action potential data recorded from one neuron to help understand the firing of other neurons. Spike trains are both data that must be explained by any neural theory of a behavior and data that also can be used to help explain the neural substrate of the behavior.

In this section, we will first discuss the general issues of coding and function and then discuss more specifically the experimental use of sensory-behavioral firing relations.

1. Codes and Function

Sensory-behavioral firing relations can never, in and of themselves, tell us about neural codes or function. This is because sensory-behavioral firing relations express correlations and as such can never indicate cause and effect. It will be useful to get some idea of what a neural code ought to be and how a variety of types of data, including sensory-behavioral firing relations, can help us decipher neural codes.

(i) Codes

Single Neuron Codes. First, let us limit our discussion to codes of single neurons. A code can be thought of as a transform table with two columns. In the case of single neuron codes, one of the columns includes the various patterns of action potentials the neuron can exhibit. The second is a column of equivalents to these action potential patterns. A single neuron may be part of many codes. For each code, all the entries of the second column should be in one "domain." There are two categories of domains for the second column. One is action potentials, the action potentials of sets of neurons projecting to the neuron. The second category is system variables. These can be internal variables, such as error signals, or external variables, such as sensory-behavioral variables. For the relationship between the pattern of firing of a neuron and system variable to be a *bona fide* code, it must meet two criteria; (1) the correlation must be high, (2) it must be demonstrated that the signal encoded in the action potential train is used by downstream neurons. The second criterion is perhaps impossible to satisfy, but partial answers may be possible, for instance, from lesion study.

The determination of a neuron's sensory-behavioral correlates is a useful step in deciphering codes. When a neuron has crisp sensory-behavioral correlates, then these correlates can be used to generate hypotheses about the code. An example comes from the hippocampus. Many projection cells of the hippocampus are "place cells"—they fire fastest when a rat is in a particular place in its environment (O'Keefe, 1979). Although the magnitude of the correlation is not yet known, the impression is that, for many cells, it is quite high. Such a high correlation does not, however, prove that the nervous system makes use of the spatial information in the spike train, but it certainly motivates further research. In this regard, lesion studies can be quite valuable; if tasks that require use of spatial information are not disrupted by hippocampal lesions, the hypothesis that these neurons encode place would, of necessity, be rejected (O'Keefe & Nadel, 1978).

In several areas of sensory and motor physiology, candidate codes are better established. One can argue, for example, that the location of tactile stimulation is encoded in the firing of single neurons in the nucleus cuneatus. Not only is there a high correlation of unit firing with the region of skin stimulation, but one can diagram a realistic model of the neural connections that cause the firing. In addition, one can argue from lesion data and recordings from other levels of the nervous system that cuneate nucleus activity is used by higher brain regions for precise tactile localization.

It should be noted that many neurons may encode variables that are poorly correlated with sensory-behavioral events. Examples we can imagine are error signals or states of the internal environment. For these neurons, sensory-behavioral firing relations will not suggest codes.

Distributed or Crossfiber Codes. Erickson (1978) and others have argued that much information processing in the nervous system may be distributed. In distributed systems, information is not encoded in the firing of single neurons, but can only be detected when a group of related neurons is considered. Consider the nucleus cuneatus again. The location of somatic stimulation is encoded in the firing of single neurons and, therefore, is not a distributed code. The shape of tactile stimuli is not encoded in the firing of any single neuron, but is, in principle, detectable from the firing of a group of neurons in the nucleus cuneatus. The code for the shape, therefore, is distributed in the nucleus cuneatus. (It may be nondistributed upstream.) We do not intend to get involved in the debate about the extent of distributed codes and function, although we will have more to say about distributed function below. We suspect that sensory-behavioral firing relations will say little about distributed codes. Distributed codes might be suggested if several individual neurons are recorded simultaneously.

In summary, sensory-behavioral firing relations suggest, at best, a limited set of neural codes. They may be useful in deciphering some codes, but useless in others.

(ii) Function

The function of a neuron can be described in two senses. *Local function* is the difference between what is encoded on the inputs to the neuron and what the output of the neuron encodes, i.e., information processing. *Global function* is the way in which this information processing is used by the whole animal. In either sense, the function of a neuron is not its sensory-behavioral firing relation. The receptive field of a neuron in the mammalian lateral geniculate is (roughly) an annulus or a spot of light, but the function of these neurons is not to respond to annuli or spots of light. The function of these neurons is poorly understood, but seems (roughly) to be the transmission of information from the optic tract to the optic radiations without much change, and to block this transmission at certain times.

In cases when sensory-behavioral correlates are considered to be fair reflections of what is encoded, we can try to follow the cell-to-cell transformation of the sensory-behavioral correlates of maximal firing rate into the brain to project an informal picture of information processing. In the visual and somatosensory systems, the results of this kind of analysis of passive receptive fields have been impressive. However, the sensory-behavioral correlate is at best only an approximation of what is encoded, and the analysis is only valid for the limited case of passive receptive fields, ignoring centrifugal control, so the result is at best approximate and incomplete (see Section C, 2, iii). The line of reasoning used in determining information flow from data on sensory-behavioral correlates is superficially similar to that used in the method of sensory-behavioral correlates as neural tags (discussed in Section D, 2, iii). However, a big difference between these two approaches is that when correlates are used as tags, we are only interested in the extent to which they are the same or overlap. Otherwise, we do not attend to their content. On the other hand, in the approximation of information flow analysis, we attend very much to the details of the content of the sensory-behavioral correlates and what this content suggests about codes and function.

No matter how accurate and complete this kind of analysis of local information processing is, it does not tell us how the rest of the brain uses the processed information; that is, it does not speak to the nature of the global function of a neuron or a region of the brain. To ask about the global function of a region of the brain is to ask about the relations of this region with other regions of the brain.

To some extent, global function can be approached by determining the sensory-behavioral correlates of neurons to which a group of neurons project. However, there are limitations to the method, because this next region of the brain will also receive other inputs. Furthermore, sensory-behavioral correlates may not be similar to what is encoded. In working out how a given area interacts with the rest of the brain, lesion experiments tell us something about neural function and about the behavior of an animal deprived of a certain region of brain, but they tell us nothing about what that region of brain does or what goes on inside it. Thus, experiments on animals with brain lesions and studies of sensory-behavioral firing relations are complementary. The strengths of one approach are the weaknesses of the other.

We see, therefore, that sensory-behavioral firing relations cannot be relied on to provide simple information on codes or function. We must develop models to explain codes and function. Sensory-behavioral firing relations may give some clues for these models, but they have no direct relation to the model itself, although they are among the most important data to be explained by any model. A model generates ideas for further paradigmatic experiments on sensory-behavioral firing relations that test and further refine the model.

(iii) Distributed Function

For over 150 years, since the introduction of phrenology, a recurrent theme in neuroscience has been the contrast between views of neural organization that stress localization and specificity of function as opposed to views that stress diffuse representation of function. We discuss this issue for two reasons. First, any method tends to bias studies in which the method is used toward a particular view of the nervous system. Electrical recording from single neurons would seem to introduce bias toward the localization point of view. Indeed, much of the work that has been done seems to reflect this bias; this work might be called *microphrenology*. We want to avoid any unintentional bias introduced by method. Second, we think there is much truth in the diffusely distributed function point of view and want to suggest how the method of recording from single neurons in behaving animals can be used in a way consistent with this point of view. We think that a proper perspective on sensory-behavioral firing relations can lead to a balanced view of localized and distributed function. Some data from single neurons in behaving animals, which indeed suggest distributed function, will be discussed.

Many views of the nervous system stress localization and specificity of function. The proponents of some of these views often consider an individual neuron to be a feature detector and they attempt to interpret the function of a single neuron, stress stability of function, and try to assign a single function to a neuron (Barlow, 1972). Again, some assign a function to a region of the brain, or a tract, or try to associate a global function with a particular neurotransmitter (*chemophrenology*).

There are many forms of the view that there is diffuse representation of function. Some proponents stress that the brain uses distributed codes or that it has probablistic network properties, that there is parallel processing, and that there is lability or multiplicity of function of a single neuron. Presentations of these views often emphasize that it is impossible to interpret the firing of a single neuron without having information about the firing of many other neurons. They often emphasize that a particular global function is performed in many regions of the brain and that one region of the brain may be involved in many functions. John and Schwartz (1978) have strongly argued this position. Pellionisz and Llinás (1979), Kohonen (1978), and Anderson, Silverstein, Ritz, and Jones (1977), among others, have developed this position mathematically, making some of the same points we make and expressing them in the language of linear algebra.

We will not consider the relative merits of these views in detail. In general, we believe that there is much that is correct in both views. Neuroscience has been much more successful using localization rather than diffuse representation as a conceptual cornerstone, since the experiments it suggests are often workable and interpretable. Diffuse representation views, on the other hand, often do not lead to helpful experiments, but rather have a net effect of being somewhat negative and discouraging about the prospect of understanding brain mechanisms (Kandel, 1977).

In the course of recording from single neurons in many parts of brain, we have been struck by a general observation that can be stated two ways: (1) A given neuron has a relatively rapid rate of firing during many events, and (2) during any given situation, many and perhaps most neurons seem to fire relatively rapidly at some time. It is as if most of the neurons were used much or most of the time. This is not true for all neurons. For instance, Siegel and McGinty (1976) have reported neurons in the reticular formation that are off for long periods of time (minutes) and that fire only in relation to specific events. Kubie and Ranck (1982) have seen neurons in the hippocampus that are off for minutes at a time. Perhaps many neurons fire only intermittently, and we are not aware of their existence because they are not firing when we are searching for neurons. Nevertheless we think that most neurons do increase their firing rates in many behaviors and that most neurons are firing relatively rapidly at some time in most situations. There are many possible reasons for this, but the one that seems most likely to us is that the brain's functions are extensively distributed. Distributed function implies that single neurons would be used in many functions and, hence, show change in their firing in association with many events; they would have multiple sensory-behavioral correlates. It would also imply that the brain uses many or most of its neurons in each behavior, regardless of whether the behavior is simple or complicated.

We can use the general approach developed in this chapter to address at least some of the issues of diffuse representation as follows. Our emphasis that a neuron can be fired by many different subsets of its inputs and our emphasis on looking for a range of sensory-behavioral correlates acknowledge that a neuron's activity may be related to many kinds of events. We do not deny specificity, but rather urge looking for multiple specificities of a neuron. Our emphasis on looking for differences in sensory-behavioral correlates between neurons and our interest in broadly tuned neurons also fit the theory of a distributed code. Attention to steady background firing may also be important. The care we have taken with regard to the inferences that can be made from sensory-behavioral correlates with respect to code, cause, and function may help to prevent some unwarranted conclusions about localization and specificity. We believe that the overall organization and network properties of the brain may vary in different behaviors and that this variation can be examined. We also stress that the network properties mentioned above can be at least partially controlled by behavior clamping.

2. Mechanisms, Circuits, and the Use of Tags

(i) Reconstructing Temporal Firing Relationships Using Data from Single Neurons

A first step in working out interactions among neurons with known sensory-behavioral firing relations is to specify the relative timing of action potentials associated with a given event. In sensory systems, a standard strategy is to collect data on the firing of single neurons, one neuron at a time, in the same and different structures, in response to a certain stimulus. When this procedure is used, it can be argued that we know how all these cells are firing in response to a stimulus by comparing their peristimulus histograms. Those cells that fire with the shortest latency must be activated first, those with the second shortest latency next, and so on. The strategy is also used in motor systems by comparing the firing times of cells relative to some constant event in a stereotyped motor sequence.

For some spontaneously occurring behavior, we can use this method by time locking with respect to a chosen external event (e.g., pressing a bar, receiving a pellet, or starting to drink). However, some sensory-behavioral variables vary too slowly to easily be used in this way. Internal events, especially periodic ones, can sometimes be used to work out temporal relations between neurons in spontaneously occurring behavior. For instance, the hippocampal theta rhythm is a slow-wave, which occurs during certain specific behavioral states. The firing of hippocampal neurons has a strong phase relation to the theta rhythm. Knowing the relation of the firing of each neuron to the phase of the theta rhythm can then help us time the firing of neurons relative to each other (Bland, Andersen, Ganes, & Sveen, 1980).

A word of caution about methods for reconstructing timing sequences: The relationships found can only be statistical. Consider two neurons that fire slowly and with much variability, so that the time-related firing pattern must be derived from extensive averaging. Even if the average event-related firing patterns of these two neurons are very similar, the action potentials of each cell may not be time locked to each other. For instance, in the extreme case, neuron A might fire with a fixed latency every other time after an event, and neuron B might fire with the same latency only on the trials when A does not fire. The two neurons would have identical post-stimulus histograms, but the firing of A would have a strong *negative* correlation with the firing of B. Even for two relatively rapidly firing neurons with similar, average, event-related firing patterns, there may be additional constraints on the timing of discharges of the two neurons that are not apparent from their averages. For this reason, it is useful to have data from two or more single neurons recorded simultaneously.

(ii) Cellular Mechanisms and Circuits

Even if the firing of a neuron can be correlated with the sensory input and/or behavioral output of the animal, a causal relationship need not exist. It is unwise to refer to firing correlated with sensory-behavioral variables as "responses" of the neuron, as is often done, because of the causality implied. Causal relationships exist, in fact, at the levels of neuronal circuits and cellular mechanisms. Each neuron is part of one or many local circuits or global circuits. We cannot mechanistically explain the behavior of one neuron unless we understand it as one element in a circuit.

We can study cell biological characteristics of neurons and the circuits involving neurons that have known sensory-behavioral firing relations. We can do this either by doing the studies in behaving animals by studying the cell biology, circuits, and sensory-behavioral firing relation on the same neuron (see Section B) or by not using a behaving animal, but having a neural tag that can identify the class of the sensory-behavioral firing relation of the neuron. Two aspects of neuronal circuits, however, must be studied in behaving animals. (1) There are circuits which change their mode of operation in different behaviors (examples of this are given in Section B above). (2) No matter how well the neuronal level interactions are specified, we still may not understand the function of that machinery. For instance, two of the circuits we know best, those in the hippocampus and the cerebellum, are among those whose function we understand least well.

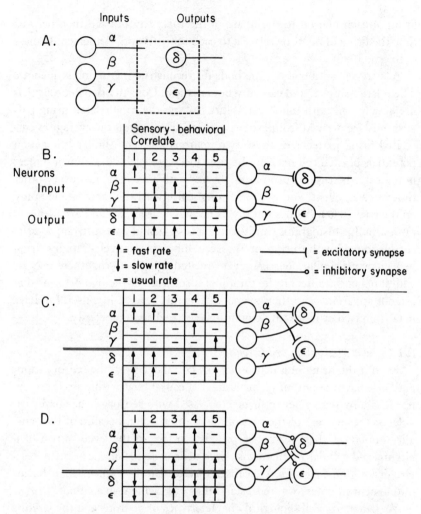

FIGURE 5.2. The use of sensory-behavioral correlates as neural tags. For a description, see text.

(iii) Neural Tags and Microcircuitry

In Figure 5.2A we show three input neurons (α, β, and γ) projecting to a brain region with two output neurons (δ and ε), in which the details of the interconnections of α, β, and γ to δ and ε are unknown. These five neurons are meant to represent five groups of neurons that have been sorted by their sensory-behavioral correlates. In Figure 5.2B we show a table of the sensory-behavioral correlates and firing of each of these five neurons. To the right of the table, we show one possible connectivity suggested by the data in the table (ignoring interneurons). Figures 5.2C and 5.2D show other combinations of sensory-behavioral correlates and the connectivity they suggest. The sensory-behavioral correlate is being used as a neural tag in this method. The sensory-behavioral correlate identifies a neuron and the time at which it fires at particular rates or patterns. One should note that this line of reasoning holds, regardless of the content of the sensory-behavioral events. This method of neural tags is frequently used, especially in sensory systems.

Similar reasoning can be used to suggest interactions of neurons within an area or patterns of convergence and divergence or the nature of a topographical projection from one region onto another. The method of neural tags only suggests relations, but many such suggestions can be further tested by other methods. Conversely, the use of sensory-behavioral correlates as neural tags is helpful in checking on microcircuitry that has been worked out by other methods.

When sensory-behavioral correlates in one region of brain are known, then the use of tags may be helpful in making preliminary guesses about what sensory-behavioral correlates to look for in regions that are afferent or efferent to it. When used along with some of the methods of Section D, 2, i (reconstruction of temporal firing relationships using data from single neurons), the method can be used to examine processes in some detail. Our explicit statement of this method of neural tags helps to make clear the great advantage of examining neurons in related areas with the same sensory behavioral variables.

E. CONCLUSION

1. SUMMARY

We discuss the relationships between sensory-behavioral variables and neuronal firing, and develop the idea of a sensory-behavioral firing relation. This concept then allows us to describe neuronal firing as a function of multiple interacting sensory-behavioral variables. Many cell biological characteristics of neurons can be studied in behaving mammals; and we discuss strategies for the studies. Some facets of cellular neurobiology can only be studied in behaving mammals. We suggest ways of discovering and describing basic neuronal variables and basic sensory-behavioral variables in order to determine a sensory-behavioral firing relation. Both phasic firing and steady background firing are related to sensory-behavioral variables. Neurons can be classified by their firing relations. A sensory-behavioral correlate is not what a neuron encodes, nor is it the function of a neuron. The relationship of sensory-behavioral firing relations to coding and function is discussed. We suggest how firing relations can be used to study both localized function and distributed function of the brain. There are some conservative, but useful ways to apply sensory behavioral firing relations in working out neural mechanisms of behavior; for instance, sensory-behavioral correlates may be used as tags to generate hypotheses of synaptic connectivity.

2. GLOSSARY

Behavioral situation. A situation specified by a set of constraints on sensory-behavioral variables. Some variables are held constant for the duration of the situation; others are allowed to vary, but their variation is constrained by certain rules, which do not change for the duration of the situation.

Firing repertoire of a neuron. The rates and patterns of firing that occur; it also includes the shape of the action potentials of the neuron.

Neural tag. One, or a group of, characteristic(s) of a class of neurons that can be used experimentally to identify a neuron as a member of that class.

Sensory-behavioral correlate of neural firing. That part of the domain of a sensory-behavioral variable over which there is a high correlation with the firing of a neuron.

Sensory-behavioral event. One, or a group of, sensory-behavioral variable(s) that changes its value rapidly.

Sensory-behavioral firing correlation. A statistical relationship between some representation of neural firing and a sensory-behavioral variable (or some transform of such a variable).

Sensory-behavioral firing relation. A statistical relationship between some representation of neural firing and all sensory-behavioral variables known to correlate with it.

Sensory-behavioral state. One, or a group of, sensory-behavioral variable(s) that has a constant value.

Sensory-behavioral variable. An externally observable dimension of sensory inputs or motor outputs or combinations of inputs and outputs. Description of discrete or continuous changes in the values of the variables along this dimension must be possible.

In the course of this chapter we define other terms, but they are used only in the section in which they are defined; the above terms are used in several sections.

ACKNOWLEDGMENTS

Dr. Richard Feinman and Dr. Howard Eichenbaum read early versions of this paper and our discussions with them were valuable. We are grateful to Drs. Deirdre Batson, Robert P. Erickson, Richard I. Hirsh, J. Allan Hobson, Herbert H. Jasper, Gerald E. Loeb, David S. Olton, Jerome M. Siegel, Mircea Steriade, William R. Uttal, and Donald J. Weisz for commentary on a not quite final version. We hope we have met the criticisms each raised. JoAnn Bracht, Shirley Schwartz, Shirley Fortner, and Jacquelyn Richardson typed innumerable versions of the chapter. John Kubie was supported by NIH Fellowship NS06152; Sloane Wolfson by NIH Training Grant NS07117; and James Ranck and Steve Fox partially by NIH Grant NS14497.

6 | A Behavioral Approach to the Analysis of Reticular Formation Unit Activity

JEROME M. SIEGEL

A. INTRODUCTION

The brainstem reticular formation (RF) was one of the first structures to be investigated using single unit recording techniques. One procedure common to all the early studies was the attempt to eliminate spontaneous behavior prior to commencing unit studies. This was not done because investigators thought that behavior was unworthy of study. Rather, it was a direct result of the unit recording technology, which required the complete immobility of the animal. Immobility was most readily achieved with the use of barbiturate anesthesia. A major drawback of this anesthetic is that it almost completely eliminates spontaneous activity of cells in RF and many other regions. The subsequent use of chloralose anesthesia, which does not produce so severe a depression of spontaneous and elicited unit activity, was a great advance. More recently, techniques for recording from unanesthetized, head-restrained animals became available. These techniques allowed unit activity in the waking state to be observed for the first time. However, it is still necessary to eliminate most spontaneous behavior when using these procedures, since motor activity tends to produce small brain movements that cause the experimenter to "lose" the recorded cell. Thus, the behavioral expertise of researchers interested in unit activity in the RF and in many other areas has been largely devoted to teaching rats, cats, and monkeys to hold still during recording sessions. In many studies, this same goal was achieved by the use of curariform agents. The development of microwire and other recording techniques now allow unit recording in completely unrestrained, behaving animals. However, the adoption of this new methodology has been slow for several reasons. One is that many experimenters now have a considerable investment in the technology of recording from restrained animals. The apparent simplicity and lack of variability in the unit activity of the restrained preparation makes interpretation easier, although, as I will show below, this simplicity may be quite misleading. Perhaps the fundamental reason that researchers have been slow to adopt the new unit recording methodologies is that procedures for relating unit activity to spontaneous behaviors have been slow to develop. Indeed, even most of those working with *unrestrained* animals have been content to use the methodologies developed for the restrained preparation, often presenting stimuli and observing unit response without describing or even observing the intervening behavior. Direct study of the relation between spontaneous unit activity and behavior has been rare (also see Ranck et al., Chapter 5, this volume).

The history of unit studies of the RF illustrates how divergent concepts of unit function can develop in the absence of extensive behavioral observation. The different theoretical views with which investigators approached the study of RF cells have produced widely different and apparently conflicting conclusions about the functional role of these cells. In the following discussion, I will review these conclusions. Procedures for studying these cells in unrestrained, behaving animals will then be presented. The findings in unrestrained animals suggest ways of harmonizing some of the conclusions reached in restrained animals.

B. REVIEW OF RETICULAR FORMATION UNIT LITERATURE

Most medial RF neurons respond to stimuli presented via one or more sensory modalities. Reticular formation responses to vestibular (Peterson et al., 1975), somatic (Segundo et al., 1967), vaginal (Rose, 1978), thermal (Cronin & Baker, 1977; Lee et al., 1977), auditory (Amassian & Devito, 1954; Bach-y-Rita, 1964; Ingle & Sprague, 1975), visual (Bell et al., 1964; Faingold & Caspary, 1977; Groves et al., 1973), and olfactory (Motokizawa, 1974) stimuli have been reported.

Casey (1971) studied the discharge of RF cells in cats trained to escape painful electrical shock. He found that unit discharge rates increased as stimulation intensities were raised to levels eliciting escape behavior. Procedures that reduce pain responses, such as morphine administration, are effective in reducing RF responses to noxious stimuli (Pearl & Anderson, 1977; Sun & Gatipon, 1976; Yokota & Hashimoto, 1976). The activation of RF neurons by painful stimuli has been interpreted as indicating that medial RF cells are specifically concerned with the sensory and motivational aspects of pain (Burton, 1968; Casey, 1971; Young & Gottschaldt, 1976).

Buchwald et al. (1966) observed multiple unit activity in RF and sensory and motor systems during classical conditioning of a hindlimb flexion response. They concluded that "activation of the conditioned stimulus and reticular systems are primary events in conditioning." Most RF neurons show a progressive decrease in their response to repeated stimuli. This "habituation" process has been studied by several investigators (Bell et al., 1964; Groves et al., 1973; Peterson et al., 1976; Scheibel & Scheibel, 1965; Segundo et al., 1967).

In 1949, Moruzzi and Magoun reported that midbrain reticular formation (MRF) stimulation in intact cats produced a long-lasting cortical desynchrony. Further work developed and refined the concept of an ascending reticular activating system contributing to both behavioral and electroencephalographic arousal. The advent of unit recording techniques allowed investigators to explore the RF for the neural substrate of these phenomena. An early study by Machne et al. (1955) reported a marked increase in the activity of most MRF units in response to arousal by either sciatic nerve or brainstem stimulation. Podvoll and Goodman (1967), Bambridge and Gijsgers (1977), and Beyer et al. (1971) reported a strong positive correlation between behavioral arousal and the level of MRF and pontine reticular formation (PRF) multiple unit activity (MUA) in the unrestrained cat. More detailed behavioral analyses have been directed at further defining the motivational variables responsible for relations between RF activity and arousal. Olds et al. (1969) found a marked acceleration in activity in every MRF unit studied as reinforcement became imminent. They conclude that the MRF activity increase is specifically related to *anticipation of reward*. This conclusion can be contrasted with the findings of Vertes and Miller (1976) and Best et al. (1973) (in rats) and Umemoto et al. (1970) (in cats). These workers studied the activity of PRF and MRF units during a conditioned emotional response (CER). These studies reported an increased firing rate in these units during anticipation of the shock. The increased RF activity was hypothesized to relate to *fear of the shock*. Umemoto et al. reported that 68% of encountered neurons discharged *specifically in relation to the CER*.

Hobson and McCarley and their co-workers reported, in a series of studies, that cells in the "gigantocellular tegmental field" (FTG), which constitutes most of the PRF, discharge at much higher rates in REM sleep than in either waking or slow wave sleep (SWS). During waking and SWS, "most FTG neurons either showed very low discharge rates (< 1 impulse per second) or were silent," whereas during REM sleep, they discharged in rapid bursts (McCarley & Hobson, 1971). Therefore, the ratio of REM sleep rates to waking and SWS rates or "selectivity" was very high. It was concluded that because of this high selectivity "FTG units are at present the best candidates" for REM sleep generator neurons (Hobson et al., 1974).

Studies in the head-restrained monkey have demonstrated relationships between the discharge of medial RF cells and eye movement. A variety of cell types have been reported in both midbrain and pontine regions (Buttner et al., 1977; Cohen & Henn, 1972; Fuchs & Luschei, 1972; Keller, 1974). Eye movement cell types similar to those seen in the monkey have been found in dorsomedial portions of the cat RF (Hikosaka & Kawakami, 1977). It has been concluded that discharge in PRF cells is "predominantly related to eye movement" (Cohen, 1978).

The relationship of RF unit activity to respiration has been extensively studied in acute preparations. Typically, respiratory related units are sought in cats that are paralyzed with Flaxedil and artificially ventilated. Units related to respiration are detected by visual observation of periodicities in discharge rate, or more frequently, by computer analysis of temporal relations in unit firing. Units related to respiration have been found throughout the RF. The proportion of units that are related to respiration in the cat ranges from 21% in the MRF to 36% in the PRF (Bertrand et al., 1973).

It has been found that stimulation of a circumscribed "midbrain locomotion region" (MLR) produces rhythmic stepping behavior in a decerebrate cat placed on a treadmill (Grillner & Shik, 1973) and speeds locomotion in the intact cat (Sterman & Fairchild, 1966). Since there are no strong direct connections between the MLR and the spinal cord, and since spinal cord areas containing reticular projections show a marked activity increase during locomotion, it was hypothesized that reticulospinal pathways might form part of the system producing both spontaneous and MLR-induced locomotion (Orlovskii, 1970). Orlovskii has, therefore, studied the activity of reticulospinal neurons during locomotion. It was shown that 69% of reticulospinal neurons were activated during MLR-induced locomotion and that the "transfer phase" of limb movement was the most active point for reticulospinal cells.

When one considers the variety of different findings made in RF studies, one naturally assumes that there are several different cell populations within the RF responding either during pain, reward, sensory stimuli, REM sleep or any of the other investigated conditions. However an analysis of the locations of the cells recorded, the proportions of cells sampled in each study, and other technical issues (Siegel, 1979a) lead to the conclusion that all of these studies are reporting on different aspects of *the same cells* (Fig. 6.1; Table 6.1).

C.   RETICULAR FORMATION UNIT ACTIVITY IN THE UNRESTRAINED CAT

To try to explain how the same cells can have so many apparently different roles, we have attempted to get the "big picture" of what aspects of behavior these cells were related to by observing these units in unre-

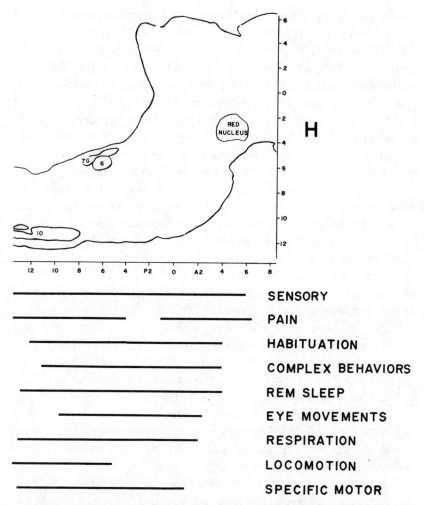

FIGURE 6.1. Anatomical distribution of cell types within the reticular formation, sagittal view of the brainstem of the cat. The bars (bottom) indicate the anterior-posterior distribution of cells identified as having specific behavioral functions. Cells with different behavioral properties are not localized to different RF areas. Key: 6, abducens nucleus; 7G genu of the facial nerve; I.O., inferior olive. From Siegel (1979a), by permission.

strained cats. It soon became obvious that simply categorizing the behavior the animal engaged in when RF units were active would be misleading. Thus, for example, certain RF cells would discharge when the cat was eating, suggesting that they be labeled "eating cells." However, closer study revealed that this was not the case. These cells would only discharge when

TABLE 6.1. A PARTIAL LIST OF THE BEHAVIORAL FUNCTIONS ATTRIBUTED TO RF CELLS

Cat stereotaxic coordinates were estimated from figures or taken from the authors' description. General anatomical terms were used in rat and monkey studies and in cat studies where precise anterior-posterior levels were not available. Third column lists percentage of encountered cells having function listed in column one.

Function or Stimulus	Cat A-P Stereotaxic Coordinate or Anatomical Designation	Percentage of Encountered Cells	Reference
Vestibular	P15-A0	75	Peterson et al., 1975
Somatosensory	P18.5-P8.5	77	Segundo et al., 1967
	P8-P3	71	Siegel & McGinty, 1977
	A2-A4	68	Bell et al., 1964
Auditory	P8-P3	40	Siegel & McGinty, 1977
	BRF, MRF	23	Scheibel et al., 1955
Olfactory	AP0-A6	58	Motokizawa, 1974
Pain	P18.3-P12.1	82	Burton, 1968
	P11-P6	57	Casey et al., 1974
	A0-A3	88	Barnes, 1976
Habituation	BRF	75	Scheibel and Scheibel, 1965
	A2-A4	75	Bell et al., 1964
Reinforcement	MRF†	100	Olds et al., 1969
Fear	MRF†	85	Best et al., 1973
	MRF	68	Umemoto et al., 1970
REM sleep	P7-A0	100	Hobson et al., 1974
	P9-P3	72	Siegel et al., 1977
Eye movements	MRF*	70	Buttner et al., 1977
	PRF*	92	Luschei & Fuchs, 1972
Locomotion	P15-P5	69	Orlovskii, 1970
Respiration	PRF	36	Bertrand et al., 1973
	MRF	21	Bertrand et al., 1973
Specific movements	P8-P3	91	Siegel & McGinty, 1977

From Siegel (1979a), by permission. †Rat studies. *Monkey studies.

the cat was eating food pellets placed in a bowl on the floor, not when it was eating pellets from a bowl lifted a few centimeters off the floor, or when it was chewing food pellets placed in its mouth. Conversely this same cell might fire when the cat was sniffing or exploring the floor and not eating, i.e., this cell type was related to the neck-extended posture, not to the behavioral category of eating. We have found that this is the case for most RF cells. Their activity is related to specific postures or movements.

In seeking to describe the underlying relation between RF unit activity and behavior, we have found that there is no substitute for the trained human observer carefully watching the behaving cat, listening to an audio monitor of the unit signal, and systematically (Siegel & McGinty, 1976, 1977; Siegel et al., 1977) noting the behaviors that occur when the unit is firing. Although such an approach may seem crude, it can produce a much more accurate picture of the behavioral role of units than can other more quantitative techniques. To take the example mentioned above, one could precisely describe the correlation between discharge in certain RF cells and food consumption and still completely miss the underlying postural relationship. The use of the full powers of human perception is, in reality, a very sophisticated and necessary methodology for determining the nature of the interrelations between unit activity and behavior. Only after a general understanding of the behavioral role has been achieved will the appropriate quantitative measures to correlate with unit activity become apparent (also see O'Keefe & Nadal, 1978, pp. 190–96; Ranck et al., Chapter 5, this volume).

After observing a variety of spontaneous behaviors for a minimum of 2 hours, we administered the discrete auditory, visual, and somatic stimuli that have been used in restrained animals to determine response modalities and latencies. A series of vestibular and proprioceptive stimuli, including active and passive movements of the vertebral column, EMG recording of selected muscles, and AC and DC EOG recording, were also used (Siegel & McGinty, 1976, 1977). In addition, all cells were recorded during both REM and non-REM sleep. This behavioral analysis takes a total of 4- to 6-hours per cell, far longer than the 5- to 10-minute observation common in acute studies. Therefore this technique is basically one of substituting intensive examination of a relatively small number of cells for a more superficial screening of a larger number of units.

In addition to this standard observation routine, we have developed other techniques to document behavioral relations. These include operant reinforcement of increased unit discharge and photographic analyses of the relation between unit activity and behavior. I will first describe the major behavioral subtypes we have seen in the medial RF and then outline the techniques for analyzing these relationships with photographic and operant reinforcement techniques.

1. CELL TYPES IN THE RETICULAR FORMATION

Table 6.2 lists the frequency of occurrence of the major cell types that we have found in the feline RF.

(i) Eye Movement Related Cells

These cells have previously been described by others in studies in the monkey and cat. They were found in the dorsomedial RF (Fig. 6.2) in the vicinity of the abducens and trochlear nuclei (we have not recorded exten-

TABLE 6.2. BEHAVIORAL RELATIONS OF RETICULAR CELLS

Type		Number		Percentage
Eye movement		28		10.0
Pinna		21		7.5
Facial		17		6.1
Head, neck, and back		150		53.4
ipsilateral active movements	39		13.9	
contralateral active movements	6		2.1	
stretch	16		5.7	
dorsoflexion	11		3.9	
other head or vertebral	78		27.9	
Proximal limb		17		6.1
Other specific stimuli or movements		33		11.8
Behavioral correlate unknown		14		5.0
Total		280		100

sively in the RF in the region of the oculomotor nucleus). They constituted 10.0% of the total number of cells we have analyzed.

Eye movement cells do not respond to cutaneous, discrete auditory or visual stimuli or to punctate or natural somatic stimuli. They do not respond to manipulation of the limbs or axial musculature (unless these manipulations cause the specific eye movement associated with discharge). Most cells in the vicinity of the abducens nucleus (but not histologically localized to the nucleus itself) discharge in relation to ipsilateral movement of the eyes, although we have seen the previously reported omniburst and omnipause cell types. Cells in the region of the trochlear nucleus (but lateral to it) discharged maximally during ventral eye movement.

All cells were tested during passive head movements, which induce vestibular compensatory slow eye movements. All abducens cells discharged in relation to ipsilateral slow phase and saccadic eye movements. Reticular formation eye movement cells in the region of the trochlear nucleus all discharged during ventral slow phases as well as during spontaneous ventral saccadic movements. On the basis of response to passive lateral head movement, the RF cells near the trochlear nucleus cells could be further subdivided into cells responding to passive contralateral or ipsilateral head movement. The latter group ($n = 8$) was located 1.6 mm lateral to the midline; the former group ($n = 3$) was 1.2 mm from midline.

(ii) Cells Related to Pinna Movement

Sherrington first demonstrated that structures caudal to the inferior colliculus were sufficient to control a variety of protective reflex movements of the pinna. We have seen that cats with the brainstem transected just in front of the abducens nucleus also show vigorous pinna movement reflexes. However, although it is known that the motoneurons innervating the auricular musculature are located in the medial facial nucleus, the specific lower brainstem regions that might be involved in the regulation of pinna movements have not been localized. We have discovered a group of cells in the pontine RF that discharge in relation to specific movements of the pinna (Siegel et al., 1980). They constituted 7.5% of the cells that we sampled.

All pinna movement cells discharged specifically in relation to movements of the ipsilateral pinna, relating to caudal, ventro-caudal, or rostral movements. These cells were silent even during very vigorous eye, head, neck, or limb movements. None of these cells responded to punctate stimulation of the pinna region with an aesthesiometer or discrete 0.5-msec electric shock stimulation sufficient to cause a muscle twitch. Passive movement of the pinna was also ineffective. No pinna cells responded to auditory or visual stimuli. Pinna movement cells were scattered throughout the PRF in the nucleus gigantocellularis and reticularis pontis caudalis (FTG in Berman's terminology) and also in the vicinity of the retrotrigeminal, accessory facial, and accessory abducens nuclei (Fig. 6.2). Most were located 2.3 mm or more lateral to midline, more lateral than other facial movement and head and neck movement cells.

(iii) Cells Related to Facial Movements

These cells, which constitute 6.0% of our sample, were related to specific movements of the facial musculature, especially of the ipsilateral vibrissae or eyelid. They were concentrated in the nucleus reticularis pontis caudalis, medial to the pinna movement cells (Fig. 6.2). None were in or

---

FIGURE 6.2. Anatomical distribution in sagittal plane of major behavioral cell types. *All cells*: This represents the locations of all units on which behavioral analysis has been completed. *Eye*: This represents the locations of all cells related to eye movement: cells related to ipsilateral eye movements (○), cells related to ventral eye movements (□). *Facial and Pinna*: Cells related to pinna movement (○), cells related to facial movements (△). *Ipsilateral Movement*: Cells discharging during ipsilateral movement and active during reflex head shake (○); cells discharging during ipsilateral movement, but silent during head shake (●). *Stretch*: Cells related to head extension (○). *Limb*: All limb movement cells discharged in relation to movements of proximal portions of the limb: Cells related to movement of ipsilateral forelimb (●); cells related to movement of the contralateral forelimb (○); cells related to movement of the ipsilateral hindlimb (■); cells related to movement of the contralateral hindlimb (□); cells related to movement of both ipsilateral limbs (▲). Key to abbreviations: FTG, FTM, FTC, gigantocellular, magnocellular and central tegmental fields; I.O., inferior olive; TB, trapezoid body; TR, tegmental reticular nucleus; PG, pontine gray.

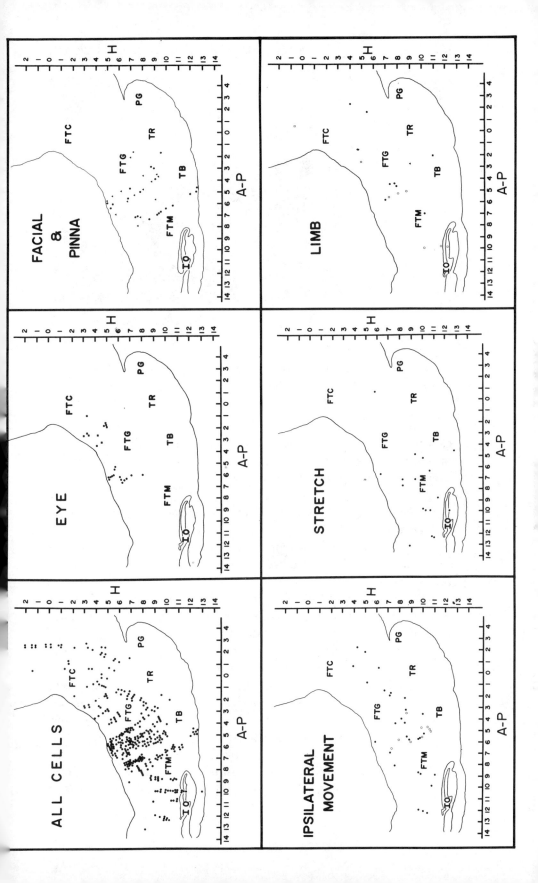

FIGURE 6.3. Head stretch cells were maximally activated when the cat assumed posture pictured, but not with lateral or dorsal head movements.

close to the facial nucleus or nerve. These cells resembled the pinna movement cells in their lack of sleep activity and in the absence of response to auditory, visual, and somatic stimulation.

(iv) Cells Discharging in Relation to a Variety of Specific Movements of the Head or Axial Musculature

These were the most common cell type in the medial RF, constituting 53.4% of our sample. To date we have been able to distinguish three distinct subtypes.

Ipsilateral Movement Cells. The largest subtype of cells related to movements of the vertebral column was cells related to active ipsilateral movement of the head or ipsilateral curvature of cervical and thoracic vertebrae. These cells, constituting 13.9% of our total sample, were also *the most common cell type in the RF*, more common than eye or facial movement related cells. Fifty-six percent of these cells discharged during *passive* movement of the head to the *contralateral* side, the remainder having no response to passive head movement. Brainstem cells with opposite active and passive head movement relations have also been reported in the rabbit (Duensing & Schaefer, 1960). Ipsilateral movement cells were scattered throughout the area explored. In contrast to facial, pinna, and eye movement cells, 50% of these cells responded to auditory stimulation, 60% of those tested responded to electrical or punctate stimulation of the skin, and 70% were active during sleep.

Head Extension Cells. The second largest group, 5.7% of the total sample, was cells that discharged during active head extension. Figure 6.3 illustrates the posture associated with discharge in these cells. None of these cells responded to passive head movement in any direction. None responded to auditory or somatic stimuli. In contrast to adjacent lateral head movement related cells, 80% had little or no tonic activity during sleep. These cells were concentrated between 1.2 and 1.6 mm lateral to midline in the nucleus gigantocellularis and reticularis pontis caudalis (Fig. 6.2).

Head-Neck Dorsoflexion Cells. These cells constituted 3.9% of our total sample ($n = 11$). They were silent when the cat sat in the sphinx position with its head lowered. They increased their discharge rate when the head was raised. Highest rates were achieved when the cat was standing and rapidly dorsoflexed its head. Active head-neck movements of the same speed ventrally or to the cats left or right did not produce discharge. Two of these cells had both tonic sleep activity and auditory response, the rest had neither. These cells were restricted to between 1.2 and 1.6 mm from the midline, but were widely scattered in the A-P dimension (Fig. 6.2).

(v) Cells Related to Movement of Proximal Limb Joints

A total of 6.1% ($n = 17$) of the cells studied were related to active and/ or passive movement of one or more limb joints. In every case, these cells were related to active or passive movement of the proximal portion of the limb (i.e., movement that involved the scapula or pelvic girdle). We saw no RF cells related to movement of more distal portions of the limbs. The largest subgroup was related to passive flexion and active extension of the ipsilateral forelimb. All but one of the cells related to ipsilateral forelimb movement were located at or lateral to 1.9 mm from the midline, whereas all those related to contralateral forelimb movement were located at or medial to 1.6 mm from the midline. They were widely distributed in the A-P dimension in medullary, pontine, and caudal midbrain regions. Forty-seven percent of these cells ($n = 8$) were type 2 cells (i.e., had high rates of tonic sleep activity). Three of the cells (18%) responded to auditory stimuli. Three of the four cells tested responded to shock stimulation of the skin in contrast to facial, eye, and head extension cells, none of which responded to this same stimulus.

(vi) Cells Related to Other Behaviors

A small number of cells discharged in relation to one of a variety of specific behaviors. As a group, these cells constituted 11.8% of the total number studied. Three cells were related to protrusion of the tongue. One of these was remarkably specific in its behavioral relations, discharging only with tongue protrusions to the ipsilateral side; the other two discharged with any tongue protrusion. These three cells were spread over a 9-mm A-P region, but were all located less than 1.6 mm from the midline and more than 4 mm from the hypoglossal nucleus. One cell was related to swallowing. Eight were related to vestibular stimulation, discharging with certain head movements, whether active or passive, and not responding if the head was held and the body moved to produce the same neck stimulation. Twenty-seven cells had somatosensory, auditory, or visual responses, which could account for all their activity. Four cells were related to jaw movement, and three to respiration.

It is important to point out that *all* the cells that were studied with our complete testing procedure ($n = 280$) were tested for *all* the behaviors we have described; all were observed during tongue movements induced by manipulating the tongue with a cotton swab, all were observed during swallowing while lapping, and all were tested for response to vestibular stimuli induced by passive head movement. Thus, the low frequencies of the cells described in this section do not reflect selective testing procedures, but rather the rarity of these cell types in the RF cell population.

(vii) Cells Unrelated to Tested Behaviors

Five percent of the cells encountered ($n = 14$) did not discharge in specific relation to any of the sensory tests or the motor observations we made. Many of these cells had considerable variability of discharge rate. However, despite extended periods of observation, their discharge could not be related to any specific sensory or motor event.

2. OPERANT REINFORCEMENT OF UNIT DISCHARGE

Our finding that activity in RF cells was related to specific movements was derived from systematic sensory stimulation and behavioral observation in unrestrained cats. We sought to document these observations using a different technique. Therefore, we developed procedures for operantly reinforcing increased discharge in RF units (Breedlove et al., 1979). This procedure, in a sense, requires the cat to do the behavioral analysis, figuring out what, if any, behaviors are required to gain reinforcement. Lateral hypothalamic stimulating and pontine gigantocellular microwire recording electrodes were implanted in three cats. After the cats recovered from surgery, current levels for reinforcing brain stimulation were determined by reinforcing the absence of eye movements with 400-msec trains of 0.3-msec pulses. Increased discharge was then reinforced in a total of 22 cells. During 12 of these experiments, a second nonreinforced control

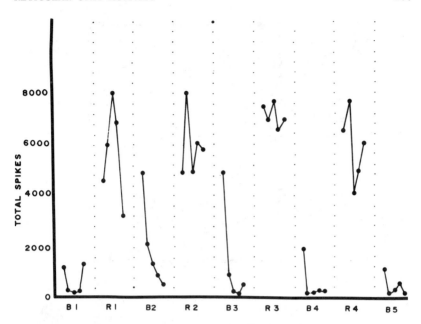

FIGURE 6.4. Unit discharge of a reinforced FTG cell. Each point represents
2 minutes. Key: B, base line (no reinforcement) periods; R, reinforcement
periods. The cat was presented with a discriminative stimulus signaling
reinforcement periods. Note the increased discharge during reinforcement
and successive extinction curves in base line periods. From Breedlove et al.
(1979) by permission.

cell was also recorded. Ten-minute reinforcing sessions alternated with
ten-minute time out periods. Unit discharge was significantly increased
by the procedure (Fig. 6.4) and experimental cells had a significantly greater
increase in discharge during reinforcement than simultaneously recorded
control cells.

The initial stages of training were accompanied by a general increase
in motor activity. However, as reinforcement sessions progressed, the
movement pattern became more specific. For example, during the later
reinforcing sessions in one experiment, the cat sat quietly in its litter box
bobbing its head up and down and receiving reinforcement. Before and
during conditioning, the cell reinforced in this experiment was observed
to fire whenever the animal moved its head up. The repetitive movements
associated with conditioning corresponded well with the behaviorally determined correlate of discharge.

We attempted to determine if proprioceptive feedback is necessary for
operant control of RF unit activity in further studies. Two cats, after having been trained to increase unit discharge as described above, were anesthetized with Halothane. We then inserted an endotracheal tube and in-

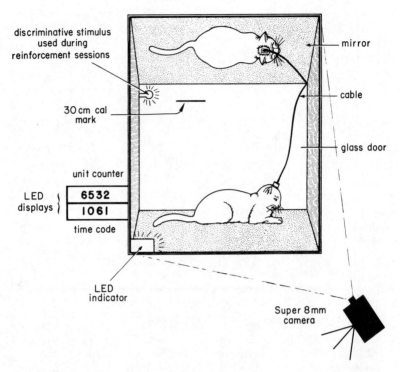

FIGURE 6.5. Arrangement of equipment used for filming unit discharge movement relations. From Siegel et al (1979a) by permission.

travenous catheter. After placing the cat in a comfortable position, we injected Flaxedil, discontinued the Halothane, and began artificial respiration, monitoring CO_2 and EEG as well as unit activity. We found that even in these conditions it was possible to reinforce RF unit activity with hypothalamic stimulation. Therefore, at least in some units, proprioceptive feedback is not essential for achieving operant control of RF activity.

3. PHOTOGRAPHIC ANALYSIS OF THE RELATION BETWEEN UNIT ACTIVITY AND MOVEMENT

We have developed a photographic procedure that allows us to more quantitatively describe the time-course and topography of RF unit activity-movement relations in unrestrained cats (Siegel et al., 1979). Two LED counters are attached to the side of an experimental chamber equipped with a mirror to allow simultaneous observation of top and side views of the cat (Fig. 6.5). One counter is set to increment whenever the unit discharges; the other displays a time code to allow correlation with a simultaneous tape recording of unit and other electrophysiological data. The chamber and counters are then filmed with an 8-mm "existing light" projector. Frame by frame analysis on a viewer allows one to plot movement vectors accompanying unit discharge. The simultaneously recorded time code signal allows the experimenter to verify that no noise has triggered the unit counter.

We found that unit discharge was accompanied by movements of from 10 to 30 mm within the same 56-msec interframe interval (Siegel et al., 1979). The movements associated with activity in each unit shared a common directional vector, which was in close agreement with the visually observed movement relation of the cell (Fig. 6.6). In the interframe interval preceeding unit discharge, the movement vectors were randomly distributed. The differences were significant.

Both the photographic and operant reinforcement techniques independently confirm our behavioral analysis procedures. However, since our behavioral procedures can provide much of the same information in less time, we do not use photographic and reinforcement techniques on all cells we encounter. We do, however, continue to use them to document new cell types.

4. SLEEP STUDIES

We observe all the units we record during sleep. The sleep studies have two overlapping goals. The first is to identify cells that might have a role in generating one or more states of sleep. The second is to observe the sleep activity of a cell with known behavioral correlates in waking and, therefore, allow us to make inferences about the interrelations between brain activity in these two states. It is generally accepted that REM sleep is generated by brainstem mechanisms, although the exact anatomical location of the cells underlying these mechanisms is uncertain. One would expect cells involved in the control of REM sleep to have a unique pattern of discharge during this state. They might fire only or mainly during this state, they might be silent only at this time, or they might change their pattern of discharge in some way. Previous reports had indicated that virtually all cells in the medial PRF [or "FTG" in Berman's (1968) terminology] discharged selectively in REM sleep (Hobson et al., 1974). We have not found this to be the case (Siegel et al., 1977, 1979; Siegel & McGinty, 1977). We found three cell types in the FTG region. Type 1 had no spontaneous activity during quiet waking and sleep, discharging only during movements. Type 2 had high rates of tonic activity during both quiet waking and SWS, which further increased during waking movement and REM sleep. Type 3 had low activity rates during quiet waking and SWS, but discharged in bursts during both waking movements and REM sleep.

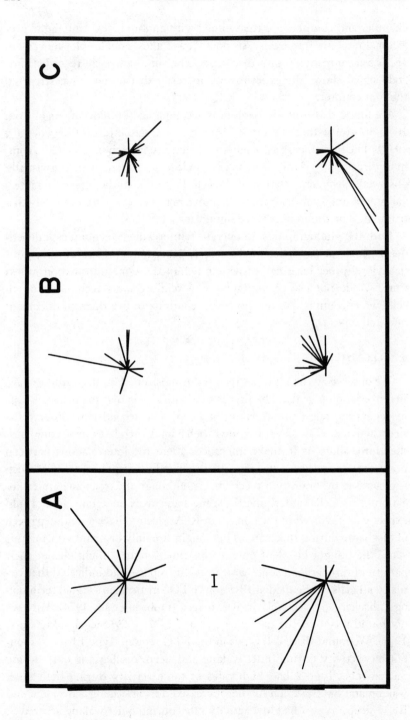

In every cell we have so far encountered with substantial REM sleep activity, we also observed comparable levels of waking activity. Indeed, there was a very strong positive correlation between waking and REM sleep activity rates (Fig. 6.7). The reason previous researchers reported that these cells discharge selectively in REM sleep was apparently because they used cats that were adapted to quietly tolerate head restraint. These procedures effectively eliminated most waking movement and correlated unit discharge, thus making the cells appear to be selectively active in REM sleep. These studies provide a good illustration of how the elimination of behavior from a preparation, far from clarifying the situation, can be misleading.

In studies of unit activity, experimenters will often give a value for waking discharge rate and other values for REM and non-REM sleep rates. In some cases, two waking rates are given, one for "active" and another for "quiet" waking. However, it should be obvious that because of the relation of PRF cells to specific movements, rates in "active" waking are a very crude, variable measure and may vary considerably depending on exactly what kinds of movements the animal is making (Fig. 6.8). We have tried to deal with this problem by providing maximum and minimum rates for the waking state, to give numerical expression to the range of activity visible in waking. However, ultimately there is no substitute for systematic observation and stimulation in determining the range of unit activity.

The positive correlation between RF activity rates in active waking and REM sleep can be most parsimoniously understood as a correlate of the motor activation of REM sleep. During this state, the eyes move rapidly as in active waking, the facial muscles and distal limb muscles twitch, and units throughout the brain's motor systems become active. Thus, the positive correlation between the waking and REM sleep activity of medial RF

FIGURE 6.6. A. _Upper_: Vectors describing the movement of the cat's head during the film frames spanning the 56-msec period before the onset of unit activity. Center point for each vector plot represents initial head position and terminations of lines represent head position one frame later. Calibration mark is 10 mm. _Lower_: vectors describing the movement of the cat's head during the film frames spanning 56 msec period in which the unit began to discharge. Note the nearly random distribution of vectors in the upper portion of the figure, and the preponderance of movements toward the upper left-hand quadrant accompanying the onset of unit activity in the lower portion of the figure. B. Note the shift in movement to upper right-hand quadrant during onset of unit activity. C. Note the shift in movement in the left-hand quadrants during the onset of unit activity. From Siegel et al (1979a) by permission.

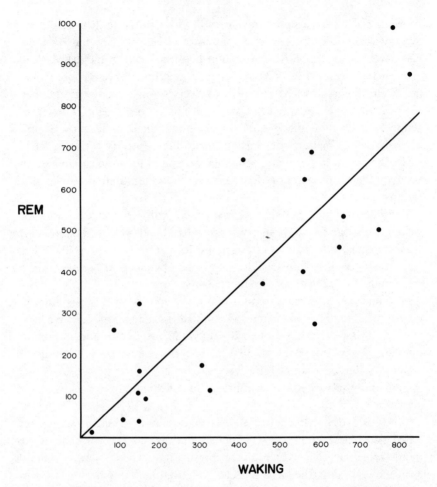

FIGURE 6.7. A scatter plot showing the positive correlation of waking and REM sleep rates in medullary cells, and the least squares best fit line. Maximum 10-sec REM sleep and waking counts are plotted. From Siegel et al (1979b) by permission.

cells provides a quantitative measure of the similarity of central motor activation in these states.

D. DISCUSSION

There is little doubt that as the mechanical and behavioral technology for the behavioral study of unit activity in unrestrained animals becomes better understood these procedures will become an indispensable starting point for the investigation of neural activity. The great advantage of the behavioral approach is that it allows one to describe the cell's relation to

Waking

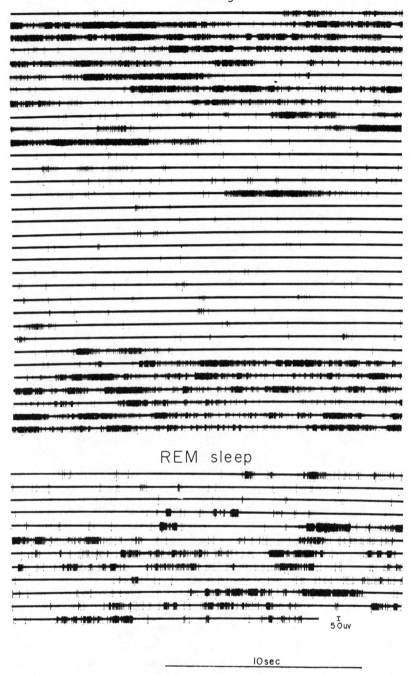

REM sleep

5 0uv

10 sec

FIGURE 6.8. Two continuous samples of the amplified unit recording of an FTG cell. The upper portion is an 11-min waking sample, and the lower is a 4-min recording spanning an entire REM sleep period. Note the variability of rate. "Average" waking rates would be a function of the cat's behavior during the sample period. From Siegel et al (1977) by permission.

behavior in the broadest possible terms, on the basis of direct observation. This is preferable to the premature use of highly controlled and restricted studies (also see Ranck et al., Chapter 5, this volume). Concepts of the role of RF cells in behavior as diverse and vague as arousal, sensory integration, anxiety, and reward anticipation have advanced largely as a result of studies in restrained or motionless animals. Our observation that these cells discharge in relation to specific movements in the unrestrained cat suggest a new perspective for interpreting prior studies. The response of RF cells to sensory stimuli and pain may reflect motor responses to these stimuli. Similarly, changes in RF activity during the emotional states created in previous studies may reflect alterations in muscle tone and movement patterns caused by the experimental situations. Only careful observation of and control for the exact movements correlated with unit activity in these situations can determine if our explanation is valid. In one recent study, in which movements were quantified, it was found that midbrain RF activity changes during learning could be precisely explained by the correlation between midbrain RF unit activity and specific head movements occurring during the task (Lecas and Malmo, 1981). Observation of unit activity during behavior is the most direct way of identifying the functional relations of cells. Behavioral control, after all, is not just one of the many functions a cell has. Rather, behavioral control, defined in its broadest sense, is *the* function of brain cells (also see Sperry, Chapter 3, this volume).

In many brain regions, anatomically adjacent cells can have completely different patterns of inputs and outputs and, presumably, completely different functional roles. Thus, the usual acute electrophysiological techniques are often difficult to interpret. Electrical stimulation not only excites fibers of passage, but may also recruit adjacent, functionally distinct, cells and may therefore create a misleading impression of diffuse control. Antidromic identification is another valuable technique for identifying cell projections. However, it is virtually impossible to gauge the relative importance of various projections or to infer the behavioral role of these cells from such studies. Often the monosynaptic effects caused by a cell's activity are minor relative to its polysynaptic effects (Peterson, 1979; Jankowska et al., 1968). However, acute neurophysiological studies are often limited to an analysis of monosynaptic effects. It therefore should not be surprising that much of the electrophysiological data, which emphasizes the diffuse, nonspecific effects of RF activation, stands in such dramatic contrast to the highly specific motor relations that can be seen in behavioral studies.

Although careful observation in the unrestrained animal can help identify the behavioral role of a cell, one must be cautious in interpreting the data obtained. A cell that discharges whenever the animal makes a specific movement need not be causing that movement. Experimental analysis is needed to determine the cell's precise role. If a cell can also be activated when the muscles involved contract isometrically and when the animal is curarized, one can rule out an essential role of proprioceptive and tactile feedback in its activation. These sorts of experiments can considerably narrow the range of possible functions of the cell. However, one must still be cautious in inferring the synaptic mechanisms underlying the behavior. Even latency studies are not definitive. If one can show that unit firing precedes the observed movement by some constant duration, one need not conclude that this activity is causing the movement. Most body movements result from complex sequences of muscle contractions. If one is monitoring a muscle, or a movement that occurs late in some specific sequence, and records a unit that is related to a muscle contraction early in the sequence, one will see a clear, relatively invariant lead that might suggest that the unit was causing the observed movement, even if, in fact, it was *responding* to an early aspect of the movement. This is a particularly likely error if the movement is related to axial musculature, since the action of this musculature may not be obvious, even though it often contracts in conjunction with or prior to (Bizzi et al., 1971) limb and other movements. Since most RF cells are related to axial movements (Siegel, 1979a, b), one must be especially cautious in implying their synaptic mechanisms from behavioral data. One should also consider the possibility that activity early in the movement sequence may have roles other than the excitation of motorneurons. Various kinds of corollary discharge to sensory receptors and the excitation and inhibition of specific interneuron pools may occur prior to or in conjunction with motoneuron depolarization.

Thus, both behavioral and acute electrophysiological techniques used alone have serious drawbacks. Just as one cannot determine the synaptic connections of a cell by using only behavioral techniques, one cannot determine the behavioral role of a cell solely through knowledge of its synaptic connections. However, when used together, behavioral and anatomical techniques can complement each other. For example, we need to know how the projection pattern of an RF cell related to tongue movement differs (we hope) from those of an adjacent cell related to limb movement. Recent findings (e.g., Evinger et al., 1979) suggest that the apparently obvious answers to these types of questions may not be correct. Anatomical projections may not always be simply related to behavioral role. Conversely, we need to know how the behavioral correlates of RF cells with ascending projections differ from those of adjacent cells with descending projections. We need to know if behavioral correlates are pharmacologically coded, i.e., Do cholinergic cells have different behavioral relations than adjacent adrenergic cells? We must also determine if there are morphological correlates of a cell's behavioral relations. These questions can only be answered by performing behavioral, electrophysiological, pharmacological, and anatomical studies of the same cells.

ACKNOWLEDGMENT

Supported by the Medical Research Service of the Veterans Administration USPHS Grant NS14610 and NSF Grant BNS8200023.

7 | Behavioral Insights into Neural Changes Accompanying Visual Development and Deprivation

DOUGLAS C. SMITH

A. INTRODUCTION

When is a finding in brain research significant? Although statistics can be used to determine if two groups of numbers differ to an extent that can be called "significant," this tells us nothing of real functional import. For, if the numbers of single cells, molecules of neurotransmitters, dendritic spines, etc., differ statistically, but if these differences are not reflected behaviorally, how can the result be "significant?" If it is our purpose to understand the functioning of the brain we cannot omit behavior, for it is behavior that is the ultimate expression of how the brain works (see Sperry, Chapter 3, this volume).

It is, of course, interesting and important to know how these individual components function, but these molecular approaches, in and of themselves, will never tell us how the brain works. For the brain is an organ composed of millions of cells gathered together, as in all organs, for a common purpose. The purpose of the heart is to pump blood. The purpose of the brain is to maintain homeostasis and to enable the organism to respond as appropriately as possible to its environment. Thus, the function of the brain is behavior and to ignore or denounce behavior as an appropriate measure is to be blind to the purpose of its very existence. Ah, but the critic might respond: "To correlate behavioral measurements of the crudity of better-worse, more-less, with physiological variables measured to two decimal places in micrograms, is, to say the least, faintly ridiculous" (Hutt & Hutt, 1970, p. 12). This statement was not meant to imply that behavior is an inappropriate measure, but rather, that improved behavioral measures were needed. Since the above quote was published, behavioral techniques have been refined, partly through the application of psychophysical methods in animals (also see Goodale, Chapter

4, this volume). It is the purpose of this chapter to demonstrate how some of these behavioral measures correlate with the physiological and anatomical changes known to occur during normal ontogeny, as well as how the behavior and correlated physiology change if the normal course of development is altered. It is my hope that the reader of this chapter would conclude that the behavioral information actually gives meaning to the physiological and anatomical data and that to ignore behavior would be ridiculous.

In attempting to achieve this end, I will concentrate on recent advances in the understanding of the physiological, anatomical, and behavioral changes that occur during normal and abnormal development of the visual system. The visual system has been chosen because a tremendous amount of research over the past two decades has been done on this system. Indeed, the visual system has become the battleground upon which the age-old controversies of innate vs. environmental factors in development, structure-function relationships, and plasticity have been, and continue to be, debated. This chapter will concentrate on the cat visual system, since much of the research addressing these questions have been performed in this species; however, data from monkeys and humans will also be mentioned when appropriate. I do not pretend to be able to review all the developmental and deprivation-induced changes within a single chapter; however, several excellent recent references exist to which the reader is referred (Aslin et al., 1981; Barlow, 1975; Daniels & Pettigrew, 1976; Freeman, 1979; Movshon & Van Sluyters, 1981). Rather, I will focus on specific behaviors, such as visual acuity, visual orienting, and depth and pattern discrimination, and describe the correlation between changes in these behavioral measures and the physiological and anatomical changes known to occur in the brain under conditions of normal and abnormal development.

B.   BEHAVIORAL MEASURES

Throughout this chapter, reference will be made to several behavioral tests and the measurements used in these tests. In general, it is most parsimonious to divide these into unlearned and learned behaviors.

Behaviors are considered unlearned when they appear during development without requiring the acquisition of an association between a stimulus and a particular response. As we will see, this does not imply that visual experience is not required for the behavior to develop normally. Unlearned behaviors to be discussed include visual orienting, visual following, visual placing, obstacle avoidance, visually guided jumping, visual cliff behavior, and optokinetic nystagmus. Unfortunately, most of the tests of unlearned behaviors only assess the presence or absence of the behavior. The most informative tests in understanding how the development of the brain correlates with these behaviors are those that allow one to determine the quality and/or quantity of these responses. An example of such an approach is the visual perimetry technique (Sherman, 1973; Sprague & Meikle, 1965), which uses visual orientation to determine the extent of the monocular or binocular visual field. As we will see, a quantitative index of the visual field can then be used to demonstrate changes in these fields related to different developmental and/or deprivation-induced alterations in the physiology of the brain.

In recent years, investigators who wanted to uncover isomorphisms between physiology and behavior in the visual system turned to learned behaviors. Initially, most studies required the animal to learn an association between a stimulus and a response, and used trials to a criterion as a dependent measure in an attempt to determine how perception correlated with known neurophysiological changes (cf., for example, Chow & Stewart, 1972; Ganz & Fitch, 1968; Ganz & Haffner, 1974; Rizzolatti & Tradardi, 1971). Although these studies provide information on what can be learned, as well as the relative degree of difficulty of a particular problem, it is difficult to know how to interpret correlations between these measures and neural changes because retarded learning can be brought about by a number of extremely different causes. These include, among many, sensory, motivational, and visuomotor changes. Further, it is not immediately apparent how perceptual changes correlate with developmental and/ or deprivation-induced changes in cells in the sensory projection areas in the brain. Indeed, to date, most studies have examined developmental and deprivation-induced changes in the visual system in primary sensory structures in the brain (i.e., striate cortex–area 17, the lateral geniculate nucleus, and the superior colliculus.)

For these reasons, many recent investigations directed at uncovering neural and behavioral isomorphisms have employed measurements of psychophysical threshold functions. Typically, these involve teaching the animal a two-choice discrimination. Once the discrimination is acquired, one stimulus is changed along some single dimension until the animal can no longer reliably discriminate between the two stimuli. As a result, a function that relates the animal's performance to systematic changes along some stimulus dimension is obtained. Threshold is arbitrarily defined as some point along this function (see Berkley, 1976). By way of example, in measuring visual acuity (a sensory process), the cat is taught to discriminate between a stimulus that has a high-contrast square-wave grating of a certain spatial frequency (i.e., the number of black and white stripes, or cycles per degree, of visual arc) and a homogeneous gray stimulus of the same luminance. Initially, a low spatial frequency stimulus is used. Once criterion is reached, the spatial frequency of the grating is systematically increased until the cat's performance falls to chance (50% correct), indicating that the spatial frequency of the grating is beyond the cat's threshold. Once it is certain that the cat's performance has reached an asymptote, the animal is given several trials at each of three to five spatial frequencies in random order in order to establish a quantitative index of threshold visual acuity. For most of the studies discussed in this chapter, threshold has been arbitrarily defined as the 70% correct level. A typical acuity function, called a frequency of seeing curve, is then plotted as shown in Figure 7.1. As can be seen, performance varies from near perfect performance to chance, as spatial frequency is increased past threshold.

The advantages of such psychophysical measurement of thresholds are that (1) a quantitative estimate is obtained, which can then be used to assess the effects of various manipulations; (2) when the threshold response function of neural elements derived electrophysiologically is found to be isomorphic with the psychophysical threshold function, those elements are considered to be one of the neural substrates of the behavior (Berkley, 1976); and (3) changes in sensory thresholds measured behaviorally are more readily interpretable than other measures. For example, since discrimination performance for suprathreshold stimuli is essentially perfect, we know that the animal remembers the task and is capable of accurately performing the behavioral response. In light of these advantages and the potential for revealing brain-behavior isomorphisms by obtaining psychophysical threshold functions electrophysiologically and behaviorally, this chapter will emphasize this approach, especially as it has been applied to the measurement of visual acuity and depth perception. Additional behavioral tests emphasized will include measurements of visual fields and obstacle avoidance, as these methods have been developed and allow quantitative assessment of behavior.

C. DEVELOPMENTAL CHANGES

The visual system of the cat, as in other species, demonstrates considerable postnatal anatomical and physiological changes. The surface area of the neonatal kitten retina is only around 40% of what it will be in the adult (Rusoff, 1979). Further, although all ganglion cells are present within

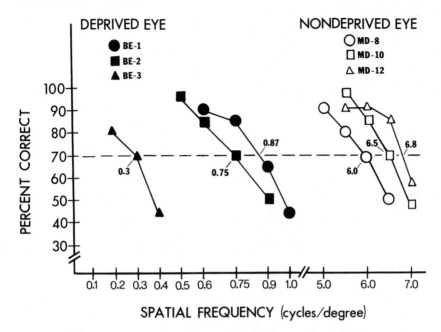

FIGURE 7.1. Frequency of seeing curves for three monocularly deprived cats. Open symbols represent data gathered using the experienced eye alone, closed symbols the deprived eye alone. Each frequency of seeing curve represents the percent of correct responses out of a minimum of 20 trials presented at each of three to four spatial frequencies. Threshold visual acuity is arbitrarily defined as the 70% correct level (dotted line). Bold numbers within the graph give acuity values for each animal (from Smith, 1981a).

24 hours of birth, these ganglion cells redistribute themselves over the next several weeks (Rusoff, 1979). Morphologically, ganglion cells in the central retina do not reach adult form until the 3rd week, whereas those in the peripheral retina are not fully mature until even later (Rusoff, 1979). The myelination of the ganglion cells' axons in the optic nerve increases dramatically during the first 4 weeks and is not fully complete until 12 weeks of age (Moore, Kalil, & Richards, 1976). Cells in the central geniculostriate pathway grow rapidly during the first 4 weeks (Kalil, 1980; Hickey, 1980) and synapses rapidly increase in number (Cragg, 1975).

Electrophysiologically, at 3 weeks of age both retinal ganglion cells and cells in the dorsal lateral geniculate nucleus (LGN) require higher stimulus intensities, show weak antagonism between the receptive field center and surround, and have receptive fields larger than those in the adult (Daniels, Pettigrew, & Norman, 1978; Hamasaki & Flynn, 1977; Rusoff & Dubin, 1977). Most important to the scope of this chapter is the spatial

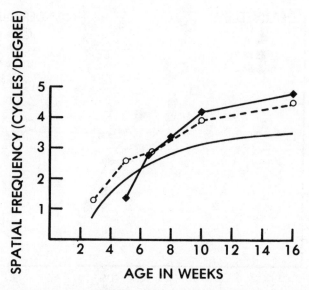

FIGURE 7.2. Changes in spatial resolution as a function of the age of the kitten. The average high frequency cutoff of neurons in the LGN of the kitten is indicated from the data of Ikeda & Tremain (1978) (-). The most sensitive (i.e., highest acuity) LGN cell found at each age is plotted (O——O) by Ikeda & Tremain (1978). A replot of the behavioral measures of visual acuity at each age is from the data of Mitchell et al. (1976) (■—■). Note the striking similarity between behavioral measures of visual acuity and electrophysiological measures of the most sensitive LGN cell at 6 weeks of age and older. See text for additional discussion.

resolving power (i.e., "visual acuity") of these cells. Curiously, no one has described the development of spatial resolution in retinal ganglion cells, although such data are available for the LGN and striate cortex. Ikeda and Tremain (1978) reported that the spatial resolution of cells in the representation of the area centralis (the cat homologue of the human fovea) as measured electrophysiologically in the LGN gradually increased from a mean value of 1 cycle/degree in 3-week-old kittens to 3 cycles/degree in 16-week-old kittens (see Fig. 7.2). Although the ocular media are cloudy until 4 weeks of age in the kitten (Thorn et al., 1976) and the optical quality improves during development, these factors only minimally affect these acuity measurements (Bonds & Freeman, 1978; Derrington, 1979), as the difference in transmission of the spatial frequencies shown in Figure 7.2 is small.

Like the neurons in the LGN, single cells in the striate cortex of the kitten show a steady improvement in spatial resolution, which increases with age and experience between 2 to 12 weeks of age (Derrington &

Fuchs, 1981). These authors state "the observed increases in spatial frequency and acuity are almost certainly a consequence of the increase in the range of spatial frequencies being transmitted through the LGN with age" (p. 8). Inspection of the single unit data from the striate cortex presented by Derrington and Fuchs (1981) indicates the highest resolving capability of any cell in the most mature kitten studied (80 days old) to be only 3.25 cycles/degree. In contrast, Ikeda and Tremain (1978) report the average acuity of LGN cells to be slightly above 3 cycles/degree at 70 days of age, whereas the most sensitive cell had an acuity of 4 cycles/degree. Although this apparent discrepancy could indicate that development of LGN acuity precedes that of cells in area 17, it is much more likely due to the fact that Derrington and Fuchs (1981) sampled cells *at least* 2 to 3 degrees (range 2 to 10°) away from the area centralis (where the cells with highest acuity would be found). In addition, sampling bias may have been an important factor, as only around 12 cells were studied per animal (seven cats, age 55–80 days, 79 cells, Derrington & Fuchs, 1981) and only three kittens older than 70 days of age were studied. It is also possible that different criterion measures of the cell's acuity were used between these studies.

The only other electrophysiological study of developmental changes in visual acuity in the cat was reported by Freeman and Marg (1975). These authors investigated the change in acuity in kittens ranging from 3 weeks of age to adult using the visual evoked response (VER) and found a consistent improvement in acuity throughout the 3rd to the 16th week. These acuity estimates are consistently lower than those for single cells in the LGN (Ikeda & Tremain, 1978); however, this is not surprising in view of the fact that the VER is an averaging technique that measures the response of a population of cells, thereby reducing sensitivity.

Given these developmental changes in electrophysiologically determined visual acuity, how might behavioral measures of visual acuity change during development? Mitchell, Griffin, Wilkinson, Anderson, & Smith (1976) described behavioral increases in visual acuity in the kitten; these are shown in comparison with the data from Ikeda and Tremain (1978) in Figure 7.2 (the comparison is with these data rather than the data of Derrington & Fuchs, 1981, for reasons discussed above). Inspection of Figure 7.2 reveals that behavioral measures of visual acuity are consistently higher than the average acuity of LGN cells after 5 weeks of age. Nevertheless, from 5 weeks of age on, the behavioral estimates of acuity agree very closely with the most sensitive cells in the LGN (Fig. 7.2). Prior to 5 weeks of age, the behavioral estimates of visual acuity are probably lower due to hypermetropia and divergence of the visual axes found in kittens this young. These problems are corrected in physiological, but not in behavioral, experiments.

Lesions of area 17 reduce visual acuity, as measured behaviorally (Berkley & Sprague, 1979; Kaye, Mitchell, & Cynader, 1981). Further, the increases in spatial resolution of single cells in the striate cortex during development almost certainly reflect the increases in acuity in the LGN (Derrington & Fuchs, 1981). Thus, electrophysiological measures of visual acuity in the representation of area centralis of the striate cortex would be expected to show the same relationship with the behavioral data as do LGN cells; this hypothesis awaits testing.

Visual acuity is only one point on a function that describes the response of the visual system, or its elements, throughout the spatial frequency range as a function of contrast. This function is called the contrast sensitivity function and is used to determine the minimal stimulus contrast necessary for the cell (or group of cells) being studied to detect a grating of a fixed spatial frequency and luminance. Visual acuity is specified as the greatest spatial resolution obtained at the highest contrast—the high frequency cutoff. An elegant demonstration of behavioral and electrophysiological isomorphisms in the developing visual system would be to demonstrate that behavioral and electrophysiological measures of contrast sensitivity covary throughout development. Although behavioral measures of contrast sensitivity in the adult cat (Blake, Cool, & Crawford, 1974; Bisti & Maffei, 1974) fit nicely with the range of electrophysiologically measured contrast sensitivity functions of LGN and area 17 neurons (Maffei & Fiorentini, 1976), such isomorphisms will be technologically difficult to accomplish for the developing kitten. Electrophysiological contrast sensitivity functions are available for cells in the LGN and striate cortex of the developing kitten (Ikeda & Tremain, 1978; Derrington & Fuchs, 1981), but behavioral measures take a great deal of time to collect. The fact that the cells' contrast sensitivity functions change with age would then confound any behavioral measures that could not be determined quickly. B. Timney (personal communication) is currently attempting these behavioral measures and it will be interesting to follow his progress. As our behavioral techniques advance, so also will our knowledge and ability to demonstrate behavioral and electrophysiological isomorphisms. Nevertheless, this should not detract from the importance of the findings, already reviewed, that demonstrate that the improvement in acuity for cells in the LGN and striate cortex of the developing kitten are reflected behaviorally and are thus, functionally "significant." Interestingly, analogous increases in visual acuity with age are seen in both the monkey and human infant both electrophysiologically (Atkinson, Braddick, & Moar, 1977; Pirchio, Spinelli, Fiorentini, & Maffei, 1978) and behaviorally (Boothe,

Williams, Kiorpes, & Teller, 1980; Braddick & Atkinson, 1979; Gwiazda, Brill, Mohindra, & Held, 1980).

Like visual acuity, depth perception is an important function of the visual system that improves during development. Electrophysiological studies of single cells in the visual cortex of the kitten have linked depth perception with neurons selective for specific retinal disparities. Such disparity-specific neurons are known to be present in both the kitten and monkey striate cortex (Barlow, Blakemore, & Pettigrew, 1967; Cynader & Regan, 1978; Pettigrew, 1974; Poggio & Fisher, 1977). That these neurons are probably required for binocular depth perception has been demonstrated by Kaye et al. (1981). These authors found that lesions of area 17, 18, and portions of area 19 eliminate behavioral evidence of binocular depth perception (stereopsis) in the cat.

During development, the sensitivity of the retinal disparity cells in the striate cortex approaches adult levels after the 5th week (Pettigrew, 1974). Recently, Timney (1981) demonstrated a very rapid improvement in behavioral measures of binocular depth perception during the 5th and 6th week. Taken together, these behavioral and electrophysiological studies provide compelling support for the view that the disparity-specific neurons in the visual cortex underlie stereopsis and that the development of these neurons is responsible for the improvement in depth perception with age. Again, a similar developmental change has been reported to occur in human infants (Held, Birch, & Gwiazda, 1980).

As mentioned earlier, many studies have investigated the development of unlearned visual behaviors. Due to space limitations, it is not practical to describe all of these; however, an excellent recent article details most of these changes and reviews the available data (Villablanca & Olmstad, 1979). Instead, the present discussion will be limited to a brief review of the electrophysiological properties of the developing superior colliculus and behavioral responses known to depend on its integrity. The superior colliculi (SC) receive a direct retinal input, but cannot be visually driven until 7 days of age (Stein, Labos, & Kruger, 1973), despite the fact that electrical stimulation produces organized eye movements prior to this age (Stein, Clamann, & Goldberg, 1980). Up to the 2nd week, the SC cells lack direction selectivity, respond to stimulation of only the contralateral eye, fatigue rapidly, and respond better to stationary rather than moving stimuli (Norton, 1974; Stein et al., 1973). During the 3rd to 5th weeks of life, these cells rapidly develop direction selectivity, become binocular, and respond better to moving than to stationary stimuli.

Seeking behavioral correlates of these developmental changes in the electrophysiological properties of cells in the SC, Norton (1974) investigated the onset of many behaviors, only some of which depended on an intact SC to be elicited. Lesion studies have implicated the SC as being essential for the normal development of orienting to and following stimuli moving into the visual field; however, other behaviors, such as visual placing, visual cliff performance, obstacle avoidance, and pattern discrimination, are unaffected by removal of the SC (Norton, 1974; Norton & Lindsley, 1971; see Goodale, Chapter 4, this volume). Norton (1974) found that orienting to a visual stimulus and following a moving stimulus could first be elicited between 16 to 18 days of age. The age at which these behavioral capacities appear correlates well with the rapid change in SC receptive field properties to a more adult-like state. Furthermore, visual cliff judgments, obstacle avoidance, and visually triggered or guided placing do not occur until after 25 days of age (Norton, 1974). Thus, those behaviors, shown to depend on an intact SC to develop normally, have a developmental onset related to maturation of the receptive field properties of SC cells. In contrast, visual behaviors unaffected by SC lesions do not correlate with these neurophysiological changes. One might predict that behaviors with an onset that correlates with the maturation of SC receptive field properties would also become more accurate over the next 3 weeks, since direction selectivity, binocularity, and reliability of the responses continue to improve over this period and are fully mature by around 40 days (Norton, 1974; Stein et al., 1973). This prediction requires one to be able to describe the quality of the responses and awaits investigation.

D. VISUAL DEPRIVATION

1. BINOCULAR COMPETITION AND THE CRITICAL PERIOD

From the pioneering work of Nobel Prize winners David Hubel and Torsten Wiesel, which involved monocular and binocular deprivation of patterned visual input, two neurophysiologically determined concepts that now pervade developmental neurobiology emerged: binocular competition and the critical period.

The theory of binocular competition states that, during development, LGN axons serving each eye compete for postsynaptic space on cells in the striate cortex and that the degree to which these afferents successfully form and maintain these connections depends upon competitive interactions between the eyes (Wiesel & Hubel, 1965). In a normally reared kitten, patterned visual input falls on the retina of both eyes, allowing each eye to compete successfully for cells in the striate cortex. Normally, around 80% of the cells in area 17 are binocularly driven. In contrast, monocular deprivation (MD) of patterned visual input during development accomplished by lid-suture places the nondeprived eye at a tremendous competitive advantage over the deprived eye. This competitive advantage is reflected by the fact that in MD cats 95% of the cells respond exclusively to the nondeprived eye, and only 5% are driven by the deprived (competed against) eye (Wiesel & Hubel, 1963, 1965). Further, the few cells that do respond to the deprived eye typically lack the specificity for the direction of movement and orientation of line stimuli, normally characteristic of striate cortical cells (Kratz et al., 1976). When kittens are binocularly deprived (BD) of patterned visual input, it was found that many more cells were responsive to a deprived eye than were found following MD (Wiesel & Hubel, 1965). During rearing, one eye of a BD cat has no decided competitive advantage over the other. Thus, the effects of BD are less severe than MD in terms of the reductions in responsivity and selectivity of the cells in the striate cortex (Kratz & Spear, 1976; Wiesel & Hubel, 1965). Nevertheless, BD does significantly reduce both the percent of responsive cells as well as the percent of the responsive cells that are orientation and direction selective as compared to normally reared cats (Kratz & Spear, 1976).

In the absence of any obvious competitive advantage given either eye in a BD cat, there must be another mechanism that contributes to the deleterious effects of binocular deprivation of patterned visual input. The additional operative mechanism is believed to be deprivation *per se* (i.e., disuse). Kratz and Spear (1976) investigated the effects of deprivation *per se* by suturing the lids of one eye closed prior to natural parting of the lids, while simultaneously removing the other eye (MDE—monocularly deprived and enucleated). In the absence of any competitive interactions, the deprived eye in these MDE cats drives significantly more cells in the striate cortex and has more cells that are orientation and direction selective than are found in either MD or BD cats (Kratz & Spear, 1976). Moreover, behavioral measures of visual acuity reflect these electrophysiological differences. Smith (1981a) found that mean visual acuity measured behaviorally for a single deprived eye was 0.64 cycle/degree in MD cats, 3.2 cycles/degree in BD cats, and 3.72 cycles/degree in MDE cats (normal visual acuities range from 4 to 7 cycles/degree). These studies indicate that the physiological and behaviorally measured acuity deficits found in MD cats are much more a result of competitive imbalances during development than of the effects of deprivation *per se*. That is, the deprived eye in both MD and MDE cats is subject to the same amount of deprivation *per se*, but only MD cats develop competitive interactions between the eyes.

Another behavioral measure has also been shown to reflect the physiological and anatomical effects of MD. Physiologically and anatomically,

the deleterious effects of MD are largely limited to the areas of the visual
system representing the binocular visual field (i.e., 45° contralateral to 45°
ipsilateral). These findings themselves support the theory of binocular
competition (Guillery, 1972; Guillery & Stelzner, 1970; Sherman et al.,
1974; Wilson & Sherman, 1977). Indeed, this is what would be expected
given that the monocular segment (nasal retina, 45°–90°, ipsilateral) cannot, by definition, be subject to binocular competitive interactions. Using
behavioral measures of visual perimetry for the deprived eye, Sherman
(1973) reported that MD cats will orient to visual stimuli rapidly entering
the visual field from above only when the stimulus is introduced into the
monocular visual field of the deprived eye. In contrast, using the nondeprived eye, the same cat orients to visual stimuli in both the monocular
and binocular portions of the visual field. Although recent studies have
questioned this correlation (Heitlander & Hoffman, 1978; Van Hof-Van
Duin, 1977), Smith, Holdefer, and Reeves (1982a) have replicated Sherman's findings.

   In an experiment with behavioral, anatomical, and physiological parameters, Sherman, Guillery, Kaas, and Sanderson (1974) elegantly demonstrated the effects of binocular competition within animals. Sherman et
al. (1974) used MD cats with a central retinal lesion made in the nondeprived eye at the same time as MD. This was a so-called critical segment
MD cat, in which the deprived eye was not competitively influenced by
the nondeprived eye in that portion of the normally binocular, central
visual pathways representing the area destroyed in the nondeprived retina. In these cats, cells in the deprived lamina of the LGN showed the
typical reduction in cell size, which normally accompanies MD, in all
areas except that representing the homologous region of the critical segment. Physiologically, multiple unit recording in striate cortex indicated
an increased efficacy of the deprived eye only within the critical segment.
Finally, behavioral tests of visual perimetry indicated that the only portion
of the binocular field in which the animal would demonstrate visual orientation using the deprived eye was that portion of the visual field that
represented the area of the visual field corresponding retinotopically to
the area removed by the retinal lesion in the nondeprived eye. A more
powerful demonstration is difficult to imagine.

   Although evidence will be discussed to indicate that competitive interactions between the eyes continue to play a role even in adult MD cats,
there is a developmental period when these interactions are at their peak.
This has been called the "critical period" or sensitive period. During the
critical period, the cells in the visual cortex are highly plastic in terms of
their receptive-field properties and binocularity. The critical period begins
at around 2 weeks of age, reaches a peak during the 5th week, and grad-

ually declines until about 4 months of age (Hubel & Wiesel, 1970; Van Sluyters & Freeman, 1977). Even after 4 months, some slight susceptibility to the effects of MD remains (Cynader, Timney, & Mitchell, 1980). During the critical period, the cortex is highly susceptible to pattern vision deprivation. Indeed, during the peak of the critical period, a day or less of MD treatment has been reported to reduce the number of binocular cells in the striate cortex (Movshon & Dursteler, 1977). Interestingly, the peak of this period is associated with a burst of synaptogenesis in the striate cortex, which is followed by a reduction in the number of synapses until adult levels are reached at about 3 months of age (Cragg, 1975). Further, ocular dominance columns, demonstrated autoradiographically, also undergo marked changes within this time and reach adult form at around 3 months of age (LeVay, Stryker, & Shatz, 1978).

Behaviorally, kittens deprived of patterned visual input throughout the critical period show gross disturbances of visual placing, jumping, obstacle avoidance, depth perception (visual cliff), optokinetic nystagmus (OKN), and the visual startle response (Dews & Wiesel, 1970; Movshon, 1976a; Wiesel & Hubel, 1963). Indeed, for all intents and purposes, the kittens appear behaviorally blind following parting of the lids. Furthermore, both MD and BD cats have difficulty learning tasks that require discriminations on the basis of complex spatial cues (i.e., poor pattern vision), and although BD cats are not as retarded as MD cats using the deprived eye alone, both are clearly deficient compared to normal. The severity and reversibility of all these behaviors depends upon the age of onset, duration of deprivation, and type of recovery both within and outside of the critical period. A behavioral demonstration of these effects has been published by Wilkinson (1980), who demonstrated that when only the age of MD is varied (the duration is kept constant), visual acuity is less severely affected the older the animal at the onset of deprivation.

2. REVERSAL WITHIN THE CRITICAL PERIOD

During the first 3 to 4 months of life, deprivation-induced changes in the visual system have a marked capacity for reversal. If an MD kitten has the lids of the deprived eye opened and those of the experienced eye closed (i.e., reverse-suture), the initially deprived eye will come to physiologically dominate or recapture cells in the striate cortex and receptive-field specificity will be restored. Exactly the opposite is found for the initially experienced, late-deprived eye (Blakemore & Van Sluyters, 1974; Hubel & Wiesel, 1970; Mitchell, Cynader, & Movshon, 1977; Movshon, 1976b; Olson & Freeman, 1978; Van Sluyters, 1978). This reversal is accomplished most easily during the peak of the critical period, and thereafter the capacity for reversal gradually declines. Anatomical studies also demonstrate this relationship (see Cragg et al., 1976; Movshon & Dursteler, 1977; Wan & Cragg, 1976).

Movshon (1976a) demonstrated that the behavioral deficits on OKN, visual startle, visual following, negotiation of a visual cliff, and visually guided placing dissipated for the initially deprived eye following reverse-suture, whereas they began to appear for the initially experienced, late deprived eye. This complementary improvement and deterioration depended on the age of the animal. It was maximal in kittens who were reverse-sutured at 5 weeks of age, and was less rapid as reverse-suturing was further delayed.

In behavioral measures of visual acuity, Mitchell, Cynader, and Movshon (1977) and Giffin and Mitchel (1978) demonstrated very nice correlations with the physiological and anatomical effects of MD and its reversal. In both these studies, the final level of acuity reached using a deprived eye is a function of the duration of deprivation (inverse relationship) and whether reverse-suture or simple binocular experience took place during recovery. As would be predicted from the theory of binocular competition, after a given duration of MD, recovery of visual acuity was always greater following reverse-suture than when only binocular experience took place during recovery. In a combined electrophysiological and behavioral investigation, Mitchell et al. (1977) obtained the following results: animals monocularly deprived until 45 days of age and then reverse-sutured had 94% of the cells in the striate cortex responsive to the initially deprived eye following reverse-suture and an acuity of 6.6 cycles/degree; the animal given binocular experience had 55% of the striate cortex cells responsive and an acuity of 4.9 cycles/degree. If animals were monocularly deprived for 60 days, following reverse-suture, 47% of the cells in the striate cortex responded to the initially deprived eye and visual acuity was 4.7 cycles/degree; 39% of the cells were responsive following binocular experience, and visual acuity was 4.4 cycle/degree. Mitchell et al. (1977) reported their data in terms of the number of cells and stated that visual acuity was *not* related to the number of cells in the striate cortex that responded to the initially deprived eye. However, this was not an appropriate comparison, since all the animals studied differed in the total number of cells sampled. Indeed, if one calculates the correlation between visual acuity and the *percentage* of striate cortex cells responsive to the initially deprived eye (as reported above), one finds a very high correlation ($r = +.98$.)

Although visual acuity might reflect the specificity of cells in the striate cortex, in these reverse-sutured kittens, the percentage of responsive cells must also be involved. This follows from the finding that, unlike the restoration of the deprived eye's capacity to drive cells in striate cortex, res-

toration of receptive-field specificity depends only upon the initial duration of MD and not upon the degree of competitive advantage given the
deprived eye during recovery (Mitchell et al., 1977; Olson & Freeman,
1978; Van Sluyters, 1978). Thus, the finding that, following the same
duration of MD, reverse-sutured animals consistently achieve higher levels of visual acuity than binocular experienced animals, indicates that the
percent of cells responding to the initially deprived eye is directly involved in mediating visual acuity. This must be the case, since no differences in receptive-field specificity are observed between these animals.
The only demonstrable differences are in the percent of striate cortical
cells that respond to the initially deprived eye. As we shall see, these
relationships are also found using behavioral measures of visual acuity and
the percent of responsive cells in striate cortex in kittens that were deprived well past the critical period (see Section 4).

3. Reversal Outside of the Critical Period

As one approaches the end of the critical period, the cells in the visual
cortex become less plastic. Initially, it was believed that although some
behavioral recovery occurred in MD cats reverse-sutured outside of the
end of the sensitive period, no physiological recovery could be demonstrated (Blakemore & Van Sluyters, 1974; Dews & Wiesel, 1970; Hubel
& Wiesel, 1970). This view, however, does not agree with more recent
studies in which the ability to reverse the physiological effects of MD
outside of the classically defined critical period has been investigated; here,
many more animals were studied and more striate cortical cells were sampled
than in the past.

Although binocular experience following MD is sufficient to produce
physiological recovery within the critical period, no such recovery is obvious once the MD cat is outside this period (Hubel & Wiesel, 1970).
Nevertheless, if an animal is reverse-sutured following 4 months of MD,
there is a significant increase in the percent of striate cortical cells responsive to the deprived eye compared to monocularly deprived controls (Smith,
Spear, & Kratz, 1978). Furthermore, if the nondeprived eye is removed
after the critical period, one sees an immediate increase in the percent of
cells in the striate cortex responding to the deprived eye (from 5% following MD to 31% following enucleation, Kratz, Spear, & Smith, 1976). The
rapid increase in the percent of striate cortical cells responding to the
deprived eye brought about by the removal of the nondeprived eye persists in MD animals up to at least 2 years of age (Spear, Langsetmo, &
Smith, 1980) and is also effective in increasing the percent of cells in the
superior colliculus that respond to the deprived eye (Hoffmann & Cy-

nader, 1977). These results indicate that the experienced eye of an MD cat suppresses the input from the deprived eye in the striate cortex and that the efficacy of the deprived eye depends on continued competitive interactions between the eyes just as it does during the critical period (Kratz et al., 1976; Smith et al., 1978). That is, if the deprived eye is placed at the greatest postcritical-period competitive advantage possible (i.e., by complete removal of the experienced eye), more cells in the striate cortex respond to the deprived eye than when reverse-suture is performed at the same age. Further, although the effects of removing the experienced eye are immediate, reverse-suture effects take time to develop (Smith et al., 1978). Finally, forced usage of the deprived eye, brought about by postcritical-period reverse-suture, puts the initially deprived eye at a greater competitive advantage than when simple binocular experience is allowed during recovery and significantly increases the percent of responsive cells in the striate cortex (Smith et al., 1978).

It is interesting that although the "responsivity" of cells in the striate cortex can be restored to some extent by altering the competitive interactions between the eyes well past the critical period, receptive field specificity cannot be restored. Following MD, which continues through the critical period, most of the few cells that respond to the deprived eye lack direction and orientation selectivity (Kratz et al., 1976). Although reverse-suture and removal of the experienced eye increase the percent of cells responding to the deprived eye, no analogous increase in the incidence of cells displaying direction and/or orientation selectivity can be found, even when forced usage of the deprived eye follows removal of the experienced eye for an extended period (Smith et al., 1978). Thus, the critical period is not completely "critical" with respect to the responsiveness of striate cortical cells to the deprived eye; it is more completely so for the restoration of receptive-field selectivity.

Recent behavioral studies in my laboratory have focused upon the relationship between these electrophysiological results and behavioral measures of obstacle avoidance, visual perimetry, and visual acuity. As mentioned earlier, MD cats using their deprived eye will consistently fail to avoid objects in their path. Although all previous reports of obstacle avoidance deficits have been essentially qualitative in nature, I wish to describe a quantitative test of obstacle avoidance, developed in this laboratory, which detects changes in this ability that might go undetected in casual observation. The test was developed in an enclosed room, where several 1-ft boards were stood on end approximately 1 ft apart (see Fig. 7.3A). A cat was released somewhere on the perimeter (variable position) and was required to find a bowl of highly palatable food hidden, again in a variable position, somewhere among the blocks. It was necessary to clip the vibrissae and restrict the movement of the ears in order to ensure that avoidances were based on visual, and not tactile, input. An investigator stood in the room and counted the number of avoidances out of 20 confrontations. Three sets of these trials were run daily, and the sessions were videotaped from above, to be scored later, in random order, by a "blind" observer. Failure to avoid was easily scored in both the videotapes and in the actual situation, as the kittens always gave an obvious startle response when they bumped into one of the obstacles. The results of such obstacle avoidance testing for one MD cat are illustrated in Figure 7.3B. Using only its deprived eye, this MD cat (deprived for 7 months) consistently bumped into the obstacles (days 1–4). Note that the conditions of testing (i.e., vibrissae cut, ears restricted) did not affect the performance using the nondeprived eye alone (open square). On day 5, the experienced eye was removed and animal MD-DE2 showed an immediate improvement in obstacle avoidance ability, which continued to improve over the next 4 days. Three findings are important to note: (1) no analogous improvement was seen so quickly in reverse-sutured animals, (2) if the deprived eye was occluded, the cat bumped into practically every block confronted (day 11) (thus, the cat was visually avoiding the blocks using the deprived eye post-enucleation), and (3) the cat never becomes as proficient in using the deprived eye as it was with the experienced eye. Casual observation, therefore, would have led to the conclusion that the animal was bumping into objects, thereby missing an important change in behavior correlated with physiological changes in the visual system.

In a second series of experiments, we determined whether the visual field of the deprived eye, measured by the visual perimetry techniques of Sherman (1973), might change following removal of the experienced eye, since the superior colliculus has been implicated in this ability. Also, an increase in the ability of the deprived eye to drive single cells in this structure occurs following removal of the nondeprived eye (Hoffmann & Cynader, 1977). As reviewed above, using the deprived eye, MD cats orient to stimuli only when they fall within the monocular segment of the deprived eye (see Fig. 7.4A). In this study (Smith, Holdefer, & Reeves, 1982a), four MD cats were tested. Each cat had base line perimetry measures using the deprived eye. After this, two of the cats had the experienced eye removed. The other two cats were reverse-sutured for several months prior to removal of the initially experienced eye. In agreement with Sherman (1974), reverse-suture does not change the extent of the visual field of the deprived eye (illustrated in Fig. 7.4B). In contrast, removal of the nondeprived eye resulted in an expansion of the deprived eye's visual field up to the midline (Fig. 7.4C). This finding was true for every cat tested and always involved the cat's demonstrating evidence of

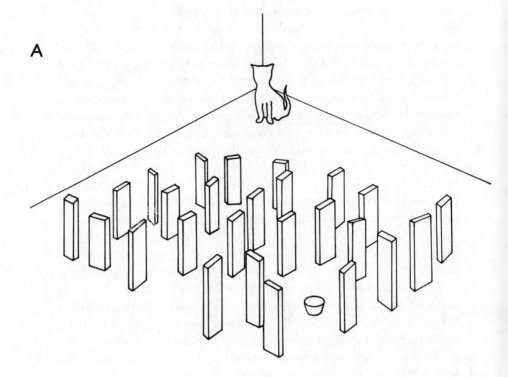

A

B

MD-DE-2

□ nondeprived eye
● deprived eye alone
☆ deprived eye occluded

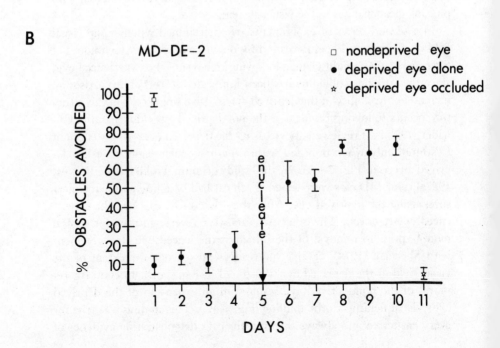

% OBSTACLES AVOIDED

enucleate

DAYS

visual orienting using the deprived eye in areas of the visual field in which they had never responded prior to removal of the experienced eye. Here again, careful quantitative assessment of a visual behavior indicates that a change in behavior systematically accompanies known physiological changes that would otherwise be virtually impossible to detect.

The final set of experiments examining the behavioral correlates of postcritical-period reversal of the electrophysiological effects of MD used visual acuity as a measure (Smith, 1981b). The visual acuity of a MD cat using the deprived eye following at least 7 months of deprivation is very poor (Fig. 7.1, BE cats). The average acuity of three MD cats deprived for 7 to 12 months was 0.64 cycle/degree (Smith, 1981a). This behavioral acuity value is much lower than that predicted from an assessment of the electrophysiological acuities of neurons in the deprived laminae of the LGN (Derrington & Hawken, 1981; Lehmkuhle et al., 1978). Thus, this finding provides behavioral evidence for suppression of the deprived eye's input to the striate cortex.

As mentioned, postcritical-period reverse-suture increases the percent of cells in the striate cortex that respond to the initially deprived eye from 5% in MD controls to 18% following several months of reverse-suture without any measurable return of receptive-field specificity (Smith et al., 1978). Visual acuity for animals reverse-sutured after 7 to 12 months of MD eventually reached a mean of 1.45 cycles/degree, a significant increase over MD controls (Smith, 1981b). In addition, following removal of the nondeprived eye in a MD cat, mean visual acuity is 2.4 cycles/degree. Thus, these behavioral measures of visual acuity reflect the increased efficacy of the deprived eye in driving cells in the striate cortex. Even more revealing are the effects of removal of the initially experienced eye in an MD cat that has already attained a stable postreverse-suture acuity estimate (which always takes much longer to attain than it does when the nondeprived eye is removed). Four such animals have been studied. Three of the four cats demonstrated rapid increases (within 1 to 5 days) in visual acuity using the deprived eye. This improvement could

---

FIGURE 7.3. Obstacle avoidance testing situation designed to allow quantitative assessment. A. The cat was placed in a random position outside the perimeter of the blocks so that he would visually guide his movements in order to find a bowl of highly palatable food hidden (in random positions) somewhere among the blocks. See text for details of testing and scoring. B. Obstacle avoidance results for cat MD-DE-2. Each point represents the mean (± 1 S.D.) percent of obstacles avoided for three daily sets of trials, each consisting of 20 confrontations with the blocks. Each point was calculated from the observations of both the experimenter in the situation and from the blind observer scoring the video tapes. See text for additional details.

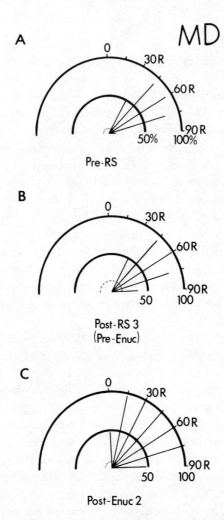

FIGURE 7.4. Quantitative assessment of the extent of the visual field of an MD cat A. Using the deprived (right) eye measured with the visual perimetry technique of Sherman (1973). The visual field is divided into 12, 15° segments, and the percent of orientations to a visual stimulus rapidly entering the visual field from above is calculated from a minimum of 60 presentations at each guideline. Using the deprived eye, this cat orients to visual stimuli only when they are introduced into the monocular field of the deprived eye. In contrast, using the nondeprived eye (not shown), the cat demonstrates a full visual field (i.e., from 90° ipsilateral to 45° contralateral). B. The visual field using the deprived eye following several months of reverse-suture. Note that no change has occurred from that shown in A. C. Visual field of the deprived eye following removal of the initially experienced eye. Note the expansion of the visual field up to the midline, which was present in the first testing session postenucleation. Prior to enucleation, visual orientations had never been observed in the central visual field (compare A and B) (redrawn from Smith et al., 1982a).

not be due to practice (Smith, 1981b) and must, therefore be related to the electrophysiological increases in responsivity known to occur following removal of the nondeprived eye (Kratz et al., 1976). Interestingly, the one reverse-sutured cat who did not demonstrate any additional improvement in visual acuity following enucleation had already attained a final level of acuity following reverse-suture that was equal to or above that found in the MD enucleated cats. In this regard, the electrophysiological effects of postcritical-period reverse-suture are apparently quite variable among animals (Smith et al., 1978). Indeed, Smith et al. (1978) found one animal in which more cells responded to the deprived eye following reverse-suture than were found in any animal following removal of the nondeprived eye (Kratz et al., 1976; Smith et al., 1978). Thus, the one reverse-suture animal who did not show any additional improvement following removal of the initially experienced eye may not have had any further increase in the ability of the deprived eye to drive cells in striate cortex, and, thus, would not be expected to show any change in acuity. Of course, this line of reasoning assumes that visual acuity in these visually deprived cats is related to the ability of the deprived eye to drive cells in the striate cortex. Is there any support for such a view? Some evidence has already been suggested (see Section D, 2), but this concerned kittens during the critical period when receptive-field specificity can be restored. Can evidence be found that relates visual acuity to the percent of responsive cells in the striate cortex of cats who are deprived well past the critical period? Evidence presented in the following section suggests the answer is yes.

4. Mass Action and Visual Acuity

The reasoning behind the visual acuity measures I have reported in recent years has been presented as the separate results were discussed. One consequence of obtaining these acuity measures is that information has been accumulated concerning the visual acuity of many different groups of cats, each of which has a striate cortex quite different from all the others. If one combines these behavioral measures of visual acuity with what is known about the physiological effects of these different rearing and recovery conditions, a quite remarkable relationship emerges. Figure 7.5 illustrates the visual acuity for *every* cat in each condition tested to date. Below the labeled bar graphs, in parentheses, are the mean percent of striate cortical cells responding to the deprived eye obtained from electrophysiological recordings from a minimum of five cats in each condition by Kratz and Spear (1976), Kratz et al. (1976), and Smith et al. (1978). Perhaps you can imagine my astonishment when I put all this information together. The conclusion seems inescapable: As the percent of visually

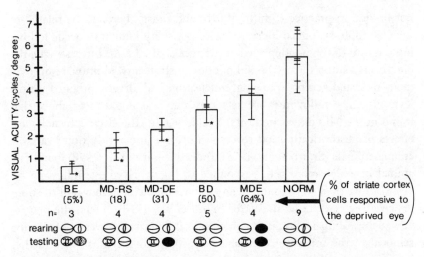

FIGURE 7.5. Visual acuity for each rearing or recovery condition as a function of the percent of responsive cells in striate cortex. The bar graphs indicate the average visual acuity for each group, the slash marks within the
bar graphs the results of individual cats in each condition. The label under
each bar indicates the name of each group and the rearing and testing conditions for each of these is illustrated at the bottom of the figure. BE, monocularly deprived during rearing and then given binocular experience.
Testing was performed with an occluder in the nondeprived eye. MD-RS,
monocularly deprived and then reverse-sutured; MD-DE, monocularly deprived during rearing with the nondeprived eye removed well past the critical period; BD, binocularly deprived during rearing via lid-sutre, with acuity assessed monocularly; MDE, monocularly deprived with the other eye
removed at the same age as the original lid-suture, NORM, visual acuity
using the nondeprived eye in MD cats (shown for comparison only). For all
kittens, deprivation was initiated prior to the age of natural eye opening and
lasted for 7 months, except when deprivation lasted 12 months (indicated
by an asterisk next to the animal's acuity). The numbers in parentheses
indicate the mean percent of striate cortical cells responsive to a single deprived eye for cats in each condition. These data come from a minimum of
five cats in each condition from the electrophysiological studies of Kratz
and Spear (1976), Kratz et al., (1976), and Smith et al. (1978).

responsive cells increases, so does visual acuity, and the relationship is
linear! Although these data do not deal with postlesion retention of learned
responses, they remarkably resemble those that served as the basis for
Lashley's (1938) concept of mass action.

It is commonly assumed that acuity reflects the spatial resolution of the
most sensitive neuron (Mitchell et al., 1977). However, this cannot be the
case for MD cats deprived through the critical period, since cells in the
LGN have a higher spatial resolution than is measured behaviorally (Der-

rington & Hawken, 1981; Lehmkuhle et al., 1978; Maffei & Fiorentini, 1976). It is very interesting in this regard that, following removal of the nondeprived eye in MD cats, behavioral measures of visual acuity increase to values that are closely associated with the acuity of LGN cells in the deprived laminae (Lehmkuhle et.al., 1978; Maffei & Fiorentini, 1976). Thus, removal of suppression mediated by the nondeprived eye may now allow the LGN output from the deprived eye to be relayed faithfully to cells in the striate cortex. One could test this by measuring spatial contrast sensitivity functions for cells in the striate cortex of MD cats before and after enucleation. Unfortunately, such measurements are not available.

In the absence of electrophysiological measures of acuity from single cells in the striate cortex of visually deprived cats, it might be that other measures of receptive-field specificity correlate with behavioral measures of visual acuity. Indeed, MD animals in which the other eye is removed at the same age MD is imposed (MDE cats, Fig. 7.5) have significantly more cells responsive to a single deprived eye and more of these cells are direction and/or orientation selective than in BD cats (Kratz & Spear, 1976). The same relationships hold for BD cats over the deprived eye of MD cats. Thus, the differences in acuity in these cats could reflect differences in the percent of cells with highly selective receptive-field properties. However, this seems unlikely when one examines the reversal of the effects of MD. That is, both reverse-suture and removal of the nondeprived eye are effective in increasing the percent of responsive cells, but not in restoring receptive field specificity (Smith et al., 1978). Yet, both manipulations improve visual acuity (Fig. 7.5). Thus, for visually pattern deprived cats, behavioral measures of visual acuity apparently reflect the percent of responsive cells in the striate cortex.

It should be mentioned that this relationship between percent responsive cells and visual acuity is limited to kittens totally deprived of patterned visual input during development. An experiment by Smith, Holdefer, & Reeves (1982b) investigated whether visual acuity is related to the percent of responsive cells in the striate cortex when patterned visual input is present during development. Smith et al. (1982b) raised kittens in the dark until 5 weeks of age and then exposed them to unequal periods of alternating monocular occlusion (AMO) for the next 8 months. On one day, the right eye was allowed 8 hours of normal visual experience, on the next day, the left eye was allowed 1 hour of visual experience. The kittens were kept in the dark at all other times. Electrophysiological recordings from single cells in the striate cortex revealed that 84% of the cells responded to the more experienced eye, whereas only 17% responded to the less experienced eye; nevertheless, neither eye differed in the selectivity of the cells' response to moving and/or oriented slits of light. In these

AMO kittens, behavioral measures of visual acuity did not reveal any differences in acuity between the eyes. Thus, unlike the relationship described above for pattern deprived cats, in cats which experience patterned visual input during development visual acuity is not related to the percent of responsive cells in the striate cortex.

E. SUMMARY

In this chapter I have reviewed many physiological and anatomical changes that occur during normal development and following visual deprivation and demonstrated the power of careful, quantitative behavioral investigations in demonstrating these changes in the organization of the brain. These behavioral measures thus give meaning to the more molecular changes in the brain and demonstrate that they are, indeed, functionally significant. Thus, we have begun to uncover brain-behavior interactions, but our quest has only begun. In writing this chapter, and indeed, this entire book, we hope to convince the readers that quantitative behavioral measures can serve as sensitive indices of changes occurring in the brain. Perhaps one day we will have many thousands of brain-behavior associations such as those reviewed in this book. It is my firm belief that with the development of appropriate behavioral tests one can uncover "brain-behavior" isomorphisms. If we have been successful in our quest, we will have convinced you of the validity of this approach and perhaps you will become a contributor. We hope so.

ACKNOWLEDGMENTS

The author expresses his gratitude to Drs. Robert Jensen, Steve Lehmkuhle, Fred Lit, Ken Kratz, and Brian Timney for their helpful comments on this chapter. The assistance in testing animals provided by M. Boyd, J. Dorsett, J. Endeley, A. Fitzgerald, R. Holdefer, M. Jackson, M.S. Loop, T. Reeves, and H. Schwark is also gratefully acknowledged. I also thank Les Sellers for typing the manuscript and Patricia Ryba for her editorial assistance.

Research from this laboratory was supported in part by a Vision Training Grant from NIH (EYO-7005), a NSF grant (BNS-8002251), and a Research General Grant (210396) from the Office of Research Development and Administration-Southern Illinois University-Carbondale.

8 | The Analysis of Behavior in the Laboratory Rat

IAN Q. WHISHAW, BRYAN KOLB,
and ROBERT J. SUTHERLAND

A. INTRODUCTION

The problem the physiological psychologist has in analyzing brain-behavior relations is made difficult not only because it demands the patient observational skill of the ethologist and the sophisticated technology of the physiologist, but also because psychologists often bring to the laboratory a prejudice that can be self-defeating. This is illustrated by the behavior of senior undergraduate students when they enter our physiological psychology laboratory class. Each student is given two rats and is told that one has brain damage and the other is normal. Their task is to determine which rat is brain damaged and, if possible, to come to some conclusion about the extent and location of the damage. They are encouraged to read any textbook or paper, design any test, or build any special equipment they feel might be useful. At the end of the semester they submit their findings to the class.

The results of this assignment are invariably the same. Most of the students see only two rats that seem surprisingly similar and that belong to a species whose behavioral repertoire is unfamiliar to everyone except some scientists and rat-catchers. They design some novel experiments, speculate extensively, but only occasionally make the correct diagnosis. Most often they devise a learning task and conclude that the animal with the poorer performance has brain damage. Then, by reading the literature, they suggest that a structure such as the hippocampus has been destroyed. Surprisingly, most of the students say that their "clinical" impression more validly indicates which animal has brain damage. Accordingly, they say, "This one just does not seem to be as normal as the other one, but I just can't put my finger on what the difference is." Their appreciation of the difficulty of diagnosing brain damage and the inadequacy of their technique is heightened when they find on histological examination that one of the rats they were given had been decorticated, that is, it had lost the 30% of its brain that they are prejudiced to believe is the most important part.

Of course, the results of the assignment are not surprising. As well as a reluctance to really "get to know" their rats because of the image of the species,[1] the students are reflecting their training in lower division experimental psychology and methodology courses. There they learned a bias that stems from a tradition in twentieth-century North American psychology that focuses on one particular way of proceeding in science. According to this view, proper science involves (1) stating a theory consisting of a set of postulates with all terms operationally defined; (2) logically deducing predictions about behavioral outcomes; (3) comparing the predictions with the results of carefully controlled experiments, which leads to a revision or confirmation of the theory (Wolman & Nagel, 1965). As a result of this bias, students (and a good number of scientists) are less concerned with what discoveries they can make about brain-behavior relations than with what *form* these discoveries must have. In keeping with this bias, good form includes animals that are naive, that receive the same life experience before and during the experiment, and that are no longer useful once the experiment is completed. This procedure, also called the hypothetico-deductive method, is somewhat akin to a surgical operation in which every precaution is made to maintain sterility. Unfortunately, all too often the findings generated by this type of experiment are also sterile.

There are features of brain-behavioral relations that severely limit the usefulness of the hypothetico-deductive method. As becomes apparent to our students, if the number of animals is small, or if the type of damage is unknown, this procedure is not helpful. Most importantly, despite the intimate interaction between brain events and behavioral events, there is no one-to-one correspondence between behavioral concepts (e.g., attention) and our concepts of the anatomical or chemical components of the brain (e.g., the dorsal noradrenergic bundle). This can be called the principle of non-congruence. Stated differently, in every experiment a selective manipulation within the physiological sphere generates a multitude of consequences in behavior. For example, feeding behavior has been studied by making lesions in hypothalamic "feeding centers," but damage to these same centers also produces such varied effects as somnolence, sensory unresponsiveness, movement abnormalities, licking and chewing abnormalities, electroencephalographic abnormalities, gastric ulceration, cardiac abnormalities, pulmonary edema, blood-brain barrier perforation, etc.

---

1. "The Norway rat is undoubtedly hated and feared by more people in more countries in the world than is any other animal. These people see in it a filthy animal, destroyer of property, spoiler of food, carrier of bubonic plague and many other terrible diseases, attacker of human beings, particularly defenseless babies." (Richter, 1968, p. 403).

Acknowledgment of these "unwanted" consequences is frequently reflected in the discussion section of papers when comments are made about the "side effects" of the experimental manipulation. It is not uncommon to read that the rats' performance might have been more in keeping with the predictions of the experiment had they not suffered a motor impairment or had they had more time to recover. Physiological psychology textbooks have still greater difficulty with the side effects of such manipulations because the side effects do not readily fit within such traditional chapter headings as motivation, emotion, arousal, etc. Consequently, side effects are simply ignored or the experimental technique, e.g., lesions, are criticized as being inadequate, crude, or nonspecific. The impression given is that an ideal technique would allow the mechanisms supporting such features of behavior as attention or motivation to be selectively taken from the brain without untoward changes occurring in any other aspect of behavior.

Is there an alternate way of studying behavior, one that avoids the pitfalls of the hypothetico-deductive method and still permits extensive study of small numbers of animals or study of animals whose deficits are not initially obvious? Yes, there is a method, which we can call the empirico-inductive method. It is empirical in the sense that reliance is on experience and observation, without regard to systems and theories, and inductive in the sense that meaningful generalizations or patterns are derived from observations.

This approach is particularly useful in cases in which the effects of toxins, pharmacological treatment, or dietary manipulation are to be investigated, when there is no clear expectancy with regard to outcome. It is also useful with more traditional approaches to brain and behavioral relations that use brain lesions, neurotoxins, and brain stimulation. Finally, this approach can be used to understand the occurrence and changes in such phasic events as heart rate, respiration, vibrissae movement, electroencephalographic (EEG) activity, single cell activity, and evoked potential activity. For example, Vanderwolf and his coworkers (Bland & Vanderwolf, 1972; Vanderwolf, 1969; Whishaw and Vanderwolf, 1973) came to their understanding of how EEG activity is related to behavior by simply observing what the animals were doing when certain patterns of EEG activity occurred. Similarly, O'Keefe's informal observations of single cell firing in the hippocampus suggested to him that the hippocampus might function as a cognitive map (O'Keefe & Nadel, 1978). Further examples of how the empirico-inductive method has been used to understand the activity of neurons in the hippocampus and brainstem can be found in the papers by Siegel [Chapter 6, this volume] and by Ranck et al. [Chapter 5, this volume].

The most important feature of the empirico-inductive approach is that it requires careful observation of what animals are actually doing and careful assessment of the many ways they change after brain manipulations. This means that many aspects of their behavior must be studied and that many tests must be designed to more completely and selectively isolate one or another feature of behavior. It also means that good descriptions of normal behavior must be available, or made, against which abnormalities can be contrasted. Since the number of behaviors to be studied becomes large, one wag has described the procedure as "the study of the side effects." Of course, it might be argued that once the animals are used for one test they are "spoiled" for use in any others. We feel that this criticism loses much of its force if the behaviors studied are those the animals will normally be engaged in daily, in their home environment.

An empirico-inductive methodology for studying the behavior of rats does not have to be invented anew. The methodology for studying appearance and general behavioral potential has long been a traditional part of human clinical medicine (see Hutt & Hutt, 1970). Furthermore, the methodology for an assessment of more complex cognitive functions does not have to be invented anew either. It is well established in human neuropsychology (see Kolb & Whishaw, 1980). The techniques need only be modified to be useful with laboratory animals such as the rat.

What should be studied? The selection of behaviors for study in the approach we are proposing can be greatly influenced by the experimenter's view of behavior. Behavior can be categorized in terms of functional end points, e.g., feeding, fighting, fleeing. It can be based upon hypothetical constructs, e.g., motivation, arousal, or fear. It could also be based upon putative functions of certain brain structures, e.g., the hippocampus, for memory. We suggest that the emphasis should be upon the animal's appearance and actual behavior. In Appendix A we summarize those features of behavior we have routinely studied in our own investigations. The list is not exhaustive, but it is comprehensive. The tests and methods used to study these behaviors are simple and inexpensive, they are easily modified, they are easily scored, they can be given quickly, and for the most part, little or no special training of the animal is required. Furthermore, behavioral abnormalities can be detected with the tests. A decorticate rat, for example, would distinguish itself by appearing abnormal on virtually every aspect of behavior described in Appendix A. Animals with less drastic treatments are found to be abnormal on one or another of the tests, depending upon the exact locus of the damage. The methodology for our own research usually involves a procedure similar to the one we assign the students. One or two animals are studied using the assessment procedure described in Appendix A, and then later more formal studies of the hypothetico-deductive type may be used to confirm initial findings.

B. THE RAT[2]

The rationale for using animals for neuropsychological research, and for using the rat, in particular, has been described elsewhere (Kolb & Whishaw, Chapter 10, this volume), and so only some general comments need be made here. First, as we have pointed out, the rat is widely used in both physiological and behavioral research. As early as 1924, Donaldson was able to compile a bibliography of over 2200 studies of the rat (Donaldson, 1924). The number of studies in which the rat has been used would be enormous. As Richter (1968) has stated, the similarity of the rat's and human's dietary needs first made it a defensible choice for nutritional studies. But it also has many other features that make it an ideal animal for neuropsychological research. It is an economically easy animal to maintain in a laboratory. It is stable and reliable, both behaviorally and physiologically, thus facilitating repeated observations. It is a simple animal for surgical purposes, and it is very resistant to infection. It has a short life-span, about three years, and so is ideal for development and aging studies. Its size makes it easy to handle, and when handled it has a gentle disposition. Finally, it keeps itself extremely clean under laboratory conditions. Richter has stated that "If someone were to give me the power to create an animal most useful for all types of studies on problems concerned directly or indirectly with human welfare, I could not possibly improve on the Norway rat" (Richter, 1968, p. 404). Most scientists who have used the rat would agree with Richter. Caution in the selection of the strain of rat is warranted. In particular, albino rats display a number of abnormalities (sensory-neural, biochemical-metabolic, and physiological) that precludes their use in certain types of experiments or at least limits the generalizability of the results (Creel, 1980). The only other ma-

2. "The Norway rat was the first animal to be domesticated for strictly scientific purposes. Domesticated rats were first used in Europe for scientific studies over one hundred years ago. They were brought from Europe [the Department of Zoology at the University of Geneva] to this country [the United States] in 1890 for studies on the brain by Adolf Meyer, then a newly arrived Swiss neuropathologist, later Professor of Psychiatry and Head of the Phipps Psychiatric Clinc at the Johns Hopkins Hospital and long time Dean of American Psychiatry. When H.H. Donaldson, Professor of Anatomy at the University of Chicago, first saw Meyer's rats, he at once recognized their possibilities for scientific research in general, and later established the famous colony of albino rats at the Wistar Institute in Philadelphia that until recently supplied rats to laboratories all over the world" (Richter, 1968, p. 403–404).

jor drawback to using the rat that we know is that it is not uncommon for scientists to develop allergies to it, particularly its saliva, which it spreads on its fur and body, and for this reason it is important that it be housed in well-ventilated quarters.

C. EXAMINATION OF APPEARANCE

The appearance of an animal provides important clues to its functional status. Examination procedures have been well worked out by neurologists for the study of human patients, and many of these are applicable to the rat. The guiding principle of the human neurological examination is to assume that every function is abnormal until examined and found to be normal. This requires that all areas of the skin and mucous membranes, and each orifice, be examined, and that the functions of each sensory system and the motor system be assessed (DeMyer, 1974). There is no standard neurological or neuropsychological examination procedure for assessing appearance of the rat, but the procedure we favor is to (1) examine the posture and the details of the rat's features while it is undisturbed in its home cage, (2) examine the contents of the cage and the droppings from the cage, and (3) remove the rat from its cage to weigh it and to assess its response to handling. Any interesting features of the rat's appearance can be studied further, as we shall illustrate with a number of examples. Some other relevant studies and observations are summarized in Appendix B.

1. Home Cage Observations

We first examine the rat's appearance by observing it in its home cage. For many of our studies, the cages we favor are wire-mesh hanging cages that provide easy observation and access to the animals. Some of the cages are modified with one Plexiglas side through which the animals can be filmed. A normal rat usually sits sideways to an observer, toward the rear of the cage, and looks toward the front. Often it will approach the front in response to any kind of disturbance. Deviations from this pattern after experimental manipulations may suggest a dysfunction warranting further investigation. In an extreme case, an animal may be akinetic, and fail to move (Balagura, Wilcox, & Coscina, 1969; Robinson & Whishaw, 1974), or be hyperkinetic and move continuously (Nauta, 1946; Maire & Patton, 1954; Morrison, 1968b; Whishaw & Robinson, 1974; Whishaw & Kolb, 1979). There may also be more subtle deviations. For example, we have observed that rats with orbital cortex lesions typically sit facing the back of their cage during the first few days after surgery (Kolb, Whishaw, & Schallert, 1977). This propensity is reflected in their behavior outside the cage, for when they are placed near a can or other small enclosure, they enter it and remain facing inward. Normal rats enter the can, turn around, and repeatedly poke their head out. The frontal-lesioned rats only turn around and emerge when the lights are turned off. The reason for this behavior is not readily obvious, but it suggests an enhancement of normal light avoidance behavior. It may also reflect a heightened aversion reaction to other aspects of the world; for example, Butter and Snyder (1972) report heightened aversive reactions in social interactions by orbital frontal-lesioned monkeys.

Many other details of the rat's appearance can be checked while it remains in its home cage. Rats keep themselves extremely clean and so dirty fur or the appearance of Harderian material (a reddish fluid around the eyes, which animals spread on their fur while grooming) will indicate changes in grooming behavior. Decorticate rats, for example, are relatively efficient at grooming in their home cage, yet the base of their tail appears dirty. Formal observations of the animals' grooming has shown that they spend less time grooming the rear of their body than do normal rats (Kolb & Whishaw, 1981a; Vanderwolf, Kolb, & Cooley, 1978). The examination should include inspection of the eyes, since many types of midbrain damage produce changes in pupillary response to light (Legg, 1975); inspection of the teeth, since absence of chewing results in increased tooth length; examination of the genitals, since inflammation may reveal persistent licking, as occurs after amygdala damage (Sutherland, 1974); examination of the fur, since piloerection can indicate fever or other signs of change in thermoregulatory functions (Satinoff, Valentino, & Teitelbaum, 1976).

While the rat remains in its home cage it is useful to watch its feeding behavior; the observations can be facilitated by depriving the rat of food during the previous night. Such simple observations have led to the findings that decorticate rats do not pick up their food in their paws to eat it, but rather eat directly from the floor (Vanderwolf, Kolb, & Cooley, 1978), and that lateral hypothalamic-lesioned rats prandial drink; that is, they take many small drinks while they eat, rather than one or two periodic large drinks (Kissileff & Epstein, 1969). They prandial drink, as it turns out, because the lesions reduce salivation.

2. EXAMINATION OF THE CAGE AND CAGE RESIDUE

The rat's cage should be examined to determine whether it has eaten and whether it is drinking normal amounts of water. We need not review here the many studies on hyperphagia and hypophagia, and on polydipsia and adipsia (for reviews see Epstein, Kissileff, & Stellar, 1973; Novin,

Wyrwicka, & Bray, 1976). If food is placed in the rat's cage, it is also possible to see whether it hoards its food by placing it in one corner of the cage. Hoarding, however, may not always be a feature of a normal rat's behavior (see species-specific behavior, below).

Clues to some aspects of a rat's behavior are also easily obtained by placing a piece of paper beneath its cage and examining the contents. Figure 8.1 shows the contents of papers from a normal rat and from a decorticate rat. The crumbs and broken pieces of food beneath the cage of the decorticate rat indicate that it has difficulty chewing and swallowing food. The random location of feces and urine indicate it does not compartmentalize its home cage with respect to its activities, as does the normal rat. Examination of the contents of the paper can reveal abnormalities in eating through the absence or presence of excess food; in drinking by changes in the extent of urine stains; in sexual behavior through the appearance of numerous sperm plugs, such as follows amygdala lesions (Sutherland, 1974); in pathological changes in the kidneys or digestive system as shown by blood in the urine or feces, such as follows lesions of the locus coreleus (Amaral & Foss, 1975; Kolb & Whishaw, 1977) or lateral hypothalamus (Lindholm, Shumway, Grijalva, Schallert, & Ruppel, 1975); or in salivary function as revealed by salivary stains, such as follows preoptic lesions (Toth, 1973). Abnormalities in intestinal motility and bladder efficiency can also be detected as there is a conspicuous 5-hr rhythm in defecation and a 2-hr rhythm in urination in normal rats (Richter, 1927).

3. Weighing and Asessing Responses to Handling

Removing the rat from its home cage each day for weighing is advisable. Rats, particularly male rats, continue to grow throughout their life and so their body weight is a sensitive indicator of their health, in general, and their feeding behavior, in particular. After the rat has been weighed its temperature can be taken with a rectal thermometer. Abnormalities in temperature are common after many types of hypothalamic damage and thus can be a useful diagnostic indicator of the physiological and metabolic status of an animal (see for example, Nagel & Satinoff, 1980).

FIGURE 8.1. Residue collected on a paper towel from beneath the cage of a normal (right) and a decorticated (left) rat. The normal rat piled its food at the front of its cage, where it ate. It defecated and urinated at the rear. Stains on the front part of the towel are caused by spillage from the water spout. Feces and food droppings are not compartmentalized beneath the cage of the decorticated rat. The volume of crumbs indicate the difficulty the decorticate rat has in biting, chewing, and swallowing food (from Whishaw, Nonneman, & Kolb, 1981).

DECORTICATE

NORMAL

149

We make it a point to ensure that all our animals are handled periodically prior to their use in experiments. This guarantees that they are used to being removed from their home cage, weighed, handled, etc. After an experimental manipulation, handling becomes a way to assess changes in some aspects of an animal's motor status. If the rat is held in an open palm and gently bounced, an indication of its motor tone can be obtained. For example, posterior hypothalamic lesions produce increases in motor tone, as indicated by a feeling of rigidity in the limbs, whereas more anterior hypothalamic lesions decrease tone, as indicated by a feeling of softness in the limbs and trunk (unpublished observations, Whishaw & Robinson, 1974). During handling, an animal's vocalizations may express its functional status. We have observed that rats depleted of dopamine (with the neurotoxin 6-hydroxydopamine) show reduced vocalization, whereas rats depleted of both dopamine and noradrenaline show increased vocalization (unpublished observations). Some drugs also affect vocalization, for example, haloperidol potentiates, whereas chlordiazepoxide reduces, vocalization (Schallert & Whishaw, unpublished observations). While the rat is held still, it is also possible to listen to its breathing, since wheezing may indicate an abnormality, such as pulmonary edema (Maire & Patton, 1954). A rating scale for the rat's responses to handling when it is removed from its cage has been developed (see King, 1956) and has been used to assess the behavior of rats after a number of experimental manipulations (Kolb, 1974b; Brady & Nauta, 1953; 1955; Cytawa & Teitelbaum, 1968).

4. FOLLOW-UP ANALYSES OF ABNORMALITIES IN APPEARANCE

As compared with the neurologist or physician, the psychologist has the advantage that an animal's condition can be carefully monitored daily. Since a neurologist usually sees a patient for just a few appointments, only occasionally are daily observations made on human features by observant individuals. These provide a treasury of insight into phenomena that might not otherwise have been studied. Such is Bean's (1980) 35-year study on the growth of his fingernails, particularly his left thumbnail. Bean observed that each nail grows at a fixed rate; that the growth of one nail could be predicted from that of another; that growth changed in relation to his health and travel; that loss of growth at one point could be made up by increased growth at a later date; and that limb use potentiated growth, etc.

Observations on nail growth in the rat have been similarly revealing (Whishaw, Schallert, & Kolb, 1981; Whishaw, Kolb, Sutherland & Becker, 1982; unpublished observations). We were initially attracted to the observation that decorticate rats had long nails because their feet "clicked" when

HIND FEET

Normal   Decorticate

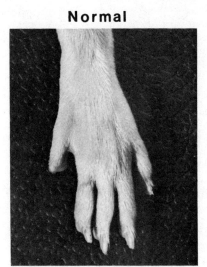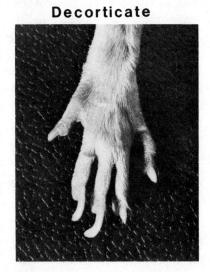

FIGURE 8.2. Hindfoot toenails of a normal, 18-month-old rat and an 18-month-old rat Decorticated at 6 months of age. In the absence of periodic nibbling, the decorticated rat's toenails continue to grow until they become so long that they break, as has already occurred for the first and third and fourth nails (from Whishaw, Kolb, Sutherland, & Becker, 1983).

they walked about on the floor. Figure 8.2 shows the length of toenails in an 18-month-old normal male rat and its littermate control, which had been decorticate since 6 months of age. The only limitation in length of the decorticate rat's nails is that when the nails become very long they break. We studied the use of toenails in grooming and found that decorticate rats scratched as often as control rats, so that growth was not due to decreased use in this activity. After scratching with a rear foot, however, both normal and decorticate rats groom the foot, but decorticate rats do not bite their nails at this time as do normal rats. This is an indication that they have oral-manipulatory deficiencies in grooming just as they do in feeding behavior.

By observing the nail length of rats with more restricted cortical lesions, we found that long nails are consistently associated with frontal cortex damage, particularly if the damage includes the lateral surface of the frontal cortex. When we examined the nails of rats in which frontal cortex damage had been received in infancy, as compared with adulthood, we found that the early lesions did not spare function; both groups had long nails. This finding was counterintuitive because it is widely known that rats subjected to lesions in infancy show sparing of function (Kolb & Nonneman, 1978;, Kolb & Whishaw, 1981b). The toenail length observations supported the view that the sparing of function that follows early lesions is behavior dependent; learned behavior shows sparing, whereas species typical behaviors, such as toenail biting, do not (Kolb & Whishaw, 1981b). The comparative observations on toenail biting and learned behaviors suggest that there are fundamental differences in the way the functions relevant to these two behaviors are organized in neocortical circuitry. For a further discussion of the importance of such distinctions in behavioral analysis, see Kolb and Whishaw [Chapter 10, this volume].

D. SENSORY AND SENSORIMOTOR BEHAVIOR

The object of sensory tests is to assess the functional status of the sensory systems, i.e., fine touch and pressure, vision, olfaction. With humans, tests are easy to administer because people can tell the examiner if a given stimulus is perceived. In the rat, assessment procedures are necessarily more indirect. There are two types of procedures for testing sensory functions in the rat. The first involve formal tests, usually as part of a learning paradigm, and is usually directed toward the study of the function of the pathways and primary projection areas of the sensory systems (see Smith, Chapter 7, this volume). The second type is more informal and is often directed toward studying the effects of damage outside the primary sensory areas. The latter tests are often referred to as sensorimotor tests.

There is a significant body of literature on the sensory systems, which is reviewed in most textbooks on physiological psychology. Much of this literature is based upon species other than the rat, presumably because other species are more convenient for studying some aspects of sensory function. This literature does not fall within the scope of the present paper (see Smith, Chapter 7, this volume). The vibrissae of the rat play a special role in the guidance of behavior and summaries of their function can be found in the literature (Gustafson & Felbain-Keramidas, 1922; Vincent, 1912; 1913; Welker, 1964).

1. SENSORIMOTOR TESTS

Sensorimotor tests are tests that can be quickly and easily administered; they are also useful for gaining a quick impression of the functional status of a sensory system, motor systems, or the relation between sensory and motor systems of animals. The usual procedure in administering the tests is to take the rat from its cage and place it in a larger open cage, on a small platform, or simply on an open counter. It is then touched with a cotton-tipped applicator or with von Frey hairs to determine if it will respond by orienting to touches on various parts of its body. A response, at its weakest, can consist of a head turn, and at its strongest a head turn and a bite at the stimulus. In the same test sessions, visual, olfactory, taste and auditory stimuli can be used to assess orienting to other modalities of stimulation. Furthermore, by varying the stimuli presented, the rat's response to pleasant (e.g., sucrose), neutral (e.g., water), or aversive (e.g., quinine) stimuli can be assessed. A number of separate issues must be considered with respect to sensorimotor testing. These include (1) the question of what the tests are measuring and (2) differentiating responses when tests are given to rats in their home cage, vs. an open field or novel environment.

A valuable addition to the von Frey hair technique is the Schallert dot test of sensorimotor behavior (Schallert et al., 1982). In the test, small pieces of adhesive paper are placed on various parts of the rat's limbs or snout and the latency and method of removal is observed. Neglect is diagnosed if a rat does not remove an adhesive dot. An asymmetry is indicated if a dot on one body part is removed before that on a corresponding contralateral body part. Tactile extinction, or at least an analogue of the human condition, can be demonstrated if an animal neglects a dot on one side of its body only when a similar-sized dot is located on the corresponding contralateral body part. We have been able to observe each of these phenomena occurring sequentially as rats recover from hemi-neocortex removal (Schallert & Whishaw, unpublished observations). The test can be modified in numerous ways. We have placed paper clips on the fur, objects on the vibrissae, objects in an animal's mouth, and objects, such as wire, string, or elastic bands, around the limbs of an animal. The advantages of the test are that it is easy for a novice to administer and scoring is objective and quantitative, and it is less subject to interference from certain types of motor asymmetry than the von Frey method. Still, care must be exercised in its use. We have noted, for example, that rats with orbital frontal neocortex lesions, which cannot open their mouths to grasp objects, not unexpectedly do poorly at this test.

2. WHAT DO SENSORIMOTOR TESTS TEST?

Rats may show any of a number of behaviors or abnormalities on sensorimotor tests, and the different possibilities should be considered when the test results are interpreted. The following are a few of the effects, or changes, that could, or have been, observed with sensorimotor testing. A summary of studies that have used sensorimotor test techniques using the rat as the subject is given in Appendix C.

(i) Anesthesia

Animals may show an anesthesia, or an inability to detect stimulation. An anesthesia could be indicated if an animal showed no motor abnormalities, could orient to stimulation on some body part, but not on another, or could orient to some types of stimulation, but not to other types.

(ii) Paresis

Paresis is a slight or incomplete loss of movement. It is possible that animals could show a loss of movement in a part of the body that precludes orienting to stimulation. Presumably, a paresis would be apparent in many aspects of a rat's motor behavior and not just in sensorimotor testing situations. Many procedures that produce sensory neglect also produce catalepsy (see below), which is characterized by rigidity, akinesia (a poverty of movement), and waxy flexibility (a tendency to maintain awkward postures). In many ways it is possible to view sensory neglect as secondary to catalepsy, but it is equally possible to interpret catalepsy as a neglect to somatosensory stimulation that normally informs the rat of the location of its trunk and limbs. Because of the difficulty in making such distinctions great care is necessary in interpreting findings successfully.

(iii) Contralateral Neglect

Animals may show a generalized neglect of all stimulation given on the side of the body contralateral to a lesion. This phenomenon is referred to as contralateral neglect, unilateral neglect, unilateral inattention, etc. (for a review, see Heilman & Watson, 1977). Although animals fail to orient to stimulation, failure is usually not thought of as due to either anesthesia or paresis. Anesthesia may be ruled out if an animal increases muscle tone or changes posture when touched. Sensory stimulation may also be found to activate the neocortical or hippocampal EEG, despite the absence of orienting (Robinson & Whishaw, 1974). Paresis can be ruled out by carefully observing the rats to see if they move appropriately during some other behavior. For example, during grooming, animals will turn to groom a part of their body they otherwise neglected during sensorimotor testing (Turner, 1973). One qualification should be made with respect to the latter point. It is possible that certain classes of movements, such as voluntary movements used in orienting, are lost to the animal, whereas other movements, such as automatic movement used in grooming, are spared (Robinson & Whishaw, 1974; Vanderwolf, 1971). The many studies on contralateral neglect following lateral hypothalamic damage suggest that it may be best thought of as a disconnection between sensory systems and the motor systems that mediate orienting (Appendix C). Studies on the nigrostriatal system implicate the absence of dopamine as being an important link in sensorimotor inattention (Appendix C). Studies on the recovery from sensory neglect show that recovery always proceeds from nose to tail (rostro-caudal). The significance of this is unclear, but it is an important clue to nervous system organization with respect to orienting.

(iv) Spatial Orienting

Many tests that require the rat to orient measure orienting to a place in space, rather than orienting to a part of the body. For example, if a normal rat is touched on the base of its tail, it does not turn to examine its tail (which is moved away from the stimulus when the rat turns), but it turns to locate the object at the place where it was encountered. We have found that we can distinguish between body orienting and place orienting in the following way. A touch from an object, such as a cotton-tipped applicator, causes the rat to turn and locate it. This measures orienting to a place in space. A paper clip attached to the rat's fur causes it to remove it, either by scratching or by seizing it with its mouth. This measures orienting to a body part (unpublished observations). Decorticate rats are deficient in turning to locate objects that have touched them, but they will remove paper clips either by licking or scratching (unpublished manuscript, Whishaw, Schallert, & Kolb, 1981).

(v) Release of Orienting

Animals may show a "release" of orienting as illustrated by more vigorous or more persistent orienting. Release of orienting has been reported to follow ventromedial or anterior hypothalamic lesions (Marshall, 1975; Whishaw & Robinson, 1974).

(vi) Hyperesthesias

Animals may display apparent hyperesthesia that causes them to find stimulation noxious; that is, rather than orient to objects and grasp them, they orient and reject the object by pushing it away (Schallert & Whishaw, 1978). The reason for this behavior is not well understood. It has been thought of as a release of avoidance (as compared with approach) behavior (see also Stellar, Brooks, & Mills, 1979). Hyperesthesias may also underlie self-mutilation, as has been reported after dorsal rhizotomy (Dennis & Melzack, 1979).

(vii) Displacement

Animals may show a displacement of reference in that they turn to the side of the body opposite to that which receives stimulation. Such an effect has been reported in rats with unilateral superior colliculus lesions (Kirvel, 1975).

(viii) Response to Novelty

Animals may be unable to orient to novel stimuli, while still showing sensory control of locomotion. Goodale and Murison (1975) found that rats with superior colliculus lesions show normal locomotion to a visual stimulus, but no shift in visual fixation, orienting, rearing, or freezing responses to novel visual or auditory stimuli. Animals with an intact superior colliculus, but a lesioned visual cortex, were impaired in visually guided locomotion, but not in orienting.

3. Home Cage versus Open Field Tests

Sensorimotor testing procedures have been criticized as crude and awkward to administer and difficult to quantify. We have found that these criticisms derive largely from attempts to test rats after they have been removed from their home cage. Despite the fact that in most studies the rats are adapted to the testing location or tested on small platforms that inhibit locomotion, best results are obtained when rats are tested in their home cage (Whishaw, Schallert, & Kolb, 1981). If hanging mesh cages, which provide easy insertion of stimulus objects, are not available, it may be necessary to construct special cages for the tests.

In their home cage, normal rats will pursue objects with a great deal of vigor, apparently viewing capture of the object as a type of "game," as when a kitten chases a moving object. In this "game," the experimenter will usually tire long before the rat. If the rat is removed from its cage, it will begin to engage in exploratory behavior, which competes with the type of orienting behavior the experimenter is attempting to elicit with the sensorimotor tests. To demonstrate this difference, we have presented a palatable mash, on a spatula, to rats in their home environment and recorded their latency to begin eating. They were then placed on a counter for 1 minute, where the tests were repeated. Over 10 days of testing, every rat accepted the food within 5 seconds in its home cage, and no rat accepted the food within 1 minute when it was removed from its home cage. Similar results were obtained with tactile or other sensory stimuli. Rats in an open field even tolerated paper clips attached to their fur, but they removed them immediately upon being replaced in their home cage.

Although sensorimotor testing is best done with the rat in its home cage, open field tests are useful for testing a rat's perception of a novel environment. If the rat continues to orient vigorously outside its home cage, it can be concluded that it is *not* making a distinction normal rats immediately make. We have found that anterior-lateral hypothalamic lesioned rats apparently fail to make such distinctions. They will pursue objects in open fields with as much vigor as they pursue them in their home cage (Robinson & Whishaw, 1974). Chasing such an object is a response that both lesioned and normal rats display in their home cages. Possibly the lesion disrupts connections to the cortex or hippocampus, which may be involved in "cognitive mapping" of the rat's home environment, rendering the rat unable to distinguish familiar places from novel places. "Neglect" of a novel environment may also account for some of the puzzling findings in other studies. Normal rats that are food or water deprived will explore a novel or partly novel environment before accepting readily available food or water (Hebb & Mahut, 1955; Zimbardo & Montgomery, 1957). Recovered lateral hypothalamic lesioned rats, however, although thought of as having reduced motivation for food, will accept food more quickly than normal rats in similar situations. Their speedy acceptance may not be due to increased motivation, as has been suggested (Devenport & Balagura, 1971), but rather to decreased perception of the change in their location. In summary, because of the differences in responses displayed by animals in their home cage and in novel environments, we suggest that for maximum effectiveness, tests should be given in both situations.

E. POSTURE AND IMMOBILITY

Animals spend a great deal of their waking time partly or completely immobile. Often, the importance of immobility as a behavior may not become obvious unless an animal is found to be unable to move or unable to remain immobile. In humans, depression and Parkinson's disease might be taken as examples of the first type of disability, whereas hyperactivity, mania, Huntington's chorea, Gilles de la Tourette's syndrome, and the incessant walking displayed by some old or senile people can be taken as examples of the second. Many of the experiments undertaken on immobility have been justified, in part, as being directed toward developing animal models of one or the other of these pathological conditions. Although immobility is complex, its analysis can be facilitated by subdividing it to direct attention at one or another of the following aspects: (1) The types of immobility, (2) restraint-induced immobility, and (3) environmental influences on immobility. Appendix D summarizes some relevant studies on these various aspects of immobility in the rat.

1. Types of Immobility

Animals display a number of types of immobility. These can be seen embedded in their normal behavior, and they may also appear as aberrations or abnormalities that come to dominate the animal's behavior. The following sections describe a number of types of immobility, their aberrations, and the ways in which they can be studied.

(i) Immobility with Postural Support

Immobility with postural support is displayed by animals when they stand still and maintain their weight off the ground (supported on their legs). Postural support is thought to be a prerequisite for normal locomotion, but postural support is also necessary for standing still, rearing, shivering, eating, grooming, lapping water, all aspects of social behavior, etc.

Immobility with postural support can occur as an aberration, referred to as "catalepsy." In this condition, the animal remains in an upright posture of "static equilibrium," with all other behaviors virtually absent. Catalepsy has three characteristics: akinesia (poverty of movement), muscular rigidity (which contributes to the sustained support), and waxy flexibility (the animal will remain in the awkward position in which it is placed). Akinesia is usually measured by placing an animal on an open surface and determining its latency to move. Rigidity is assessed by placing the animal on a vertical mesh or on two horizontal bars and determining how long it hangs there before climbing down. Waxy flexibility is measured by placing the animal in awkward postures and determining how long they are retained, i.e., one foot, or two feet, placed upon a small platform, or the body is contorted into strange positions. Cataleptic animals show "bracing reactions" by which they actively resist being moved from their static upright posture (Schallert, DeRyck, Whishaw, Ramirez, & Teitelbaum, 1978). When pushed from the back or side, or when pushed along with the front feet only, against the floor (wheel-barrow position), they remain rigid and push back rather than stepping in the direction in which they are pushed, as do normal rats.

Catalepsy commonly occurs in animals treated with major tranquilizers, such as haloperidol, in animals with hypothalamic lesions in which the ascending nigrostriatal dopamine fibers are severed, and in animals depleted of brain dopamine (see Appendix C). Catalepsy is also seen in such human diseases as Parkinson's disease and some other types of motor system diseases (Denny-Brown, 1968; Jung & Hassler, 1960; Martin, 1967).

Catalepsy can be considered as the result of exaggerated activity in a system that normally maintains an animal immobile in an upright position. What would happen, however, if this system were absent or severely damaged? The most likely consequence is that the animal would no longer be able to remain still in an upright posture. Lesions in the pontine reticular formation appear to produce just such a consequence. Whenever such an animal is placed upon the ground it begins to gallop forward; it is as if central inhibitory systems that allow normal animals to remain still are absent (Teitelbaum, Schallert, DeRyck, Whishaw, & Golani, 1980). Haloperidol, which produces catalepsy in normal animals, fails to produce immobility or even to block the locomotion of this animal. This may be an analogue of human "festination" or the running forward seen in some Parkinson patients (Sacks, 1976) and some old people. For example, we have seen an old patient who walked incessantly up and down the corridors of a nursing home repeating over and over again "I'm so tired." Haloperidol in doses that would immobilize a normal person had no effect on her ceaseless forward locomotion.

(ii) Localized Catalepsy

Localized catalepsy, that is, catalepsy restricted to a particular part of the body, is rarely seen. In the early stages of Parkinson's disease, catalepsy may be more obvious in a hand or in one-half of the body than in the remainder of the body. Blepharospasm, which is sustained closure of one of both eyelids, is an example of a localized catalepsy. In human blepharospasm, eyelid closure can last hours or days or it can be permanent. Activating stimulation, such as a visit to a new place, can sometimes produce temporary relief, but treatment for the condition is quite ineffective (Henderson, 1956). We have observed blepharospasm in rats after lateral hypothalamic damage (Schallert & Whishaw, 1978), after Haloperidol treatment, and after depletion of central dopamine by reserpine. We have also observed blepharospasm in old rats and in some decorticate rats (unpublished observations). In Figure 8.3, an example of blepharospasm in a decorticate rat is shown. Brushing the eye of a normal rat with a cotton-tipped applicator produces eyelid closure, but the eyelid opens as soon as the stimulus is removed. In the decorticate rat, the eye remains closed for seconds or minutes after the stimulus. Blepharospasm in the rat has an interesting relation to behavior. It can be induced during immobility and during more automatic movements, such as lapping water, chewing food, and grooming, but it cannot be induced during more "voluntary" movements, such as head turns, rearing, or walking. As in some people, activating stimulation (such as removing the rat from its home cage to walk around) blocks the occurrence of blepharospasm (unpublished observations). We suggest watching for isolated immobilities of body parts, or catalepsies, because they may provide useful models for the study of neural circuitry involved in the production and maintenance of immobility.

NORMAL   BLEPHAROSPASM

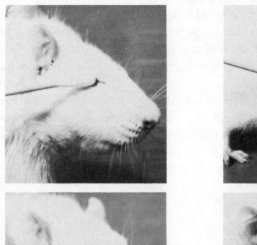
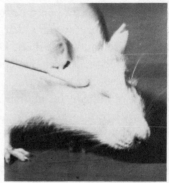

FIGURE 8.3. A stimulus applied to the eyelid of a normal rat produces eyelid closure, followed by eyelid opening the moment the stimulus is removed. Blepharospasm or eyelid catalepsy is manifest by sustained eyelid closure lasting from seconds to minutes after the stimulus is removed. The demonstration is from a decorticate (cortex plus hippocampus removed) rat.

(iii) Immobility without Support

Immobility without postural support occurs when animals lie down in resting or sleeping postures. This type of immobility is readily produced by low doses of minor tranquilizers or anesthetic agents. After such low doses, animals are still capable of walking, but when they stop they immediately subside to the surface. Human narcolepsy can be considered a condition in which there are repeated bouts of loss of support, and in these instances, the afflicted people also fall asleep. Martin (1967) has described Parkinson patients as being able to maintain postural support for a period of time. They can even balance upon one leg. In more advanced cases of Parkinson's disease, however, the patients may lose postural fixation of one part of the body on another. The head may fall forward in relation to the shoulders; the shoulders and the trunk may droop in relation to the legs; or the knees may fold, resulting in a loss of bipedal posture. Examples of loss of support or loss of fixation of one part of the body upon another are commonly seen in animals with damage in the posterior diencephalon. Generally, this loss is more obvious in the early recovery period (see Golani, Wolgin, & Teitelbaum, 1979).

Loss of postural fixation of one part of the body upon another can be potentiated by certain procedures. Teitelbaum, Wolgin, DeRyck, and Maire (1976) report that bandaging parts of the body can cause the loss of postural support of that body part. If the head of a rat which is clinging to a vertically oriented grid is bandaged, it will fall back from an upright position even though the rat will continue to cling with its feet. The mechanism here is unknown, but it presumably involves the contribution of sensory stimulation from body segments to postural support.

(iv) Immobility without Muscle Tone

So-called paradoxical sleep or REM sleep in the rat is characterized by the absence of muscle tone.[3] The absence of muscle tone has been shown to be produced by inhibition of spinal motor neurons by descending brainstem pathways (Pompeiano, 1970). Humans may suffer attacks in which they lose all motor tone and collapse onto the floor in a state resembling paradoxical sleep. This condition is called cataplexy. At present there are no rat analogues of this condition, but there is a dog analogue (Lucas, Foutz, Dement, & Mitter, 1979). We have removed brain-damaged rats from their cages and occasionally found them completely limp as if they had suffered an attack of cataplexy (Robinson & Whishaw, 1974), but they could be aroused by shaking them.

2. RESTRAINT-INDUCED IMMOBILITY

Restraint immobility, or as it is more popularly called, "animal hypnosis" or "tonic immobility," now comprises a rather large literature (see Maser & Gallup, 1977). Animals are placed in bizarre postures on their sides or upon their backs and restrained for from 5 to 15 seconds and then released. The length of time they are immobile is recorded. Thus, the term restraint-induced immobility describes the procedure and its consequence. This research is widely thought to model natural situations in which an animal has been caught by a predator and remains immobile or "plays possum" as a defense against being killed and eaten. More recent

3. Even though rats in active sleep display no muscle tone, they do show frequent, brief movements of the vibrissae, eyes, back, digits, and tail. The details of these movements have not been thoroughly analyzed, but Lapointe and Nosal (1979) have documented some aspects of their change during the first 17 days of life.

studies have been directed toward understanding the neural mechanisms that underlie and sustain the strange postures of immobility produced by restraint. Some researchers have suggested that the same mechanisms underlie pathological types of immobility, such as the catalepsy seen in advanced schizophrenia (Gallup & Maser, 1977).

Unfortunately, although the rat would be a convenient animal to use for such research, it does not display this type of immobility as readily as do lizards, chickens, and rabbits. However, immobility can be produced by some types of brain lesions, and in infant rats within the first two postnatal weeks (see Appendix D). We have found one natural situation in which rats readily show "animal hypnosis." If a male rat is introduced into the territory of another male rat he will engage in combat, but if he loses, and if no escape is available, he will lie immobile in a posture such as that illustrated by Barnett (1963). Klause Miczak (personal communication) demonstrated to us that if the intruder is returned to the situation some time later, he will immediately become immobile. In studying this phenomenon, we have found that this immobility will occur even if the tenant male is removed before the intruder is reintroduced. Furthermore, if the intruder is placed in any of the "animal hypnosis" positions (on its back or side) and restrained briefly, it will remain immobile for seconds or minutes (unpublished observations). Thus, "animal hypnosis" may be part of the rat's behavioral repertoire, but it may be more important for defense in intraspecies conflict than for interspecies defense. This conclusion is especially supported by findings that the bites made by a resident against an intruder are non-random and are generally not directed to the snout and ventral surface of the trunk (Blanchard & Blanchard, 1977; Blanchard, Blanchard, Takahashi, & Kelley, 1977). It is unlikely that a predator's attack would be constrained in just the same way. In experiments in which difficulties are encountered in obtaining restraint-induced immobility in the rat, this intraspecies conflict situation might prove useful.

3. ENVIRONMENTAL INFLUENCE ON IMMOBILITY

The incidence and postures of immobility are sensitive to a wide variety of environmental influences, many of which are, in turn, affected by brain damage or other types of neurological manipulation. Generally, influences that move an animal toward homeostasis for a physiological function facilitate the occurrence of immobility, whereas influences that move an animal away from homeostasis will reduce the tendency of an animal to remain immobile. The behavioral inactivation that follows a large turkey dinner at Christmas time is a widely recognized example of such an influence. Although these types of effects are well known, what might not be as well known is the profound influences they may have on brain-damaged animals. For example, Levitt and Teitelbaum (1975) report that gastric intubations of food into a lateral hypothalamic lesioned animal in the early postsurgical period can so inactivate the animal that it goes limp and remains limp even when it is suspended by its tail. Slight warming of the skin can similarly inactivate brain-damaged rats (Schallert, Whishaw, DeRyck, & Teitelbaum, 1978).

The profound effect environmental manipulation seems to have on brain-damaged rats may result from the fact that the brain lesions reduce the number of behavioral options the animals have. Two examples will suffice to illustrate this point. Rats with lateral hypothalamic lesions lose their operant thermoregulatory functions, while their more reflexive physiological responses are retained (Satinoff & Shan, 1971). The usual response of a normal animal to increased environmental temperature is, in the following sequence, to walk away, to saliva spread, and then to sprawl (Roberts, Mooney, & Martin, 1974). If brain damage removes walking and saliva spreading, an animal will sprawl quickly to increased environmental temperature because this is its remaining behavioral option. A similar phenomenon is seen in infant rats. When warmed they sprawl (see Fig. 8.4) both because they are brought to thermoregulatory neutrality and because being unable to walk well and saliva spread and groom well, this is their best defense against hyperthermia (Whishaw, Schallert, & Kolb, 1979). The seemingly bizarre posture of catalepsy seen after some other brain manipulations may be a posture for shivering thermogenesis; it might be displayed because the rat has lost the ability to generate heat by locomotion or increased fat metabolism (Schallert, Whishaw, DeRyck, & Teitelbaum, 1978).

F. MOVEMENT

Analysis of locomotion in the rat requires first that the animals be observed as they walk, run, jump, turn, swim, etc. There are very few manipulations of the brain that will not reveal some abnormality in one or another of these movements. The change may be subtle, and therefore exhaustive analysis requires filming or videotaping the movements for subsequent slow motion study, recording of electromyographic activity, or measuring with force transducers, etc. Ultimately, a refined description can be obtained by using a notation system to document the movement of every joint and limb, which allows computer analysis of the results. An example of such a system is the Eshkol and Wachmann (1958) notation developed for describing classical ballet, but recently adapted for describ-

NORMAL

WARMED

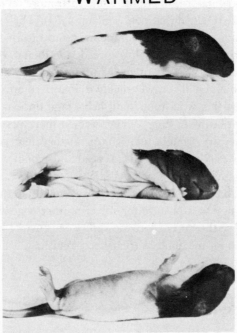

FIGURE 8.4. The effects of skin warming on the posture and behavior of a six-day-old infant rat. Mild warmth inactivates postural support; consequently the rat can be placed in a variety of postures that it maintains for seconds to minutes (after Whishaw, Schallert, & Kolb, 1979).

ing animal movements (Golani, 1976). It allows not only for a description of how parts of the body move in relation to each other or in relation to any other frame of reference, but also of how the movements are influenced by such features of the environment as visual stimuli and surfaces the body contacts.

The error in using visual inspection only, without follow-up measures, can be illustrated with the following example. The close relation between hippocampal rhythmical slow activity (RSA) and movement has led to the suggestion that the hippocampus plays some role in the guidance and execution of movement (Vanderwolf, 1969). A particularly striking demonstration of this relation is seen in the increased frequency of RSA associated with the execution of increasingly higher standing jumps, over heights of 28 to 56 cm (Whishaw & Vanderwolf, 1973). Nevertheless, the supposition that the hippocampus has a motor function has been questioned a number of times on the evidence that its destruction does not result in paresis. Myhrer (1975a,b), in particular, has reported that fimbria-fornix lesions, which disrupt hippocampal RSA, produce no change in learning or performance of a jump response. Myhrer, however, simply recorded trials to acquisition and jump latency. But Hagan and Morris (1981) repeated Myhrer's experiment with normal and fimbria-fornix lesioned rats. Using strain gauges to record jump latency, peak force, velocity, and flight time they found that the fimbria-fornix lesioned rats jumped in a qualitatively different manner and with a shorter force duration than did normal rats. The fimbria-fornix lesioned rats were also impaired in jumping heights over 45 cm, heights attained with ease by a normal rat. To argue from this evidence that these abnormalities are attributable to the absence of hippocampal RSA may be premature, but to argue that fimbria-fornix damage leads to abnormalities in jumping in supportable. These experiments demonstrate the importance of developing and using refined measures of movement before concluding that abnormalities of movement have not occurred.

The following sections describe movement and procedures for its analysis under the headings of (1) general activity, (2) movement initiation, (3) turning and climbing, (4) walking, (5) righting responses, (6) limb movements, (7) oral movements, and (8) environmental influences. Studies directed at analyzing movement are summarized in Appendix E.

1. GENERAL ACTIVITY

(i) Activity Rhythms

A fundamental, but frequently ignored, aspect of behavior is that all activities performed by the rat exhibit temporal rhythms. The most conspicuous of these has a cycle duration of about one day; hence, it is called the circadian rhythm. General activity and sleep exhibit rhythms of shorter cycle duration (ultradian) and a great many behaviors have cycle durations much longer than a day (estrous, lunar, and circannual rhythms). Al-

though under typical conditions these rhythms are synchronized to lighting or feeding or noise schedules, the endogenous nature of the rat's internal clocks has been well established under invariant environmental
conditions (Rusak & Zucker, 1975).

Endogenous rhythms pose at least three fundamental problems for the
neuropsychologist: (1) She/he must be sensitive to the rhythmical aspect
of the behaviors under study so that endogenously generated fluctuations
are not mistaken for the effects of some neurological or pharmacological
manipulation, (2) the effects of drugs (Reinberg & Halberg, 1971) or brain
stimulation or the spontaneous and evoked electrical activity of the brain
(Barnes, McNaughton, Goddard, Douglas, & Adamec, 1977; Margules,
Lewis, Dragovich, & Margules, 1972) vary according to the time in the
rat's cycles the measurements are taken, and (3) the neural mechanisms of
the biological clocks themselves must be determined. Work on the suprachiasmatic nucleus of the hypothalamus indicates that this tiny group of
cells may be involved in measuring photoperiod, coupling together a variety of rhythmical activities, or actually performing the timing functions
of the circadian clock (Rusak & Zucker, 1975).

(ii) Videorecording

One of the most effective ways of measuring general activity in the rat
is to videotape the animal's behavior for 24 hours or more. This can be
done with a time lapse videorecorder that records for 24 hours on a 1-hour
tape and that permits a 1-hour playback. On the playback, instances and
durations of any of an animal's behaviors can be recorded on counters,
clocks, and with pens on a paper chart. With such a system, virtually
every act an animal performs can be observed. Using this technique, we
have found that normal rats show two activity peaks of grooming, eating
and drinking, walking, rearing, and head movements. During the intervening periods, the animals were largely inactive. However, animals depleted of brain dopamine with the neurotoxin 6-hydroxydopamine did not
show the normal rhythm in their activity and did not eat, drink, rear, or
make head movements. Activity consisted of incessant postural adjustments throughout the entire recording session (Whishaw, Robinson,
Schallert, DeRyck, & Ramirez, 1978). In human Parkinson patients and
patients treated with major tranquilizers, such as Haloperidol, this type
of restless activity has been referred to as akathesia or "cruel restlessness"
(Byck, 1975; Sachs, 1976). The point to be made here is that the Parkinson-
analogue animal is so extremely akinetic that, in more limited observation
periods, it appears not to move at all. Had the videorecording with rapid
playback not been done, the phenomenon of "cruel restlessness" in the rat
would have been very difficult to observe.

A weakness of the videorecording technique is that it is difficult to maintain normal light-dark cycles during filming. In experiments in which this might be an important variable, a low-level lighting camera can be used and adjustments made as the room lighting changes.

(iii) Movement Sensors

General activity can also be recorded with photoelectric tranducers (Morrison, 1968a) or capacitance sensors (Decsi, Gacs, Zambo, & Nagy, 1979). A problem is that the record is hard to interpret with respect to the actual behavior in which the rat was engaged.

(iv) Activity Wheel

A popular method of measuring general activity is to use activity wheels (Richter, 1965). Although they give a useful measure of one type of activity they have some drawbacks; three are mentioned here. First, we have found that the effect of a lesion on wheel running activity and activity that is videorecorded in the rat's home cage environment are often different. For example, decorticate rats are more active in wheels than normal rats, but the two groups do not differ in videorecording situations (Kolb & Whishaw, 1981a). Second, some animals have specific disabilities with respect to walking in wheels. Lateral hypothalamic lesioned rats show decreased locomotor activity in wheels. To find out why, we tested them in a motor-driven wheel and found they were completely unable to run on the wheel, even at slow speeds and even after months of testing (unpublished observations). This occurs because such rats, if they are on a curved and moving surface, brace against the movement of the wheel in much the same way dopamine-depleted rats brace against body displacement (Schallert, DeRyck, Whishaw, Ramirez, & Teitelbaum, 1978). This resistance to a moving surface was specific to the wheel, and presumably its curved surface, because the same animals would walk in a treadmill, as has been reported by Sembello and Gladfelter (1974). Third, activity in rats is not constant over their lifetime. In fact, if only wheel measures of activity were used, old male rats would appear never to move at all (Slonaker, 1912).

(v) Open Field Tests

Another popular way to measure the effect of a treatment on the general activity of a rat is in an open field test. These tests involve putting an animal in a small room or large box and recording the distance it locomotes, its rearing behavior, whether it defecates, whether it leaves the wall of the field, etc. The test usually lasts 5 or 10 minutes. Despite its popularity, the usefulness of the open field test, used alone as a measure of activity, is limited by other variables that may have very similar effects upon performance. If used in conjunction with other measures, or if given a number of times under varying conditions, it is useful, as well as rapid and easily administered. It can be modified as an exploratory test by the addition of novel objects, different lighting, different floor substrates, etc. We have found the test an excellent way of examining the activity of normal, decorticated, and decorticated and hippocampectomized rats (unpublished studies). As is shown in Figure 8.5, the locomotor behavior of normal rats and deneocorticate (neocortex removed) rats is similar in both light and dark. The animals begin exploratory behavior in the corner in which they are first placed, and they continue exploration by making increasingly longer excursions, all the while remaining close to the wall of the field. Rats with the hippocampus removed in addition to the neocortex behave in a similar way, but are less active in the light. In the dark, however, they run quickly about the room, sometimes at a gallop, in an apparently random fashion. This is an excellent demonstration that the open field, when used in a parametric design, reveals an important dimension of the role of the hippocampus in modulating the motor activity of the rat in response to such changing sensory events as intensity of illumination. Curiously, this phenomenon is more pronounced in albino than in pigmented rats.

2. MOVEMENT INITIATION

Evidence from some brain lesion studies (Robinson & Whishaw, 1974; Vanderwolf, 1971), pharmocological studies (Bindra & Reichert, 1966), EEG studies (Bland & Vanderwolf, 1972; Whishaw & Vanderwolf, 1973), as well as observational studies (Golani, Wolgin, & Teitelbaum, 1979), suggests that movement initiation involves neural processes that are, in part, different from those involved in sustaining locomotion. One process of movement initiation, the "warm-up," has been described in detail by Golani et al. (1979) for lateral hypothalamic lesioned rats and has provided a number of insights into the dimensions of the neural organization seemingly involved in movement initiation.

If a rat is placed on a flat surface, it begins to move in a characteristic way: first with a number of head movements, then with movements of the forepart of the body, finally pivoting on one hindleg. The components of this warm-up are easier to see in lateral hypothalamic lesioned rats because they appear gradually and sequentially during the stages of recovery from the brain damage. Study of these lesioned rats shows that the warm-up movements are organized in several separate dimensions: (1) A vertical dimension that first involves obtaining postural support, second,

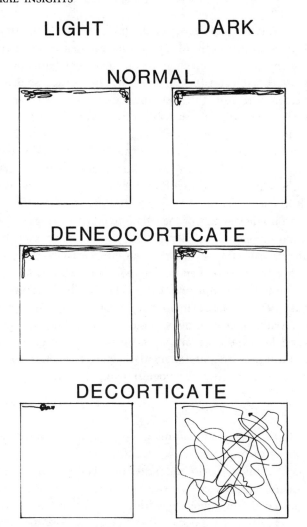

FIGURE 8.5. Patterns of locomotion in 5-minute tests by normal, deneocorticate (neocortex removed) and decorticate (neocortex and hippocampus removed) rats in a 8 foot square open field under conditions of normal room lighting or darkness. The exploratory patterns and the distance traveled by normal and deneocorticate rats are similar (beginning upper left and confined to the wall of the open field). Decorticate rats, however, are inactive in the light, but locomote at random in the dark.

raising the head provided it maintains some contact with a surface, and third, raising the head without surface contact; (2) a longitudinal dimension that initially involves backward and forward movements of the head, and finally backward movements of the entire body; and (3) a horizontal dimension that first involves small lateral movements of the head, second, lateral movements of the forepart of the body including the front limbs, and third, pivoting the entire body on the rear foot contralateral to the direction of the pivot. The sequence of movement initiation is always head to tail (cephalo-caudal). Golani et al. (1979) suggest that the first small movements "recruit" the subsequent movements, so that the animal is sequentially released from immobility and propelled into movement a segment at a time. They envisage the process as analogous to the rat being released from a straitjacket beginning at the head and working backwards. Concomitantly, it is easy to see that the scanning movements that precede walking are ideally designed to inform the animal about the environment in which it has been placed.

The warm-up movements of the lateral hypothalamic rat are character-istic of the movements of normal rats. However, there are exceptions. The movements made by the normal rat are quite varied, for they can begin movement in any dimension and at any point in the sequence. They may also move through the sequences extremely rapidly. As pointed out by Golani et al. (1979), in some situations, such as when a rat is placed in its home cage, walking may begin without the preceding warm-up move-ments. Nevertheless, the warm-up process is easily recognized in normal animals and can provide a useful standard against which to compare ani-mals subjected to different physiological manipulations.

3. TURNING AND CLIMBING

Rats perform turning and climbing movements to negotiate a remark-able number of environmental obstacles (Barnett, 1963). How can these movements be studied? Levitt and Teitelbaum (1975) devised a procedure in which an animal is placed in a situation that requires it to make a par-ticular sequence of movements to extricate itself. The situations are rela-tively simple and they have been called "traps," because they trap or iso-late specific movements and also because if the animal is unable to perform the movement it is literally trapped. Theoretically, the number of traps that can be devised is determined only by the ingenuity of the experimen-ter; we have used tubes, jars, cans, bags, grids, and other common labo-ratory apparatus. The two types of traps described below are those that have been most widely used, and they also most readily illustrate the principles of constructing and using traps.

(i) The Cage

One of the most useful, accessible, and versatile apparatus for studying movements is the wire mesh hanging cage. If a decorticate rat is placed on top of an inverted cage, it will not quickly climb down like a normal rat, but is trapped on top of the cage (Whishaw et al., 1981). The reason for its predicament is that, rather than stretching over the edge and climbing down, it backs away each time it encounters an edge. Eventually, it ends up sitting in a characteristic posture with its rear hanging over the edge, where it may remain indefinitely. The rat, placed in the cage, is trapped because it does not follow the contour of the cage and climb up and then down; rather it persistently rears or turns in circles. Even if the rat is food deprived, it fails to climb out of the cage to obtain food, but rather persists in trying to reach the food through the grids of the cage. The decorticate rat can perform two movements. If it is placed on the wall of the inverted cage, facing upward, it can climb up. If it is placed on the wall of the cage facing down, it can climb down. Other types of movement disabilities that can be identified on a hanging cage include the inability to climb up or down, as mentioned, the inability to climb down only, or catalepsy as measured by prolonged clinging to the cage.

(ii) Alleys

Two types of alleys have been used to isolate and study movements of turning; the V and the straight alley (Golani, Wolgin, & Teitelbaum, 1979; Schallert, DeRyck & Teitelbaum, 1980; Schallert, Whishaw, Ramirez, & Teitelbaum, 1978 a,b; Whishaw, Schallert, & Kolb, 1981). The use of the V for studying and isolating the movement abilities of catecholamine-depleted, Parkinson-analogue rats is illustrated in Fig. 8.6. The catecholamine-depleted rat engages in little spontaneous locomotion, but if treated with an anticholinergic drug, such as atropine, it becomes very active and walks for a number of hours. With the use of the V-trap we were able to observe a unique feature of the animal's locomotion. Once the animal walked into the trap, it was unable to rear against the corner, as does a normal rat (but it could sit up in order to facewash), and it was unable to turn and walk out of the trap. In the absence of the ability to rear or turn, it remains in the trap indefinitely and can only begin to walk again if the trap is removed. Thus, the form of locomotion released by atropine is forward locomotion. The locomotor abilities of the rat are in this way analogous to the locomotor abilities of some Parkinson patients, who after walking into the corner of a room, are unable to turn around and walk out (Martin, 1967). By treating the same rats with the dopamine precursor L-dopa, we were able to isolate another pattern of movement: turning. When given L-dopa, the animal is able to rear in the trap and to turn against the surface of the trap in order to escape (Fig. 8.6). Thus, the form of locomotion released by L-dopa includes rearing and turning. The straight alley can also be used to study and isolate various types of rearing

ATROPINE   L-DOPA

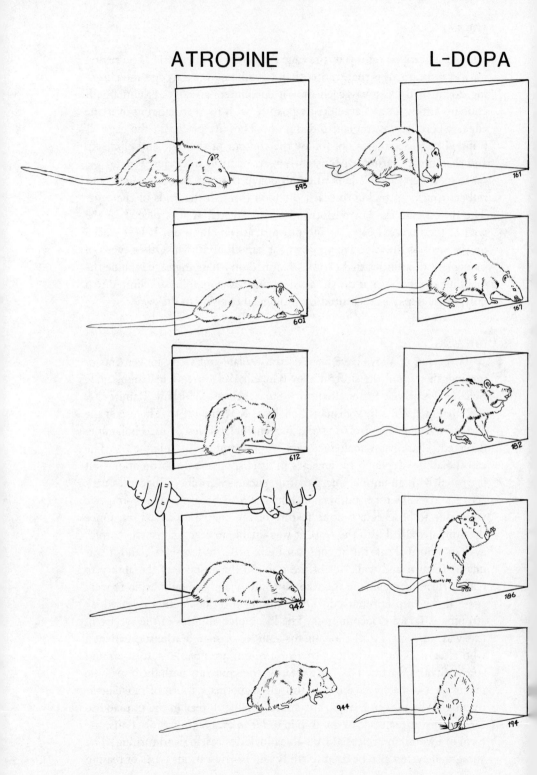

and turning movements. Furthermore, if a lid is placed over the alley, rearing and turning can be prevented, and the ability of an animal to back out can be studied. Atropine-treated rats, for example, are unable to back out of such an alley. The actual movement deficiency that prevents rats from extricating themselves from alleys differs depending upon the type of brain damage that they have, so the behavior in the traps requires careful observations. For example, lateral hypothalamic lesioned rats are not able to escape from an alley early in recovery because they cannot rear and turn. Decorticate rats can rear and turn, but fail to escape an alley because they do not walk far enough into the alley to rear against its far wall and turn; instead they stop when they encounter the wall with their vibrissae and make no further attempt to extricate themselves.

4. WALKING

There are a number of simple techniques for studying walking. The most complete analyses of walking in the rat are those of Hruska, Kennedy, and Silbergeld (1979) and Ganor and Golani (1980). The former study describes what can be called the "biasable" properties of a movement, duration of a movement and its amplitude, whereas the latter study describes the more invariant intralimb actions. Hruska et al. (1979) find that walking can be described spatially, in terms of the displacement of the four feet, and temporally, in terms of stride duration (swing time and stance time). They find that normal walking is a lateral sequence, diagonal couplet, which does not vary with the speed of locomotion within the normal range of walking. As the rats walk more quickly, their stance time decreases and their stride length increases, but swing time does not change. The measures made by Hruska et al. (1979) were obtained from video records and footprints. The footprints were made by greasing the rat's feet, having it walk on polygraph paper, and dusting the footprints with fingerprint powder. Ganor and Golani (1980) used the Eshkol-Wachmann system of movement notation to describe limb movements recorded with high speed photography. Their description is directed toward the changes

---

FIGURE 8.6. The demonstration of different subsets of movement released by atropine and L-dopa in the catecholamine-depleted, Parkinson-analogue, rat. Atropine releases forward locomotion, but not rearing and turning. Thus, the atropine-treated rat, which would otherwise walk inexorably forward, is "trapped" in a V-shaped alley. The rat, however, is able to sit up to groom. L-dopa releases walking and also rearing and turning, which allow the rat to escape from the alley. Note also the differences in posture produced by the two drugs; neither drug releases the animal from maintaining "snout-contact" with surfaces. Numbers refer to 1-second intervals of film (after Schallert, Whishaw, Ramirez, & Teitelbaum, 1978a,b).

a limb undergoes when it moves. The action of a limb is described within two frames of reference: movements, the change in orientation of a segment in relation to the next serially connected segment; and displacements, the change in the segment in relation to gravity. Each limb movement cycle is composed of seven relatively independent synergies. During swing, the distal segments do not affect the kinematics of proximal ones, in support they do affect the proximal segments. This description emphasizes intralimb coordination and integration, not flexion and extension, and the authors suggest that this language is more appropriate for neurophysiological investigation than descriptions that are solely concerned with flexion and extension.

With the use of techniques such as those of Hruska et al. (1979), walking has been studied in animals with basal ganglia damage produced by intrastriatal injections of kainic acid. These rats show an abnormally long swing time and a shortened stance time (Hruska & Silbergeld, 1979). In dopamine-depleted, Parkinson-analogue rats, stride length is decreased (Schallert, Whishaw, Ramirez, & Teitelbaum, 1978b); after parietal lesions, lift is decreased, but stride length is unaffected (Gentile, Green, Nieburgs, Schmelzer, & Stein, 1978); and after cortical X-irradiation, hopping or waddling locomotor gaits are observed (Hicks & D'Amato, 1975, 1980; Mullenix, Norton, & Culver, 1975).

Walking has also been studied in rats with elevated platforms that are quite narrow to make walking more difficult. The use of such a technique has revealed abnormalities in walking in brain-damaged animals that were not apparent if the animals walked on flat, open surfaces (for example, Gentile et al., 1978; Maier, 1935). In experiments of this kind, there has been a tendency to measure only the details of limb use, and overall carriage has been neglected. It is possible, however, that a change in limb use can be a consequence of changes in body posture. We have observed control rats and decorticate rats walking on a narrow beam and have found that the entire posture of the decorticate rat is different from that of control rats. The control rat walks with its head thrust forward and with its back relatively straight, but the decorticate rat walks with its head inclined with the snout down to the surface and with its back arched. The decorticate rat appears to sniff its way along the platform, forcing a change in its body posture, hence, it walks with a waddle; it also grips the sides of the platform. This behavior has also been described following denervation of vibrissae (Vincent, 1912), which suggests that the decortication interrupts the guidance of walking by sensory information from the vibrissae. In conclusion, although measurement of the details of limb movement alone may suffice to reveal a deficit after brain damage, the significance of a change in the way a limb moves during walking may only be appreciated after assessing overall body posture or guidance by one sensory modality or another.

5. SWIMMING

Rats are good swimmers, and feral rats often live near water and dive underwater to obtain food (Galef, 1980).

There have been a number of recent studies of swimming in the rat. This seems attributable to the fact that swimming movements are relatively stereotyped, simple, and easy to elicit. The adult rat swims with long, alternating thrusts of its hindlimbs, while the front limbs are held fairly still, tucked up under its chin. The front limbs are not always immobile, however, because they make sculling movements to help the rat turn and to balance the forepart of its body when it slows down or moves its head.

Swimming is a useful way of studying the ontogeny of movement because during maturation the different components of swimming emerge in a predictable temporal sequence. For example, initially, rats paddle with all four limbs, with their heads under the water, but after the first two weeks of life, the nose is held out of the water and forepaw paddling is inhibited. The adult pattern is evident by about 25 days of age (Schapiro, Salas, & Vukovich, 1970). This ontogenetic sequence is a useful standard against which to compare animals subjected to various pharmacological or dietary treatments (M. Salas, 1972).

The pattern of movements during swimming has been also studied in brain-damaged rats. Vanderwolf, Kolb, and Cooley (1978) have reported that decorticate rats do not show the adult pattern of swimming, but rather they paddle with all four limbs, as do infant rats. This finding seems to be true, however, only if relatively warm water, in which the rats are not greatly motivated to swim, is used (Whishaw, Nonneman, & Kolb, 1981). If the rats are placed in cold (18°C) water, they swim very vigorously and inhibit forepaw movement. Observations of the posture of the decorticate rat's swimming suggest that they use their forepaws to keep their head above water; normal rats keep their head above water by paddling more vigorously and by thrusting their head forward.

Swimming has been used to study at least five other features of rat behavior. (1) Swimming has been used in learning tasks such as mazes, prompted by the fact that rats are highly motivated to escape from water. Thus the usual motivating procedures of food deprivation, adaption, pretraining, etc., need not be used. (2) Swimming has been used to study social learning, that is, to determine how one rat "tells" other rats where food is hidden under the water. (3) Swimming has been used to study the rat's responses to stress. There has been some suggestion in the literature that if rats are unable to cope with a novel situation, such as being placed in a water tank from which there is no escape, they will suddenly die, a phenomenon termed sudden death (Binik, 1977; Binik, Theriault, & Shustack, 1977; Richter, 1957). (4) Swimming has been used to study diving bradycardia, a sudden slowing of the heart that occurs in all diving mammals when they are submerged in water (Lin, 1974; Lin & Baker, 1975; Whishaw & Schallert, 1977). (5) Swimming has been used to study the motor abilities and the response of rats to activating stimulation after various types of brain damage, or of old rats (Levitt & Teitelbaum, 1975; Marshall & Berrios, 1979; Marshall, Levitan, & Stricker, 1976; Robinson & Whishaw, 1974. For example, lateral hypothalamic or posterior-lateral hypothalamic lesioned rats, who are akinetic and cataleptic, will sink when placed in warm water, but will swim vigorously when placed in cold water (Robinson, Whishaw, & Wishart, 1974).

6. Righting Responses

Broadly defined, righting responses consist of the movements animals make to return to a static upright posture. They are different from loco-motor behaviors by which an animal moves from a static upright posture to another location. Nevertheless, they are necessary precursors for loco-motion, and they are also necessary for the maintenance of many aspects of normal locomotion (for example, see Bard, 1968). Righting responses consist of a number of different movements; each of these can be influenced by different sensory systems, and each require the function of most levels of the brain.

(i) Supporting Reactions

Supporting reactions involve changing a movable limb into a solid pillar, to support body weight. These reactions are elicited by the stretch placed on extensor musculature, which derives from placing the feet on the ground. Slight movements of the limb to activate joint receptors also contribute to the supporting reactions. Supporting reactions are markedly exaggerated in the Haloperidol-treated rat. In response to any touch or slight displacement (even in response to an approaching visual stimulus), the animal braces to counteract the displacement (Schallert, DeRyck, Whishaw, Ramirez, & Teitelbaum, 1978). Supporting reactions can be tested quite simply by observing whether an animal will support its weight on its limbs.

(ii) Righting Reactions

Righting reactions involve movements that bring an animal into a normal upright posture from any of a variety of positions. Usually, an animal is held upside down and dropped to test its ability to turn and land on its feet, but other movements, such as getting up when placed on one side or returning a limb that has been placed in an awkward position to a normal position, should be considered part of a rat's repertoire of righting responses.

(iii) Placing Reactions

Placing reactions involve movements that are intended to obtain a base of support for the limbs. Tactile placing responses can be tested by touching the forelimb of an animal to a horizontal surface. Visual placing can be tested by holding the animal above a surface: the limbs should stretch forward to touch the surface. Vestibular placing can be tested by suddenly dropping a blindfolded animal: its limbs should extend suddenly downward to meet the surface. Placing reactions can also be tested by drawing an animal's limbs into awkward postures to see if they will be moved to a normal position. For example, a limb can be hung over a table edge, placed up on a small stand, lifted on a finger, or pulled out from the animal's body.

(iv) Hopping Reactions

Hopping reactions involve movements made by the limbs to regain support of the body after its weight has suddenly been displaced. If a rat is held under the forelimbs and pushed to one side it will hop to replace its feet beneath its body.

As mentioned, most of the sensory systems, as well as different functional levels of the nervous system, contribute to righting responses. For this reason, a comprehensive test of righting responses requires that the contribution of each sensory system be examined. For example, a Haloperidol-treated rat placed gently on its side and held still will remain there for many minutes after it is released. It can then be observed that touches, vestibular displacement by tilting, sounds, etc., will elicit righting back to a normal upright posture.

It is often naively thought that righting responses are mediated only by lower brainstem mechanisms. However, the contribution of the neocortex to placing responses is well documented (Bard & Brooks, 1934). The cortex also helps maintain an animal in an optimal posture for performing righting responses. Figure 8.7 shows some abnormal postures of decorticated rats after they have been lifted from a surface. When dropped, the

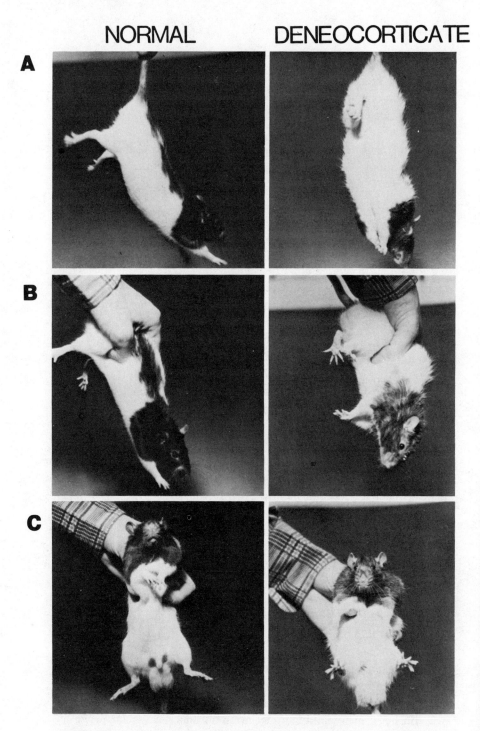

FIGURE 8.7. Comparisons of the postures shown by normal rats and decorticate rats lifted up in three different ways (A, B, and C) (from Whishaw, Schallert, & Kolb, 1981).

decorticate animals make a righting response, but it is often incomplete because they are not posturally "prepared" to adequately effect the response (Whishaw, Schallert, & Kolb, 1981).

7. INDEPENDENT LIMB MOVEMENTS

In the foregoing section, the discussion of limb movements has centered on movements that effect a change in the rat's orientation to a surface or substrate. A second class of limb movements is involved in changing the position or orientation of an object relative to the rat's body.

There are at least two reasons for giving special attention to this class of limb movements. They allow the animal to make precise and refined manipulations of objects, movements that are essential for many of its behaviors, including eating. They are also most likely controlled by anatomical systems that appeared rather late in phylogeny and that differ in some ways from those that control whole body movements. In particular, the pyramidal tract, which projects from the neocortex to the motor nuclei of the cranial nerves and to the spinal cord, appears to be especially important for the strength and dexterity of these movements (Castro, 1978; Lawrence & Kuypers, 1968). Limb movements are used for two general functions; obtaining objects in the environment and rejecting objects in the environment. They can also be studied in two ways: in formal test situations or as they are used by animals as they engage in such natural behaviors as eating, grooming, and nest building. In the following sections, we discuss each aspects of their use.

Limb movements have been studied in four types of tasks: (1) latch box opening, (2) bar pressing, (3) reaching and retrieving, and (4) spontaneous behaviors, such as eating and grooming.

Lashley (1935) conducted the earliest study on latch box opening and, although it was extensive in terms of the range of puzzles given to the rats, it suffered from the weakness that performance was conceptualized in terms of learning, motivation to open latches, aggressiveness of responding, etc. As a result, Lashley did not describe the details of the rat's motor responses or even localize a cortical area that, when lesioned, produced major deficits. Rats have been filmed opening puzzles before and after frontal cortex lesions were received (Gentile et al., 1978). Frontal cortex removal produced three types of deficits: (1) the limb was displaced from the target, (2) the temporal ordering of the movements was erratic, and (3) the movements were often more repetitive. By their description, these abnormalities resemble apraxia (abnormality in purposeful movement in the absence of paralyses) more than simple inability to use the limb musculature; to our knowledge, this is the best demonstration of this phenomenon in the rat. Rats with parietal cortex lesions were not deficient in opening the latches.

In studies in which bar pressing was used to measure limb use, the task is arranged so that the animals can manipulate the bar with only one limb. Rats with globus pallidus and entopeduncular lesions, which would interrupt the major output from the striatum, show weakness, reduced muscle tone, and an inability to press a bar with the limb contralateral to the lesion. Rats with cortical lesions and lateral hypothalamic lesions are able to manipulate the bar (Levine, Ferguson, Kreinick, Gustafson, & Schwartzbaum, 1971). Although this task seems to detect a functional deficiency of a limb, it is less informative with respect to the nature of the abnormality.

The most instructive of the formal tasks assessing limb function is the reaching and retrieving task (Castro, 1972 a,b; Castro, 1977, 1978; Kartje-Tillotson & Castro, 1980). The task itself is rather simple; the rat must reach through a small hole in its cage to grasp a food pellet and retrieve it. A good analogy is therefore available to the kind of studies of the grasp response using monkeys and humans (Lawrence & Kuypers, 1968; Twitchell, 1951, 1965). The deficit Castro describes following lesions in the motor area of the frontal cortex of the rat is also so like that reported to follow motor cortex damage in monkeys and humans (Lawrence & Kuypers, 1968; Twitchell, 1951) that it is worth quoting:

> During the early stages of postoperative testing, animals showed an apparent inertia of movement. More specifically, they would characteristically stand in front of the food tray and attempt to lift their forelimb into the slot but initially would be able to raise it only slightly off the floor of the cage. Then after several such movements in succession, they would with seemingly great effort be able to place their forelimb at the edge of the slot. With varying rates of recovery, animals were in time able to extend their forelimbs further into the slot and eventually make contact with the pellets. There occurred a general shift toward an increasing frequency of full extensions with less of the abortive short extensions or slaps at the edge of the slot. Ability to extend increased to the point where animals would occasionally overextend beyond the pellets, and they frequently exhibited poor direction of movement. For example, a rat might accidentally push a pellet toward the side of a slot and toward the displaced pellet. A normal rat was able to retrieve a displaced pellet quite effectively. After an unsuccessful attempt, frontal lesion animals would frequently bring their empty hands to their mouth as though they contained a pellet and would do this even if they had not touched a pellet. Conversely, experimental animals would occasionally grasp a pellet and not react to it but would proceed to the next slot in search of another pellet with one already in their grasp. . . . Rats with frontal cortex lesions recovered the ability to perform each specific movement in the sequence required to successfully grasp a pellet. At the time of sacrifice, all animals were able to extend their forelimbs the proper distance and grasp a pellet. However, marked incoordination frequently occurred as the animals brought their hands to their mouths. In some in-

stances, they took 15–20 sec attempting to place a successfully grasped pellet into their mouths. As a compensatory process, rats would very noticeably turn their heads toward their hands and thus minimize the distance required to carry the pellets (Castro, 1972a,b, pp. 181–182).

The importance of Castro's observations, as compared with Lashley's study, lies in the choice of an appropriate task and in the choice of appropriate measures to assess the animal's deficit. Still more important, however, these observations demonstrate that the rat can be effectively used to study reaching and grasping, and that the degree of motor disability is comparable to that found in such species as monkeys and humans. Such studies with the rat have not been pursued enthusiastically by psychologists in the past because there has been a long standing belief that such lower mammals display little impairment following cortical motor area lesions (Walker & Fulton, 1938). However, Bures and his co-workers have studied single cell activity, EEG activity and the effects of dopamine depletion on limb use (cf. Siegfried & Bures, 1980).

Rats more frequently use their front limbs for a variety of movements as part of their repertoire of species-specific behaviors (see next section). The behaviors provide a cornucopia for behavioral analysis, but in fact very few researchers have availed themselves of the opportunity to use spontaneous acts for movement analysis. An exception to this statement is a report by Barron (1934) describing abnormalities of paw use in placing, grooming, and feeding in rats that had received unilateral pyramidal tract section. Following frontal cortex lesions, rats stop using their paws for eating for a short time and eat directly from the floor with their mouths (Castro, 1972b; Kolb & Nonneman, 1975a; Kolb, Schallert, & Whishaw, 1977; Vanderwolf, Kolb, & Cooley, 1978). Following decortication, when rats eat large food pellets, this limb use is permanently absent (Vanderwolf, Kolb, & Cooley, 1978; Kolb & Whishaw, 1981a). A more detailed analysis shows, however, that the characteristics of the food that the decorticate is given is important in determining how it eats. If the rat is given large pellets of food, it eats in the way illustrated in Fig. 8.8C, without using its front limbs, or, as illustrated in Fig. 8.8B, it jams the food under its body to hold it. If the rat is given small pellets of food, it picks them up and eats using the normal eating posture as is shown in Fig. 8.8D. The rat is markedly deficient in eating even small pellets of food: It frequently drops them, it often fails to grasp them properly, and it is often unaware that it has dropped them. Unlike the normal rat (Fig. 8.8A), the decorticate rat is also not able to sit up and look away. This deficit occurs because basic postural reflexes intrude, causing the rat to drop the food; when the decorticate rat looks up, its front limbs extend and the digits clasp. This limb extension is characteristic of a postural

FIGURE 8.8. Eating postures of normal (A) and decorticate (B, C, D) rats. 1. A normal rat can sit up and hold a small piece of food, and even avert its head (A) without dropping the food. 2. Decorticate rats do not pick up large pieces of food, but rather push them under their body (B) or eat them directly from the floor (C). 3. Decorticate rats can sit up and eat small pieces of food in the normal way (C) (from Whishaw, Nonneman, & Kolb, 1981).

adjustment associated with head elevation in decerebrate animals and as such can be considered a release of a brainstem postural reflex.

Limb use can be studied quite simply in a number of other behaviors of normal rats, and these deserve mention. If a noxious substance, such as ammonia, is introduced into a rat's home cage on a spatula, the rat will back up into the corner of a cage and bat at the spatula with rapidly alternating movements of its front limbs. It may also use one limb to push the spatula away. Similarly, if a paper clip is attached to its fur, it will pull it off with its teeth and bat at it with its front paws (unpublished observations). Furthermore, if noxious objects are introduced into the rat's home cage and if there is sawdust in the cage, the rat will bury the object by pushing sawdust over it using the forepaws [see Pinel and Treit, Chapter 9, this volume]. Changes in limb use after brain damage have not been studied for any of these behaviors, yet each provides a simple way of examining the integrity of limb function.

8. ORAL MOVEMENTS

Movements of the mouth and tongue are seemingly difficult to study because the movements are quite fast, between 4 and 7 cycles/sec and because a clear view of the mouth and tongue is not always obtained. Deficits in chewing have generally been inferred from spillage of food or from peculiar chewing patterns on food pellets (Kolb & Nonneman, 1975a; Zeigler & Karten, 1974). However, very detailed descriptions of movements of the lingual, masticatory, and facial musculature made by rats to reject noxious food have been published by Grill and his co-workers (Grill & Norgren, 1978a,b,c,d). Grill observed these movements by filming the movements through a mirror placed beneath the rat's cage. The movements consist of rhythmic tongue protrusions, lateral tongue movements, gapes, and rhythmic mouth movements. Rats also show five body movements associated with the rejection of noxious food: (1) chin rubbing, rubbing the chin along the floor with the lower lip retracted; (2) head shakes, a rapid side to side movement of the head to throw food from the mouth; (3) face washing; (4) flailing of the forelimbs, to remove food from the mouth, face, and paws; and (5) paw pushing, a back and forth movement of the paws against the substrate, a behavior that might be used to remove food from the paws. All these behaviors can be seen in some lateral hypothalamic lesioned rats and in rats who have previously been food poisoned and then reoffered the noxious food (see Schallert & Whishaw, 1978). The behaviors generally occur as a constellation, and can be evoked in the home cage simply by offering the animal noxious food on a spatula.

A number of studies have been directed at the use of the tongue in picking up food and lapping water, and the extent to which the tongue can be protruded. Castro (1972c) found that rats with frontal lesions were unable to protrude their tongue sufficiently to grasp a food pellet in a slot in a glass tray. It should be noted that this is as much a deficit in tongue protrusion as in tongue use. We have observed that decorticate rats, although unable to protrude their tongues extensively, can lap crumbs from a counter top and can lap food or water from a spatula. Brimley and Mogenson (1979) have made an extensive study of tongue protrusion. They had rats lap food from a tray that could be gradually lowered away from the rat's cage. Thus, the rat has to extend its tongue further and further to reach the food. Damage in a surprisingly large number of structures produced deficits in tongue extension, including the zona incerta, the globus pallidus, the medial lateral hypothalamus, the far-lateral hypothalamus, and the central amygdaloid complex. The most severe deficit occurred after globus pallidus lesions, when tongue extension was reduced by about 50%. In the same study, the authors measured lap volume (the ratio of the number of laps to the volume of water consumed). Again they found that the zona incerta, the globus pallidus, the far lateral hypothalamus, and the central amygdaloid lesions reduced lap volume.

We have found that some very simple preliminary measures of oral and tongue use can be obtained by testing the rats in their home cage. We presented food or water on a spatula and observed whether the rats can bite or lick the food from the spatula. We then smeared mash or water on the wall or on the grids of the rat's cage to see if they could lick it off. Finally, we measured tongue protrusion by holding a spatula containing mash or water just outside the rat's cage so that it had to protrude its tongue to reach the spatula. An actual measure of tongue protrusion can be obtained by placing the mash on a ruler and simply reading off the distance the rat licks mash along the ruler. We performed similar types of tests with different-sized food pellets. First we observed how the rats eat the food, and then we retracted the food from the cage to see whether they could reach through the grids to obtain it. For example, decorticate rats can chew mash from a spatula, but they are unable to protrude their tongue very far through a grid to reach the mash. They can also bite food offered to them in their cage, but they cannot reach through the grids for a food pellet. We also observed how the animals drank from a water spout. Initially, decorticate rats must be taught to drink. Subsequently, they have a difficult time lapping water, and they alternate chewing and lapping at the spout. They also drink with their heads inverted in a way described in rats with globus pallidus lesions (Levine & Schwartzbaum, 1973). Again, we emphasize that these are simple tests that can be quickly given to rats while they are in their home cage, and with a few changes in procedure, they can be quantified almost as accurately as more elaborate tests.

9. ENVIRONMENTAL INFLUENCES ON MOVEMENT

Early views of brain function in sleep and waking were dominated by the notion that waking behavior was produced by afferent activity and that sleep was a result of passive deafferentation. According to this view, the brain functioned as a complex reflexive system the only function of which was to mediate activity between the sensory receptors and the muscles. Moruzzi and Magoun (1949) completely changed this view. Moruzzi and Magoun stimulated the brainstem of cats and found that the waking EEG produced in the cortex outlasted the stimulation. It was clear, therefore, that intrinsic mechanisms of the brain could maintain central activation in the absence of further sensory stimulation.

The current view of brain function holds that both endogenous neural processes and sensory events are important for initiating and maintaining behavior. However, after brain damage, the normal relation between internal and external influences can be changed. The question to be asked then is, Does the change in behavior of an animal reflect a changed sensitivity to sensory events or to changes in endogenous neural processes? Often the answer is both, but determining the relative weight to be placed on each can be difficult. An example will serve to illustrate this point. Rats who received large posterior lateral hypothalamic lesions were initially somnolent and akinetic, but they subsequently recovered to the point where they ate, drank, groomed, etc., and otherwise maintained themselves. They remained akinetic, however, and hardly ever walked, which made conventional learning tests difficult to conduct. Even if they were placed in a water maze (37 °C), they sank to the bottom of the maze and made little attempt to swim, although they periodically rose to the surface to breath (Fig. 8.9). In 18°C water, they swam vigorously in the normal swimming pattern and even mastered a T-maze. In subsequent tests, we found that the lesioned rats could swim in both hot and cold water; in fact, swimming improved in direct proportion to the deviation of water temperature from normal body temperature. These results suggest that after the lesion the motor systems prerequisite for a motor activity such as swimming are intact, but that their threshold for activation is raised (Robinson & Whishaw, 1974; Robinson, Whishaw, & Wishart, 1974). Other lesions might damage the motor systems, sensory systems, or internal connecting networks in different ways, but repeating tests under different environmental influences should help provide a better assessment of how neural systems concerned with movement are changed.

G.   SPECIES-SPECIFIC BEHAVIORS

Ethologists have long recognized a class of behaviors that is characteristic of a particular species and initially described it in such terms as "instinctive" behavior. In 1951, Tinbergen described these behaviors as "fixed action patterns," by which he meant innate, stereotyped movements, specific to a species, that can be performed in the absence of sensory feedback. Although Tinbergen primarily chose examples from the behavior of birds and fish to illustrate this class of behaviors, mammals exhibit many fixed action patterns. For example, the behavioral sequence utilized by a mouse to wash its face is relatively inflexible, is characteristic of the species, and is performed in the absence of sensory feedback (Fentress, 1972).

The concept of fixed action pattern is generally taken to imply that the

WATER TEMPERATURE 37° C

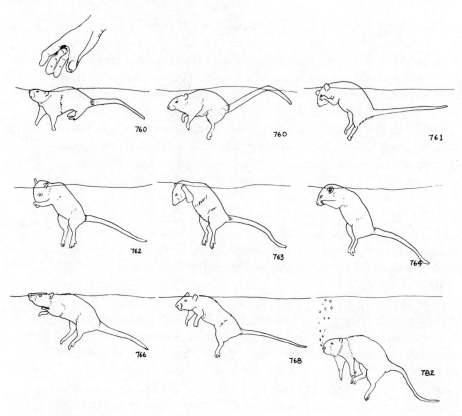

WATER TEMPERATURE 18° C

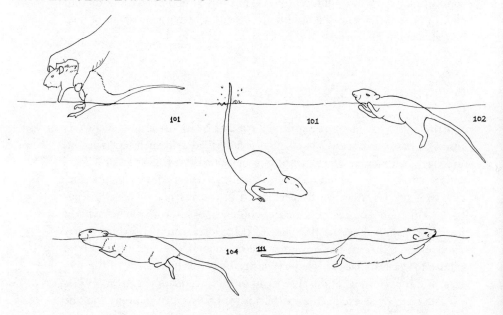

186

behaviors are relatively unmodified by experience and that their form or patterning is independent of environmental control once the sequence is initiated (cf. Hinde, 1970). Many behaviors typical of a given species, however, significantly depend upon prior experience and are modulated by concurrent environmental events. For example, food hoarding by laboratory rats is virtually absent if rats have never experienced food deprivation (Morgan, Stellar, & Johnson, 1943), and the movement patterns of hoarding at any given time are modified by a variety of environmental factors, such as time of day, brightness of lighting, and size and weight of food available. It is with this in mind that the term "species-specific behavior" is often used by neuropsychologists to include those "fixed" action patterns, characteristic of a species, that may be modified by the environment and prior experience.

We define species-specific behavior as the repertoire of "fixed" action patterns characteristically observed in all individuals of a particular species. This repertoire has, in all species, been shaped by factors involved in survival in a unique niche and in a particular way of life.

1. WHY STUDY SPECIES-SPECIFIC BEHAVIORS?

At least four aspects of species-specific behaviors make them especially important in neuropsychological study. (1) Species-specific behaviors are essential for the survival of an animal, and therefore, any disruption of these behaviors must be seen as significant. An understanding of the neurological control of species-specific behaviors is thus an important step in understanding brain-behavior relationships in animals. (2) Species-specific behaviors are complex, certainly more complex than many of the behaviors we have discussed so far. For many behaviors, the animals must combine distinct behavioral units to form complex behavioral chains or they must respond to complex sensory stimuli. For example, when rats groom they produce a series of behavioral units such as shaking the paws, licking the paws, and rubbing the paws over the snout. These movements are chained together to produce very long sequences of movements that may continue uninterruptedly for several minutes. Behavioral chaining has long

FIGURE 8.9. Behavior of a posterior lateral hypothalamic lesioned rat upon being placed in warm (37°C) and cold (18°C) water. In warm water, the rat slowly sinks while engaging in a face grooming sequence. At the end of the sequence it raises its head, takes a breath, and then slowly sinks while exhaling. Its buoyancy when first placed in the water is attributable to air bubbles trapped in its fur. Upon first being placed in cold water, the animal becomes extremely activated and dives. After surfacing, it paddles backwards and forward across the swim tank in a normal swimming posture. Numbers indicate seconds of film (after Robinson & Whishaw, 1974).

been recognized as a significant problem in ethology (Eibl-Eibesfeldt, 1970), as well as in brain-behavior relationships (Lashley, 1951). Similarly, ethologists have recognized the unique capacity of certain complex sensory arrays to elicit species-specific behaviors (Tinbergen, 1951), and the neurological mechanisms for the perception of these stimuli and the production of the appropriate behavioral responses are just now beginning to be appreciated (cf. Ewert, 1980; see Goodale, Chapter 4, this volume). (3) Many species-specific behaviors are affected by experience. Therefore, it is possible to vary the experience of animals to determine how neurological manipulations interact with experiential factors. For example, we have noted that food hoarding in normal rats is significantly affected by experience. The hoarding by decorticate rats is relatively unaffected by experiencing food deprivation, whereas the hoarding of rats with frontal lesions is affected more than normal by the experience of deprivation (cf. Kolb, 1974a). (4) Species-specific behaviors develop in a particular sequence during ontogeny and it is therefore possible to document carefully the effects of neurological manipulations upon the development of behaviors. For example, hamsters do not hoard food prior to about 25 days of age, at which time they abruptly begin to hoard food. Hamsters with neonatal removal of the frontal cortex, however, begin hoarding normally at the usual time and only subsequently do they show an impairment, that is, they appear to "grow into their behavioral deficit" as they become worse and worse relative to their littermate controls (Kolb & Whishaw, 1979).

To date, neuropsychologists have paid little attention to the study of species-specific behaviors, instead, they have tended to focus on "simpler" behaviors, such as those described in the previous sections, or on behaviors that involve the learning of some new habit. In the following pages and in Appendix F we identify the species-specific behaviors of the rat that can be studied easily in the laboratory. We also give references of examples of neuropsychological findings regarding the neural bases of species-specific behaviors. These references are not intended to be exhaustive, but rather to provide a general summary and to direct the interested reader to the relevant literature. With reference to this literature, however, we wish to emphasize the following point. Given the relative inflexibility of species-specific behaviors, it might be thought that detailed and quantified descriptions of each of the behaviors would be available for easy reference. With some exceptions, this is not the case. Most descriptions are rather informal, i.e., "when hoarding food, the rat picks up the food in its mouth and then walks with a hopping gait that differs from the gait of normal walking," or "when building a nest the rat first picks up the material in its mouth, etc.".. Although these are good descriptions of the events, better descriptions of the actual movements are necessary for many species-specific behaviors.

2. GROOMING

Grooming is a relatively stereotyped activity in the rat and is simple to observe, to record, and to score.[4] We frequently use the study of grooming behavior to teach students the techniques of behavioral recording in rats. Grooming is a highly reliable behavior that is typical of both sexes and of all age animals after weaning. The animal does not wait until the fur is dirty to groom. The behavior *seems* to be performed in the absence of peripheral stimulation or feedback. In mice, whose grooming is similar to that of the rat, grooming occurs when the forepaws and face are anesthetized, and even if the forepaws are amputated at birth. Furthermore, during a component behavior, such as face washing, the mice with amputations make licking movements at the fictive location of the missing forepaws, and not on the stump of the forearm. There can be variations in the movements, however, for there are compensatory changes in muscular force brought about by altering the load on the forelimbs during even the fastest sequences of face washing (Fentress, 1980).

Grooming behavior can be easily elicited by soaking a rat in water. It is then observed and scored by placing the soaked rat in a familiar cage or box and recording each behavior as it occurs in sequence for 20 to 30 minutes. The following notes were taken from 5 minutes of observation of a normal soaked rat: "Walks. Shakes body. Shakes paws. Washes face. Walks, rears, shakes body. Shakes paws. Washes face. Walks. Shakes body. Shakes paws. Washes face. Licks paws. Shakes paws. Licks back. Shakes body. Shakes paws. Licks left foreleg. Washes face. Licks back. Licks right rear leg. Washes face. Licks paws. Shakes paws. Washes face. Shakes paws. Licks back. Shakes body. Walks away."

Scoring of this grooming sequence can be done in a number of ways. This 5-minute period included three bouts of grooming behavior, which were each terminated by walking. There were a total of 26 grooming components (3,3,20), yielding an average grooming sequence of 8.67 groom-

---

4. The purpose of grooming is not just to keep the fur clean, but also to treat cuts and scratches such as might be incurred in fights, to clean the sensory systems (e.g., wiping the ears, the eyes, or the nose, after sniffing), to spread Harderian fluid from the eyes over the fur for thermoregulatory purposes, and to remove body vermin. Richter (1968) reports that each wild rat may carry as many as 30 fleas, which it quickly disposes of when housed in a clean laboratory. Even in the laboratory, however, lice are removed with greater difficulty as witnessed by their presence on animals in some domestic colonies (personal observations). An account of the role of rats and lice in human disease has been given by Zinsser (1934).

ing components. The sequences lasted 7 seconds, 11 seconds, and 4 minutes, 16 seconds, respectively, giving a total duration of 4 minutes 34 seconds of grooming behavior in 5 minutes. The grooming included five body shakes, seven paw shakes, and six face washes. Each grooming sequence was begun by a body shake and was terminated by walking. In a more detailed analysis the order of the behavioral components within the chains could be considered, to establish the probabilities of particular behaviors occurring at particular points in a sequence.

Grooming behavior may be disrupted in a number of ways: (1) The occurrence of grooming behavior may be abolished all together. (2) The duration of grooming may be reduced; that is, the rat engages in grooming activity, but does less grooming than normal. (3) The distribution of grooming to various body parts is altered. For example, decorticate rats tend to spend very little time grooming the caudal parts of their bodies (Kolb & Whishaw, 1981a), but amygdala lesioned rats spend more time grooming the anogenital region (Sutherland, 1974). (4) The length of grooming sequences may be reduced [i.e., the rat may have a normal total amount of grooming, but with shorter episodes both in terms of time and number of grooming components, as occurs in decorticate rats (Vanderwolf et al., 1978)]. (5) Animals may exhibit "groom arrest"; that is, the rat may be grooming normally, pause for up to a few minutes without moving, and then continue grooming once again where it had left off. Groom arrest is often observed in rats exhibiting somnolence or catalepsy after a large lateral hypothalamic lesion (Levitt & Teitelbaum, 1975). (6) Animals may assume unusual postures when grooming. For example, decorticate rats often face wash by sitting up with the lumbar spine held abnormally erect or extended and the thoracic spine abnormally flexed, giving the back a peculiar right-angled appearance (Vanderwolf et al., 1978). (7) Animals may continually lose their balance when grooming the face or back. Thalamic rats often topple over backward when grooming the back and, in some cases, may appear unable to inhibit standing while grooming the face, again resulting in loss of balance (unpublished observations).

3. FOOD-RELATED BEHAVIORS

Rats exhibit a variety of behaviors related to food: food hoarding, eating, neophobia, taste aversion, foraging, and diet selection. We will discuss each of these behaviors separately.

(i) Food Hoarding

Rats do not ordinarily eat out in the open unless they have been deprived of food: when they encounter food they will usually carry it home to eat. In the laboratory, hoarding behavior is commonly assessed in one of two ways using standard laboratory chow chunks, each weighing about 10 grams. (1) Food is placed into the home cage of the rat and the number of pellets touching or piled up over various time intervals are counted. (2) Rats are housed in special cages attached to runways. The food is scattered in the runways and the rat is allowed access to the runway either for a short time (e.g., 1 hour/day) or for an indefinite time (e.g., 48 hours). The measure of hoarding is the number of pellets carried home. We have found a runway with unlimited access to be the better procedure. Here the rats are required to perform a complex behavior (i.e., leave the home cage, explore the runway, pick up the food in the mouth, carry it home). Performance can be disrupted for a number of reasons: the rats may not enter the runway, they may eat the food in the runway, they may pick up the food, but not carry it home, etc. Decorticate rats fail to initiate hoarding, whereas a hippocampal rat will pick up the pellet in its mouth and run up and down the alley before dropping the pellet in a random location (cf. Vanderwolf et al., 1978). Our view of food hoarding in domestic rats may have to be modified by recent observations of feral rats. Takahashi and Lore (1980) report that wild rats neither carry food to nor eat food in their burrows, but they may carry it to other protected areas or "shucking stations." The hoarding seen in laboratory rats may reflect the latter behavior rather than the storage of food in a home larder per se.

(ii) Eating

When normal rats eat food pellets, they begin by picking up a pellet in the mouth. They often walk a couple of steps, stop, adopt a sitting posture, transfer the food pellet to the forepaws, bite off a piece, chew while holding the pellet motionless, rotate the pellet with the forepaws, bite off another piece, and so on.[5] Many neurological manipulations disrupt this relatively stereotyped sequence of behaviors. Decorticate rats do not pick the food up in the forepaws, but rather attempt to eat the food where it lies on the cage floor (cf. Vanderwolf et al., 1978). Similarly, rats with orbital frontal lesions initially appear unable to eat normally, instead they eat like the decorticate rat, but over a period of several months they gradually recover the ability to eat in the normal manner (Kolb, Whishaw, & Schallert, 1977). Periodic study of eating behavior can be made by depriving rats of food for 24 hours and then giving them a few food pellets and observing their behavior.

---

5. Forepaw and biting movements made by rats while eating have received little detailed description. Eibl-Eibesfeldt (1961) raised European red squirrels by hand and studied the movements involved in opening hazelnuts, which are normally a staple part of their diet. The basic action patterns of gnawing, splitting, and turning the nut appeared the first time the inexperienced red squirrels were given a nut. Initially the movements were varied and ineffective, but after practice they became more stereotyped and efficient.

(iii) Neophobia

Wild rats are notorious for their elusive and wary behavior towards new foods and as a result they can be poisoned or trapped only with difficulty.[6] Features of this behavior are residual in domestic rats. If rats are given a new food they generally consume very little on the first presentation, even if they are hungry. Wild rats will not even eat familiar food if the food hopper has been significantly altered. The decline in food consumption observed with new food or some alteration in a familiar one is known as neophobia. Lesions of the amygdala are consistently associated with reduced neophobia (Rolls & Rolls, 1973).

(iv) Taste Aversion

If rats are presented with a novel food and they later become ill they will avoid that food in the future, that is, they display bait-shyness or taste aversion learning. In this regard, Richter's (1968) account of the development of the rat poison alpha-naphtyl thiourea makes fascinating reading.

At the outbreak of World War II, North America's sole supply of rat poison was cut off by the Axis powers. Fearing that an uncontrolled rat population might be used against them, the U.S. government enlisted the aid of Richter (1968), who has recounted the quite successful campaign to discover a highly toxic, but tasteless rat poison.

In the laboratory, taste aversion is usually studied by pairing a novel flavor or odor, such as apple juice, with subsequent intraperitoneal injection of some agent that induces illness, such as apomorphine or lithium chloride. The measure of taste aversion is the amount of the food consumed on a second presentation, hour, days, or even weeks later. Lesions of the amygdala or certain areas of the hypothalamus are known to disrupt taste aversion learning (cf. Nachman & Ashe, 1974). Conditioned taste preferences can also be produced by pairing consumption of a tasty substance with recovery from illness (Garcia, Ervin, Yorke, & Koelling, 1967) or with rewarding brain stimulation (Ettenberg & White, 1978; Sutherland & Nakajima, 1980).

(v) Foraging and Diet Selection

If rats have access to two or more foods they usually sample all of them. Sampling appears to be important in maintaining normal nutritional bal-

---

6. Many studies on rat behavior received their impetus from the necessity of controlling wild rat populations, which in some cities can be as high as 300 per city block. Rat catchers studied behavior feeding habits in the wild and also often found it necessary to conduct more controlled experiments in the laboratory. Neophobia behavior in particular became obvious and had to be circumvented lest it frustrate poisoning and trapping operations (Barnett & Spencer, 1951; Richter, 1968).

ance in rats, since they will adjust their intake of different foods to counteract different nutritional deficiencies (cf. Barnett, 1963). There are few
systematic studies of diet selection in rats with neurological deficits, but
it is likely that lesions of the amygdala, hypothalamus, or gustatory cortex, among other areas, would interfere with normal diet selection (see
Nachman & Ashe, 1974).

4. SLEEP

Most mammals spend a considerable amount of their inactive periods
in sleep, although the amount of sleep different species engage in varies
widely (Allison & Cicchetti, 1976). At least two qualitatively different
stages of sleep can be identified from electroencephalographic (EEG) activity, electromyographic activity (EMG), and behavioral observations. (1)
Quiet sleep refers to that stage during sleep when the EEG record taken
from the cerebral cortex consists primarily of large amplitude slow frequency waves. (2) Active sleep or REM sleep refers to that stage of sleep
when the EEG shows a desynchronized pattern, usually characteristic of
the waking state, but when the animal is deeply asleep behaviorally. Skeletal muscle tone is reduced and movement is inhibited except for rapid eye
movements and twitches of the vibrissae, digits, ears, etc. Active sleep is
correlated with dreaming in humans and presumably in the rat as well,
although a method for determining this is not available.[7] Two types of
active sleep that are pharmacologically distinct can be identified from the
EEG record in rats (cf. Robinson, Kramis, & Vanderwolf, 1977).

Investigators have studied several aspects of sleep in rats. These include the following: (1) Occurrence of normal amounts of both types of
sleep. In the laboratory, rats normally sleep about 12 hours, of which
about 20 to 25% is paradoxical sleep. Treatments may alter or even eliminate one type of sleep. For example, Jones (1979) abolished paradoxical
sleep by lesions in the pontine tegmentum. (2) The distribution of sleep
and waking periods during the day. Although rats are active primarily in
the night cycle, they do have brief periods of activity during the light
cycle as well. Some neurological manipulations, such as lesions of the
suprachiasmatic nucleus of the hypothalamus (Richter, 1967; Rusak &
Zucker, 1975), may disrupt the distribution of the sleep and activity periods, as well as their duration. (3) Sleep postures. Although seldom studied, it is reasonable to presume that sleep postures could be disturbed
following various manipulations, especially in animals showing postural

7. Using a bar-pressing technique, Beninger, Kendall, and Vanderwolf (1974) have shown
rats can discriminate between their own behaviors including face-washing, walking, rearing,
and immobility. It is theoretically and technically possible that rats trained in this way can
"self-report" their "behavior" during quiet and active sleep, etc. Results from such an experiment could be used to make inferences about the occurrence of dreaming.

abnormalities during waking. (4) Relationship between neocortical and hippocampal EEG, sleep, and sleep postures and movement. Different EEG patterns in both the neocortex and the hippocampus accompany slow wave sleep and paradoxical sleep. In addition, during paradoxical sleep, the EEG patterns are normally correlated with such movements as twitches and eye movements. Treatments that disrupt waking EEG are likely to also disrupt sleeping EEG (cf. Vanderwolf, 1983). (5) Places of sleep. Rats normally sleep in their home nest, or in the absence of a nest, in a dark, well-protected place. We have observed that decorticate rats sometimes sleep out in the open in hoarding alleys (unpublished observations). It is likely that other treatments may have similar effects upon the choice of places to sleep, but to date this has not been examined.

5. Nest-Building

Given access to suitable material, rats will usually make a nest that fits its body (cf. Barnett, 1963). Materials such as paper, cloth, straw, or string are picked up with the mouth and carried to a sheltered spot, if available. They are then piled with the paws and snout into a heap and may be torn up, shredded, or split to a manageable size before nest construction begins. Rats shape the material into a cup-shaped nest by using the forepaws and teeth to manipulate the material and by repeatedly walking in tight circles to obtain a circular shape. Thus, nest-building requires that the rat perform a relatively complex sequence of movements involving whole body movements and limb movements, as well as fine movements of the digits and mouth. In addition, the intensity of nest-building in the female waxes and wanes in a 4-day cycle, showing an inverse relation to the more widely known 4-day cycle of locomotor activity (Kinder, 1927).

Nest-building appears to have two primary functions in rats: (1) It contributes to the maintenance of a constant body temperature. The intensity of nest-building is directly related to the temperature and the initiation of nest-building activity is affected by treatments that affect behavioral thermoregulation in other ways (cf. Barnett, 1963). (2) It provides a home for the young, functioning both to keep the young warm, and less importantly, to keep the young together in a safe place. Neurological treatments that disrupt maternal behavior are thus often found to disrupt nest-building as well (cf. Slotnick, 1967).

Nest-building is normally assessed in two different ways: in an enclosed area and in an open area.

(i) Enclosed Area

Here, the rat is placed in a relatively confined cage (e.g., 20 cm³) and is provided with nesting material of some sort. We have found pieces of twine and/or strips of paper toweling to be the best. Each behavior can be recorded as it occurs (e.g., pick up material, push, walk) or progress can be quantified by rating the nest quality (e.g., Shipley & Kolb, 1977). In the latter case, it is best to rate the nest-building frequently over the first hour and then periodically over the ensuing 24 or 48 hours. Some animals may appear disorganized and clumsy over the first hour, but given enough time, they may build rather good nests. Damage to the septum has particularly severe effects upon nest-building in enclosed areas (cf. Shipley & Kolb, 1977).

(ii) Open Area

Here, the rat is placed in a cage attached to a large open area, such as an alley similar to those used in studies of hoarding behavior (see above). The nesting material is scattered about in the alley so that the rat must find the material, pick it up in its mouth, and carry it to the home cage in order to build a nest. This test is more complex than the enclosed-area test, since it includes a component of gathering or hoarding behavior. As in the enclosed-area test, behavior can be recorded either by describing each behavior as it occurs or by using a nest rating scale. In addition, we have found it useful to record the latencies of various components of the behaviors, such as time to carry the material home and latency to start nest-building. The location of the nest site should also be recorded. We have observed rats with septal lesions who built nests in the alleys rather than carrying the materials home (unpublished observations). In hamsters, damage to the septum, hippocampus, medial frontal cortex, and hypothalamus may abolish or severely disrupt nest-building in the open area (cf. Shipley & Kolb, 1977).

6. MATERNAL BEHAVIOR

In the rat, maternal behavior begins at parturition and continues for 3 or 4 weeks. It consists of two stages: (1) behavior related to the delivery of the young and (2) behavior related to the care and nursing of the young. In the first stage, the mother is concerned primarily with the delivery of the young, licking and cleaning the pups, licking birth fluids from her body and her immediate vicinity, and eating the placentas (Rosenblatt, 1970). Some elements of maternal care may also appear: the female may retrieve and clean pups, lie down over them, and even nurse them.[8] In

8. There are complex interactions in the behavior between infant and mother rats; these include suckling initiation on the part of the pups, first by amniotic fluid deposited by the mother on the nipples and then by saliva deposited by the infants on the nipples (Blass & Teicher, 1980), and the initiation and termination of nursing on the part of the mother, by cooling when she is away from the pups and by warming after she has been nursing the pups, respectively, of her ventral surface (Croskerry, Smith, & Leon, 1978).

the second stage, the mother's behavior is directed toward nursing, cleaning, protecting (including retrieval of errant pups, defense of the pups, keeping pups warm) the pups and maintaining the nest (see nest-building above). Maternal behavior can also be induced in virgin female rats by providing continuous exposure to pups for about 1 week. The virgin female will then retrieve and clean pups and adopt a nursing posture over them, although she does not actually nurse them (cf. Rosenblatt, Siegal, & Mayer, 1979).

In principle, neuropsychological studies of maternal behavior in the rat would be expected to include both stages of maternal behavior, as well as the maternal behavior of virgin rats. To date, however, neuropsychological studies of maternal behavior have focused on pup retrieval and nest-building with only passing notice of other aspects of maternal care (cf. Terlecki & Sainsbury, 1978). Behavioral measures usually include the latency to retrieve pups scattered by the experimenter, the number of pups retrieved, the length of time to retrieve all pups, the time spent licking, nursing, or manipulating pups, and the total time the mother spends in the nesting area, in addition to measures of nest-building (see above). Further, a crude measure of maternal efficiency can be obtained by recording the mortality rate in each litter.

To date, neuropsychological studies have focused on the effects of lesions of either the limbic system (cf. Slotnick, 1967; Kolb & Whishaw, 1979; Steele, Rowland, & Moltz, 1979) or the sensory systems (cf. Beach & Jaynes, 1956a,b; Fleming, Vaccarino, Tambosso, & Chee, 1979) upon maternal behavior. Deficits in pup retrieval are correlated with deficits in food hoarding, suggesting a common dysfunction. Although not systematically studied to date, it is likely that the size of the nesting area will affect maternal behavior, since the difficulty of pup retrieval should increase with cage size.

7. SOCIAL BEHAVIOR

Social behavior can be defined as "all behavior which influences, or is influenced by, other members of the same species. The term thus covers all sexual and reproductive activities, all behavior which tends to bring individuals together and also all intraspecific conflict" (Barnett, 1963, p. 72). It is beyond the scope of this chapter to describe the social behavior of the rat in detail, so the reader is referred to Barnett (1963), Grant (1963), and Grant and Mackintosh (1963). In this section, we will briefly describe the social behavior of the rat and the most common laboratory situations used to assess it. We have chosen to describe sexual behavior separately (see below), since for practical purposes most neuropsychologists treat sexual behavior as a type of behavior separate from social behavior.

Rats form social groups described by Eibl-Eibesfeldt (1970) as "closed anonymous groups": individual members do not know each other individually, but they can tell if an individual belongs to the group from various cues, especially olfactory cues. Since individual animals are anonymous, there is no rank order, although sometimes an especially large individual male may dominate the other rats. Although the rats in a group are anonymous, they have a very complex pattern of behaviors toward one another and toward rats from outside the group. These include what Barnett (1963) describes as amicable behavior (e.g., contact, nuzzling, grooming one another), fighting and threat behavior, and defensive behavior. Neurological manipulations may alter these behaviors in a variety of ways, such as (1) increasing or decreasing the frequency of the behaviors, (2) changing the response thresholds to the stimuli that elicit the behaviors, or (3) qualitatively alternating the behavioral responses to particular socially relevant stimuli.

It is generally recognized that social behavior is not a unitary behavior with a unitary neurological basis. Rather, different aspects of social behavior have different neural and endocrine bases (cf. Moyer, 1968). It is therefore necessary to examine social behavior in a number of different situations before concluding that a particular treatment has produced a general change in social behavior, since changes may be situation-specific. Neuropsychological studies of social behavior in rats usually utilize one or more of the following procedures: (1) free interaction, (2) structured interaction, (3) territorial interaction, and (4) irritable aggression. We describe each of these situations separately.

(i) Free Interaction

A group of subjects (usually five to ten) are housed in a large group cage, often with several interconnected chambers. The rats are individually and distinctively marked so that the behavior of each one can easily be observed and recorded using ethological recording techniques. In this situation, the experimenter does not interfere with the animals and may observe interactions for days or weeks sometimes both before and after some neurological manipulation (cf. Lubar, Herrmann, Moore, & Shouse, 1973). One difficulty with this procedure is that it is possible to record a tremendous amount of data in a very short time and computer analysis may be necessary to draw any conclusions.

(ii) Structured Interaction

Here, two rats are placed in a compartment that is novel to both of them. Their behavior is then recorded, usually by using a time-sampling procedure, for up to 30 minutes (cf. Kolb, 1974b). Pairings may be made repeatedly over days (cf. Latane, 1970) and may either be between rats with the same neurological manipulations or with different manipulations.

(iii) Territorial Interaction

If a normal rat is placed into the territory of another normal rat, they both behave in characteristic ways: The intruder is very defensive and attempts to escape, whereas the territorial occupant is rather more aggressive and may seriously harm the intruder. Research that uses this situation to study intraspecies aggression refer to the situation as the "colony-intruder model of aggression" (Blanchard & Blanchard, 1977; Lore, Nikoletseas, & Flannelly, 1980).[9] To study the effect of a particular neurological manipulation upon territorial aggression, it is therefore necessary to study the behavior of both control and experimental rats in the role of both the intruder and the territorial occupant (cf. Kolb, 1974b, Lau & Miczek, 1977).

(iv) Irritable Aggression

Sometimes rats will not display many social behaviors unless provoked by a strong stimulation, such as an electric shock to the feet. Typically, two rats are placed in a compartment with a grid floor and electric shock is applied to the feet through the grid. Even rats that display virtually no social behavior (e.g., decorticate rats, see Vanderwolf, Kolb, & Cooley, 1978) fight in this situation, although the predominant behavior by both rats is often escape related. The social behavior observed in this situation is obviously not very normal, but the task allows social behavior to be demonstrated in rats who show virtually no social behavior in more natural situations.

(v) Miscellaneous Social Behaviors

The behavioral situations described above represent the most common situations in which the social behavior of rats is studied by neuropsychologists. These situations ignore a number of social behaviors that rats also

9. The colony intruder model can be used to study the rat's response to other species of animals. To a potential predator, such as a cat, they freeze or if possible make avoidance responses even upon the first encounter (Blanchard & Blanchard, 1971). They will bury a hole leading into their cage to block the entrance of an intruder such as a pigeon (Pinel, personal communication). They will also kill some animals: Bandler and Moyer (1970) report 100% of domestic rats kill frogs and turtles, 45% kill chicks, and 15% kill mice. The cues used by rats to make the discriminations that guide these behaviors are poorly understood. Pheromones may be involved: Alberts and Galef (1973) introduced an anesthetized rat in a plastic bag into the home cage of another male. The anesthetized intruder was attacked only if the bag was perforated, which suggests the presence of a pheromone. The characteristics of female intruders that inhibit male attack may also be olfactory related (Grant & Chance, 1958).

exhibit, but that to date have not been systematically studied in rats with neurological manipulations. These include ultrasonic vocalizations (cf. Francis, 1977) and urine marking (cf. Brown, 1975).

8. SEXUAL BEHAVIOR

Although relatively simple in function, sexual behavior is a very complex behavior requiring the integrity of various hormonal and neural systems. The complexity of sexual behavior becomes apparent when one realizes that copulation itself is a rather small part of sexual behavior. Most sexual behavior occurs prior to (courtship) or following copulation. In addition, at least in the male rat, there are daily bouts of autosexual behavior, involving unsheathing and thrusting of the penis, pelvic movements, genital licking, ejaculation, and consumption of the sperm plug (Orbach, 1961; Orbach, Miller, Billimoria, & Solhkah, 1967). Each component of autosexual behavior depends upon an adequate level of circulating testosterone (Orbach et al., 1967), but brain lesions that suppress copulatory behavior (such as amygdala or preoptic area lesions) do not affect or facilitate this pattern of autosexual behavior in the rat (Agmo, Soulairac, & Soulairac, 1977; Sutherland, 1974). Interestingly, these autosexual ejaculations persist after sectioning of the spinal cord in rats (and man) and are not affected by anesthetization of the penis; thus, they may simply reflect the level of endogenous activity in a spinal reflex. Administration of certain drugs, such as *para*-chloroamphetamine (Humphries, O'Brien, & Paxinos, 1980), amantadine (Baraldi & Bertolini, 1974), epinephrine, and methocyl (Orbach, 1961), is followed within several minutes by "spontaneous" ejaculation.

A thorough study of sexual behavior requires that all behavior of the male and female rat be studied, including exploration, sniffing, grooming, and soliciting behaviors, such as ear wiggling, hopping, and darting in estrous females, genital and nongenital grooming, mounting, pelvic thrusting, ejaculation, lordosis, immobility, ultrasonic songs, and postejaculatory urination (Dewsbury, 1967). Unfortunately, these behaviors have not been carefully studied in rats with neurological manipulations.

In most neuropsychological studies of sexual behavior, all the behaviors have not been studied; only the copulatory patterns have. Thus, the study of female sexual behavior frequently involves the duration and frequency of the lordosis response in ovariectomized, hormone-primed females. Similarly, studies of male sexual behavior concentrate upon the number of mounts, intromissions, interejaculatory intervals, etc. Lesions of the preoptic region of the hypothalamus abolish many of these behaviors (cf. Whalen, 1970).

Sexual behavior may also be studied in other ways, depending upon the question being asked. For example, in his study of the preferred rate of sexual contact in females, Bermant (1961) provided female rats with a lever they could press to produce a male rat. Following a mount, the male was removed and Bermant studied the time until the next lever press in females. Lesions of the habenular complex reduced the preferred rate of sexual contact by females and suppressed lordosis and soliciting as well (cf. Sutherland, 1982). In other studies, it was merely observed whether or not rats with certain neurological manipulations engaged in sexual behavior. Beach (1940) has reported that male rats with extensive areas of neocortex removed (35 to 75%) failed to copulate. Beach's study was extensive and systematic and used experienced male rats and hormone treatments to facilitate the occurrence of sexual behavior. Davis (1939), however, reported that some males with as much as 75% of the cortex removed did copulate. Since, in Beach's study, males were left with female rats for only a single test session, or in a few cases as long as 10 days, we wondered if extensive pairing would facilitate the occurrence of mating. We have left decorticated male rats with female rats up to 1 year. Six of ten totally (>97%) decorticate rats sired litters, and four of these six rats sired four litters during the year. Thus, it is clear that decorticated male rats can copulate successfully, but the factors that affect their success have not been adequately worked out.

9. OTHER BEHAVIORS

We have described those species-specific behaviors that are usually studied by neuropsychologists, but we have not exhausted the species-specific behaviors of the rat. In this section, we will briefly mention several other behaviors that are common to rats, but that have not been studied extensively in rats with neurological manipulations. In particular, these include high frequency vocalizations, burrowing, burying, exploratory behavior, and play behavior.

(i) Vocalizations

Rats emit high frequency vocalizations in a number of social situations. For example, calls at 40 to 60 kHz are emitted by males investigating estrous females (Salas, 1972), calls at 22 kHz are emitted by male rats after ejaculation (Barfield & Gayer, 1972; Brown, 1979), hissing with ultrasonic components is emitted by rats during fighting (Berg & Baenninger, 1973), and calls at 22 kHz are emitted by males when defeated or when left in isolation (Lore, Flannelly, & Farina, 1976; Francis, 1977). The functions and neurophysiological bases of these vocalizations are unknown.

(ii) Burrowing

Laboratory rats are proficient at burrowing and can construct elaborate underground burrow systems (Barnett, 1963). Indeed, even if the earth provided is loose and will not support a burrow, rats spend a great deal of time digging. We are unaware of any neuropsychological studies of burrowing, however.

(iii) Burying

Rats will bury a variety of objects, if allowed to. Much of the burying may be incidental to digging activity, but Pinel and his colleagues (see Chapter 8, this volume) have shown that rats will bury noxious objects, such as those that shock or startle the animals. Although only Pinel and his colleagues have carefully studied this behavior, it appears to be a reliable and sensitive measure of the avoidance behavior of the rat and may be a far better measure of response to aversive events than standard shock avoidance.

(iv) Investigatory Behavior

Rats regularly explore their surroundings by approaching and entering every accessible place or moving and manipulating objects around their nesting place. By doing so, the animals learn shortest routes from one place to another in their environment, are able to sample all the edible items in the vicinity of the nest area, and leave trails of odors on the routes they regularly use; these odors can be detected by other rats. If novel objects are detected they may be avoided, buried, or marked with urine. Although many experiments may claim to study "exploration," the primary measure is of activity in a novel environment. We are unaware of any neuropsycholgoical studies that have systematically examined the "spontaneous" investigation of home cages or novel objects. There is, however, an extensive literature on this behavior in normal rats (cf. Glickman & Scroges, 1966; Berlyne, 1966; Barnett, 1958), and little reason why it has not been studied in rats with neurological manipulations.

(v) Play Behavior

Play is frequently seen in rats and other mammals, but it is seldom studied. Play may take many forms and it is difficult to define satisfactorily (see Eibl-Eiblesfeldt, 1970). In most instances, however, play behavior is indistinguishable from more serious behavior. For example, when rats play, they may chase one another around or engage in "rough and tumble" fighting. The "serious" aspects of these behaviors are lacking, however, since we know that a rat escaping a serious threat would not immediately return for more; during rough and tumble play-fighting, there is an inhibition of biting and no threat behavior. The occurrence of biting or threat displays indicate that the fighting is real. Play behavior has been studied in normal rats and in rats subjected to hormonal manipulations (Meany & Stewart, 1979, 1981; Olioff & Stewart, 1978; Poole & Fish, 1976), but there have been no systematic investigations in rats subjected to brain manipulations other than those hormonally induced.

H. CONCLUSION

In this chapter, we have described the appearance and behavior of the rat within the context of some of the many relevant neuropsychological studies in which the animal has been used as subject. It was not possible to describe every behavior in detail, it was not possible to refer to all relevant literature, and it was definitely not possible to describe in any detail the neural systems thought to be involved in the control of different behaviors. In our introduction we argued that it is premature to formulate and test theories of behavior, but instead that it is more appropriate to make careful observations and careful descriptions of behavior from which meaningful generalizations about the organization of the nervous system could later be made. We have called this approach an empirico-inductive method, and it is loosely patterned on the model of the clinical neurological and neuropsychological batteries for humans. In fact, Hutt and Hutt (Chapter 2, this volume; also see Vanderwolf, Chapter 1, and Ranck et al., Chapter 5) have argued that this approach to behavior is a necessary precursor to more a formal science of the hypothetico-deductive type. In our introduction, we listed the types of problems that can be addressed with an empirico-inductive method; we also gave examples of some problems that were successfully solved with such a methodology. We now suggest that through the use of this approach, and with attention to the behavioral repertoire of the rat and its many possible modifications, the neuropsychologist can gain an intimate knowledge of the behavior of the laboratory rat from which will flow insights into the neural organization underlying that behavior.

ACKNOWLEDGEMENT

This research was supported by research grants from the Natural Sciences and Engineering Research Council of Canada to Ian Q. Whishaw and Bryan Kolb. Robert J. Sutherland was supported by a NSERC Postdoctoral Fellowship. We thank Adria Allen for typing the manuscript.

APPENDIX A.

BEHAVIORAL ASSESSMENT OF THE RAT: A SUMMARY OF FEATURES OF BEHAVIOR FOR EXAMINATION

Appearance
Body weight, core temperature, eyes, feces, fur, genitals, muscle tone, pupils, responsiveness, saliva, teeth, toenails, vocalizations

Sensory and Sensorimotor Behavior
   Home Cage: Response to auditory, olfactory, somatosensory, taste, vestibular, and visual stimuli
   Open Field: Response to auditory, olfactory, somatosensory, taste, vestibular, and visual stimuli

Posture and Immobility
   Types of Immobility: Immobility with posture, without posture, of body parts, without muscle tone
   Restraint-Induced Immobility: Animal hypnosis or tonic immobility
   Environmental Influences on Immobility: Food, temperature, etc.

Movement
   General Activity: Videorecording, movement sensors, activity wheels, open field tests
   Movement Initiation: The warm-up effect
   Turning and Climbing: Cages, alleys, tunnels, etc.
   Walking and Swimming
   Righting responses: Supporting, righting, placing, hopping reactions
   Limb movements: Bar-pressing, reading and retrieving, spontaneous behaviors
   Oral movements: Mouth and tongue movements in acceptance or rejection of food
   Environmental Influences on Movement

Species-Specific Behaviors
   Grooming, food hoarding, eating, neophobia, taste aversion, foraging and diet selection, sleep, nest-building, maternal behavior, social behavior, sexual behavior, vocalizing, burrowing, burying, exploratory behavior, play behavior

Learning (classical conditioning, instrumental conditioning, learning sets)
   Spatial learning: Morris water maze, radial arm maze, Grice box
   Avoidance learning: Defensive shock prod burying, conditioned taste aversion
   Response learning: Latch puzzles
   Working vs. reference memory: Radial arm maze

APPENDIX B.

A PARTIAL LIST OF STUDIES ON THE APPEARANCE AND PHYSIOLOGICAL
FUNCTIONS OF THE RAT

Behavior	Lesion	Reference
Cage residue	Cortex	Brandes & Johnson, 1978; Kolb & Nonneman, 1975a, b; Kolb, Whishaw, & Schallert, 1977; Whishaw, Nonneman, & Kolb, 1981; Whishaw, 1974
	Amygdala	Sutherland, 1974
	Hypothalamus	Reynolds & Kimm, 1972; Toth, 1973
Cardiac function	Hypothalamus	Boyko, Galabru, McGeer, & McGeer, 1979; Nagel & Satinoff, 1980
Gastrointestinal pathology	Amygdala	Henke, 1980
	Hypothalamus	Grijalva, Lindholm, & Novin, 1980; Lindholm, Shumway, Grijalva, Schallert, & Ruppel, 1975; England, Marks, Paxinos, & Atrens, 1979; Nobrega, Weiner, & Ossenkopp, 1980; Ossenkopp, Weiner, & Nobrega, 1980; Schallert, Whishaw, and Flannigan, 1977
Grooming	Cortex	Kolb & Whishaw, 1981a; Whishaw, Nonneman, & Kolb, 1981; Vanderwolf, Kolb, & Cooley, 1978
	Basal ganglia	Grill & Norgren, 1978
	Hypothalamus	Levitt & Teitelbaum, 1975; Robinson & Whishaw, 1974; Woods, 1954
Activity	Hypothlamus	Balagura, Wilcox, & Coscina, 1969; Morrison, 1968b; Whishaw & Robinson, 1974; McGinty, 1969; Nauta, 1946; Wiener, Nobrega, Ossenkopp, & Shilman, 1980
Kidney pathology	Locus Coeruleus	Amaral & Foss, 1975; Kolb & Whishaw, 1977

Behavior	Lesion	Reference
Light sensitivity	Visual and extravisual	Altman, 1962; Whishaw, 1974
Pupils	Midbrain	Legg, 1975
Polydipsia	Hypothalamus	Rolls, 1970; Simons, 1968; Wishart & Walls, 1975
Pulmonary edema	Hypothalamus	Maire & Patton, 1954, 1965
Responsiveness to handling	Cortex	Kolb, 1974b
	Isolated normals	Hatch, Wiberg, Balazs, & Grice, 1963
	Limbic system	Brady & Nauta, 1953, 1955; Cytawa & Teitelbaum, 1968; King, 1956; Yutzey, Meyer, & Meyer, 1964
Salivation	Hypothalamus	Chapman & Epstein, 1970; Hainsworth & Epstein, 1966; Kissileff & Epstein, 1969; Schallert, Leach, & Braun, 1978; Toth, 1973; Epstein, Blass, Batshaw, & Parks, 1970
Thermoregulatory change	Hypothalamus	Satinoff & Henderson, 1977; Satinoff, Valentino, & Teitelbaum, 1976; Schallert & Whishaw, 1978

APPENDIX C.

A PARTIAL LIST OF STUDIES ON SENSORIMOTOR FUNCTIONS IN THE RAT

Lesion	Reference
Cortex	Goodale & Murison, 1975; Vanderwolf, Kolb, & Cooley, 1978; Whishaw, Schallert, & Kolb, 1981
Amygdala	Kirvel, 1975; Turner, 1973
Lateral hypothalamus	Almli & Fisher, 1977; Almli, Fisher & Hill, 1979; Almli, Hill, McMullen, & Fisher, 1979; Marshall & Teitelbaum, 1974; Marshall, Turner, & Teitelbaum, 1971; McMullin & Almli, 1980; Robinson & Whishaw, 1974; Schallert & Whishaw, 1978; Stellar, Brooks, &

Lesion	Reference
	Mills, 1979; Stricker, Cooper, Marshall, & Zigmond, 1979; Turner, 1973; Whishaw & Robinson, 1974
Medial hypothalamus	Marshall, 1975
Anterior hypothalamus	Whishaw & Robinson, 1974
Nigrostriatal system	Ljungberg & Ungerstedt, 1976; Marshall, 1979; Marshall, Berrios, & Sawyer, 1980; Marshall & Gotthelf, 1979; Marshall, Levitan, & Stricker, 1976; Marshall, Richardson, & Teitelbaum, 1974; Pelham, Lippa, & Sano, 1977
Superior colliculus	Goodale & Lister, 1974; Goodale & Murison, 1975; Kirvel, 1975; Marshall, 1978

Appendix D.

A Partial List of Studies on Immobility in the Rat

Immobility	References
Types	Costall & Naylor, 1974; DeJong, 1945; DeRyck, Schallert, & Teitelbaum, 1980; Fog, 1972; Golani, Wolgin, & Teitelbaum, 1979; Kuschinsky & Hornykiewicz, 1972; Robinson & Whishaw, 1974; Schallert, DeRyck, Whishaw, Ramirez, & Teitelbaum, 1979; Schallert & Whishaw, 1978
Restraint induced	DeRyck, Schallert, & Teitelbaum, 1980; McGraw & Klemm, 1969, 1973; Prestrude, 1977; Schallert, DeRyck, Whishaw, & Teitelbaum, 1978; Svorad, 1957; Teschke, Maser, & Gallup, 1975; Whishaw, Schallert, & Kolb, 1979; Woodruff & Bailey, 1979
Environmental influences	Alberts, 1978; Fishman & Roffwaig, 1971; Komisaruk & Larsson, 1971; Levitt & Teitelbaum, 1975; Roberts, Mooney, & Martin, 1974; Robinson & Whishaw, 1974; Ross, Komisaruk, & O'Donnell, 1979; Schallert, Whishaw, DeRyck, & Teitelbaum, 1978; Teitelbaum, Wolgin, DeRyck, & Marin, 1976; Wagner & Woods, 1950; Whishaw, Schallert, & Kolb, 1979

APPENDIX E.

SUMMARY OF STUDIES OF MOVEMENT IN THE RAT

Movement	References
General activity	Kolb & Whishaw, 1981a; Morrison, 1968a; Richter, 1965; Slonaker, 1912; Whishaw, Robinson, Schallert, DeRyck, & Ramirez, 1978
Initiation	Bland & Vanderwolf, 1972; Golani, Wolgin, & Teitelbaum, 1979; Vanderwolf, 1971; Whishaw & Vanderwolf, 1973
Turning and climbing	Almli & Fisher, 1977; Golani, Wolgin, & Teitelbaum, 1979; Levitt & Teitelbaum, 1975; Schallert, DeRyck, & Teitelbaum, 1980; Schallert, Whishaw, Ramirez, & Teitelbaum, 1978a,b; Whishaw, Schallert, & Kolb, 1981
Righting responses	Bard, 1968; Bard and Brooks, 1934; Bignall, 1974; DeRyck, Schallert, & Teitelbaum, 1980; Hicks & D'Amato, 1975; Schallert, DeRyck, Whishaw, Ramirez, & Teitelbaum, 1979; Sechzer, Ervin, & Smith, 1973; Whishaw, Schallert, & Kolb, 1981
Walking	Chapin, Loeb, & Woodward, 1980; Ganor & Golani, 1980; Gentile, Green, Nieburgs, Schmelzer, & Stein, 1978; Gruner, Altman, & Spivac 1980; Hicks & D'Amato, 1975, 1980; Hruska, Kennedy, & Silbergeld, 1979; Hruska & Silbergeld, 1979; Maier, 1935; Mullenix, Norton, & Culver, 1975; Schallert, Whishaw, Ramirez, & Teitelbaum, 1978a,b
Swimming	Bekoff & Trainer, 1979; Binik, 1977; Binik, Theriault & Shustack, 1977; Gruner & Altman, 1980; Levitt & Teitelbaum, 1975; Lin, 1974; Lin, 1975; Marshall & Berrios, 1979; Marshall, Levitan, & Stricker, 1976; Richter, 1957; Robinson & Whishaw, 1974; Robinson, Whishaw, & Wishart, 1974; Rosellini, Binik, & Seligman, 1976; Salas, 1972; Schapiro, Salas, & Vukovich, 1970; Vanderwolf, Kolb, & Cooley, 1978; Whishaw, Nonneman, & Kolb, 1981
Limb	Castro, 1972b, 1977, 1978; Kartje-Tillotson & Castro, 1980; Kolb, Schallert & Whishaw, 1977; Kolb & Whishaw, 1981a,b; Lashley, 1935; Levine, Ferguson, Kreinick, Gustafson,

Movement	References
	& Schwartzbaum, 1971; Levine & Schwartzbaum, 1973; Siegfried & Bures, 1980; Siegfried, Fisher, & Bures, 1980; Spiliotis & Thompson, 1973; Thompson, Gates, & Gross, 1979; Vanderwolf, Kolb, & Cooley, 1978; Whishaw, Nonneman, & Kolb, 1981.
Oral	Brimley & Mogenson, 1979; Castro, 1972a, 1975; Grill & Norgren, 1978a,b,c,d; Keehn & Arnold, 1960; Kolb & Nonneman, 1975; Levine, Ferguson, Kreinick, Gustafson, & Schwartzbaum, 1971; Levine & Schwartzbaum, 1973; Zeigler & Karten, 1974
Development	Adolph, 1957; Almli, 1978; Altman & Sudarshan, 1975; Bolles & Woods, 1964; Cambell & Spear, 1972; Johannsen & Hall, 1980; Pellegrino & Altman, 1979

APPENDIX F.

A LIST OF REPRESENTATIVE LESION STUDIES OF SPECIES-SPECIFIC BEHAVIOR IN THE RAT

Behavior	Lesion	Reference
Grooming	None	Woolridge, 1975
	Decorticate	Vanderwolf, Kolb, & Cooley, 1978; Kolb & Whishaw, 1981a; Whishaw, Nonneman, & Kolb, 1981
	Decerebrate	Freed & Grill, 1979
	Orbital frontal	Kolb, Whishaw, & Schallert, 1977
	Thalamic	Grill & Norgren, 1978a
Food-related hoarding	None	Barnett, 1963
	Decorticate	Vanderwolf, Kolb, & Cooley, 1978; Kolb & Whishaw, 1981a
	Caudate	Kolb, 1977
	Hippocampal	Wishart, Brohman, & Mogenson, 1969; Wallace & Tigner, 1972; Vanderwolf, Kolb, & Cooley, 1978

Behavior	Lesion	Reference
	Medial frontal	Kolb, 1974a; Kolb & Whishaw, 1981b
	Medial thalamus	Vanderwolf, 1967; Kolb, 1977
	Midbrain	Phillips, 1975
	Orbital frontal	Kolb, 1974a
	Septal	Wishart, Brohman, & Mogenson, 1969
	Ventromedial hypothalamus	Herberg & Blundell, 1970
Eating movements	None	Barnett, 1963
	Decorticate	Whishaw, Nonneman, & Kolb, 1981
	Frontal	Kolb, Whishaw, & Schallert, 1977
Neophobia and taste aversion	None	Richter, 1968
	Amygdala	Nachman & Ashe, 1974; Sutherland, 1974
	Caudate	Kolb, Nonneman, & Abplanalp, 1977
	Decerebrate	Grill & Norgren, 1978b
	Gustatory cortex	Braun, Slick, & Lorden, 1972; Kiefer & Braun, 1979; Lorden, 1976
	Hippocampus	Best & Orr, 1973; Murphy & Brown, 1974; Krane, Sinnamon, & Thomas, 1976
	Lateral hypothalamus	Roth, Schwartz, & Teitelbaum, 1973
	Medial frontal cortex	Divac, Gade, & Wikmark, 1975; Kolb, Nonneman, & Abplanalp, 1977
	Medial thalamus	Kolb, Nonneman, & Abplanalp, 1977
	Olfactory bulbs	Hankins, Garcia, & Rusinak, 1973
	Orbital frontal cortex	Divac, Gade & Wikmark, 1975; Kolb, Nonneman, & Abplanalp, 1977
	Septum	McGowan, Garcia, Ervin, & Schwartz, 1969

Behavior	Lesion	Reference
	Ventromedial hypothalamus	Gold & Proulx, 1972; Weisman, Hamilton, & Carlton, 1972
Foraging and diet selection	None	Richter, Holt & Barelare, 1938; Young, 1943; Calhoun, 1949
	Amygdala	Nachman & Ashe, 1974
Sleep	Posterior hypothalamus	McGinty, 1969; Robinson & Whishaw, 1974
Nest-building	None	Barnett, 1963; Kinder, 1927
	Cingulate cortex	Slotnick, 1967
	Medial frontal cortex	Kolb & Whishaw, 1979
	Hippocampus	Kimble, Rogers, & Hendrickson, 1967
	Fimbria-fornix	Terlecki & Sainbury, 1978
	Septum	Knight, 1970
Maternal behavior	None	Weisner & Sheard, 1933; Rosenblatt & Lehrman, 1963
	Cingulate cortex	Slotnick, 1967; Stamm, 1955
	Decorticate	Beach, 1937; Kolb & Whishaw, 1978
	Fimbria-fornix	Terlecki & Sainsbury, 1978
	Hippocampus	Kimble, Rogers, & Hendrickson, 1967
	Medial frontal cortex	Kolb & Whishaw, 1979
	Olfactory bulb	Fleming, Vaccarino, Tambosso, & Chee, 1979
Social behavior	None	Barnett, 1963
	Amygdala	Jonason & Enloe, 1971; Eichelman, 1971; Kolb & Nonneman, 1974
	Caudate	Kolb, 1977
	Decorticate	Vanderwolf, Kolb, & Cooley, 1978
	Hippocampus	Kolb & Nonneman, 1974
	Hypothalamus	Paxinos & Bindra, 1972, 1973
	Medial frontal cortex	Kolb, 1974b; Kolb & Nonneman, 1974; Lubar, Herrmann, Moore, & Shouse, 1973

Behavior	Lesion	Reference
	Medial thalamus	Kolb, 1977
	Orbital frontal cortex	Kolb, 1974b; Kolb & Nonneman, 1974
	Septal	Albert & Chew, 1980; Jonason & Enloe, 1971; Johnson, Poplawsky, & Bieliauskas, 1972; Lau & Miczek, 1977; Lubar, Herrmann, Moore, & Shouse, 1973; Eichelman, 1971; Kolb & Nonneman, 1974
Sexual behavior	None	Anisko, Adler, & Suer, 1979; Dewsbury, 1967
	Amygdala	Michal, 1973; Schwartz & Kling, 1964
	Brainstem	Heimer & Larssen, 1964; Goodman, Jansen, & Dewsbury, 1971; Paxinos & Bindra, 1972, 1973
	Decorticate	Beach, 1940, 1944; Carter, Witt, Kolb, & Whishaw, 1982; Whishaw & Kolb, 1982
	Habenula	Sutherland, 1981
	Hippocampus	Michal, 1973; Kimble, Rogers, & Hendrickson, 1967
	Midline cortex	Michal, 1973
	Medial frontal	Larssen, 1964
	Septum	Michal, 1973
	Preoptic	Heimer & Larssen, 1966, 1967; Chen & Bliss, 1974
Miscellaneous		
vocalizations	None	See text
burrowing	None	Barnett, 1963
burying	None	Pinel, this volume
	Decorticate	Kolb & Whishaw, 1981a
	Frontal	Kolb & Whishaw, 1981b
Exploration	None	Nau, 1980
	Hippocampus	Leaton, 1965
Play	Septum	Nielson, McIver, & Boswell, 1965

9 | The Conditioned Defensive Burying Paradigm and Behavioral Neuroscience

JOHN P.J. PINEL and DALLAS TREIT

A. INTRODUCTION

Attempts to identify the neural correlates of learning and memory have focused, for the most part, on the performance of animals in a limited number of simple learning situations, i.e., in variations of those conditioning paradigms developed by early psychologists in animal learning laboratories. Because these paradigms have had, and will continue to have, a substantial impact on the direction of research in behavioral neuroscience, it is important to be aware of some of the reasons why these particular conditioning paradigms were developed.

> Sometimes we forget why psychologists ever trained white rats to press bars for little pellets of flour or sounded metronomes followed by meat powder for domestic dogs. After all, when in the real world do rats encounter levers which they learn to press in order to eat, and when do our pet dogs ever come across metronomes whose clicking signals meat powder? (Seligman, 1970, p. 406).

One premise that served as the basis for the development of many of the traditional conditioning paradigms was that learning in all its forms can ultimately be understood in terms of a few simple principles that govern the learning of associations between stimuli (respondent conditioning) or between responses and reinforcers (operant conditioning). Because these general principles were assumed to be the same regardless of the events under investigation (e.g., Estes, 1959; Pavlov, 1927; Skinner, 1938), early "learning" psychologists tended to favor artificial learning environments, which were assumed to be uncontaminated by the past experience or by the species-specific propensities of the subjects (cf. Seligman, 1970). Thus, to a large degree, the study of animal learning became the study of responses, such as lever presses, key pecks, and shuttles, made in response to such stimuli as buzzes, lights, clicking, and geometric patterns.

Such investigations have contributed greatly to our understanding of the principles of learning and have provided a valuable automated technology for the investigation of a variety of psychological processes. However, we believe that basing the investigation of the neural basis of learning *entirely* on such conditioning paradigms might lead to two kinds of problems. First, the "artificial" forms of animal learning devised by learning psychologists may have a particularly complex neural basis. Natural forms of learning may be related more directly to their underlying neural mechanisms. Second, theories based *solely* on data from "artificial learning" paradigms may hold for only "artificial" forms of learning (Seligman, 1970). For example, learning in most respondent conditioning paradigms is a slow, step-by-step process that occurs only when the conditioned stimulus is immediately followed by the unconditioned stimulus over many trials. Therefore, it has been assumed in many physiological theories of learning that there is a progressive synaptic facilitation between the neural representation of two stimuli when they repeatedly occur close together in time (e.g., Hebb, 1949). Although such a process is presumed to account for learning in general, it is quite clear that it cannot account for more natural forms of learning without considerable revision. For example, in the conditioned taste aversion paradigm, rats reliably learn to avoid a taste followed by toxicosis in a single trial, even when the interval between the conditioned stimulus (taste) and the unconditioned stimulus (toxicosis) is several hours (Garcia & Koelling, 1966).

In the last decade, interest in more natural forms of animal learning increased substantially, largely in response to the important contributions being made through the study of conditioned taste aversion. Comparisons between taste aversion conditioning and more traditional forms of conditioning have been the primary impetus in numerous psychological investigations. Furthermore, the conditioned taste aversion paradigm has been used in behavioral neuroscience to study the neural correlates of learning (e.g., Grupp, Linseman, & Cappell, 1976), to identify the illness-producing side effects of various pharmacological and physiological treatments (e.g., Deutsch, Molino, & Puerto, 1976), and to help understand the capacity of organisms to correct dietary deficiency (e.g., Rozin & Kalat, 1971).

In this chapter, we describe the development of another aversive conditioning paradigm, that involves a form of learning that seems to be important for the survival of rats in the wild rather than minimize the contribution of such adaptive predispositions. This paradigm is discussed in two major sections: (1) its initial observation and major characteristics and (2) its preliminary applications in neuroscience research.

B. CONDITIONED DEFENSIVE BURYING: MAJOR CHARACTERISTICS

Two features are shared by most traditional aversive conditioning chambers that constrain an animal's ability to cope with the aversive stimulation. First, in most conventional aversive conditioning environments, few, if any, objects are present that can be incorporated into a defensive response. Unlike more natural settings, most test chambers are constructed with floors of fixed metal rods through which feces and other extraneous materials pass. Second, the exact source of the noxious agent is almost always disguised; the aversive stimulus is typically a diffuse electric shock administered through a poorly defined source, the grid floor.

1. INITIAL OBSERVATION AND MEASUREMENT OF CONDITIONED DEFENSIVE BURYING

In 1978, we reported a series of aversive conditioning experiments in which the usual constraints were circumvented (Pinel & Treit, 1978). First, the aversive stimulus was not a generalized shock administered through a grid floor; it was a localized electric shock administered from a well-defined source, a small, wooden, wire-wrapped dowel (i.e., a shock prod) mounted on the wall of the test chamber. Second, the floor was covered with a layer of commercial bedding material.

The subjects were handled and pre-exposed, in groups of four or five, to the $44 \times 30 \times 44$ cm Plexiglas test chamber for 30-minute periods on each of four consecutive days. During all phases of the experiment, the chamber floor was covered evenly with 5 cm of regular grade San-i-cel, a commercial bedding material made of ground corncob. On Day 5, the rats were randomly assigned as experimental or control. The experimental animals were placed individually in the center of the chamber facing away from the $6.5 \times .5 \times .5$ cm wire-wrapped wooden prod that had been fixed to the center of the wall at one end, 2 cm above the level of the bedding material. When the rats in this group first touched the prod with a forepaw, a brief shock, initiated by the experimenter and terminated by the withdrawal of the subject, was delivered between the two uninsulated wires. This shock circuit delivers shocks averaging 7.9 mA (SD = 1.47 mA) in intensity and 42.9 msec (SD = 9.8 msec) in duration. Following the shock, each subject was observed for 15 minutes during which no further shocks were administered. Control rats were not shocked, but otherwise were treated in the same manner.

The immediate reaction of the experimental rats to the shock was to reflexively withdraw to the back of the chamber where they remained relatively, but not completely immobile, for a minute or so. Then almost every subject cautiously approached the prod and began pushing the bedding material from the floor of the chamber at and over it. It is this behavior that has been termed conditioned defensive burying. Each burying sequence typically began with the rat facing the shock prod from the back of the apparatus. Then the rat moved directly toward the prod, pushing and spraying a pile of bedding material ahead with rapid shoveling movements of its snout and alternating pushing movements of its forepaws.

This burying behavior is typically measured in two different ways. First, the total amount of time that each rat engages in *directed* forelimb spraying is recorded. The occasional movement of material with responses other than forelimb spraying and/or in directions other than at the test object(s) is noted separately, but does not contribute to the duration-of-burying score. This duration measure has proven to be remarkably reliable. For example, Pinel, Treit, and Wilkie (1980) and Davis and Rossheim (1980) have reported high correlations, .988 and .93, respectively, between the scores of independent observers. The second measure of burying is not taken until the test session is over. Once the rat is removed from the test chamber, it is a simple matter to measure the height of the bedding material at the test object. Not surprisingly, this height measure is frequently highly correlated (e.g., $r = .89$, Pinel & Treit, 1979) with the duration measure.

It is important to note that the term "burying" is more descriptive of the behavior rather than of its consequences. Whereas directed forelimb spraying (i.e., burying) is a reliable response of rats to prod shock in the presence of bedding material, not every subject accumulates a pile of bedding sufficiently large to completely cover the prod mounted 2 cm above the original level of the bedding during the usual 15-minute test period.

2. Conditioned and Unconditioned Burying

Our original assumption was that the burying behavior of the shocked rats was controlled by a conditioned association between the shock and the prod; in other words, we assumed that the shocked rats buried the prod because they had learned in a single trial that the prod was a potential source of aversive stimulation. However, on the basis of our first experiment, we could not rule out the possibility that the shocked rats buried the prod more than did the unshocked controls simply because it was the only novel object in the shock chamber.

The fact that rats shocked on a grid before the test did not bury the prod in the test chamber, whereas those shocked by the prod in their home cages did (Pinel & Treit, 1978), supported our view that burying

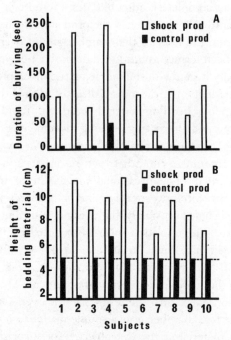

FIGURE 9.1. Duration of burying (panel A) directed at the shock prod and control prod and the final height of the bedding material at the shock prod and control prod (panel B) for each of the subjects (Pinel & Treit, 1978).

shock sources was a conditioned behavior. However, the best evidence for this view came from a study (Pinel & Treit, 1978) in which 10 rats were shocked by one of two identical prods mounted at opposite ends of the chamber. The scores of individual subjects rather than group means are presented in Figure 9.1 to illustrate the robustness of the conditioned defensive burying phenomenon. All 10 subjects spent time burying the prod by which they had been shocked. Only one subject briefly attempted to bury the control prod, but not until it had completely covered the shock prod. Similarly, all 10 subjects accumulated higher piles of bedding material at the shock prod than at the control prod (see Fig. 9.1).

Investigation of the stimulus control of conditioned defensive burying (Pinel, Treit, & Wilkie, 1980) provided further evidence of the associative nature of this phenomenon. The amount of burying was significantly reduced if either the position (front or back of the chamber) or brightness (black or white) of the prod was changed while the rat was removed from the chamber during a 1-minute shock-test interval. Unexpectedly, these studies of stimulus control also provided an impressive demonstration of just how much a rat can learn in a single conditioning trial when it is free from some of the constraints inherent in traditional aversive-conditioning paradigms. Although we have only rarely observed shocked rats to push burying material in any direction other than at the shock source, eight shocked rats in one stimulus-control experiment directed bedding material at a hole in the wall of the apparatus directly opposite the prod position. However, such responses were restricted to a group ($n = 20$) in which the position of the prod had been changed between the shock and the test. After burying the prod in its new position, subjects sprayed bedding material at the hole through which the prod had been inserted during shock administration.

Paradoxically, it was during a series of experiments designed to establish the generality of *conditioned* defensive burying that Terlecki, Pinel, and Treit (1979) determined that burying can also appear as an *unconditioned* component of a rat's neophobic reaction to some objects. The original purpose of these experiments was to establish that aversive stimuli other than footshock can serve as unconditioned stimuli in the conditioned defensive burying paradigm. Thus, following the usual 4 days of habituation to the test chamber, one of four different sources of aversive stimulation was mounted on the end wall before each subject was placed in the chamber for conditioning. Mounted on the wall were a prod, a length of polyethylene tubing, a flashbulb in a protective collar, or a mouse trap with the springs loosened to lessen impact. When each experimental subject touched one of these sources with a forepaw, it received a shock, a airblast, a flash, or a physical blow, respectively, followed immediately by a 15-minute test. The four respective control groups were treated in exactly the same fashion except that the aversive stimulation did not occur when the source was contacted.

The results in the shock and airblast conditions were consistent with our previous observations. Control rats engaged in little or no burying, whereas almost every experimental rat buried the prod or air tube. However, in both the trap and flashbulb conditions, the control animals spent so much time burying the test objects that it was difficult to demonstrate significant increases in burying in response to the aversive stimulation. Moreover, subjects in the experimental groups began burying before aversive stimulation occurred. In the trap condition, this unconditioned burying made it impossible to have an experimental group ($n = 10$). One rat triggered the trap from a distance with the bedding material, and another three rats completely buried the trap without contacting it, thus making it impossible to spring the trap.

The high incidence of unconditioned burying in the trap and flash control conditions, although interesting, left unanswered part of the original question. Will rats bury a neutral stimulus paired with a sudden flash of

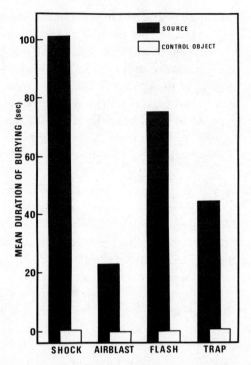

FIGURE 9.2. Mean duration of burying directed at the source of aversive stimulation and at a comparable control object (Terlecki, Pinel, & Treit, 1979).

light or physical impact? Accordingly, Terlecki et al. (1979) conducted further experiments to show that rats previously habituated to the flash-bulb assembly or to the trap would not bury these objects until they had been paired with aversive stimulation. In one experiment, two comparable test objects (prods, tubes, flashbulbs, or traps), one white and one black, were mounted on opposite walls of the test chamber during all phases of the experiment, including the 4 days of habituation—in all the previous experiments the source of aversive stimulation had not been positioned in the test chamber until the test day. In this experiment, there was no unconditioned burying during conditioning and testing, i.e., no rats buried the test objects on the test day prior to receiving the aversive stimulation. Moreover, after the single conditioning trial, the rats in all four conditions directed almost all their burying at the source of aversive stimulation (white or black) rather than at the comparable control object (Fig. 9.2). Thus, the phenomenon of defensive burying is not restricted to situations in which neutral objects serve as the source of painful electric shock. Rats seem to enter the experimental environment with an already established tendency to bury some objects (unconditioned defensive burying), but not others, and they readily learn to selectively bury an object that has been the source of any one of a variety of aversive stimuli (conditioned defensive burying).

3. BURIAL OF THE DEAD

Pinel, Gorzalka, and Ladak (1981) reported a particularly interesting form of unconditioned burying. They found that rats would use the forelimb burying response to accumulate bedding material over the bodies of dead conspecifics. The fact that rats would bury neither fresh corpses nor anesthetized rats suggested that the stimuli responsible for initiating the burial of dead conspecifics might be olfactory cues created during the course of putrefaction. In particular, Pinel et al. (1981) hypothesized that burying behavior could be initiated by the accumulation of putrescine (1,4-diaminobutane) and cadaverine (1,5-diaminopentane), polyamines that, as their names imply, contribute to the characteristic odor of decaying tissue. In support of this hypothesis, they found (1) that rats would bury anesthetized conspecifics sprinkled with putrescine or cadaverine or even wooden dowels treated in the same manner and (2) that rats first rendered anosmic by intranasal injections of zinc sulfate buried neither aged carcasses nor dowels sprinkled with either of the two nidorous compounds.

4. CONDITIONING-TEST INTERVAL

Can a single shock from a well-defined source produce an enduring change in behavior, or is conditioned defensive burying a transient phenomenon? Certainly the utility of the conditioned defensive burying paradigm in the investigation of memory would be severely limited if there were no evidence of long-term retention. Two quite different experiments have a bearing on this question. In the first (Pinel & Treit, 1978), experimental rats were shocked by the single prod that had been mounted on the wall after the habituation phase of the experiment. Each rat was removed immediately from the test chamber and retested at one of five shock-test intervals: 10 seconds, 5 minutes, 5 hours, 3 days, or 20 days. At each of the five intervals, the experimental rats spent more time burying the prod than did unshocked controls. Thus, the elevated levels of prod burying produced by a single conditioning trial appear to last for at least 20 days when only a single prod is present during conditioning and testing.

The second study of the retention of conditioned defensive burying assessed the ability of rats to selectively bury one of two comparable prods (white or black) mounted on opposite walls of the test chamber (Pinel, Treit, & Wilkie, 1980). The habituated subjects were shocked by one of the prods, removed immediately from the chamber, and returned 30 seconds, 5 minutes, 1 hour, 8 hours, 24 hours, or 7 days later for a 15-minute test of retention. These rats buried the shock prod substantially more than they did the control prod ($p < .05$) at all but the 7-day interval. Thus, even though the two prods were identical except for brightness, the discriminative burying of the rats lasted for at least 24 hours. Presumably retention of the discrimination could have been extended by making the differences between the test and control objects more marked.

5. AVAILABILITY OF BURYING MATERIAL

Although the stereotypical nature of the directed forelimb spraying response facilitated the initial investigation of defensive burying, it also raised some serious questions concerning the adaptiveness of burying in the rat's natural habitat. Such an unvarying response pattern would be of marginal utility in habitats where available burying materials require more varied responses for their disposition. However, the stereotypical nature of the burying sequence may simply have been a reflection of the homogeneity of the commercial bedding that had served as the only available burying material in most of the studies of defensive burying.

To clarify this issue, Pinel and Treit (1979) shocked rats through one of two wall-mounted prods in the presence of bedding, sand, or wooden blocks. The wooden blocks were large enough so that a rat could not pile them over the prod using the forepaw pushing motions characteristic of burying with commercial bedding. In this experiment, any behavior that moved materials toward the shock prod or control prod was scored as burying. In all three conditions, the rats spent a substantial proportion of time engaging in burying behavior, and in each condition this behavior was directed almost exclusively at the prod that was the source of aversive stimulation. In both the sand and bedding conditions, the topography of the burying response was the same. The rats began each burying episode facing the prod from a distant part of the chamber. Then they moved directly toward the prod, pushing and spraying the material toward the prod with snout and forepaws.

Similar behaviors were also observed in those animals burying with blocks. They would sometimes move toward the prod pushing blocks ahead of them with snout and forepaws. Although this behavior was effective in accumulating blocks near the prod, it was necessary for the subjects to pick the blocks up in order to form a pile. Thus, most of the subjects in the "blocks condition" also picked blocks up in their teeth and threw or placed them in a pile with teeth and forepaws. Moreover, careful observation of this behavior suggested that it was far from haphazard. On several occasions, a block positioned on the pile to cover the last exposed portion of the shock prod toppled to the floor, from which it was quickly retrieved and returned to its original position on the pile.

What do rats do if there is no available burying material in the vicinity of the shock source? If there is burying material available somewhere else in the chamber, they may transport it to the prod for use in its burial. In one study, rats carried wooden blocks piled beneath the control prod to the other end of the chamber where they were used to bury the shock prod (Pinel & Treit, 1979). We have also seen rats pile their own feces on shock sources when other materials were unavailable, and Silverman (1978) reported that rats used their own feces to block an intake duct carrying cigarette smoke into a barren test environment. Whillans and Shettleworth (1981), Arnaut and Shettleworth (1981), and Moser, Tait, and Kirby (1980) have all reported that rats will use sawdust to bury shock sources.

6. Conditioned Burying in Rats Free to Escape

Although demonstrations of conditioned defensive burying can serve as a basis for questioning the restrictive methodology of traditional aversive conditioning paradigms, the burying paradigm itself is restrictive in at least one important way. The ability of subjects to flee from the source of aversive stimulation is always restricted by the conditioning chamber. Our 44 × 30 cm test chambers, although not inordinately small by usual standards, did not afford the subject an opportunity to leave the immediate vicinity of the shock prod. As a result, an important question remained concerning the generality of the conditioned burying response. Is conditioned burying a reaction that occurs only in those cases in which rats have no opportunity for flight?

To answer this question Pinel, Treit, Ladak, and MacLennan (1980) compared the conditioned defensive burying of rats in chambers of different size: 25 × 20 cm, 50 × 40 cm, 100 × 60 cm, or 200 × 80 cm. The results are summarized in Fig. 9.3. Although burying behavior was rare in the no-shock control groups, the rats in each of the four experimental groups spent significant ($p < .05$) amounts of time burying the prod. Thus, increases in the floor dimensions of the test chamber up to 200 × 80 cm, 12 times the floor area of the apparatus used by Pinel and Treit (1978), were not sufficient to eliminate the conditioned defensive burying of a well-defined shock source. There was, however, an obvious tendency (see Fig. 9.3) for the rats tested in the smaller chambers to spend more time burying. In the same vein, Pinel, Treit, Ladak, and MacLennan (1980) and Moser, Tait, and Kirby (1980) have reported conditioned defensive burying in rats free to flee to a separate "safe" compartment in the appa-

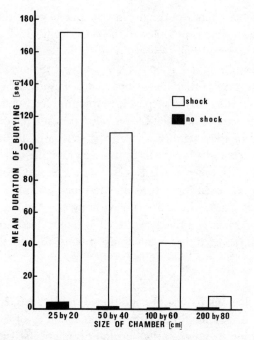

FIGURE 9.3. Mean duration of burying by shock and no-shock animals tested in each of the four chambers of different size (Pinel, Treit, Ladak, & MacLennan, 1980).

ratus. Thus, although the amount of conditioned defensive burying does appear to be influenced by the opportunity for flight, it is not limited to situations in which rats are restricted to the immediate vicinity of the source of aversive stimulation.

7. SHOCK INTENSITY AND CONDITIONED DEFENSIVE BURYING

The relationship between shock intensity and conditioned defensive burying is illustrated in Fig. 9.4 (Treit, Pinel, & Terlecki, 1980). Although burying behavior was observed at a wide range of shock intensities, more time was spent burying the prod and bedding was piled higher at the higher intensities.

During the course of this experiment, Treit et al. (1980) noticed an interesting relationship between the subjects' latencies to return to the vicinity of the prod and the amount of burying they engaged in. Those subjects returning to the prod most quickly tended to engage in the most conditioned burying. The correlation between each experimental animal's latency to enter the 7-cm^2 area around the prod and the amount of time

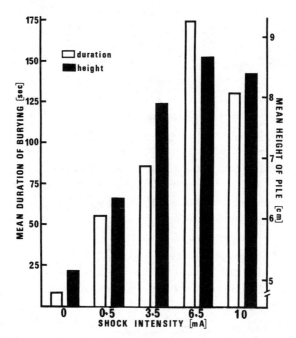

FIGURE 9.4. Mean duration of burying and the mean height of the bedding material accumulated by rats shocked at different intensities (Treit, Pinel, & Terlecki, 1980).

spent burying was − .380. This significant ($p < .05$) negative correlation is particularly interesting in view of the fact that latency has been the accepted measure of retention in comparable situations (one-trial passive avoidance; cf. Pinel, 1968). It is assumed that subjects approaching a shock source do not remember the previous consequences of such behavior. The observation that those rats returning to the prod sooner engaged in more defensive burying constitutes a direct challenge to this common assumption.

8. ORGANISMIC VARIABLES

Adult, male, hooded rats have been the subjects in most studies of defensive burying. To what extent do the results of these investigations hold for subjects of a different age, sex, species, or strain? The effects of these organismic variables on defensive burying were systematically investigated in three experiments by Treit, Terlecki, and Pinel (1980).

In one of the three experiments, males and females of four different species of rodent were studied in the discriminated defensive burying paradigm. Male and female Long-Evans hooded rats, CD-1 albino mice, Mongolian gerbils, and Syrian golden hamsters ($n = 10$) were habituated to the standard 44×30 cm test chamber in the usual fashion on the first four days of the experiment. On the fifth day, each subject was shocked by one of two prods (white or black) mounted on opposite end walls of the chamber. The 15-minute test began as soon as the shock was administered. Both rats and mice selectively buried the shock prod. However, the burying response was absent in gerbils and hamsters. There were no significant differences in burying between males and females of any of the four species. It has been confirmed in other laboratories that neither hamsters (Whillans & Shettleworth, 1981) nor gerbils (Davis & Whiteside, 1980) engage in conditioned defensive burying. These results suggest that burying behavior is a defensive response typical of some types of rodent (rats and mice), but not others (hamsters and gerbils). However, it is premature to rule out the possibility that hamsters and/or gerbils may display defensive burying under other experimental conditions.

In the second study, significant levels of conditioned burying were observed in three strains of rats (i.e., Long-Evans, Wistar, and Fischer) and three strains of mice (i.e., CD-1, CF-1, and BALB/c). The Fischer rats engaged in burying activity significantly longer ($p < .05$) than did the Long-Evans rats, but neither of these strains were significantly different from the Wistar rats. The mice of the CF-1 strain buried significantly longer than did the CD-1 and BALB mice. Conditioned defensive burying has also been observed in Sprague-Dawley (McKim & Lett, 1979) and Holtzman rats (Davis & Rossheim, 1980).

In a third and final study of organismic variables by Treit et al. (1980), the effect of age on the conditioned defensive burying of rats was assessed. An equal number of male and female Long-Evans hooded rats ($n = 10$) were tested in the single-prod paradigm at 30, 60, and 90 days of age. The most important finding was that almost every rat displayed some burying behavior—even those 30 days of age. However, both the 60 and the 90-day-old rats buried significantly ($p < .05$) more than did the 30-day-old rats. Again, there were no significant differences between the burying behavior of males and females.

Thus, early in development, just 9 days after weaning, the rat is capable of burying sources of aversive stimulation. It is interesting to note that by 30 days of age, wild rats already spend time outside their burrow systems and thus could benefit from the protection from predation afforded by defensive behaviors (Calhoun, 1962). Owings and Coss (1977) found that young, laboratory-reared ground squirrels directed more burying behavior at a snake than at a comparable control object (a long, green, string-pulled nylon bag) at first encounter. The fact that very young laboratory-reared rodents will display defensive burying is consistent with Bolles's hypothesis that defensive reactions are innate (Bolles, 1970).

9. Is Burying Defensive?

Pinel and Treit (1978), in their initial report, gave two reasons for their assumption that burying can be a defensive behavior. First, burying was reliably elicited by foot shock. Second, burying behavior directed at well-defined sources of painful stimulation in the rat's natural environment could reasonably be expected to reduce the chance of subsequent injury. However, since then, several other lines of research have provided additional evidence that the label "defensive burying" is indeed appropriate.

Several experiments have established that burying is the reliable response to a variety of potentially hazardous objects other than sources of painful foot shock. In laboratory experiments, rats have buried such complex novel stimuli as traps, flashbulbs (Terlecki et al., 1979), or stimulus cards (Hudson, 1950) when they were first encountered in the test environment. Even the wall-mounted prod may attract some burying activity when it first appears in a familiar test chamber (McKim & Lett, 1979; Moser et al., 1980; Pinel & Treit, 1978). Laboratory rats also bury "neutral" objects that have previously been the source of any one of a number of aversive stimuli, such as a shock (Treit, Pinel, & Terlecki, 1980), an airblast, a light flash, a physical blow (Terlecki et al., 1979), or cigarette smoke (Silverman, 1978). Moreover, Pinel, Hoyer, and Terlecki (1980) showed that approach-avoidance behavior was observed in conjunction with burying behavior in several different contexts.

Further support for the idea that burying can serve a defensive function in the rat's natural environment comes from reports that burying occurs in a variety of test environments designed to mimic certain aspects of the natural environment. Burying has been observed in test chambers large enough to permit some degree of flight (Pinel, Treit, Ladak, & MacLennan, 1980), in chambers where burying materials were not readily available in the vicinity of the prod (Pinel & Treit, 1979), or in chambers where burying materials were restricted to natural (e.g., sand, Pinel & Treit, 1979; feces, Silverman, 1978) or cumbersome (e.g., blocks, Pinel & Treit, 1979) materials. Also relevant are reports of burying in experiments in which the conditioning and/or testing phases were conducted in the rats' home laboratory environment (Pinel & Treit, 1978; Wilkie et al., 1979).

The best evidence that burying by rodents can serve a defensive function in the wild comes from a series of studies of the reaction of California ground squirrels to snakes by Owings and Coss (e.g., Owings & Coss,

1977; Coss & Owings, 1978). They reported that the ground squirrels elicited defensive behaviors in the snakes by spraying sand at them with a forelimb spraying response comparable to that used by domestic rats to bury aversive objects in laboratory studies. Because the amount of defensive burying by the ground squirrels was correlated with the number of hisses, but not the number of strikes by the snake, Owings and Coss suggested that burying may be the only way that ground squirrels can harass snakes without increasing the probability of being bitten.

It should be emphasized that support for the view that burying behavior can serve a defensive function in some contexts does not imply that it cannot also serve other functions. For example, running can clearly be viewed as a defensive behavior in some contexts and yet it undeniably serves a variety of other functions in nonthreatening situations. Three lines of research have a bearing on this issue. First, Wilkie et al. (1979) questioned whether the burial of noxious food sources is defensive. Because rats so readily learn to avoid consuming aversive substances it is difficult to see how an individual rat would be protected by burying a noxious food that it would not consume in any case. Wilkie et al. (1979) and Whillans and Shettleworth (1981) have suggested that burying in such situations might serve an altruistic function, i.e., that its primary benefit might be to other members of the species. Second, Poling, Cleary, and Monaghan (1981) observed that rats would sometimes bury such non-threatening objects as food pellets and glass marbles, and on this basis they concluded that in some contexts burying is most appropriately viewed as a component of hoarding behavior. Third, Pinel, Gorzalka, and Ladak (1981) argued that the burial of dead conspecifics by rats is not a simple case of the rats protecting themselves from the aversive odor of the carcass. Carr, Landauer, Wiese, Marasco, and Thor (1979) found that food-deprived rats were more likely to eat aged carcasses than fresh ones, and Montoya, Sutherland, and Whishaw (1981) found that rats would consume more cadaverine-soaked food pellets than normal pellets. Thus, although aged rat carcasses and cadaverine-soaked objects are undeniably aversive to humans and are extremely effective in eliciting burying responses in rats, the fact that the rat seems to find such odors appetizing in some contexts suggests that such instances of burying do not serve the simple function of protecting the rat from irritating odors.

C. NEUROSCIENTIFIC APPLICATIONS OF THE CONDITIONED DEFENSIVE BURYING PARADIGM

To date, the conditioned defensive burying phenomenon has been used in our laboratory to study brain-behavior relations in three quite different ways: (1) to assess the effects of pimozide on learning and memory, (2) to explore the role of the septum in defensive behavior, and (3) to assess the anxiolytic effects of drugs. These three applications will be discussed separately in the following three sections.

1. Effect of Pimozide on Conditioned Defensive Burying

A number of recent neuropharmacological studies have examined the role played by dopamine in the mediation of learned responses (e.g., Fibiger, Zis, & Phillips, 1975; Neimegeers, Vanbruggen, & Janssen, 1969; Ranje & Ungerstedt, 1977). By administering neuroleptics, which interfere with the functioning of dopaminergic pathways, neuropharmacologists have disrupted the performance of learned responses. However, before these data can be taken as evidence for the involvement of dopamine in associative learning, alternative, simpler interpretations must be ruled out. For example, the commonly employed neuroleptics pimozide and haloperidol have powerful effects on motor functioning that could in themselves account for many observed deficits in performance.

One simple way of differentiating between the motor-deficit and the learning-deficit interpretation of the impairments displayed by neuroleptic-treated subjects is to separate the learning and testing phases in time so that the pharmacological state of subjects during these two stages can be independently manipulated. If the test performance of drug-free subjects injected with pimozide during the previous learning phase were disrupted, this would be strong evidence that the effects of pimozide were on learning per se rather than on the performance of learned responses. Unfortunately, the multiple-trial conditioning paradigms typically used to assess the effects of neuroleptic drugs on learning (e.g., shuttle box, Fibiger et al., 1975; Neimegeers et al., 1969) cannot be divided readily into separate conditioning and test phases.

In contrast to responses acquired in traditional multiple-trial conditioning procedures, the defensive burying response can be reliably elicited after only a single conditioning trial, even when the interval between conditioning and testing is as long as 20 days (Pinel & Treit, 1978). Thus, in the conditioned defensive burying paradigm, it is quite possible to administer a drug to a subject during the conditioning phase and then to test the subject at a later time when it is drug free.

This feature of the conditioned defensive burying paradigm was recently exploited in two studies by Beninger, MacLennan, and Pinel (1980) designed to assess the effects of pimozide on associative learning. In the first experiment, pimozide was injected into the experimental rats prior to both the conditioning and testing phases; the controls, however, received two injections of the vehicle. The pimozide produced a substantial deficit

BEHAVIORAL APPROACHES TO BRAIN RESEARCH

in conditioned defensive burying, thus confirming previous reports (e.g., Neimegeers et al., 1969) that the performance of learned responses is disrupted in rats under the influence of pimozide during both conditioning and testing. However, the fact that pimozide also reduced locomotor activity suggested that the deficits in defensive burying might be due to motor impairment rather than to a disruption of associative processes.

In the second experiment, Beninger et al. (1980) conditioned rats while they were under the influence of pimozide, but tested them in its absence. The results supported the hypothesis that the disruptive effects of pimozide on conditioned responding were due to motor impairment. Pimozide during the conditioning phase had no detectable effect on the amount of burying behavior displayed during the drug-free test phase. The amount of burying behavior during the test phase displayed by rats given pimozide during conditioning was not significantly different from that displayed by the vehicle controls. Thus, although pimozide does generally impair the motor processes that subserve the burying response, it does not appear to disrupt the associative learning processes that mediate conditioned defensive burying. Thus, integrity of dopamine neuronal systems does not appear to be a necessary condition for associative learning (cf. Beninger, Mason, Phillips, & Fibiger, 1980).

2. Effect of Septal Lesions on Conditioned Defensive Burying

One of the oldest and most widely used methods for determining the neural correlates of behavior is the lesion technique. Discrete areas of the brain are removed and the effects of these lesions on a specified behavior are observed. Although traditional conditioning paradigms have frequently served as assays of the effects of experimental brain lesions, interest has recently shifted to the effects of brain lesions on naturally occurring units of behavior (cf. Konishi, 1971). In particular, many neuroscientists have focused their attention on the neural mechanisms controlling defensive behaviors (e.g., Moyer, 1968). Accordingly, the purpose of two studies by Gray, Terlecki, Treit, and Pinel (1981) was to investigate the neural correlates of defensive burying. The septal area was the focus for these studies because it had previously been implicated in the regulation of other defensive behaviors (Blanchard, Blanchard, Lee, & Nakamura, 1979).

In the first experiment of Gray et al. (1981), male hooded rats received bilateral electrolytic septal lesions or sham lesions. After a 21-day recovery period, each rat was exposed individually to the apparatus on four consecutive days. On the next day, one-half of the rats in each of the two groups were assigned to a shock or no-shock condition. Each rat in the shock condition was tested in the standard one-prod paradigm. The control subjects were treated in exactly the same way, except that they were not shocked. In addition to taking the standard measures of burying, the frequency of contacts with the prod was recorded.

The major finding of this study was that septal lesions completely eliminated defensive burying. Not one of the septal-lesioned animals in either the shock or no-shock conditions engaged in defensive burying, whereas every shocked animal in the sham-lesion group displayed the burying response. In contrast, the septal lesions had no significant effect on the other measures of defensive behavior, i.e., the shock-produced suppression of prod approaches and contacts was unaffected. These results suggested that normal septal functioning is required for rats to perform the defensive burying response, but that it is not required for rats to form the association between the prod and the shock.

A second study was conducted in order to investigate the possibility that more specific anatomical areas within the septum may mediate the burying response (cf. Blanchard et al., 1979). Accordingly, the rats in Experiment 2 received anterior septal lesions, posterior septal lesions, or sham lesions before being habituated, conditioned, and tested as in the preceding experiment. As can be seen in Figure 9.5, the posterior septal lesions completely suppressed defensive burying and the anterior septal lesions had no discernible effect on the burying behavior. As in the preceding experiment, there were no other significant differences between the behavior of subjects in the experimental groups. The rats in all three shocked groups were less likely to approach and contact the prod after the shock.

The remarkable specificity of the effect of the septal lesions is difficult to explain in terms of such general deficits as impaired associative learning, decreased fear motivation, or deficits in motor function. Animals with lesions that included the posterior septum were able to passively avoid the shock source in a normal manner, suggesting that the mechanisms of associative learning and fear motivation were not grossly disrupted by the lesions. Nor were there any obvious signs of motor impairment in these rats. Their behavior in the test situation appeared to be identical in every respect to that of controls, except that they did not display the burying response. Thus, the posterior septum appears to play a specific role in the control of the defensive burying response in rats.

These results are comparable in some respects to those of Kolb and Whishaw (1981). They found that neodecortication (Kolb & Whishaw, 1981a) or frontal lesions (Kolb & Whishaw, 1981b) in either neonatal or adult rats abolished conditioned defensive burying without disrupting the tendency of the rats to avoid the shock prod. Contrary to our usual procedure, Kolb and Whishaw left the shock circuit on during the entire testing procedure, and they found that decorticate rats like intact controls rarely received more than one or two shocks during the test.

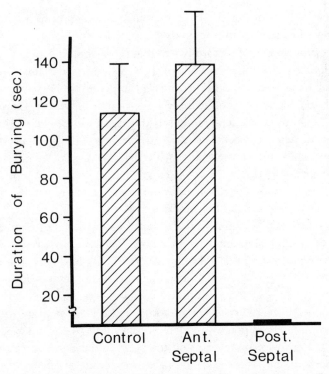

FIGURE 9.5. Mean duration (± SEM) of burying by rats given control (sham) lesions, anterior septal lesions, or posterior septal lesions (Gray, Terlecki, Treit, & Pinel, 1981).

3. EFFECT OF ANXIOLYTIC DRUGS ON CONDITIONED DEFENSIVE BURYING

The possibility that the unconditioned and conditioned defensive burying paradigms could be useful in the study of anxiolytic drug effects was assessed during a recent series of experiments by Treit, Pinel, and Fibiger (1981). The purpose of the first study in this series was to demonstrate that the burying paradigms fulfill the major criteria of a valid screening procedure for anxiolytic agents, i.e., there is a dose-dependent sensitivity to a known anxiolytic agent and the side effects (e.g., ataxia) are distinguishable from the "anxiolytic" effects (cf. Lippa, Nash, & Greenblatt, 1979). Accordingly, rats received a 0.5 mg/kg ($n = 30$), 1.0 mg/kg ($n = 30$), or 2.0 mg/kg ($n = 30$) intraperitoneal injection of diazepam (Roche) or its vehicle ($n = 30$) 30 minutes before being placed individually in the Plexiglas test chamber. One-third of the rats in each group were given a brief 1 mA shock and another one-third, a 10 mA shock when they first contacted the wire-wrapped prod that was mounted on the wall of the chamber. The remaining one-third in each group were tested in the chamber

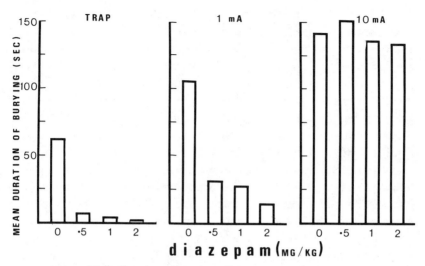

FIGURE 9.6. Mean duration of burying of a novel trap, a 1-mA shock source, or a 10-mA shock source by rats given different doses of diazepam (Treit, Pinel, & Fibiger, 1981).

with a novel object (i.e., mouse-trap) known to produce burying behavior without being paired with such aversive stimulation as shock (i.e., unconditioned burying). Thus, the design was a 4 × 3 factorial, with four levels of drug dosage and three levels of test stimuli. All subjects were observed for 15 minutes after the shock or the first contact with the trap.

Diazepam significantly reduced the duration of burying when the shock level was low or when the trap was the test object (Fig. 9.6). This suppression was significant at every dose and increased with increases in dose. In contrast, there was no significant reduction of burying at any of the doses when rats received the high-intensity shock.

These results established that burying behavior can be sensitive, in a dose-dependent fashion, to the effects of a known anxiolytic agent. The fact that burying was not suppressed in the high-intensity shock condition suggests that the suppression of responding produced by diazepam in the presence of the novel object and after low-intensity shock was not due to gross motor or perceptual deficits. Furthermore, because unconditioned burying of the trap was suppressed by diazepam, it is difficult to argue that the suppressive effects of diazepam are due to its putative analgesic properties. Taken together, these results suggest that the defensive burying procedure can be a useful paradigm for studying the anxiolytic effects of drugs.

Treit, Pinel, and Fibiger (1981) provided two further lines of evidence

for their view that conditioned defensive burying could prove to be a valuable addition to the behavioral techniques available for studying anxiolytic
effects. First. they found that the relative potencies of diazepam, chlordiazepoxide, and pentobarbital in the burying paradigm compared favor-
ably with the relative potencies of these drugs in clinical settings. Second,
they showed that the effects of anxiolytics on conditioned burying appeared to be dissociable from the effects of other drugs that disrupt this
behavior. Stimulants (picrotoxin, metrazol, *d*-amphetamine) either had no
consistent effect on the burying response or increased responding slightly.
Major tranquilizers, such as chlorpromazine, depressed responding, but
unlike anxiolytic compounds, this depression also occurred at the high
intensities of shock, suggesting that these compounds produced a general
motor impairment in the test animals (cf. Schlechter & Butcher, 1972).
Taken together, these results indicate that the conditioned defensive burying paradigm could prove to be a major improvement over the cumbersome behavioral techniques currently used to assess the potential of pro-
spective anxiolytic agents.

D. CONCLUSIONS

Although the conditioned defensive burying paradigm is a recent addition to the behavioral techniques available for studying brain-behavior
interactions, there is already considerable evidence that it will prove to be
a valuable tool in the hands of behavioral neuroscientists. The research on
conditioned defensive burying, which was comprehensively reviewed in
the preceding sections, has already revealed a number of features of the
phenomenon that indicate that continued investigation will prove to be
productive.

Robustness. A cursory inspection of any of the figures included in this
chapter stands as ample testimony to the robustness of the conditioned
defensive burying paradigm. In each experiment, there was little if any
overlap between the burying scores of unshocked control rats and those
receiving a *single* prod shock. In fact, it was not uncommon for burying
behavior to be displayed by every shocked rat in a group even when the
behavior was absent in unshocked controls.

Selectivity. Rats selectively buried a source of aversive stimulation in the
presence of comparable or even identical control objects. For example, 42
of 42 subjects in Experiment 3 of Terlecki et al. (1979), 10 of 10 subjects
in Experiment 4 of Pinel and Treit (1978), and 47 of 47 subjects in Experiments 1 and 2 of Pinel and Treit (1979) buried the source of aversive
stimulation more than they did the control object. This selectivity makes

it possible in some situations to use subjects as their own controls, eliminating the need for no-shock control groups.

Speed of Acquisition. An important attribute of defensive burying is that it can be reliably conditioned in only a single trial. Thus, the conditioned defensive burying paradigm is particularly useful in those instances when it is necessary to specify the exact time of learning.

Generality. Although there have been relatively few studies of conditioned defensive burying, it has already been established that conditioned defensive burying is not specific to situations that involve a particular level of shock, a particular type of aversive stimulus, a particular type of test environment, a particular type of burying material, or a particular strain, species, sex, or age of rodent. This generality facilitates the tailoring of the conditioned defensive burying paradigm to the demands of particular experiments. For example, Beninger et al. (1980) modified the usual paradigm to compensate for the inactivity of pimozide-treated rats during the conditioning trial. Rather than waiting for the lethargic rats to come into contact with the prod, each rat was placed on the prod by the experimenter so that it could be shocked without delay. This procedure produced the usual high levels of burying during a later test in which the subjects were tested in a drug-free state. Thus, the conditioning of defensive burying is a form of stimulus-stimulus learning that can occur even when subjects do not voluntarily contact the source of aversive stimulation; as such, the paradigm may be a particularly valuable means of producing associative learning in animals rendered temporarily immobile by various pharmacological or physiological treatments.

Retention. Although defensive burying can be conditioned in only a single trial, the conditioning has been shown to endure. Rats shocked once by a prod showed significantly more burying behavior than did unshocked controls even when they were not tested for 20 days (Pinel & Treit, 1978), and rats shocked by one of two comparable prods selectively buried the shock prod 24 hours later (Pinel, Treit, & Wilkie, 1980).

The conditioned defensive burying paradigm is not only an alternative to traditional avoidance conditioning paradigms. Traditional avoidance paradigms are arranged so that the only way a rat can reduce the probability of subsequent aversive stimulation is to flee from it (active avoidance), stay away from it (passive avoidance), or to perform an arbitrary operant response, such as a lever press. The belief that fleeing from or staying away from aversive objects is the primary method of defense for rodents is so prevalent that when rats are observed to approach sources of aversive stimulation, they are frequently assumed to have amnesia (cf. Pinel, 1968). However, the conditioned defensive burying paradigm demonstrates that rats and mice, like humans, can avoid aversive stimulation

by approaching their sources and coping with them. In view of the fact
that burying a source of aversive stimulation potentially reduces the probability of subsequent contact with it, and in so doing reduces the probability of subsequent aversive stimulation, defensive burying can be appropriately viewed as avoidance behavior. Because this form of avoidance
learning is so different from the types of avoidance learning that have been
studied extensively in neuroscientific research, its investigation provides
a new perspective from which to view defensive behavior, avoidance conditioning, and their physiological correlates.

III | Generalizing in Brain-Behavior Research

10 | Problems and Principles Underlying Interspecies Comparisons

BRYAN KOLB and IAN Q. WHISHAW

A. INTRODUCTION

The problems inherent in generalizing about brain-behavior relation-ships among species can best be understood by reviewing the history of behavioral contributions to brain research. The modern experimental study of the relationship between the brain's activity and behavior can be traced to the early 1820's, in the studies of Flourens. Gall and Spurzheim had hypothesized in their phrenology that psychological functions were local-ized in the brain in discrete regions of the neocortex. Flourens rejected the concept of localization of function and developed an experimental technique with which to buttress his philosophical arguments: he surgi-cally removed the cerebrum of animals and studied the changes in their behavior. From his experiments he concluded that there was no localiza-tion of function in the cerebrum and that all intellectual faculties resided there coextensively. Although it is now generally accepted that Flourens' experiments devastated the science of phrenology, it is ironic that they should have been so influential. Most of his experiments were performed with pigeons and chickens, animals with virtually no neocortex, and his behavioral tests were assessments of such activities as eating and wing flapping, behaviors that bore no relation to the faculties proposed for the cortex by Gall and Spurzheim. In spite of these faults Flourens' experi-ments remain important to contemporary neuropsychology because they illustrate a number of fundamental problems that have plagued neuro-psychology from Flourens' time to the present. First, Flourens' experi-ments raise the basic question of whether studies with nonhuman species can provide information about brain-behavior relations in humans. Sec-ond, they demonstrate the problem of selecting the nonhuman species that is suitable for testing a particular hypothesis. Third, they lead us to confront the issue of which behaviors in nonhumans can be considered similar enough to those observed in humans to allow generalizations. Fourth, they demonstrate the problem of how many tests of a given behavior are necessary to allow valid generalizations to be made. This chapter addresses each of these questions in turn.

B. SHOULD ANIMALS BE USED IN NEUROPSYCHOLOGY?

To many people, psychology is seen as being wholly independent of the study of animals. Psychology is the study of *human* behavior; neuropsychology involves the study of the *human* brain. In this view, it is largely assumed that both human neuroanatomy and human cognitive processes differ fundamentally from those of nonhumans. This view rests primarily upon two assumptions. First, it has been assumed that the development of human language has resulted in a fundamentally different cortical organization in humans and nonhumans, particularly in the parietal lobe. Second, it has been widely assumed that the human brain and the nonhuman brain differ in that the association areas of the frontal, temporal and parietal lobes of the cerebral cortex are asymmetrically organized in the former and symmetrically organized in the latter. Although there is no question that rats or monkeys are not merely little men in fur suits, there is no compelling evidence to support these assumptions; that is, there is no evidence of a qualitative difference in either the structure or organization of the brains of human and nonhuman mammals.

1. STRUCTURAL COMPARISONS

Neuroanatomists have long realized that a simple comparison of the brain size of different species is not a valid basis for comparison, since brain size is confounded with body size. Thus, for example, elephants would be expected to have larger brains than shrews simply because it requires more neurons to operate the much larger body of the elephant. Brain sizes can be compared, taking body size into account, by using the encephalization quotient or EQ (Jerison, 1973). The EQ is the ratio of actual brain size to expected brain size where the expected brain size is a kind of average for living mammals. Thus, the average, or typical, mammal (which incidentally is the cat) has an EQ of 1.0. Animals that deviate from 1.0 have brains larger or smaller than would be expected for a mammal of that particular body size. Thus, the rat has an EQ of 0.4, whereas the chimpanzee has an EQ of 2.48 and the human an EQ of 6.30. The rat brain is therefore only 0.4 times as large as expected for a typical mammal of that body size, the chimpanzee has a brain 2.48 times as large as expected for a typical mammal of that body size, and the human brain is 6.3 times as large as expected for a typical mammal of that body size. The

EQ makes it clear that the human brain is really larger than the brains of most other mammals. This high EQ is not unique to humans, however; the EQ of the dolphin is about 6.0, and, thus, comparable.

The question arises as to whether a larger brain is qualitatively different from a smaller brain or whether a larger brain is merely a larger (scaled-up) version of the same basic brain? According to Jerison (1973), as the EQ increases, nearly all structures of the brain increase in size, but it is the neocortex that shows the most dramatic increase. To validly compare the increase in the neocortex relative to the increase in the remaining brain structures, Stephan and Andy (1969) calculated a progression index: the ratio of actual neocortex to the expected neocortex of a typical mammal. The progression index shows that the volume of human neocortex is 3.2 times greater than the predicted volume for nonhuman primates, in general, and nearly three times greater than that predicted for a chimpanzee of the same body weight. These figures mean that the increase in neocortex volume from the apes to humans is greater than would be expected from the trends within the other primates. Where in the neocortex does this increase occur? Passingham (1973) demonstrated that the increase in volume of the human neocortex does not occur in the primary sensory or motor cortex, but rather within the association cortex. Within primate phylogeny, the association cortex increases progressively as a proportion of the total neocortex. Thus, although the association cortex makes up a greater proportion of the human neocortex than would be expected from looking at the chimpanzee brain, Passingham concludes that, given the phylogenetic trend, humans do not have more association cortex than would be predicted for a primate with so much neocortex.

Luria (1973), Geschwind (1965), and Konorski (1967) have all argued that fundamental differences exist between the parietal lobes of human and nonhuman primates. These authors have claimed that there is no homologue of the angular gyrus in nonhumans, and Konorski (1967) has questioned the existence of the arcuate fasciculus, which connects the posterior part of the parietal-temporal junction with the frontal cortex, in nonhumans. In a thorough review of this issue, Passingham and Ettlinger (1974) conclude that Konorski was in error because there is clear evidence that the arcuate fasciculus exists in nonhuman primates, and to date there is no unequivocal evidence of major differences between the angular gyrus in humans and in other primates. Indeed, they point out that the only clear anatomical difference between human and nonhuman primate brains is the larger size of the human brain. In humans, the main selection pressure was for a larger brain with more association neocortex. In other words, although the human brain is larger than would be expected for a primate of the same body weight, this increase in brain size is attributable to a general increase in association cortex. In summary, there is no compelling evidence that there is a qualitative difference between the brains of humans and those of other mammals.

2. LOCALIZATION OF CEREBRAL FUNCTIONS TO SITE AND SIDE

Two of the most striking characteristics of cerebral organization in humans are that functions are relatively localized within the cerebral cortex and that many functions are relatively lateralized to one hemisphere or the other. It has been known for over 100 years that language functions are localized primarily in the frontal and parietal-temporal zones of the left hemisphere in right-handed people. Although specific functions of the right hemisphere were not discovered until more recent times, it has been known for at least 30 years that visuospatial functions are localized primarily in the posterior regions of the right hemisphere. Today, any comprehensive discussion of human brain function will describe both the side and site of cerebral functions as fundamental principles underlying cerebral organization in humans (e.g., Luria, 1973; Kolb & Whishaw, 1980). If we are to use animals in neuropsychology, it is therefore of paramount interest to know whether or not the two basic principles of functional cerebral organization in humans (localization and lateralization) underlie functional cerebral organization in nonhumans.

(i) Localization

Although the initial studies of Lashley on the effects of cortical ablation in rats and monkeys (Lashley, 1929, 1939) did not support the concept of localization of function in the rat and monkey, subsequent work has demonstrated that not only are functions localized in the cortex of nonhuman mammals, but also that similar functions are localized in homologous regions. Thus, for example, lesions of the primary motor cortex of a variety of mammalian species are associated with remarkably similar effects. Rats, cats, and monkeys all experience deficits in the use of the distal muscles, such as manipulating objects with the forepaws (cf. Kolb & Whishaw, 1980). The principle of localization of function to specific sites within the cerebral hemispheres thus appears valid for both humans and nonhumans.

(ii) Lateralization

Evidence of lateralization of function in nonhuman mammalian brains has, however, been more difficult to obtain. Indeed, until very recently, it was commonly reported that unilateral excision of cortical tissue outside the primary sensory or motor regions of nonhumans did not significantly affect many behaviors altered by unilateral lesions (e.g., Warren, Cornwell, & Warren, 1969). Thus, although isolated reports suggested asymmetrical effects of left and right cerebral hemispheric lesions in nonhumans (e.g. Hamilton & Lund, 1970; Webster, 1972), the evidence overwhelmingly supported the view that there was a fundamental difference in the functional organization of human and nonhuman brains: functions were asymmetrically organized in the human brain and symmetrically organized in the nonhuman brain.

Recent anatomical and behavioral evidence has suggested that this conclusion may be in error; cerebral asymmetry may indeed by a characteristic of mammalian brains. Several groups have reported that lesions in the region of the cerebral artery of the right, but not the left hemisphere of rats are associated with an increase in wheel running activity (Robinson, 1979; Sherman, Garbanati, Rosen, Yutzey, & Denenberg, 1980; Kolb & Whishaw, 1980). Furthermore, there is reliable evidence of a consistent anatomical difference between the left and right hemispheres in rats, a difference that may underlie the observed behavioral asymmetry (Diamond, Johnson, & Ingham, 1975; Robinson & Coyle, 1980; Qke, Lewis, & Adams, 1980; Kolb, Sutherland, Nonneman, & Whishaw, in press). These studies have shown that the right hemisphere of the rat is larger and heavier than the left hemisphere and also that the cerebral cortex is thicker on the right than on the left. Furthermore there is a difference in the distribution of catecholamines within the two hemispheres.

Unequivocal evidence of functional asymmetry in monkeys has been elusive. Studies of the visual system have consistently yielded negative results, which is somewhat surprising considering the anatomical similarity of the visual systems in humans and other primates. Recent findings suggestive of functional asymmetry in the auditory system are somewhat more encouraging. Petersen, Beecher, Zoloth, Moody, and Stebbins (1978) studied the ability of Japanese macaques to discriminate among communicatively relevant sounds and irrelevant sounds. The animals were able to discriminate communicatively relevant sounds presented to the right ear (hence, left hemisphere) better than those presented to the left ear (hence, right hemisphere). These results suggest that Japanese macaques engage in left-hemisphere processing in a way that is analogous to that of humans.

In conclusion, although it is likely that the degree of cerebral asymmetry increases as the amount of cerebral cortex increases, it appears that lateralization of some functions commonly occurs in placental mammals. Just as the human brain is larger and has more cerebral cortex than expected for a mammal of its body size, it is probable that if a "lateralization quotient" analogous to the encephalization quotient could be calculated, the human brain would have greater lateralization of function than expected for a mammal of its body size. This increased asymmetry would not, however, be evidence of a qualitative difference in the cerebral organization of the brain of humans and the brain of other mammals, and it would not impugn the use of animals in neuropsychology.

C. SELECTING THE ANIMAL

We have argued that nonhuman species can be validly used in the study of human brain-behavior relationships. It must not be assumed, however, that all species are equally useful for all problems. The choice of species obviously depends upon the nature of the problem under study. There are three principal lines of neuropsychological research, and for each the research species is chosen for different reasons. The lines of research include:

1. Studies directed toward understanding the basic mechanisms of brain function.

2. Studies designed to produce models of human neurological disorders.

3. Studies designed to describe the phylogenetic development of the brain.

We consider each of these separately.

1. STUDIES OF BASIC MECHANISMS

To date, the chief purpose of cross-species comparisons in neuropsychology has been to understand the basic mechanisms of brain function. In this type of comparative work, the species chosen for study depend upon the nature of the question asked. For example, neurophysiologists may choose to study the neural activity of giant nerve fibers in the squid because the nerve is so large and accessible. Similarly, neuropsychologists may choose to study the role of visual association cortex in visually guided behavior in cats or monkeys because these species have large visual association areas and, like humans, the behavior of cats and monkeys depends heavily upon visual input. Sometimes species are chosen merely for convenience or cost. We have chosen to study rats in our work on a model of Parkinson's disease because the neurochemical preparation and the maintenance of the animals is relatively simple (Whishaw, 1979; Schallert, Whishaw, Ramirez, & Teitelbaum, 1978a). Owing to difficulties in caring for the animals, such experiments are impractical with cats or monkeys.

2. MODELS OF HUMAN DISORDERS

In this type of comparative work, the aim is to produce the disorder, or a condition that simulates it, and then to manipulate numerous variables in order to try to understand the cause of the disorder and its course, and ultimately, to formulate a treatment. For example, a model of Parkinson's disease has been developed in the rat—not out of an interest in Parkinsonian rats per se, but rather to find the causes of their abnormal behaviors and to find ways to eliminate these behaviors. Rats are depleted of dopamine by injecting the neurotoxin 6-hydroxydopamine and they are studied over the ensuing weeks in a number of behavioral situations and under a variety of drug conditions. We have found that symptoms of Parkinson's disease such as blepharospasm, Meyerson's sign, resistance, rigidity, and various other dyskinesias can be found in the Parkinsonian rat and manipulated with such anti-Parkinsonian drugs such as L-dopa and atropine and that valid comparisons can be made to the symptomatology of Parkinson's disease in humans (e.g., Whishaw, 1979).

3. STUDIES OF PHYLOGENETIC DEVELOPMENT

Here, particular species are chosen because of their phylogenetic relationships. In this approach, it is assumed that understanding the phylogenetic development of the brain is important if we are to make meaningful cross species comparisons. Experiments with rats, cats, and rhesus monkeys do not permit inferences regarding evolutionary development because these species do not form an evolutionary sequence: rats were never ancestral to cats, nor cats to monkeys. All these species evolved independently from some primitive mammalian ancestor (see Fig. 10.1). In order to draw inferences regarding the evolutionary development of the brain it is necessary to choose closely related species that constitute what Hodos and Campbell (1969) have termed a quasi-evolutionary sequence. Thus, a series of animals that include the living descendants of groups believed to be ancestors of the more advanced forms are used (see Fig. 10.2). For example, Ravizza and Belmore (1978) studied the phylogenetic development of auditory processing by considering opossums, hedgehogs, tree shrews, bushbabies, macaques, chimpanzees, and humans. Each succeeding species listed above is believed to have evolved from a species something like the one listed before it. Ravizza and Belmore thus created a quasi-evolutionary lineage in order to make inferences about the neurological basis of auditory processing in humans. It would have been inappropriate for them to have chosen rats, cats, and monkeys as the subjects, since, as noted, these species represent parallel forms that have evolved independently for millions of years.

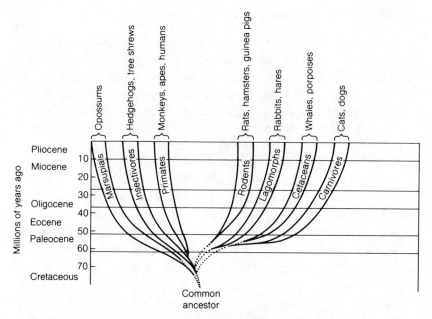

FIGURE 10.1. A phylogenetic tree showing the probable times of origin and affinities of the orders of mammals most commonly studied in neuropsychology (from Kolb & Whishaw, 1980).

4. THE RAT AS A DEFENSIBLE CHOICE

Although the most popular species used for research on the brain is the rat, there is some controversy over the appropriateness of using the rat in neuropsychological studies. Beginning with Schneirla in 1946 and Beach in 1950, there has been a continuing disenchantment with "rat runners" and periodic pronouncements that comparative and physiological psychology is rat infested (e.g., Dukes, 1960; Lockhart, 1968; Boice, 1971; Scott, 1973; Lown, 1975). For example, Lockhart (1968) documented the changes that have occurred in the domestication of feral Norway rats and concluded that the laboratory rat is an "indefensible choice" for comparative, or indeed general, behavioral research. Boice (1971) even went so far as to imply that "rat runners" have no place in contemporary psychology.

We have already noted that rats are not the best choice for studies in which the phylogenetic development of the brain is the primary interest, but we must also consider whether rats really are appropriate choices for other types of neuropsychological research. Although it is no doubt true that domesticated strains of Norway rats differ from their feral cousins, we are unaware of any compelling evidence that rats are "inferior, freaks,

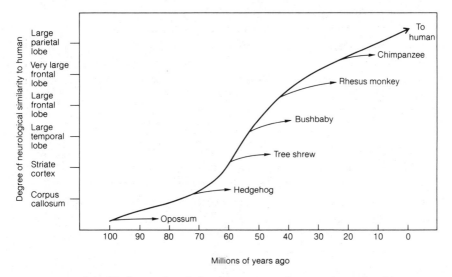

FIGURE 10.2. Phylogenetic relationships among the experimental subjects forming a quasi-evolutionary lineage. Notice that hedgehogs, tree shrews, bushbabies, monkeys, and apes are living animals taken to be close approximations of the ancestors of humans (from Kolb & Whishaw, 1980).

unnatural animals or degenerates" as Lockhart (1968) contends. For example, Dewsbury (1973) found that the basic copulatory pattern of laboratory rats is virtually identical to several non-domesticated rodent species. Similarly, Price (1972) studied learning in both feral and domestic rats and was unable to find a reliable difference in learning ability between the two varieties.

Laboratory rats became popular as subjects of psychological studies in the 1930's and they have been used in over half of the studies published in the *Journal of Comparative and Physiological Psychology* since that time (Gottlieb, 1976). Their initial popularity resulted from the widespread use of rats in conditioning and learning experiments (Beach, 1950). Although this connection might have been causal up to the 1950's or 1960's, it certainly is no longer (Gottlieb, 1976). Fewer and fewer neuropsychological studies are based on the conditioning and learning literature: rats are now the favorite choice for neuropsychological studies because most neurological studies use rats. Neuropsychologists can hardly do behavioral studies in the 1980's without carefully considering the wealth of neurophysiological, neurochemical, neuropharmacological, and neuroanatomical information available; this information is largely only available for the rat or other closely related rodent species. For example, a survey of the index listings for "hippocampus" in the 1980 Society for Neuroscience

Abstracts listed 92 papers on the hippocampus. Of these papers, 68 (72%) used rats and 12 (13%) others used closely related rodent species or rabbits. Of the remaining papers, four studied humans, two studied monkeys, and two studied cats, and in four others the species used was not specified. It is hardly any wonder that the rat is used in most neuropsychological studies of the hippocampus.

There are several advantages to this reliance upon the rat. First, as we have just noted, most research in neuroscience is done on the rat. Unless neuropsychologists are prepared to replicate the basic neurophysiological and neurochemical studies done with rats on other species that are more closely related phylogenetically to humans, it is best to use rats—at least for most studies of subcortical structures. Second, the rat has been thoroughly studied by psychologists since the 1930's, and it is now possible to describe the normal behavior of the rat (e.g., Barnett, 1963; Whishaw, Sutherland, & Kolb, Chapter 8, this volume). By comparing the normal behavior of the subject to its behavior following various neurological manipulations, behavioral abnormalities can be identified. Third, it is now possible to describe a standardized behavioral test battery analogous to neuropsychological test batteries used in clinical neuropsychology (cf. Kolb & Whishaw, 1980). The widespread use of a basic standardized test battery provides a basic framework from which to interpret other behavioral observations on the same animals across different laboratories and theoretical positions (see Whishaw et al., Chapter 8; Vanderwolf, Chapter 1, this volume).

We are not foolish enough to argue, or even to imply, that the rat is the ideal subject in neuropsychological work. We do wish to emphasize, however, that the rat is a defensible choice for many types of neuropsychological studies, and for many questions it may not only be a legitimate choice, it may be the only choice.

D. SELECTING THE BEHAVIOR TO STUDY

Each mammalian species has a unique behavioral repertoire that permits the animal to survive in its particular behavioral niche. In view of the diversity of the behavior of different species, it is necessary to identify comparable behaviors across species to allow valid cross species generalizations. Recall that Flourens chose to study eating and wing-flapping in birds in order to draw conclusions about the mental faculties suggested by Gall and Spurzheim. Few would seriously argue that Flourens chose appropriate behaviors. Still, it might be difficult to agree on which behaviors Flourens should have studied in his birds in order to challenge the propositions of the phrenologists.

There is no simple solution to this problem. Ethologists have success-fully utilized the concept of homology in their studies of behavioral evo-lution (e.g., Lorenz, 1950) and a similar approach is theoretically possible in neuropsychology, but this approach is fraught with difficulties. An al-ternate approach, that of classifying behavior in terms of general function, has been proposed recently by Warren (Warren & Kolb, 1978). This tech-nique may provide an alternative to homology that is more attractive to neuropsychologists. We shall consider each of these approaches sepa-rately.

1. HOMOLOGY

Homology has been an important concept in biology for well over 100 years, but in post-Darwinian times, "homologue" has most often been used to refer to "resemblance due to inheritance from a common ancestry" (Simpson, 1961, p. 78). From this definition we can see that the forepaws and hands of rats and humans, respectively, are homologous, whereas the wings of bats and birds are not. Forepaws and hands derive from a com-mon ancestry, but the wings of bats evolved independently as structural adaptations to permit flight. As forelimbs, the wings of birds and bats are, of course, still homologous. It is important to note that the function of the wings is not relevant in the definition; it is the evolution of the structure that is important.

Although the concept of homology has proven to be a valuable tool in comparative anatomy and systematics, its application to behavior in psy-chology is difficult and confusing for at least three reasons. First, unlike bones, neither central nervous systems nor behaviors leave fossil records. It is generally agreed that "to be homologous, two behaviors exhibited by two phylogenetically related forms must have been present as a single behavior in their common ancestor" (Atz, 1970, p. 54). This is a very difficult proposition to prove in psychological research; the difficulty is compounded by the fact that those species most suitable for laboratory research diverged from their common ancestors millions of years ago. Sec-ond, since behavior does not occur in the absence of anatomical structure, definitions of behavioral homology must include references to structure. For example, Hodos defines behavioral homology as follows: "behaviors are considered homologous to the extent that they can be related to spe-cific structures that can, in principle, be traced back through a genealogi-cal series to a stipulated ancestral precursor irrespective of morphological similarity" (Hodos, 1976, p. 156). It can be seen from this definition that head scratching in frogs and cats is accomplished with the hindlimb and therefore can be considered homologous in frogs and cats. Head scratch-ing in humans and dogs is not homologous, however, since it is accomplished with a different structure, namely the forelimb. Similarly, tail swishing or muscle twitching in horses cannot be considered homologous to scratching by other species because entirely different structural adaptations are involved. The necessity of relating structure to behavior is clearly critical if one wishes to identify the evolutionary development of behavior, but it may place an unnecessarily restrictive burden on neuropsychologists. A neuropsychologist studying maternal behavior might be unable to generalize between two species because the structures involved were not homologous. For example, grooming or cleaning of the young is accomplished by licking with the tongue in rats, but monkeys groom their young with the forepaws. This leads us to the third, and most important problem. Although neuropsychologists are acutely aware of anatomical structure, most behavioral questions in neuropsychology tend to involve function, rather than structure. In other words, neuropsychologists tend to study either the type of movement an animal makes (e.g., Vanderwolf's type I or type II behavior, voluntary or automatic behavior) or the inferred function of that behavior (e.g., sexual behavior, maternal behavior, spatial behavior, memory, learning). Although the actual details of the movements are a critical component of the behavioral analysis (cf. Goodale, Chapter 4; Whishaw et al. Chapter 8, this volume), cross species comparisons in psychology are generally made with regard to the general function of the behaviors rather than the evolutionary history of the skeletal structures involved.

Homology may prove to be as powerful a tool in the study of behavior as it is in the study of anatomy, but in view of the problems we have considered with respect to behavior, it appears that at present behavioral homology is not a suitable basis for generalizing in neuropsychology or for selecting behaviors to study in neuropsychology. It would seem that selection of behavior on functional grounds may prove to be more useful, at least in the short run.

2. CLASS-COMMON VERSUS SPECIES-SPECIFIC BEHAVIORS

Although the details of behavior may differ somewhat, mammals share many similar behavioral traits and capacities, abilities that may form the basis for functional comparisons. All mammals must detect and interpret sensory stimuli, relate this information to past experience, and act appropriately. For example, all mammalian mothers provide milk and maternal care to their young, all mammals appear to be capable of learning complex tasks under various schedules of reinforcement (Warren, 1977), and all mammals are mobile and have developed very efficient mechanisms for responding to spatial location (O'Keefe & Nadel, 1978). The details of maternal behavior, the characteristics of the behavior most easily influenced by reinforcement, and the complexity of the "spatial maps" vary widely from species to species (e.g. Seligman, 1970), but these capacities are ubiquitous among mammalian species.

There is no universally acceptable way to classify those traits and capacities common to mammals, particularly if one wishes to avoid appealing to such mental constructs as memory, attention, or cognition that defy simple definition, that are considered to be present by inference, and that are difficult to correlate with specific neural processes (see Vanderwolf, Chapter 1, this volume for a discussion of this and related problems in behavioral analysis). Recognizing this problem, Warren and Kolb (1978) proposed that behaviors and behavioral capacities demonstrable in all mammals could be designated *class-common behaviors*. In contrast, behaviors that have been selected to promote survival in a unique niche and in a particular way of life could be designated *species-specific behaviors*. The distinction and the interaction of the two sorts of behavior is apparent in the response of rats and cats to a brief novel noise from a speaker. The rat initially freezes and then tries to get away from the sound source; the cat orients to the sound source and then tries to find it. These are species-typical reactions, eminently appropriate for the rat as potential prey and the cat as predator. Note, however, that both rats and cats (and all other mammals) are well endowed with the capacity to localize accurately the sources of sound (Masterton, Heffner, & Rivizza, 1969); this is class-common behavior. The movements an animal makes in response to a sound is determined to a large extent by the niche the animal occupies (e.g., predator or prey); this is species-specific behavior.

The distinction between class-common and species-specific behaviors solves the problems inherent in the use of homology for a basis of comparison between species, but it is not without weakness of its own. At least two problems must be considered. First, it is apparent from our description that virtually every behavior an animal engages in is at once both class-common and species-specific behavior. Second, we must ask whether it is legitimate to assume that since behaviors in different species have the same function, the neural substrates of the behaviors are the same. We shall consider each of these problems separately.

3. DISTINGUISHING BETWEEN CLASS-COMMON AND SPECIES-SPECIFIC BEHAVIOR

Behaviors are class-common in the sense that they perform the same general function across the class Mammalia; they are species-specific in the sense that the details of the behavioral patterns and the structures used are unique to the species. The fact that behaviors can be classified as both class-common and species-specific at the same time is a problem both because the distinction between the two is somewhat arbitrary and because the class-common component of behavior is frequently inferred and not observed directly. Consider the following example.

Urine is used as a territorial marker by many species of mammals. Cats, for example, spray distinctive landmarks, such as bushes, large rocks, posts, walls, with a fine mist of urine that has a distinctive and, to many humans, rather strong odor. Other cats exhibit a striking behavioral sequence when they encounter urine of a conspecific (see Fig. 10.3). The most common components of the response pattern include approaching, sniffing, and touching the urine source with the nose, flicking the tip of the tongue repeatedly against the anterior palate behind the upper incisors, withdrawing the head from the urine and opening the mouth in a "gape" or Flehmen response, and licking the nose (e.g., Kolb & Nonneman, 1975a). This behavioral pattern apparently allows olfactory stimuli to reach the secondary olfactory system. When the cat "gapes," the nasal passages are closed to the flow of air and air is forced into the mouth, through the ductus incivitus on the roof of the mouth, and then across the vomernasal organ, before making its way to the trachea. It has been hypothesized that the vomeronasal organ is a special evolutionary adaptation, which functions to identify species-specific odors. Cats are apparently able to identify other individual cats by their urine markings and habituate rapidly to urine from the same cat (e.g., Kolb & Nonneman, 1975a).

In our studies of the effects of frontal cortex lesions upon the response to urine in cats (Nonneman & Kolb, 1974), we demonstrated that removal of the prefrontal cortex selectively abolished the Flehmen response in cats. Thus, cats approached the urine in the normal way and engaged in the complete normal behavioral pattern to the urine except that the gape response was omitted. Since the gape or Flehmen response was abolished, the cat was unable to utilize the vomeronasal system and hence unable to identify the urine. This result has important implications for the neurological organization of species-specific behaviors. To our knowledge, it represents the only published example in which a fixed action pattern is altered by a cortical lesion, such that one component is missing, but the remaining pattern survives, apparently intact. It may be that we have studied a very unusual action pattern, but it may also be that the neurological hard-wiring for fixed action patterns is far less fixed than previously believed. A problem arises, however, if we wish to generalize from

---

FIGURE 10.3. Composite photograph showing cat sniffing urine-soaked cotton ball (left), beginning gape response (middle), and full gape response (right).

251

our findings in cats to other species that do not have a Flehmen response (e.g., rodents, primates).

In order to generalize, we must identify the class-common component of the behavior. That is, we must identify the function of the behavior that is common across the class Mammalia. If we find that a particular neurological manipulation alters a species-specific behavior, it may do so for three reasons: (1) it abolishes the unique neural substrate of a particular species-specific behavior, (2) it abolishes the class-common neural substrate of a species-specific behavior, or (3) it abolishes both. Since we have argued that there is little compelling evidence favoring the existence of fundamental differences in cerebral organization in mammals (see above), it is unlikely that the first explanation is common. Nevertheless, we cannot rule out this possibility with respect to behaviors such as the Flehmen response, since many species (e.g., rodents and primates) do not have this behavior. If we believe that the abolition of the Flehmen response is not merely an example of a unique behavior being abolished, then we must consider which class-common behavior has been affected. This is relatively simple with many behaviors, such as maternal activity or the response to a novel noise, but it is not as simple for such behaviors as the Flehmen response. For example, we could argue that the general function affected is the analysis of socially relevant olfactory stimuli. Since all mammals appear to respond selectively to certain odors characteristic of their species (e.g., Doty, 1976), we would have identified a class-common behavior that we could make predictions about. We could predict that lesions of the frontal cortex of other species would also disrupt the response to odors of conspecifics, whether or not the species utilizes the Flehmen response. If we tested this hypothesis and found it to be untrue, we would not, however, have demonstrated a species difference. It is equally likely that we misinterpreted the nature of the function disrupted in our initial experiment. We might have proposed that the general function affected was in social behavior. It so happens that olfactory stimuli are critical for social behavior in cats and relatively less important in the species we tested. Had we examined social behavior in our test of the generalizability of our original observation, we might have indeed been able to make a valid generalization.

The problem of identifying the function studied (and hence, the class-common behavior about which to generalize) is a serious weakness in our rationale for generalizing. There is, however, no choice in the matter, since many functions neuropsychologists attempt to study are only inferred to be present. The point to emphasize here is that generalizing in neuropsychology is difficult even after we have selected the behavior to study.

4. Do Class-Common Behaviors Have Class-Common Neural Substrates?

The identification of class-common behaviors does not guarantee that the neural control of the behaviors is class-common. We have already argued, however, that there is no compelling evidence of a qualitative difference in the organization of the brain of placental mammals. In particular, there is evidence of both functional localization and lateralization in the cerebral cortex of all mammals, although the degree of localization and lateralization probably increases in proportion to the relative volume of neocortex (see above). Neurophysiological stimulation, evoked potential, and lesion studies reveal a similar topography in the motor, somatosensory, visual, and auditory cortices of the mammals, a topography that provides the basis for the class-common neural organization of fundamental capacities of mammals. Furthermore, the most sensible place to look for species-specific neural mechanisms to control species-specific behaviors is in the limbic system and hypothalamus, where lesions usually disrupt species-specific behavior. Yet even here, the experimental literature yields no convincing evidence of species-specific neural circuits. Lesions in the same regions of the hypothalamus and limbic system produce similar sorts of changes in the behavior of diverse species (e.g., Isaacson, 1974). In sum, although there may be exceptions, it appears to be a rule of thumb that class-common behaviors are indeed controlled by class-common neural circuitry.

E. SELECTION OF TESTS

In the course of studying the effects of damage to the brain of rats, cats, monkeys, and humans (as well as various other species), neuropsychologists have employed a bewildering array of tests. These neuropsychological tests may have been originally chosen more or less at random, as in the case of Halstead's original battery to test for frontal lobe damage in humans (Halstead, 1947), or they may have been chosen to quantify a subjective impression, as in the case of Milner's choice of the Thurstone word fluency test to quantify the apparent poverty of expressive speech in frontal lobe patients (Milner, 1964). In either event, the psychologist usually has little intrinsic interest in the task per se, but rather in the behavior the task is alleged to be measuring. In other words, although behavioral tests are presumed to measure the brain's capacity to produce certain behaviors under particular circumstances, it is assumed that "given" tests are measuring some more general capacity. This more general capacity is what we have described as class-common behavior. The actual details of the behavior of the subject on a given test are, however, species-specific.

The validity of generalizations in neuropsychology depends, in large part, upon the judicious choice of a battery of tests. It is hazardous at best to generalize on the basis of one or two tests, since there are many obstacles to the reliable demonstration of class-common processes within a species, let alone between species. In choosing tests, neuropsychologists must consider at least three factors: (1) It is necessary to demonstrate that different neural areas are functionally dissociable with the tests chosen. We must be certain that an observed behavioral change is not merely a nonspecific effect of damage to the brain. (2) Since the class-common capacity being measured by the test is an inferred process, it is necessary to use multiple tests of the alleged capacity to ensure that the experiments are really measuring what they appear to be measuring. Just because we believe the task measures some capacity (e.g., the ability to chain together a sequence of movements) does not mean that it actually does. (3) Since behavioral tasks may be differentially affected by different neurological manipulations, it is necessary to have a broad range of tasks in order to ensure that the effect of a manipulation is evaluated correctly. We consider each of these factors in turn.

1. A Basis for Double Dissociation

The oldest method for studying brain-behavior relationships has been to study the effects of circumscribed lesions upon behavior and to infer the function of the damaged area from behavioral deficits. There are many problems with this approach (cf. Kolb & Whishaw, 1980), one of which is that in order to demonstrate that an area has a special function, it is necessary to show that lesions in other areas of the brain do not produce a similar deficit. The method that has proven most effective for doing this is one that Teuber (1955) called "double dissociation." Here, a battery of tests is given to groups of subjects with different lesions. In the event that one group only exhibits a behavioral change on one test and another group only on another, it is possible to infer that certain functions are localized in the areas studied and that damage to these areas does not result in global impairment on every task. For example, consider two hypothetical cortical regions, areas 102 and 107. One group of animals has area 102 ablated, and another area 107. The behavior of the animals is then studied on three tests (e.g., eating, swimming, and grooming). If damage to area 102 disrupted only eating, whereas damage to 107 disrupted only swimming, then we could say that areas 102 and 107 are doubly dissociated. We are thus able to conclude that areas 102 and 107 have a different role in the control of complex movement and that this role is relatively specific to particular behaviors. The larger the battery of tests administered, the greater the possibility of double dissociation among various brain regions, and the closer we can come to making valid generalizations regarding localization of brain functions, both within and between species.

2. Cross-Test Correlation

The choice of behavioral tasks is the most important aspect of a neuropsychological experiment; a task is chosen because it is believed to measure a particular behavioral capacity. The belief that a particular behavioral test is measuring a particular capacity is, however, an inference. To be certain that a given behavioral capacity is actually being measured, it is therefore necessary to test subjects (preferably the same subjects) on more than one test of the same inferred capacity. If performance on the two tests correlates, then there is at least face validity to the idea that the inferred capacity is actually being measured. If, however, the performance on the two tests is not highly correlated, then the experimenter must rethink both the original inference as well as the choice of tests. Consider the following example.

In our study (Kolb, Sutherland, & Whishaw, in press, a), comparing the effect of parietal, medial frontal, and orbital frontal lesions on the "spatial" behavior of rats, we utilized three different behavioral tests: the Morris water maze, the radial arm maze, and the spatial reversal task. In the Morris water maze, the subject is placed in a large round water tank and its task is to locate an escape platform submerged 1 cm below the water surface. The location of the platform is constant, but the starting point in the water is varied at random. The water is tinted white and the tank is painted white so there are no cues in the maze as to the location of the platform. The rat would appear to have to use cues outside the maze in order to learn the spatial location of the platform. In the radial arm maze, food is placed in four arms of the eight-arm maze, and it is the rat's task to learn which arms contain food and which do not. Since all the arms are identical, it is assumed that the rat must use cues beyond the maze in order to identify the correct and incorrect arms. Finally, in the spatial reversal task the animal is trained to find food in one of two alleys in a Grice box. Once the animal has learned the location of the food, the location of the food is shifted to the other alley. Once this is mastered, the food is shifted back, and so on. Since the two arms are identical, except for their spatial location, it is assumed that the task is measuring some aspect of the "spatial ability" of the rat.

On the basis of previous studies in which a spatial function had been assigned to the medial frontal and parietal cortex (cf. Pohl, 1973; Kolb,

Nonneman, & Singh, 1974), we had anticipated that rats with medial frontal and parietal lesions would be impaired at all three tasks, whereas rats with orbital frontal lesions would not be impaired at any task. We also hoped that the performance of the rats with medial frontal and parietal lesions could be differentiated in some way, since it has been argued that these two cortical zones played different roles in spatial behavior (Semmes, Weinstein, Ghent, & Teuber, 1963). The results were totally unexpected and forced us to reconsider our assumption that the tests we chose were all measuring "spatial behavior," and our inference that these cortical zones are involved in spatial analysis. Rats with medial frontal lesions were impaired at the Morris water maze and the spatial reversals, rats with parietal lesions were impaired at the radial arm maze and the spatial reversals, and rats with the orbital frontal lesions were impaired at the Morris maze and the radial arm maze. Had we used only one test (e.g., spatial reversals) we would have concluded that the medial frontal and parietal cortex, but not the orbital frontal cortex, were involved in "spatial analysis." We then could have concluded that a class-common function of the medial frontal and parietal cortex is the analysis of spatial behavior. As it turns out, we were not justified in this conclusion, largely because our initial assumption that all three tests were assessing similar aspects of spatial learning ability was probably in error. Studies utilizing single tests of any function run the serious risk of this type of error.

3. THE IMPORTANCE OF A BROAD RANGE OF BEHAVIORAL TESTS

Even if we have carefully chosen tests that are known to double dissociate brain regions and are generally conceded to measure a particular behavioral capacity across species reliably, we may still be at risk in making faulty generalizations unless we choose a broad range of behavioral tests. This is particularly true in studies of recovery of function. It is widely accepted that brain injury sustained in infancy is likely to produce less severe behavioral effects than similar injury incurred at maturity. Nevertheless, it has become clear that sparing of function is not an inevitable consequence of early brain injury, and a battery of tasks is often required to determine the nature and extent of residual deficits. Our study of the effects of neonatal damage to the prefrontal cortex of rats provides an example.

Excision of the prefrontal cortex in adult rats, cats, dogs, and monkeys reliably produces deficits on a task originally designed by Jacobsen (1936). In one variant of this test, the animal is given a cue as to where food can be found, but it is not allowed to respond for a short period (e.g., 1, 3, 5 seconds). For example, a peanut may be placed under one of two food

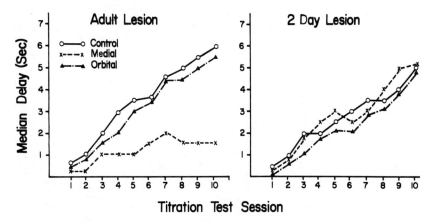

Titration Test Session

FIGURE 10.4. Delayed response performance of rats who received lesions of the medial frontal or orbital frontal cortex at 2 or 100 days of age. All testing was done in adulthood. Rats who received medial frontal lesions in adulthood are severely impaired, whereas rats operated at 2 days of age show no impairment (after Kolb, Nonneman, & Singh, 1974; Kolb & Nonneman, 1978).

wells and a light indicates to the animal which foodwell contains the peanut. After a brief delay, the animal is allowed to respond and the measure of its performance is the accuracy with which it correctly chooses the baited foodwell. Although there is disagreement over whether this test primarily measures spatial ability, memory, or some other function, it is agreed that performance of this test requires an intact frontal cortex. Laboratory rats are capable of mediating delays as long as 10 seconds, but after removal of the medial frontal cortex in adulthood they are unable to reacquire the task, even with extensive practice (see Fig. 10.4). Following similar damage in infancy, however, rats are quite capable of mediating delays of 10 seconds, suggesting that there is sparing of function following neonatal removal of the frontal cortex. Indeed, this sparing is not limited to delayed response, but also occurs in a variety of behavioral tests including spatial reversals, active avoidance, and the Morris water maze (Kolb & Whishaw, 1981a; Kolb, Sutherland, & Whishaw, in press,b). To our surprise, however, we have discovered that although there is significant sparing of function on several standard neuropsychological tests of learning, there is absolutely no evidence of sparing of function on tests of species-specific behavior (see Fig. 10.5). Had we not chosen to use a thorough battery of tests, we might have erroneously concluded that there was (or was not, depending upon the tests we chose) sparing of function. Furthermore, had we not chosen tests of both learned and species-specific

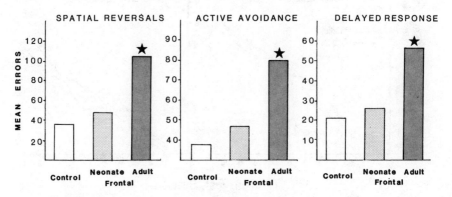

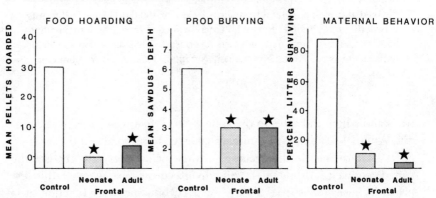

FIGURE 10.5. Summary of the relative effects of removal of the medial frontal cortex in adulthood or in infancy. Neonatal lesions allow complete sparing of performance on cognitive tests, but allow no sparing of performance of species-specific behaviors (data from Kolb & Nonneman, 1978; Kolb & Whishaw, 1981a).

behavior, we would have failed to discover that the nature of the behavioral test (that is, whether or not it involves the acquisition of a new habit) might be critical for the appearance of sparing of function.

F. OF RATS AND HUMANS: AN EXAMPLE OF GENERALIZATION

We have argued that it is possible to make valid generalizations regarding brain-behavior relationships in mammals. In considering the choice of species, the nature of behaviors to study, and the selection of behavioral tests, we have proposed that generalizations can be made on the basis of studies with rats, cats, monkeys, and other common laboratory species provided that class-common behaviors can be identified and a battery of tests is used. The idea that experiments using such standard laboratory species as rats and cats can tell us anything significant about human brain-behavior relationships is not, however, universally accepted, even among physiological psychologists. Consider the following recent quotation:

> the usefulness of current brain-behaviour comparisons which are largely *post hoc* and arbitrary (for example, experimentation and discussion of the effects of lesions of frontal cortex in those old favourites, the rat, cat and monkey, and their implications for frontal cortex function in man) is so questionable that it seems unlikely that this kind of work, which has consumed vast resources of time and effort from neuroscientists over the last thirty to forty years, will have much place when the history of the unfolding of knowledge of brain-behaviour relationships comes to be written (Plotkin, 1979, p. 71)

Plotkin goes on to conclude that the only way in which meaningful conclusions about brain-behavior relationships can be drawn is to emphasize the comparison of species "related" through a direct evolutionary lineage. As noted earlier, the use of a quasi-evolutionary lineage is most certainly a valid basis for choosing species to study, but it is by no means the only acceptable basis for choosing species. Consider the following example.

In the course of studying the effects of lesions of the frontal association cortex of rats and cats, we were impressed with two consistent observations. First, rats and cats with frontal lesions appeared to have some type of deficit in carrying out chains of movements, in the absence of any change in muscle tone or strength. For example, rats with lesions of the orbital frontal cortex were impaired at chaining together the discrete movements necessary to groom or eat (Kolb, Whishaw, & Schallert, 1977; Shipley & Kolb, 1977). Similarly, rats with medial frontal excisions had difficulty in performing the motor sequences necessary for the successful executon of such species-specific behaviors as nest building and food hoarding (cf. Kolb & Whishaw, 1981a; Shipley & Kolb, 1977), as well as opening puzzle latches (Kolb & Whishaw, in press). Similarly, it had been shown by others that removal of the dorsolateral frontal cortex in monkeys produces impairments in the acquisition and performance of various motor habits (e.g., Deuel, 1977; Passingham, 1978). Second, the social behavior of both rats and cats clearly changes following removal of the frontal cortex (Kolb, 1974b; Kolb & Nonneman, 1974; Nonneman & Kolb, 1974); and similar changes have been reported by others in monkeys (Butter & Snyder, 1972; R.E. Myers, 1972). For example, both cats and rhesus monkeys become submissive in their interactions with conspecifics and fail to respond nor-

mally to various species-specific releasers such as urine (see Fig. 10.3) and
threat postures, in the case of cats, and threat displays, in the case of
monkeys. In addition, Myers reported a reduction in the frequency of
facial expressions in monkeys with frontal lobe lesions. (Facial expressions, obviously, are important social signals in primates.)

The apparent consistency of observed changes in what we have called
"movement programming" and "social behavior" led us to study these
behaviors in humans with frontal lobe removals. Although previous studies in humans had examined the effects of large, naturally occurring lesions of the left or right hemispheres on different movement tasks and
socially relevant behaviors, little was known about the effect of frontal
lobe excisions on either movement programming or social behavior. On
the basis of the studies of "those old favourites, the rat, cat and monkey,"
we anticipated that the control of these behaviors represented class-common
functions of the frontal cortex. We therefore modeled our studies of humans on our previous studies of nonhuman species. The results showed
that our generalization from rats to humans was valid. Our studies using
rats led us to ask questions of brain-behavior relationships in humans,
questions we could not have asked without these studies. We will discuss
the movement programming and social behavior results separately.

1. MOVEMENT PROGRAMMING

In this experiment, we asked subjects with unilateral removals from
the left or right frontal, central, temporal, or parietal regions (and normal
control subjects) to copy complex movements of the arm or face (Kolb &
Milner, 1981a). The tasks were modifications of those used by Kimura
and Archibald (1974) and Mateer and Kimura (1977) in their studies of
the motor performance of patients with acquired cerebrovascular lesions
of either hemisphere. On the arm task, the largest deficit was found to
follow lesions of the left parietal lobe, although a milder impairment accompanied lesions of either frontal lobe. On the face task, in contrast, the
left parietal lobe lesions caused no impairment, whereas marked deficits
were seen after frontal lobe lesions of either side. On analysis of the facial-
movement task, the frontal lobe groups made more errors of sequence
than normal controls or other groups of patients. In other words, one
deficit observed in the frontal lobe groups was a difficulty in ordering the
various components of the sequence into a chain of movements. The components were recalled correctly, but in the wrong order. To be sure, the
frontal lobe patients made other sorts of errors as well, including intru-
sions (making movements not belonging in the sequence) and omissions
(leaving movements out).

The results of this study confirm our hypothesis based on animal studies: the control of complex movement sequences is a class-common function of the frontal lobe. Our studies of rats and cats, in conjunction with the work by others using monkeys, led us to a hypothesis we were able to test with human subjects. In addition, the somewhat unexpected demonstration of a substantial deficit in arm movements has led us to return to our animal subjects to examine the effect of parietal lesions on various complex movements, such as opening puzzle latches. It is hoped that after additional study of our animals, we will be able to return to our human subjects with new questions that may be useful in answering important questions regarding motor control in the human brain.

2. SOCIAL BEHAVIOR

Our study of social behaviors in rats and cats led us to the conclusion that frontal lobe lesions disrupted the production and perception of socially relevant stimuli. It was with these results in mind that we devised three experiments to see if similar changes also followed frontal lobe lesions in humans. In the first two experiments, we studied the production of those stimuli that would appear to be most important in human social interaction, namely facial expression and language. These studies thus involved the effects of circumscribed cortical excision of the frontal, central, parietal, or temporal cortex in the spontaneous production of facial expressions or conversational speech. Following our studies using cats (Nonneman & Kolb, 1974) and the Myers (1972) study of monkeys, an ethological recording technique was used to score the facial movements: brows raised, brows knitted, eyes closed, mouth open, slight smile, wide smile, open-mouth smile, lips tight, lips turned down at corners, lips pursed, lips pouting, tongue out and laughing, sighing, and miscellaneous.

Excisions of either the left or right frontal lobe significantly reduced the occurrence of spontaneous facial expressions, whereas central, temporal, or posterior lesions had no differential effect (Kolb & Milner, 1981b). On the other hand, during routine neuropsychological testing, left frontal lobe lesions significantly reduced the incidence of spontaneous talking, whereas right frontal lobe lesions significantly increased it (Kolb & Taylor, 1981). Lesions elsewhere in the cortex had no effect on this behavior. Thus, like rats, cats, and monkeys, frontal lobe lesions significantly alter the production of affective behavior in humans. Like monkeys, there was a dramatic decrease in the occurrence of facial expression, a decrease we were able to quantify by utilizing experimental techniques used previously with nonhumans.

In the final study, we examined the reception of affectively toned facial expression and verbal descriptions of emotional events by using two tasks: a nonverbal photograph-matching test and a sentence-matching test. In the photograph-matching test, the subject was first shown seven key photographs, each of which depicted one of the verbally categorizable emotions described by Ekman, Friesen, & Ellsworth (1973). These have been characterized as sadness, fear or terror, happiness or amusement, anger, disgust or contempt, surprise, and interest or attention. The subject was then shown a series of 24 stimulus photographs of faces taken from *Life* magazine and was asked to match each of them with the key photograph that most closely expressed the same emotion. In the sentence-matching test, the subject was given a list of verbal categories of emotion listed above. He was then read a series of 48 sentences, each of which described an event illustrated in a photograph from *Life* magazine, and then was asked to choose the emotional category that best matched the emotion of the person described in the sentence. For example, all control subjects matched "sad" with "this person is at a funeral" and "disgust" with "this person has just eaten something that tastes bad." The results showed that patients with right frontal lobe lesions were significantly impaired on the photograph-matching test, whereas patients with left frontal lobe lesions were significantly impaired on the verbal test (Kolb & Taylor, 1981).

The results of our study of receptive behavior indicate that, as in our studies of expressive behavior, we were able to generalize from studies of nonhumans and make valid predictions regarding brain-behavior relationships in humans. The failure to localize the deficits in receptive behavior to the frontal lobe was not entirely unexpected, since we have observed analogous results in our studies of cats with lesions of the visual and auditory association cortex. By using more subtle tests in both humans and cats, one ought to be able to distinguish the relative contributions of the frontal and posterior cortex to the analysis of receptive social behavior.

G. CONCLUSIONS

We have considered the rationale and problems inherent in trying to make generalizations on brain-behavior relationships in neuropsychology. Mammals have to cope with the same basic problems imposed by the environment, and the behavioral capacities to cope with problems are class-common. The evidence indicates that class-common behaviors are mediated by class-common neural mechanisms sufficiently similar among mammals to permit valid generalizations across species. The production of valid generalizations requires that both class-common and species-specific behavior be studied, however, and that a thorough test battery be used before generalizations are attempted. Finally, we echo the sentiments expressed a decade ago by Harlow when he wrote that "basically the problems of generalization of behavioral data between species are simple—one cannot generalize, but one must. If the competent do not wish to generalize, the incompetent will fill the field" (Harlow et al., 1972, p. 716).

ACKNOWLEDGMENT

We dedicate this chapter to Dr. J.M. Warren, whose application of the comparative model to neuropsychology has been both a model and inspiration to us.

References

Adams, D.B. The activity of single cells in the midbrain and hypothalamus of the cat during affective defense behavior. Archives Italiannes Biologie, 106: 243–249, 1968.

Adolph, E.F. Ontogeny of physiological regulation in the rat. The Quarterly Review of Biology, 32: 89–137, 1957.

Adrian, E.D. The physical background of perception. Clarendon Press, Oxford, 1946.

Agmo, A., Soulairac, M.-L., and Soulairac, A. Preoptic lesions, sexual behavior, and spontaneous ejaculation in the rat. Scandinavian Journal of Psychology, 18: 345–347, 1977.

Albert, D.J. and Chow, G.L. The septal forebrain and the inhibitory modulation of attack and defense in the rat. A review. Behavioral and Neural Biology, 30: 357–388, 1980.

Alberts, J.R. Huddling by rat pups: Group behavioral mechanisms of temperature regulation and energy conservation. Journal of Comparative and Physiological Psychology, 92: 231–245, 1978.

Alberts, J.R. and Galef, B.G., Jr. Olfactory cues and movement: Stimuli mediating intraspecific aggression in the wild Norway rat. Journal of Comparative and Physiological Psychology, 85: 233–242, 1973.

Allison, T. and Cicchetti, D.V. Sleep in mammals: Ecological and constitutional correlates. Science, 194: 732–735, 1976.

Almli, R.C. The ontogeny of feeding and drinking: Effects of early brain damage. Neuroscience and Biobehavioral Reviews, 2: 281–300, 1978.

Almli, R.C. and Fisher, R.S. Infant rats: Sensorimotor ontogeny and effects of substantia nigra destruction. Brain Research Bulletin, 72: 425–459, 1977.

Almli, R.C., Fisher, R.S., and Hill, D.R. Lateral hypothalamus destruction in infant rats produces consummatory deficits without sensory neglect or attenuated arousal. Experimental Neurology, 66: 146–157, 1979.

Almli, R.C., Hill, D.L., McMullen, N.T., and Fisher, R.S. Newborn rats: Lateral hypothalamic damage and consummatory sensorimotor ontogeny. Physiology and Behavior, 22: 767–773, 1979.

Altman, J. Effects of lesions in central nervous visual structures on light aversion in rats. American Journal of Physiology, 202: 1208–1210, 1962.

Altman, J. and Sudarshan, K. Postnatal development of locomotion in the laboratory rat. Animal Behavior, 23: 896–920, 1975.

Amaral, H. and Foss, J.A. Locus ceruleus lesions and learning. Science, 188: 377–378, 1975.

Amassian, V.E. and DeVito, R.V. Unit activity in reticular formation and nearby structures. Journal of Neurophysiology, 17: 575–603, 1954.

Anderson, E.E. The interrelationship of drives in the male albino rat. II. Intercorrelations between 47 measures of drive and learning. Comparative Psychology Monograph, 14(6): 1–119, 1938.

Anderson, J.A. and Hinton, G.E. (Eds.), Parallel models of associative memory. Hillsdale, NJ: Lawrence Erlbaum Assoc., 1981.

Anderson, J.A., Silverstein, J.W., Ritz, S.A., and Jones, R.S. Distinctive features, categorical perception, and probability learning: Some applications of a neural model. Psychological Review, 84: 413–451, 1977.

Anderson, K. and Symmes, D. The superior colliculus and higher visual functions in the monkey. Brain Research, 13: 37–52, 1969.

Anderson, K. and Williams, M.R. Visual pattern discrimination in cats after removal of superior colliculi. Psychonomic Science, 24: 125, 1971.

Anisko, J.J., Adler, N.T., and Suer, S. Pattern of postejaculatory urination and sociosexual behavior in the rat. Behavioral and Neural Biology, 26: 169–176, 1979.

Arnaut, L. and Shettleworth, S.J. The role of spatial and temporal contiguity in defensive burying in rats. Animal Learning and Behavior, 9: 275–280, 1981.

Aschoff, J. Circadian rhythms in man. Science, 148: 1427–1432, 1965.

Aslin, R.N., Alberts, J.R. and Petersen, M. Development of perception. New York: Academic Press, 1981.

Atkinson, J., Braddick, O. and Moar, K. Development of contrast sensitivity over the first three months of life in the human infant. Vision Research, 17: 1037–1044, 1977.

Atz, J.W. The application of the idea of homology to behavior. In L.R. Aronson, T. Tobach, D.S. Lehrman, and J.S. Rosenblatt (Eds.), Development and evolution of behavior. San Francisco: W.H. Freeman, 1970.

Ayllon, T. and Michael, J. The psychiatric nurse as a behavioral engineer. Journal of the Experimental Analysis of Behavior, 2: 323–334, 1959.

Bach-y-Rita, P. Convergent and long-latency unit response in the reticular formation of the cat. Experimental Neurology, 9: 327–344, 1964.

Balagura, S., Wilcox, R.H., and Coscina, D.V. The effects of diencephalic lesions on food intake and motor activity. Physiology and Behavior, 4: 629–633, 1969.

Bambridge, B. and Gijsbers, K. The role of tonic neural activity in motivational processes. Experimental Neurology, 56: 370–385, 1977.

Bandler, R. and Moyer, K.E. Animals spontaneously attacked by rats. Communications in Behavioral Biology, 5: 177–182, 1970.

Baraldi, M. and Bertolini, A. Penile erections induced by amantadine in male rats. Life Sciences, 14: 1231–1235, 1974.

Bard, P. Postural coordination and locomotion and their central control. In V.B. Mountcastle (Ed.), Medical physiology. St. Louis: The C.V. Mosby Co., 1968, pp. 1750–1770.

Bard, P. and Brooks, C.M. Localization of control of some postural reactions in the cat and rat together with evidence that small cortical remnants may function normally. In S.T. Orton (Ed.), Localization of function in the cerebral cortex (Vol. 13). Baltimore: Williams & Wilkins, 1934, pp. 107–157.

Barfield, R.J. and Gayer, L.A. Sexual behavior: Ultrasonic postejaculatory song of the male rat. Science, 176: 1349–1350, 1972.

Barlow, H.B. Single units and sensation: A neuron doctrine for perceptual psychology? Perception, 1: 372–394, 1972.

Barlow, H.B. Visual experience and cortical development. Nature, 258: 199–204, 1975.

Barlow, H.B., Blakemore, C., and Pettigrew, J.D. The neural mechanism of binocular depth discrimination. Journal of Physiology, 193: 327–342, 1967.

Barnes, C., McNaughton, B., Goddard, G., Douglas, R., and Adamec, R. Circadian rhythm of synaptic excitability in rat and monkey central nervous system. Science, 197: 91–92, 1977.

Barnes, K.L. A quantitative investigation of somatosensory coding in single cells of the cat mesencephalic reticular formation. Experimental Neurology, 50: 180–193, 1976.

Barnett, S.A. Exploratory behaviour. British Journal of Psychology, 49: 289–310, 1958.

Barnett, S.A. The rat: A study in behaviour. London: Methuen, 1963.

Barnett, S.A. and Spencer, M.M. Feeding, social behavior and interspecific competition in wild rats. Behavior, 3: 229–242, 1951.

Barron, D.H. The results of unilateral pyramidal section in the rat. The Journal of Comparative Neurology, 60: 45–55, 1934.

Beach, F.A. The neural basis of innate behavior. I. Effects of cortical lesions upon the maternal behavior pattern in the rat. Journal of Comparative Psychology, 24: 393–436, 1937.

Beach, F.A. Effects of cortical lesions upon the copulatory behavior of male rats. Journal of Comparative Psychology, 29: 193–244, 1940.

Beach, F.A. Effects of injury to the cerebral cortex upon sexually-receptive behavior in the female rat. Psychosomatic Medicine, 6: 40–55, 1944.

Beach, F.A. The snark was a boojum. American Psychologist, 5: 115–124, 1950.

Beach, F.A. Variables affecting "spontaneous" seminal emission in rats. Physiology and Behavior, 15: 91–95, 1975.

Beach, F.A. and Jaynes, J. Studies of maternal retrieving in rats. I. Recognition of young. Journal of Mammalogy, 37: 177–180, 1956a.

Beach, F.A. and Jaynes, J. Studies in maternal retrieving in rats. 3. Sensory cues. Behaviour, 10: 104–125, 1956b.

Bean, W.B. Nail growth: Thirty-five years of observation. Archives of Internal Medicine, 140: 73–76, 1980.

Bechterew, W. Uber die Function der Vierhugel. Archives Ges Physiology 33: 413–419, 1884.

Bekoff, A. and Trainer, W. The development of interlimbs coordination during swimming in postnatal rats. Journal of Experimental Biology, 83: 1–11, 1979.

Bell, C., Sierra, G., Buendia, N., and Segundo, J.P. Sensory properties of neurons in the mesencephalic reticular formation. Journal of Neurophysiology, 27: 961–997, 1964.

Beninger, R.J., Kendall, S.B., and Vanderwolf, C.H. The ability of rats to discriminate their own behaviors. Canadian Journal of Psychology, 28: 79–91, 1974.

Beninger, R.J., MacLennan, J.A., and Pinel, J.P.J. The use of conditioned defensive burying to test the effects of pimozide on associative learning. Pharmacology, Biochemistry and Behavior, 12: 445–448, 1980.

Beninger, R.J., Mason, S.T., Phillips, A.G., and Fibiger, H.C. The use of conditioned suppression to evaluate the nature of neuroleptic-induced avoidance deficit. Journal of Pharmacology and Experimental Therapeutics, 213: 623–627, 1980.

Bennett, T.L. The electrical activity of the hippocampus and processes of attention. In R.L. Isaacson and K.H. Pribram (Eds.), The hippocampus (Vol. 2): Neurophysiology and behavior. New York: Plenum Press, 1975, pp. 77–99.

Berg, D.S. and Baenninger, R. Hissing by laboratory rats during fighting encounters. Behavioral Biology, 8: 733–741, 1973.

Berkley, M.A. Cat visual psychophysics: Neural correlates and comparisons with man. In J.M. Sprague and A. Epstein (Eds.), Progress in psychobiology and physiological psychology (Vol. 6). New York: Academic Press, 1976, pp. 63–119.

Berkley, M.A. and Sprague, J. Striate cortex and visual acuity functions in the cat. Journal of Comparative Neurology, 187: 679–702, 1979.

Berlucchi, G., Sprague, J.M., Levy, J., and DiBerardino, A.C. Pretectum and superior colliculus in visually guided behavior and influx and form discrimination in the cat. Journal of Comparative and Physiological Psychology, 78: 123–172, 1972.

Berlyne, D.E. The arousal and satiation of perceptual curiosity in the rat. Journal of Comparative and Physiological Psychology, 48: 238–246, 1955.

Berlyne, D.E. Curiosity and exploration. Science, 153: 25–33, 1966.

Berman, A.L. The brain stem of the cat. Madison, WI: University of Wisconsin Press, 1968.

Bermant, G. Response latencies of female rats during sexual intercourse. Science, 133: 1771–1773, 1961.

Berntson, G.G. and Micco, D.J. Organization of brain stem behavioral systems. Brain Research Bulletin, 90: 898–908, 1976.

Bertrand, F., Hugelin, A., and Vibert, J.F. Quantitative study of anatomical distribution of respiration related neurons in the pons. Experimental Brain Research, 16: 383–399, 1973.

Best, P.J., Mays, L.E., and Olmstead, C.E. Activity of midbrain reticular formation units during conditioned freezing. In M.I. Phillips (Ed.), Brain unit activity during behavior. Springfield, IL: Charles C. Thomas, 1973, pp. 155–164.

Best, P.J. and Orr, J. Effects of hippocampal lesions on passive avoidance and taste aversion learning. Physiology and Behavior, 10: 193–196, 1973.

Best, P.J. and Ranck, J.B., Jr. Reliability of the relationship between hippocampal unit activity and behavior in the rat. Neuroscience Abstracts, 1: 538, 1975.

Best, P.J. and Ranck, J.B., Jr. The reliability of the relationship between hippocampal unit activity and sensory-behavioral events in the rat. Experimental Neurology, 75: 652–664, 1982.

Beyer, C., Almanza, J., DeLaTorre, L., and Guzman-Flores, C. Brain stem multiunit activity during 'relaxation' behavior in the female cat. Brain Research, 29: 213–222, 1971.

Bignall, K.E. Ontogeny of levels of neural organization: The righting reflex as a model. Experimental Neurology, 42: 566–573, 1974.

Bindra, D. and Reichert, H. Dissociation of movement initiation without dissociation of response choice. Psychonomic Science, 4: 95–96, 1966.

Bindra, D. and Thompson, W.R. An evaluation of defecation and urination as measures of fearfulness. Journal of Comparative and Physiological Psychology, 46: 43–45, 1953.

Binik, Y.M. A note on the term sudden death. Omega, 3: 41–44, 1977.

Binik, Y.M., Theriault, G., and Shustack, B. Sudden death in the laboratory rat. Cardiac function, sensory, and experiential factors in swimming deaths. Psychosomatic Medicine, 39: 82–92, 1977.

Bisti, S. and Maffei, L. Behavioral contrast sensitivity of the cat in various visual meridians. Journal of Physiology, 241: 201–210, 1974.

Bizzi, E., Kalil, R.E. and Tagliasco, V. Eye-head coordination in monkeys: Evidence for centrally patterned organization. Science, 173: 452–454, 1971.

Black, A.H. Hippocampal electrical activity and behavior. In R.L. Isaacson and K.H. Pribram (Eds.), The hippocampus (Vol. 2): Neurophysiology and behavior. New York: Plenum Press, 1975, pp. 129–167.

Blake, L. The effect of lesions of the superior colliculus on brightness and pattern discrimination in the cat. Journal of Comparative and Physiological Psychology, 52: 272–278, 1959.

Blake, R., Cool, S.J., and Crawford, M.L.J. Visual resolution in the cat. Vision Research, 14: 1211–1218, 1974.

Blakemore, C. and Van Sluyters, R.C. Reversal of the physiological effects of monocular deprivation in kittens: Further evidence for a sensitive period. Journal of Physiology, 237: 195–216, 1974.

Blanchard, D.C., Blanchard, R.J., Lee, E.M.C., and Nakamura, S. Defensive behaviours in rats following septal and septal-amygdala lesions. Journal of Comparative and Physiological Psychology, 93: 378–390, 1979.

Blanchard, R.J. and Blanchard, D.C. Defensive reactions in the albino rat. Learning and Motivation, 2: 351–362, 1971.

Blanchard, R.J. and Blanchard, D.C. Aggressive behavior in the rat. Behavioral Biology, 21: 197–224, 1977.

Blanchard, R.J., Blanchard, D.C., Takahashi, T., and Kelley, M.J. Attack and defensive behavior in the albino rat. Animal Behavior, 25: 622–634, 1977.

Bland, B.H., Andersen, P., Ganes, T., and Sveen, O. Automatic analysis of rhythmicity of physiologically identified hippocampal formation neurons. Experimental Brain Research, 38: 205–219, 1980.

Bland, B.H. and Vanderwolf, C.H. Diencephalic and hippocampal mechanisms of motor activity in the rat: Effects of posterior hypothalamic stimulation on behavior and hippocampal slow wave activity. Brain Research, 43: 89–106, 1972.

Blass, E.M. and Teicher, M.H. Suckling. Science, 210: 15–22, 1980.

Boice, R. On the fall of comparative psychology. American Psychologist, 26: 858–859, 1971.

Bolles, R.C. Group and individual performance as a function of intensity and kind of deprivation. Journal of Comparative and Physiological Psychology, 52: 579–585, 1959.

Bolles, R.C. Grooming behavior in the rat. Journal of Comparative and Physiological Psychology, 53: 306–310, 1960.

Bolles, R.C. Species-specific defense reactions and avoidance learning. Psychological Review, 77: 32–48, 1970.

Bolles, R.C. and Woods, P.J. The ontogeny of behavior in the albino rat. Animal Behavior, 12: 427–441, 1964.

Bonds, A.B. and Freeman, R.D. Development of optical quality in the kitten eye. Vision Research, 18: 391–398, 1978.

Boothe, R.G., Williams, R.A., Kiorpes, L., and Teller, D.Y., Development of contrast sensitivity in infant *Macaca nemestrina* monkeys. Science, 208: 1290–1292, 1980.

Boring, E.G. Sensation and perception in the history of experimental psychology. New York: Appleton-Century, 1942.

Boyko, W.J., Galabru, C.K., McGeer, E.G., and McGeer, P.L. Thalamic injections of kainic acid produce myocardial necrosis. Life Sciences, 25: 87–98, 1979.

Braddick, O. and Atkinson, J. Accommodation and acuity in the human infant. In R.D. Freedman (Ed.), Developmental neurobiology of vision. New York: Plenum Press, 1979, pp. 289–300.

Brady, J.K. and Nauta, W.J.H. Subcortical mechanisms in emotional behavior: Affective changes following septal forebrain lesions in the albino rat. Journal of Comparative and Physiological Psychology, 46: 339–346, 1953.

Brady, J.K. and Nauta, W.J.H. Subcortical mechanisms in emotional behavior: The duration of affective changes following septal and habenular lesions in the albino rat. Journal of Comparative and Physiological Psychology, 48: 412–420, 1955.

Brandes, J.S. and Johnson, A.K. Recovery of feeding in rats following frontal neocortical ablations. Physiology and Behavior, 20: 763–770, 1978.

Braun, J.J. Neocortex and feeding behavior in the rat. Journal of Comparative and Physiological Psychology, 89: 507–522, 1975.

Braun, J.J., Slick, T.B., and Lorden, J.F. Involvement of gustatory neocortex in the learning of taste aversion. Physiology and Behavior, 9: 637–641, 1972.

Breedlove, S.M., McGinty, D.J., and Siegel, J.M. Operant conditioning of pontine gigantocellular units. Brain Research Bulletin, 4: 663–667, 1979.

Brimley, C.C. and Mogenson, G.J. Oral motor deficits following lesions of the central nervous system in the rat. American Journal of Physiology, 237: 126–131, 1979.

Brown, R.E. Object-directed urine marking by male rats (*Rattus norvegicus*). Behavioral Biology, 15: 251–254, 1975.

Brown, R.E. The 22-kHz pre-ejaculatory vocalizations of the male rat. Physiology and Behavior, 22: 483–489, 1979.

Buchwald, J.S., Halas, E.S., and Schramm, S. Changes in cortical and subcortical unit activity during behavioral conditioning. Physiology and Behavior, 1: 11–22, 1966.

Bunnell, B.N. Mammalian behavior patterns. In D.A. Dewsbury and D.A. Rethlingshafer (Eds.), Comparative psychology. New York: McGraw-Hill, 1973, pp. 78–123.

Bureš, J., Burešová, O., and Huston, J.P. Techniques and basic experiments for the study of brain and behavior. New York: Elsevier Scientific Publishing Co., 1976.

Burton, H. Somatic sensory properties of caudal bulbar reticular neurons in the cat (*Felis domestica*). Brain Research, 11: 357–372, 1968.

Buser, P.A. and Rougeul-Buser, A. Cerebral correlates of conscious experience. Amsterdam: North-Holland Publishing Co., 1978.

Butter, C.M., Mishkin, M., and Rosvold, H.E. Stimulus generalization in monkeys with inferotemporal and lateral occipital lesions. In D. Mostofsky (Ed.), Stimulus generalization. Stanford, CA: Stanford University Press, 1965.

Butter, C.M. and Snyder, D.R. Alterations in aversive and aggressive behaviors following orbital frontal lesions in rhesus monkey. Acta Neurobiologiae Experimentalis, 32: 115–156, 1972.

Buttner, U., Buttner-Ennever, J.A., and Henn, V. Vertical eye movement related unit activity in the rostral mesencephalic reticular formation of the alert monkey. Brain Research, 130: 239–252, 1977.

Byck, R. Drugs and the treatment of psychiatric disorders. In L.S. Goodman and A. Gilman (Eds.), The pharmacological basis of therapeutics. New York: Macmillan, 1975, pp. 152–200.

Calhoun, J.B. A method for self control of population growth among mammals living in the wild. Science, 109: 333–335, 1949.

Calhoun, J.B. The ecology and sociology of the Norway rat. Bethesda, MD: U.S. Department of Health, Education, and Welfare, 1962.

Campbell, B.A. and Spear, N. Ontogeny of memory. Physiological Review, 79: 215–236, 1972.

Carpenter, R. Movements of the eyes. London: Pion Ltd., 1977.

Carr, W.J., Landauer, M.R., Wiese, R.E., Maraseo, E. and Thor, D.H. A natural food aversion in Norway rats. Journal of Comparative and Physiological Psychology, 93: 574–584, 1979.

Carter, C.S., Witt, D.M., Kolb, B., and Whishaw, I.Q. Neonatal decortication and adult female sexual behavior. Physiology and Behavior, 1982, in press.

Carthy, J.D. and Ebling, F.J. (Eds.), The natural history of aggression. New York: Academic Press, 1964.

Casagrande, J.A., Harting, J.K., Hall, W.C., Diamond, I.T., and Martin, G. Superior colliculus of the tree shrew: A structural and functional subdivision into superficial and deep layers. Science, 177: 144–147, 1972.

Casey, K.L. Responses of bulboreticular units to somatic stimuli eliciting escape behavior in the cat. International Journal of Neuroscience, 2: 14–28, 1971.

Casey, K.L., Keene, J.J., and Morrow, T. Bulboreticular and medial thalamic unit activity in relation to aversive behavior and pain. Advances in Neurology, 4: 197–205, 1974.

Castro, A.J. Motor performance in rats. The effects of pyramidal tract section. Brain Research, 44: 313–323, 1972a.

Castro, A.J. The effects of cortical ablations on digit use in the rat. Brain Research, 37: 137–185, 1972b.

Castro, A.J. The effects of cortical ablations on tongue usage in the rat. Brain Research, 45: 251–253, 1972c.

Castro, A.J. Tongue usage as a measure of cerebral cortical localization in the rat. Experimental Neurology, 47: 343–352, 1975.

Castro, A.J. Limb preference after lesions of the cerebral hemisphere in neonatal rats. Experimental Neurology, 18: 605–608, 1977.

Castro, A.J. Analysis of cortical-spinal and rubrospinal projections after neonatal pyramidotomy in rats. Brain Research, 144: 155–158, 1978.

Chapin, J.K., Loeb, G.E., and Woodward, D. A simple technique for determination of footfall patterns of animals during treadmill locomotion. Journal of Neuroscience Methods, 2: 97–102, 1980.

Chapin, J.K. and Woodward, D.J. Modulation of sensory responsiveness of single somatosensory cortical cells during movement and arousal behaviors. Experimental Neurology, 72: 164–178, 1981.

Chapman, H.W. and Epstein, A.N. Prandial drinking induced by atropine.

Physiology and Behavior, 5: 549–554, 1970.

Chen, J.J. and Bliss, D.K. Effects of sequential preoptic and mammillary lesions on male rat sexual behavior. Journal of Comparative and Physiological Psychology, 87: 841–847, 1974.

Chorover, S.L. and Schiller, P.H. Short term retrograde amnesia in rats. Journal of Comparative and Physiological Psychology, 59: 73–78, 1965.

Chow, K.L. and Stewart, D.L. Reversal of structural and functional effects of long-term visual deprivation in cats. Experimental Neurology, 34: 409–433, 1972.

Clark, W. Le Gros. Anatomical pattern as the essential basis of sensory discrimination. Springfield, IL: Charles C. Thomas, 1974.

Cohen, B. Pontine reticular formation neurons and motor activity. Science, 199: 207, 1978.

Cohen, B. and Henn, V. Unit activity in the pontine reticular formation associated with eye movements. Brain Research, 46: 403–410, 1972.

Coss, R.G. and Owings, D.H. Snake-directed behavior by snake naive and experienced California ground squirrels in a simulated burrow. Zeitschrift fuer Tierpsychologie, 48: 421–435, 1978.

Costall, B. and Naylor, R.J. On catalepsy and catatonia and the predictability of the catalepsy test for neuroleptic activity. Psychopharmacologia, 34: 133–241, 1974.

Cragg, B.G. The development of synapses in kitten visual cortex during visual deprivation. Experimental Neurology, 46: 445–451, 1975.

Cragg, B., Anker, R., and Wan, Y.K. The effect of age on the reversibility of cellular atrophy in the LGN of the cat following monocular deprivation: A test of two hypotheses about cell growth. Journal of Comparative Neurology, 168: 345–354, 1976.

Creel, D. Inapproprite use of albino animals as models in research. Pharmacology, Biochemistry, and Behavior, 12: 969–977, 1980.

Cronin, M.J. and Baker, M.A. Thermosensitive neurons in the cat. Brain Research, 128: 461–472, 1977.

Croskerry, P.G., Smith, G.K., and Leon M. Thermoregulation and the maternal behavior of the rat. Nature, 273: 299–300, 1978.

Cynader, M. and Regan, D. Neurones in cat parastriate cortex sensitive to the direction of motion in three-dimensional space. Journal of Physiology (London), 274: 549–569, 1978.

Cytawa, J. and Teitelbaum, P. Spreading depression and recovery from septal hyperemotionality. Folia Biologica, 16: 459–468, 1968.

Daniels, J.D. and Pettigrew, J.D. Development of neuronal responses in the visual system of cats. In G. Gottlieb (Ed.), Studies on the development of behavior and the nervous system (Vol. 3): Neural and behavioral specificity. New York: Academic Press, 1976, pp. 195–232.

Daniels, J.D., Pettigrew, J.D., and Norman, J.L. Development of single-neuron responses in kitten's lateral geniculate nucleus. Journal of Neurophysiology, 41: 1373–1393, 1978.

Darwin, C. Expression of the emotions in man and animals. London: Murray, 1872.

Davis, C.D. The effect of ablations of neocortex on mating, maternal behavior and the production of pseudopregnancy in the female rat and on copulatory activity in the male. American Journal of Physiology, 127: 374–380, 1939.

Davis, S.F. and Rossheim, S.A. Defensive burying as a function of insulin-induced hypoglycemia and type of aversive stimulation. Bulletin of the Psychonomic Society, 16: 229–231, 1980.

Davis, S.F. and Whiteside, D. Defensive burying: Across species evaluation. Paper read at a meeting of the Psychonomic Society, St. Louis, November, 1980.

Dean, P. Analysis of visual behavior in monkeys with inferotemporal lesions. In D. Ingle, M. Goodale, and R. Mansfield (Eds.), Analysis of visual behavior. Cambridge, MA: The MIT Press, 1982.

De Castro, J.M. Core temperature relationships with spontaneous behavior in the rat. Physiology and Behavior, 25: 69–75, 1980.

DeJong, H. Experimental catatonia. A general reaction-form of the central nervous system and its implications for human pathology. Baltimore: Williams & Wilkins, 1945.

Delius, J.D. Displacement activities and arousal. Nature, 214: 1259–1260, 1967.

Dember, W.N. and Earl, R.W. Analysis of exploratory, manipulatory and curiosity behaviours. Psychological Review, 64: 91–96, 1957.

DeMyer, W. Technique of the neurologic examination. New York: McGraw-Hill, 1974.

Dennis, S.G. and Melzack, R. Self-mutilation after dorsal rhizotomy in rats: Effects of prior pain and pattern of root lesions. Experimental Neurology, 65: 412–421, 1979.

Denny, M.R. and Thomas, J.O. Avoidance learning and relearning as a function of shuttle-box dimensions. Science, 132: 620–621, 1960.

Denny-Brown, D. Clinical symptomology of diseases of the basal ganglia. In P.J. Vinken and G.W. Bruyn (Eds.), Handbook of clinical neurology (Vol. 6): Diseases of the basal ganglia. Amsterdam: North Holland, 1968, pp. 133–172.

Denny-Brown, D. and Chambers, R.A. Visuomotor function in the cerebral cortex. Archives of Neurology and Psychiatry, 73: 566, 1955.

Derrington, A.M. Direct measurements of image quality in the kitten's eye. Journal of Physiology, 295: 16–17, 1979.

Derrington, A.M. and Fuchs, A.F. The development of spatial-frequency selectivity in kitten striate cortex. Journal of Physiology, 316: 1–10, 1981.

Derrington, A.M. and Hawken, M.P. Spatial and temporal properties of cat geniculate neurones after prolonged deprivation. Journal of Physiology, 314: 107–120, 1981.

DeRyck, M. Schallert, T., and Teitelbaum, P. Morphine versus Haloperidol catalepsy in the rat: A behavioral analysis of postural support mechanisms. Brain Research, 201: 143–172, 1980.

Descartes, R. Traite de l'homme. Paris: Angot, 1664.

DeSci, L., Gacs, E. Zambo, K. and Nagy, J. A simple device to measure stereotyped rearing of the rat in an objective and quantitative way. Neuropharmacology, 18: 723–725, 1979.

Deuel, R.K. Loss of motor habits after cortical lesions. Neuropsychologia, 15: 205–215, 1977.

Deutsch, J.A., Molina, F., and Puerto, A. Conditioned taste aversion caused by palatable nontoxic nutrients. Behavioral Biology, 16: 161–174, 1976.

Devenport, L.D. and Balagura, S. Lateral hypothalamus: Reevaluation of function in motivated feeding behavior. Science, 172: 744–746, 1971.

Dews, P.B. and Wiesel, T.N. Consequences of monocular deprivation on visual behavior in kittens. Journal of Physiology, 206: 437–455, 1970.

Dewsbury, D.A. A quantitative description of the behavior of rats during copulation. Behaviour, 29: 154–178, 1967.

Dewsbury, D.A. Comparative psychologists and their quest for uniformity. Annals of the New York Academy of Sciences, 223: 147–167, 1973.

Diamond, M.C., Johnson, R.E., and Ingham, C.A. Morphological changes in the young, adult and aging rat cerebral cortex, hippocampus, and diencephalon. Behavioral Biology, 14: 163–174, 1975.

Divac, I., Gade, A., and Wikmark, R.G.E. Taste aversion in rats with lesions in the frontal lobes: No evidence for interoceptive agnosia. Physiological Psychology, 3: 43–46, 1975.

Dodwell, P. Geometrical approaches to visual processing. In D. Ingle, M. Goodale, and R. Mansfield (Eds.), Analysis of visual behavior. Cambridge, MA: The MIT Press, 1982.

Donaldson, H.H. The rat: Data and reference tables. Philadelphia: Wistar Institute (2nd Ed.), 1924.

Doty, R.L. (Ed.). Mammalian olfaction, reproductive processes and behavior. New York: Academic Press, 1976.

Duensing, F. and Schaefer, K.P. Die aktivitat einzelner Neurone der Formatio Reticularis des nicht gefesselten Kaninchens bei Kopfwendungen und vestiburlaren Reizen. Archiv fuer Psychiatrie und Nervenkrankheiten, 201: 97–122, 1960.

Dukes, W.F. The snark revisited. American Psychologist, 15: 157, 1960.

Eibl-Eibesfeldt, I. The interactions of unlearned behavior patterns and learning in mammals. In J.F. Delafresnaye (Ed.), Brain mechanisms and learning. London: Oxford Council for International Organizations of Medical Sciences Symposium, 1961, pp. 53–73.

Eibl-Eibesfeldt, I. Ethology, the biology of behavior. New York: Holt, Rinehart and Winston, 1970.

Eichelman, B.S. Effect of subcortical lesions on shock-induced aggression in the rat. Journal of Comparative and Physiological Psychology, 74: 331–339, 1971.

Ekman, P., Friesen, M.V., and Ellsworth, P. Emotion in the human face. New York: Pergamon, 1973.

England, A.S., Marks, P.C., Paxinos, G., and Atrens, D.M. Brain hemisections induce asymmetric gastric ulceration. Physiology and Behavior, 23: 513–517, 1979.

Epstein, A.N., Blass, E.M., Batshaw, M.L., and Parks, D. The vital role of saliva as a mechanical sealant for suckling in the rat. Physiology and Behavior, 5: 1395–1398, 1970.

Epstein, A.N. Kissileff, H.R., and Stellar, E. The neuropsychology of thirst: New findings and advances in concepts. Washington, D.C.: V.H. Winston and Sons, 1973.

Erickson, R.P. Simulus coding in topographic and nontopographic afferent modalities: On the significance of the activity of individual neurons. Psychological Reviews, 75: 447–465, 1968.

Erickson, R.P. Common properties of sensory systems. In R.B. Masterton (Ed.), Handbook of behavioral neurobiology (Vol. I). New York: Plenum Press, 1978, pp. 73–90.

Eshkol, N. and Wachmann, A. Movement notation. London: Weidenfeld and Nicolson, 1958.

Esper, E.A. A history of psychology. Philadelphia: W.B. Saunders, 1964.

Estes, W.K. The statistical approach to learning theory. In S. Koch (Ed.), Psychology: A study of a science (Vol. 2). New York: McGraw-Hill, 1959.

Estes, W.K. and Skinner, B.F. Some quantitative properties of anxiety. Journal of Experimental Psychology, 29: 390–400, 1941.

Ettenberg, A. and White, N. Conditioned taste preferences in the rat induced by self-stimulation. Physiology and Behavior, 21: 363–368, 1978.

Evarts, E.V. and Tanji, J. Reflex and intended responses in motor cortex pyramidal tract neurons of monkey. Journal of Neurophysiology, 39: 1069–1080, 1976.

Evinger, C., Baker, R., and McCrea, R.A. Axon collaterals of cat medial and inferior rectus motoneurons. Neuroscience Abstracts, 5: 369, 1979.

Ewert, J.-P. Neural mechanisms of prey-catching and avoidance behavior in the toad (Bufo bufo L.). Brain, Behavior, and Evolution, 3: 36–56, 1970.

Ewert, J.-P. Neuroethology. New York: Springer-Verlag, 1980.

Ewert, J.-P. Neural basis of configurational prey selection in the common toad. In D. Ingle, M. Goodale, and R. Mansfield (Eds.), Analysis of visual behavior. Cambridge, MA: The MIT Press, 1982.

Faingold, C.L. and Caspary, D.M. Changes in reticular formation unit response patterns associated with pentylenetetrazol-induced enhancement of sensory evoked responses. Neuropharmacology, 16: 143–147, 1977.

Fentress, J.C. Development and patterning of movement sequences in inbred mice. In J.A. Kiger (Ed.), The biology of behavior: Proceedings of the thirty-second annual biology colloquium. Corvallis: Oregon State University Press, 1972.

Fentress, J.C. How can behavior be studied from a neuroethological perspective. In H.M. Pinsker and W.D. Willis, Jr. (Eds.), Information processing in the nervous system. New York: Raven Press, 1980, pp. 263–283.

Ferrier, D. The functions of the brain. London: Smith, Elder and Co., 1886.

Fetz, E.E., Finocchio, D.V., Baker, M.A., and Soso, M.J. Sensory and motor responses of precentral cortex cells during comparable passive and active joint movements. Journal of Neurophysiology, 43: 1070–1089, 1980.

Fibiger, H.C., Zis, A.P., and Phillips, A.G. Haloperidol-induced disruption of conditioned avoidance responding: Attenuation by prior training or by anticholinergic drugs. European Journal of Pharmacology, 30: 309–314, 1975.

Fischman, M.W. and Meikle, T.H., Jr. Visual discrimination training in cats after serial tectal and cortical lesions. Journal of Comparative and Physiological Psychology, 59: 193–201, 1965.

Fishman, R. and Roffwaig, H.P. Free choice of lighting and sleep behavior in the laboratory rat. Psychophysiology, 7: 304–305, 1971.

Fleming, A., Vaccarino, F., Tambosso, L., and Chee, P. Vomeronasal and olfactory system modulation of maternal behavior in the rat. Science, 203: 372–374, 1979.

Flourens, P. Investigations of the properties and the functions of the various parts which compose the cerebral mass. In G. von Bonin (Ed.), The cerebral cortex. Springfield, IL: Charles C. Thomas, 1960.

Flourens, S.I. Recherches expérimentales sur les proprieties et les fonctions du système nerveux dans les animaux vertébrés. Paris: Crevot, 1824.

Fog, R. On stereotype and catalepsy: Studies on the effect of amphetamines and neuroleptics in rats. Acta Neurologica (Scand.), 50: 1–66, 1972.

Fox, S.E. and Ranck, J.B., Jr. Electrophysiological characteristics of hippocampal complex-spike cells and theta cells. Experimental Brain Research, 41: 399–410, 1981.

Francis, R.L. 22-kHz calls by isolated rats. Nature, 265: 236–238, 1977.

Franz, S.I. On the functions of the cerebrum: The occipital lobes. Psychological Review Monograph, 13(4): 1, 1911.

Freed, E.K. and Grill, J.J. Levels of function in rat grooming behavior. Neuroscience Abstracts, 5: 468, 1979.

Freeman, D.N. and Marg, E. Visual acuity development coincides with the sensitive period in kittens. Nature, 254: 614–615, 1975.

Freeman, G.I. and Papez, J.W. The effects of subcortical lesions on visual discrimination of rats. Journal of Comparative Psychology, 11: 185–191, 1930.

Freeman, R.D. (Ed.). Developmental neurobiology of vision. New York: Plenum Press, 1979.

French, J.D. The reticular formation. In J. Field, H.W. Magoun, and V.E. Hall (Eds.), Handbook of physiology. Section 1: Neurophysiology (Vol. 2). Washington, D.C.: American Physiological Society, 1960, pp. 1281–1305.

Fuchs, A.F. and Luschei, E.S. Unit activity in the brainstem related to eye movement: Possible inputs to the motor nuclei. Bibl. ophthal (Basel), 82: 17–27, 1972.

Galef, B.G., Jr. Diving for food: Analysis of a possible case of social learning in wild rats. Journal of Comparative and Physiological Psychology, 94: 416–425, 1980.

Gall, F.J. On the functions of the brain and each of its parts (tr by W. Lewis). Boston: Marsh, Capen & Lyon, 1835.

Gall, F.J. and Spurzheim, G. Anatomie et physiologie du système nerveux en général, et du cerveau en particulier (Vol. I). Paris: Haussman et d'Hautel, 1910.

Gallup, G.G. and Maser, J.D. Tonic immobility: Evolutionary underpinnings of human catalepsy and catatonia. In J.D. Maser and M.E.P. Seligman (Eds.), Psychopathology: Experimental models. San Francisco: W.H. Freeman, 1977, pp. 334–462.

Ganor, I. and Golani, I. Coordination and integration in the hindleg step cycle of the rat: Kinematic synergies. Brain Research, 195: 57–67, 1980.

Ganz, L. and Fitch, M. The effect of visual deprivation on perceptual behavior. Experimental Neurology, 22: 638–660, 1968.

Ganz, L. and Haffner, M.E. Permanent perceptual and neurophysiological effects of visual deprivation in the cat. Experimental Brain Research, 20: 67–87, 1974.

Garcia, J., Ervin, F., Yorke, C., and Koelling, R. Conditioning with delayed vitamin injection. Science, 155: 716–718, 1967.

Garcia, J. and Koelling, R. Relation of cue to consequence in avoidance learning. Psychonomic Science, 4: 123–124, 1966.

Gellert, E. Systematic observation: A method in child study. Harvard Educational Review, 25: 179–195, 1955.

Gentile, A.M., Green, S., Nieburgs, A., Schmelzer, W., and Stein, D.G. Disruption and recovery of locomotor and manipulative behavior following cortical lesions in rats. Behavioral Biology, 22: 417–455, 1978.

Geschwind, N. Disconnexion syndromes in animals and man. Brain, 88: 237–294, 1965.

Ghiselli, E.E. The superior colliculus in vision. Journal of Comparative Neurology, 67: 451–467, 1937.

Gibson, J.J. Visually controlled locomotion and visual orientation in animals. British Journal of Psychology, 49: 182–194, 1958.

Gibson, J.J. The senses considered as perceptual systems. Boston: Houghton Mifflin, 1966.

Gibson, J.J. The ecological approach to visual perception. Boston: Houghton Mifflin, 1979.

Giffin, F. and Mitchell, D.E. The rate of recovery of vision after early monocular deprivation in kitten. Journal of Physiology (London), 274: 511–537, 1978.

Gillespie, L.A. and Cooper, R.M. Visual cortical lesions in the rat and a conditioned emotional response. Journal of Comparative and Physiological Psychology, 83: 76–91, 1973.

Ginsberg, A.P. Is the illusory triangle physical or imaginary? Nature, 157: 219–220, 1975.

Glaser, E.M. and Ruchkin, D.S. Principles of neurobiological signal analysis. New York: Academic Press, 1976.

Glickman, S.E. and Scroges, R.W. Curiosity in zoo animals. Behaviour, 24: 151–188, 1966.

Golani, I. Homeostatic motor processes in mammalian interactions: A choreography of display. In P.P.G. Bateson and P.H. Klopfer (Eds.), Perspectives in ethology (Vol. II). New York: Plenum Press, 1976.

Golani, I., Wolgin, D.L., and Teitelbaum, P. A proposed natural geometry of recovery from akinesia in the lateral hypothalamic rat. Brain Research, 164: 237–267, 1979.

Gold, R.M. and Proulx, D.M. Bait-shyness acquisition is impaired by VMH lesions that produce obesity. Journal of Comparative and Physiological Psychology, 79: 201–209, 1972.

Goldman, P.S. and Rosvold, H.E. Localization of function within the dorsolateral prefrontal cortex of the rhesus monkey. Experimental Neurology, 27: 291–305, 1970.

Goltz, F.L. Der Hund Ohne Gosshirn E. Pfluger. Archives fuer Physiologie, 13: 137–148, 1950.

Goodale, M.A. Neural mechanisms of visual orientation in rodents: Targets versus places. In A. Hein and M. Jeannerod (Eds.), Spatially oriented behavior. New York: Springer-Verlag, 1983.

Goodale, M.A. and Lister, T.M. Attention to novel stimuli in rats with lesions of the superior colliculus. Brain Research, 66: 361–362, 1974.

Goodale, M.A. and Milner, A.D. Fractionating orientation behavior in the rodent. In D. Ingle, M. Goodale, and R. Mansfield (Eds.), The analysis of visual behavior. Cambridge, MA: The MIT Press, 1982.

Goodale, M.A. and Murison, R.C.C. The effects of lesions of the superior colliculus on locomotor orientation and the orienting reflex in the rat. Brain Research, 88: 243–261, 1975.

Goodman, E., Jansen, P., and Dewsbury, D. Midbrain reticular formation lesions: habituation to stimulation and copulatory behavior in male rats. Physiology and Behavior, 6: 151–156, 1971.

Gottleib, G. Comparative psychology. American Psychologist, 31: 295–297, 1976.

Grant, E.C. An analysis of the social behaviour of the male laboratory rat. Behaviour, 21: 260–281, 1963.

Grant, E.C. and Chance, M.R.A. Rank order in caged rats. Animal Behavior, 6: 183–194, 1958.

Grant, E.C. and Mackintosh, J.H. A comparison of the social postures of some common laboratory rodents. Behaviour, 21: 246–259, 1963.

Gray, D.S., Terlecki, L.J., Treit, D., and Pinel, J.P.J. The effect of septal lesions on defensive burying in the rat. Physiology and Behavior, 27: 1051–1056, 1981.

Gregory, R. Visual illusions. Scientific American, 219: 66–76, 1968.

Gregory, R.L. The intelligent eye. London: Weidenfeld and Nicholson, 1970.

Grijalva, C.V., Lindholm, E., and Novin, D. Physiological and morphological changes in the gastrointestinal tract induced by hypothalamic intervention: An overview. Brain Research Bulletin, 5 (Suppl. 1): 19–31, 1980.

Grill, H.J. and Norgren, R. Neurological tests and behavioral deficits in chronic thalamic and chronic decerebrate rats. Brain Research, 143: 299–312, 1978a.

Grill, H.J. and Norgren, R. Chronically decerebrate rats demonstrate satiation but not baitshyness. Science, 201: 267–269, 1978b.

Grill, H.J. and Norgren, R. The taste reactivity test. I. Mimetic responses to gustatory stimuli in neurologically normal rats. Brain Research, 143: 263–279, 1978c.

Grill, H.J. and Norgren, R. The taste reactivity test. II. Mimetic responses to gustatory stimuli in chronic thalamic and chronic decerebrate rats. Brain Research, 143: 281–297, 1978d.

Grillner, S. and Shik, M.L. On the descending control of the lumbosacral spinal cord from the "mesencephalic locomotor region." Acta Physiologica (Scand), 87: 320–333, 1973.

Gross, C.G., Rocha-Miranda, C.E., and Bender, D.B. Visual properties of neurons in inferotemporal cortex of the macaque. Journal of Neurophysiology, 35: 96–111, 1972.

Grossman, S.P. Essentials of physiological psychology. New York: Wiley, 1973.

Groves, P.M., Miller, S.W., Parker, M.V., and Rebec, G.V. Organization by sensory modality in the reticular formation of the rat. Brain Research, 54: 207–224, 1973.

Groves, P.M., Rebec, G.V., and Segal, D.S. The action of D-amphetamine on spontaneous activity in the caudate nucleus and reticular formation of the rat. Behavioral Biology, 11: 33–47, 1974.

Gruner, J.A. and Altman, J. Analysis of locomotor performance in comparison to stepping. Experimental Brain Research, 40: 374–382, 1980.

Gruner, J.A., Altman, J., and Spivack, N. Effects of arrested cerebellar development on locomotion in the rat. Experimental Brain Research, 40: 361–373, 1980.

Grupp, L.A., Linseman, M.A., and Cappell, H. Effects of amygdala lesions on taste aversions produced by amphetamine and LiCl. Pharmacology, Biochemistry, and Behavior, 4: 541–544, 1976.

Guillery, R.W. Binocular competition in the control of geniculate cell growth. Journal of Comparative Neurology, 144: 117–130, 1972.

Guillery, R.W. and Stelzner, D.J. The differential effects of unilateral lid closure upon the monocular and binocular segments of the dorsal lateral geniculate nucleus in the cat. Journal of Comparative Neurology, 139: 413–422, 1970.

Gustafson, J.W. and Felbain-Keramidas, S.L. Behavioral and neural approaches to the function of the mystacial vibrissae. Psychological Bulletin, 84: 477–488, 1922.

Gwiazda, J., Brill, S., Mohindra, I., and Held, R. Preferential looking in infants from two to fifty-eight weeks of age. American Journal of Optometry, 57: 428–435, 1980.

Haaxma, R. and Kuypers, H.G.J.M. Intrahemispheric cortical connections and visual guidance of hand and finger movements in the rhesus monkey. Brain, 98: 239–260, 1975.

Hagan, J.J. and Morris, R.G.M. Fimbria-fornix lesions disrupt learning of a ballistic movement (jumping) normally associated with high-frequency hippocampal slow-wave activity. Journal of Physiology, 310: 27P, 1981.

Hainsworth, F.R. Saliva spreading, activity, and body temperature regulation in the rat. American Journal of Physiology, 212: 1288–1292, 1967.

Hainsworth, F.R. and Epstein, A.N. Severe impairment of heat-induced saliva-spreading in rats recovered from lateral hypothalamic lesions. Science, 153: 1255–1257, 1966.

Halgren, E., Babb, T.L., and Crandall, P.H. Activity of human hippocampal formation and amygdala neurons during memory testing. Electroencephalography and Clinical Neurophysiology, 45: 585–601, 1978.

Hall, C.S. Emotional behavior in the rat. I. Defecation and urination as measures of individual differences in emotionality. Journal of Comparative Psychology, 18: 385–403, 1934.

Hall, J.F. and Kobrick, J.L. The relationships among three measures of response strength. Journal of Comparative and Physiological Psychology, 45: 280–282, 1952.

Halstead, W.C. Brain and intelligence: A quantitative study of the frontal lobes. Chicago: University of Chicago Press, 1947.

Hamasaki, D.I. and Flynn, J.T. Physiological properties of retinal ganglion cells of 3-week-old kittens. Vision Research, 17: 275–284, 1977.

Hamilton, C.R. and Lund, J.S. Visual discrimination of movement: Midbrain or forebrain. Science, 170: 1428–1430, 1970.

Hankins, W.G., Garcia, J., and Rusinak, K.W. Dissociation of odor and taste in baitshyness. Behavioral Biology, 8: 407–419, 1973.

Hansen, E.L. and McKenzie, G.M. Dexamphetamine increases striatal neuronal firing in freely moving rats. Neuropharmacology, 18: 547–552, 1979.

Harlow, H.F., Gluck, J.P., and Suomi, S.J. Generalization of behavioral data between nonhuman and human animals. American Psychologist, 27: 709–716, 1972.

Harrell, N.W. and Isaac, W. Frontal lesions and illumination effects upon the activity of the albino rat. Physiology and Behavior, 4: 477–478, 1969.

Hartshorne, H. and May, M.A. Studies in the nature of character. 1. Studies in deceit. New York: Macmillan, 1928.

Hartshorne, H., May, M.A., and Maller, J.B. Studies in the nature of character. II. Studies in service and self-control. New York: Macmillan, 1929.

Hassler, R. Interaction of reticular activating system for vigilance and the truncothalamic and pallidal systems for directing awareness and attention under striatal control. In P. Buser and A. Buser-Rougeul (Eds.), Cerebral correlates of conscious experience. Amsterdam: North Holland, 1978, pp. 111–129.

Hatch, A., Wiberg, G.S., Balazs, T., and Grice, H.C. Long-term isolation stress in rats. Science, 142: 507, 1963.

Hebb, D.O. The organization of behavior: a neuropsychological theory. New York: Wiley, 1949.

Hebb, D.O. Essay on mind. Hillsdale, NJ: Lawrence Erlbaum Assoc., 1980.

Hebb, D.O. and Mahut, H. Motivation et recherche du changement perceptif chez le rat et chez l'homme. Journal Psychologie Normale Pathologique, 52: 209–211, 1955.

Hecaen, H. and Albert, M.L. Human neuropsychology. New York: Wiley, 1978.

Heilman, K.M. and Watson, R.T. The neglect syndrome—a unilateral defect of the orienting response. In S. Harnad, R.W. Doty, L. Goldstein, J. Jaynes, and G. Krauthamer (Eds.), Lateralization in the nervous system. New York: Academic Press, 1977, pp. 285–302.

Heimer, L. and Larsson, K. Drastic changes in the mating behavior of male rats following lesions in the junction of diencephalon and mesencephalon. Experientia, 20: 460–461, 1964.

Heimer, L. and Larsson, K. Impairment of mating behavior in male rats following lesions in the preoptic-anterior hypothalamic continuum. Brain Research, 3: 248–263, 1967.

Heitlander, H. and Hoffman, K.-P. The visual field of monocularly deprived cats after late closure or enucleation of the non-deprived eye. Brain Research, 145: 153–160, 1978.

Held, R., Birch, E., and Gwiazda, J. Stereoacuity of human infants. Proceedings of the National Academy of Science, USA, 27: 5572, 1980.

Henderson, J.W. Essential blepharospasm. Transactions of the American Ophthalmological Society, 54: 453–520, 1956.

Henke, P.G. The centromedial amygdala and gastric pathology in rats. Physiology and Behavior, 25: 107–112, 1980.

Herberg, L.J. and Blundell, J.E. Non-interaction of ventromedial and lateral hypothalamic mechanisms in the regulation of feeding and hoarding behaviour in the rat. Quarterly Journal of Experimental Psychology, 22: 133–141, 1970.

Hering, E. Memory: Lectures on the specific energies of the nervous system. Chicago: Open Court Publishing Co., 1913.

Hernandez-Peon, R., Scherrer, H., and Jouvet, M. Modification of electrical activity in cochlear nucleus during "attention" in unanesthetized cats. Science, 123: 331–332, 1956.

Hess, S., Burgi, S. and Bucher, V. Motor function of tectal and tegmental area. Monotsschrift fuer Psychiatrie und Neurologie, 112: 1–52, 1946.

Hickey, T.L. Development of the dorsal lateral geniculate nucleus in normal and visually deprived cats. Journal of Comparative Neurology, 189: 467–481, 1980.

Hicks, S.P. and D'Amato, C.J. Motor-sensory cortex-corticospinal system and developing locomotion and placing in rats. The American Journal of Anatomy, 143: 1–42, 1975.

Hicks, S.P. and D'Amato, C.J. Development of the motor system: Hopping rats produced by prenatal irradiation. Experimental Neurology, 70: 24–39, 1980.

Hikosaka, O. and Kawakami, T. Inhibitory reticular neurons related to the quick phase of vestibular nystagmus—their location and projection. Experimental Brain Research, 27: 377–396, 1977.

Hinde, R.A. Animal behaviour. A synthesis of ethology and comparative psychology. New York: McGraw-Hill, 1966.

Hinde, R.A. Animal behaviour (2nd Ed.). New York: McGraw-Hill, 1970.

Hobson, J.A. The cellular basis of sleep cycle control. Advances in Sleep Research, 1: 217–250, 1974.

Hobson, J.A., McCarley, R.W., Freedman, R., and Pivik, R.T. Time course of discharge rate changes by cat pontine brain stem neurons during sleep cycle. Journal of Neurophysiology, 37: 1297–1309, 1974.

Hobson, J.A., McCarley, R.W., and Wyzinski, P.W. Sleep cycle oscillation: Reciprocal discharge by two brainstem neuronal groups. Science, 189: 55–58, 1975.

Hodos, W. The concept of homology and the evolution of behavior. In R.B. Masterton, W. Hodos, and H. Jerison (Eds.), Evolution, brain and behavior: Persistent problems. Hillsdale, NJ: Lawrence Erlbaum Assoc., 1976.

Hodos, W. and Campbell, C.B.G. Scale naturae: Why there is no theory in comparative psychology. Psychological Review, 76: 337–350, 1969.

Hoffman, J.C. The influence of photoperiods on reproductive functions in female mammals. In R.O. Greep and E.B. Astwood (Eds.), Handbook of physiology; Section 7; Endocrinology (Vol. 2): Female reproductive system. Part 1. Baltimore: Williams & Wilkins, 1973, pp. 57–77.

Hoffman, K. Versuche zur Analyse der Tagesperiodik. I. Der Einfluss der Lichtintensitat. Zeit vergl Physiologie, 43: 544–566, 1960.

Hoffman, K.-P. and Cynader, M. Functional aspects of plasticity in the visual system of adult cats after early monocular deprivation. Philosophical Transactions of the Royal Society of London, 278: 411–424, 1977.

Holmes, G. Disturbances in visual orientation. British Journal of Ophthalmology, 2: 449–506, 1918. Reprinted in F. Walshe (Ed.), Selected papers of Sir Gordon Holmes. London: Macmillan, 1956.

Horel, J.A. Effects of subcortical lesions on brightness discrimination acquired by rats without visual cortex. Journal of Comparative and Physiological Psychology, 56: 103–109, 1968.

Hruska, R.E., Kennedy, S., and Silbergeld, E.K. Quantitative aspects of normal locomotion in rats. Life Sciences, 25: 171–180, 1979.

Hruska, R.E. and Silbergeld, E.K. Abnormal locomotion in rats after bilateral intrastriatal injection of kainic acid. Life Sciences, 25: 181–194, 1979.

Hubel, D.H. Single unit activity in visual cortex of the unanesthetized cat. Federation Proceedings, 16: 63, 1957.

Hubel, D.H. Cortical unit responses to visual stimuli in nonanesthetized cats. American Journal of Ophthalmology, 46: 110–121, 1958.

Hubel, D.H. and Wiesel, T.N. The period of susceptibility to the physiological effects of unilateral eye closure in kittens. Journal of Physiology, 206: 419–436, 1970.

Hubel, D.H. and Wiesel, T.N. Brain mechanisms of vision. Scientific American, 241: 150–162, 1979.

Hudson, B.B. One-trial learning in the domestic rat. Genetic Psychology Monographs, 41: 99–145, 1950.

Hull, C.L. Principles of behavior. New York: Appleton-Century-Crofts, 1943.

Humphrey, N.K. and Weiskrantz, L. Vision in monkeys after removal of the striate cortex. Nature, 215: 595–597, 1967.

Humphries, C.R., O'Brien, M., and Paxinos, G. PCA: Effects on ejaculation, thermoregulation, salivation, and irritability in rats. Pharmacology, Biochemistry, and Behavior, 12: 851–854, 1980.

Hutt, C. Exploration and play in children. Symposium of the Zoological Society of London, 18: 61–81, 1966.

Hutt, C. Temporal effects on response decrement and stimulus satiation in exploration. British Journal of Psychology, 58: 365–373, 1967.

Hutt, C. and Coxon, M. Systematic observation in clinical psychology. Archives of General Psychiatry, 12: 374–378, 1965.

Hutt, S.J. and Hutt, C. Stereotypy, arousal and autism. Human Development, 11: 277–286, 1968.

Hutt. S.J. and Hutt, C. Direct observation and measurement of behavior. Springfield, IL: Charles C. Thomas, 1970.

Hutt, C., Hutt, S.J., Lee, D., and Ounsted, C. Arousal and childhood autism. Nature, 204:908–909, 1964.

Hutt, C. Jackson, P., and Level, M. Behavioral parameters and drug effects. Epilepsia, 7:250–259, 1966.

Ikeda, H. and Tremain, K.E. Amblyopia resulting from penalisation: Neurophysiological studies of kittens reared with atropinisation of one or both eyes. British Journal of Opthalmology, 62: 21–28, 1978.

Ingle, D. Two visual systems in the frog. Science, 181: 1053–1055, 1973.

Ingle, D. Detection of stationary objects by frogs (Rana pipiens) after ablation of optic tectum. Journal of Comparative and Physiological Psychology, 91: 1359–1364, 1977a.

Ingle, D. Role of visual cortex in anticipatory orientation towards moving targets by the gerbil. Neuroscience Abstracts, 3: 68, 1977b.

Ingle, D. Organization of visuomotor behaviors in vertebrates. In D. Ingle, M. Goodale, and R. Manfield (Eds.), The analysis of visual behavior. Cambridge, MA: The MIT Press, 1982.

Ingle, D., Cheal, M., and Dizio, P. Cine analysis of visual orientation and pursuit by the Mongolian gerbil. Journal of Comparative and Physiological Psychology, 93: 919–928, 1979.

Ingle, D. and Sprague, J.M. Sensorimotor function of the midbrain tectum. Neuroscience Research Program Bulletin, 13: 169–288, 1975.

Isaacson, R.L. The limbic system. New York: Plenum Press, 1974.

Jacobs, B.L., Trulson, M.E., and Stern, W.C. Behavioral effects of LSD in the cat: Proposal of an animal behavior model for studying the actions of hallucinogenic drugs. Brain Research, 132: 301–314, 1977.

Jacobsen, C.F. Functions of frontal association areas in primates. Archives of Neurology and Psychiatry (Chicago), 33: 558–568, 1935.

Jacobsen, C.F. Studies of cerebral function in primates. Comparative Psychology Monographs, 13: 1–68, 1936.

James, W. The principles of psychology. New York: Henry Holt and Co., 1890.

Jankowska, E., Lund, S., Lundberg, A., and Pompeiano, O. Inhibitory effects evoked through ventral reticulospinal pathways. Archives Italiannes Biologie, 106: 124–140, 1968.

Jasper, H.H. Reticular-cortical systems and theories of the integrative action of the brain. In H.F. Harlow and C.N. Woolsey (Eds.), Biological and biochemical bases of behavior. Madison: University of Wisconsin Press, 1958, pp. 37–61.

Jasper, H.H. Problems of relating cellular or molecular specificity to cognitive function: Importance of state dependent relations. In F.O. Schmitt, G.F. Worden, G. Adelman, and S.G. Dennis (Eds.), The organization of the cerebral cortex. Cambridge: The MIT Press, 1981, pp. 375–393.

Jerison, H.J. Evolution of the brain and intelligence. New York: Academic Press, 1973.

Jersild, A.T. and Meigs, M.F. Direct observation as a research method. Review of Educational Research, 9: 472–482, 1939.

Johannsen, I.B. and Hall, W.G. The ontogeny of feeding in rats: III. Thermal determinants of early ingestive responding. Journal of Comparative and Physiological Psychology, 94: 977–992, 1980.

John, E.R. and Schwartz, E.L. The neurophysiology of information processing and cognition. Annual Review of Psychology, 29: 1–29, 1978.

Johnson, D.A., Poplawsky, A., and Bieliauskas, L. Alterations of social behavior in rats and hamsters following lesions of the septal forebrain. Psychonomic Science, 26: 19–20, 1972.

Jonason, R.K. and Enloe, L.J. Alterations in social behavior following septal and amygdaloid lesions in the rat. Journal of Comparative and Physiological Psychology, 75: 286–301, 1971.

Jones, B. Elimination of paradoxical sleep by lesions of the pontine gigantocellular tegmental field in the cat. Neuroscience Letters, 13: 285–293, 1979.

Jung, R. and Hassler, R. The extrapyramidal system. In J. Field et al. (Eds.), Handbook of physiology, Section 1 (Vol. 2): Neurophysiology. Chapter 35. Washington, D.C.: American Physiological Society, 1960, pp. 863–927.

Kaada, B.R., Jansen, J., Jr. and Andersen, P. Stimulation of the hippocampus and medial cortical areas in unanesthetized cats. Neurology, 3: 844–857, 1953.

Kahonen, T. Associative memory. New York: Springer-Verlag, 1978.

Kalil, R. A quantitative study of the effects of monocular enucleation and deprivation on cell growth in the dorsal lateral geniculate nucleus of the cat. Journal of Comparative Neurology, 189: 483–524, 1980.

Kandel, E.R. Neuronal plasticity and the modification of behavior. In J.M. Brookhart, V.B. Mountcastle and E.R. Kandel (Eds.), Handbook of physiology, Part 2 (Vol. 7). Bethesda: American Physiological Society, 1977, pp. 1137–1182.

Kartje-Tillotson, G. and Castro, A.J. Limb preference after unilateral pyramidotomy in adult and neonatal rats. Physiology and Behavior, 24: 293–296, 1980.

Kaye, M., Mitchell, D.E., and Cynader, M. Selective loss of binocular depth perception after ablation of cat visual cortex. Nature, 293: 60–62, 1981.

Keating, E.G. Effects of tectal lesions on peripheral field vision in the monkey.

Brain Research, 104: 316–320, 1976.

Keehn, J.D. and Arnold, E.M.M. Licking rates of albino rats. Science, 132: 739–741, 1960.

Keller, E.L. Participation of medial pontine reticular formation in eye movement generation in monkey. Journal of Neurophysiology, 37: 316–332, 1974.

Kelly, J.P. and Van Essen, D.C. Cell structure and function in the visual cortex of the cat. Journal of Physiology, 238: 515–547, 1974.

Kiefer, S.W. and Braun, J.J. Acquisition of taste avoidance habits in rats lacking gustatory neocortex. Physiological Psychology, 7: 245–250, 1979.

Kimble, D.P., Rogers, L., and Hendrickson, C.W. Hippocampal lesions disrupt maternal, not sexual behavior in the albino rat. Journal of Comparative and Physiological Psychology, 63: 401–407, 1967.

Kimura, D. and Archibald, Y. Motor functions of the left hemisphere. Brain, 97: 337–350, 1974.

Kinder, E.F. A study of the nest-building activity of the albino rat. Journal of Experimental Zoology, 47: 117–161, 1927.

King, F.A. Effects of septal and amygdaloid lesions on emotional behavior and conditioned avoidance responses in the rat. Journal of Nervous and Mental Diseases, 126: 57–63, 1956.

Kirvel, R.D. Sensorimotor responsiveness in rats with unilateral superior collicular and amygdaloid lesions. Journal of Comparative and Physiological Psychology, 89: 882–891, 1975.

Kissileff, H.R. and Epstein, A.N. Exaggerated prandial drinking in the "recovered lateral" rat without saliva. Journal of Comparative and Physiological Psychology, 67: 301–308, 1969.

Kluver, H. Certain effects of lesions of the occipital lobes in macaques. Journal of Psychology, 4: 383–401, 1937.

Kluver, H. Visual function after removal of the occipital lobes in monkeys. Journal of Psychology, 11: 23–45, 1941.

Knight, W.R. Effects of septal forebrain lesions upon nesting, temperature regulatory and maternal behaviors in ground squirrels and other rodents. Pennsylvania Academy of Science, 44: 184–191, 1970.

Koffka, K. Principles of gestalt psychology. New York: Harcourt, Brace, and Co., 1935.

Kohler, W. Gestalt psychology. New York: Liveright, 1929.

Kohler, W. and Held, R. The cortical correlate of pattern vision. Science, 110: 414–419, 1949.

Kohler, W. and Wallach, H. Figural after-effects. An investigation of visual processes. Proceedings of the American Philosophical Society, 88: 269–357, 1944.

Kolb, B. Prefrontal lesions alter eating and hoarding behavior in rats. Physiology and Behavior, 12: 507–511, 1974a.

Kolb, B. Social behavior of rats with chronic prefrontal lesions. Journal of Comparative and Physiological Psychology, 87: 466–474, 1974b.

Kolb, B. Studies on the caudate-putamen and the dorsomedial thalamic nucleus of the rat: Implications for mammalian frontal-lobe functions. Physiology and Behavior, 18: 237–244, 1977.

Kolb, B. and Milner, B. Performance of complex arm and facial movements after focal brain lesions. Neuropsychologia, 19: 491–503, 1981a.

Kolb, B. and Milner, B. Observations of spontaneous facial expression after focal cerebral excisions and after intracarotid injection of sodium amytal. Neuropsychologia, 19: 505–514, 1981b.

Kolb, B. and Nonneman, A.J. Frontolimbic lesions and social behavior in the rat. Physiology and Behavior, 13: 637–643, 1974.

Kolb, B. and Nonneman, A.J. The development of social responsiveness in kittens. Animal Behaviour, 23: 368–374, 1975a.

Kolb, B. and Nonneman, A.J. Prefrontal cortex and the regulation of food intake in the rat. Journal of Comparative and Physiological Psychology, 88: 806–815, 1975b.

Kolb, B. and Nonneman, A.J. Sparing of function in rats with early prefrontal cortex lesions. Brain Research, 151: 135–148, 1978.

Kolb, B., Nonneman, A.J., and Abplanalp, P. Studies on the neural mechanisms of baitshyness in rats. Bulletin of the Psychonomic Society, 10: 389–392, 1977.

Kolb, B., Nonneman, A.J., and Singh, R.K. Double dissociation of spatial impairments and perseveration following selective prefontal lesions in rats. Journal of Comparative and Physiological Psychology, 87: 772–780, 1974.

Kolb, B., Sutherland, R.J., Nonneman, A.J., and Whishaw, I.Q. Asymmetry in the cerebral hemispheres of the rat, mouse, rabbit and cat: The right hemisphere is larger. Experimental Neurology, 78:348–359, 1982.

Kolb, B., Sutherland, R., and Whishaw, I.Q. A comparison of the contribution of the frontal and parietal association cortex to spatial localization in rats. Behavioral Neuroscience in press. (a)

Kolb, B., Sutherland, R.J., and Whishaw, I.Q. Neonatal hemidecortication or frontal cortex ablation produce similar behavioral sparing but opposite effects upon morphogenesis of remaining cortex. Journal of Behavioral Neuroscience, in press. (b)

Kolb, B. and Taylor, L. Affective behavior in patients with localized cortical excisions: Role of lesion site and side. Science, 214: 89–91, 1981.

Kolb, B. and Whishaw, I.Q. Effects of brain lesions and atropine on hippocampal and neocortical electroencephalograms in the rat. Experimental Neurology, 56: 1–22, 1977.

Kolb, B. and Whishaw, I.Q. Decortication: Was Flourens correct? Neuroscience Abstracts, 4: 76, 1978.

Kolb, B. and Whishaw, I.Q. Failure to find sparing of species-typical behaviors following neonatal prefrontal cortex lesions. Neuroscience Abstracts, 5: 629, 1979.

Kolb, B. and Whishaw, I.Q. Fundamentals of human neuropsychology. San Francisco: W.H. Freeman and Co., 1980.

Kolb, B. and Whishaw, I.Q. Neonatal frontal lesions in the rat: Sparing of learned but not species-typical behavior in the presence of reduced brain weight and cortical thickness. Journal of Comparative and Physiological Psychology, 95: 863–879, 1981a.

Kolb, B. and Whishaw, I.Q. Decortication of rats in infancy or adulthood produced comparable functional losses on learned and species-typical behaviors. Journal of Comparative and Physiological Psychology, 95: 468–483, 1981b.

Kolb, B. and Whishaw, I.Q. Dissociation of the contributions of the prefrontal, motor and parietal cortex to the control of movement in the rat. Canadian Journal of Psychology, in press.

Kolb, B., Whishaw, I.Q., and Schallert, T. Aphagia, behavior sequencing and body weight set point following orbital frontal lesions in rats. Physiology and Behavior, 19: 93–103, 1977.

Komisaruk, B.R. and Larsson, K. Suppression of a spinal and cranial nerve reflex by vaginal or rectal probing in rats. Brain Research, 35: 231–235, 1971.

Konishi, M. Ethology and neurobiology. American Scientist, 59: 56–63, 1971.

Konorski, J. Disinhibition of inhibitory CRs after prefrontal lesions in dogs. In A. Fessard, R.W. Gerard, and J. Konorski (Eds.), Brain mechanisms and learning. Springfield, IL: Charles C. Thomas, 567–573, 1961.

Konorski, J. Integrative activity of the brain. Chicago: The University of Chicago Press, 1967.

Konorski, J. and Lawicka, W. Analysis of errors by prefrontal animals on the delayed-response test. In J.M. Warren and K. Akert (Eds.), The frontal granular cortex and behavior. New York: McGraw-Hill, 1964, pp. 271–294.

Kow, L.-M., Grill, H.J., and Pfaff, D.W. Elimination of lordosis in decerebrate female rats: Observations from acute and chronic preparations. Physiology and Behavior, 20: 171–174, 1978.

Krane, R., Sinnamon, H., and Thomas, G. Conditioned taste aversions and neophobia in rats with hippocampal lesions. Journal of Comparative and Physiological Psychology, 90: 680–693, 1976.

Kratz, K.E. and Spear, P.D. Effects of visual deprivation and alterations in binocular competition on responses of striate cortex neurons in the cat. Journal of Comparative Neurology, 170: 141–152, 1976.

Kratz, K.E., Spear, P.D., and Smith, D.C. Postcritical-period reversal of effects of monocular deprivation on striate cortex cells in the cat. Journal of Neurophysiology, 39: 501–511, 1976.

Kreezer, G.L. Technics for the investigation of behavioral phenomena in the rat. In E.J. Farris and J.Q. Griffith Jr. (Eds.), The rat in laboratory investigation. New York: Hafner Publishing Co., 1949, pp. 203–277.

Kubie, J.L. and Ranck, J.B., Jr. Sensory-behavioral correlates in individual hippocampal neurons in three situations: Space and context. In W. Seifert (Ed.), Molecular, cellular, and behavioral neurobiology of the hippocampus. New York: Academic Press, 1982.

Kuffler, S. and Nicholls, J. From neuron to brain. Sunderland, MA: Sinauer Associates, Inc., 1976.

Kuschinsky, K. and Hornykiewicz, O. Morphine catalepsy in the rat: Relation to striatal dopamine metabolism. European Journal of Pharmacology, 19: 119–122, 1972.

Lapointe, G. and Nosal, G. The postnatal evolution of muscular twitches in the developing rat. Experientia, 35: 1070–1071, 1979.

Larssen, K. Mating behavior in male rats after cerebral cortex ablation: II. Effects of lesions in the frontal lobes compared to lesions in the posterior half of the hemispheres. Journal of Experimental Zoology, 155: 203–214, 1964.

Lashley, K.S. Brain mechanisms and intelligence: A quantitative study of injuries to the brain. Chicago: The University of Chicago Press, 1929.

Lashley, K.S. The mechanism of vision. I. A method for rapid analysis of pattern-vision in the rat. Journal of Genetic Psychology, 37: 453–460, 1930.

Lashley, K.S. The mechanism of vision, XII. Nervous structures concerned in the acquisition of habits based on reactions to light. Comparative Psychology Monographs, 11: 43–79, 1935a.

Lashley, K.S. Studies of cerebral function in learning. XI. The behavior of the rat in latch-box situations. Comparative Psychology Monographs, 11: 1–42, 1935b.

Lashley, K.S. Factors limiting recovery after central nervous system lesions. Journal of Nervous and Mental Disease, 88: 733–755, 1938.

Lashley, K.S. The mechanism of vision. XVI. The functioning of small remnants of the visual cortex. Journal of Comparative Neurology, 70: 45–67, 1939.

Lashley, K.S. The problem of cerebral organization in vision. Biological Symposia, 7: 302–322, 1942.

Lashley, K.S. The problem of serial order in behavior. In L.A. Jeffress, (Ed.), Cerebral mechanisms in behavior. New York: Wiley, 1951, pp. 112–136.

Lashley, K.S. In search of the engram. In F.A. Beach, D.O. Hebb, C.T. Morgan, and H.W. Nissen (Eds.), The neuropsychology of Lashley. New York: McGraw-Hill, 1960, pp. 478–505.

Lashley, K.S., Chow, K., and Semmes, J. An examination of the electrical field theory of cerebral integration. Psychological Reviews, 58: 123–135, 1951.

Latané, B. Gregariousness and fear in laboratory rats. Journal of Experimental Social Psychology, 5: 61–69, 1970.

Lau, P. and Miczek, K.A. Differential effects of septal lesions on attack and defensive-submission reactions during intraspecies aggression in rats. Physiology and Behavior, 18: 479–485, 1977.

Lawrence, D.G. and Hopkins, D.A. The development of motor control in the rhesus monkey: Evidence concerning the role of corticomotor-neuronal connections. Brain, 99: 235–254, 1976.

Lawrence, D.G. and Kuypers, H.G.J.M. The functional organization of the motor system in the monkey. I. The effects of bilateral pyramidal lesions. Brain, 91: 1–18, 1968.

Layman, J.D. Functions of the superior colliculi in vision. Journal of Genetic Psychology, 49: 33–47, 1936.

Leaton, R.N. Exploratory behavior in rats with hippocampal lesions. Journal of Comparative and Physiological Psychology, 59: 325–330, 1965.

Lecas, J.C. and Malmo, C. Reticular multiple-unit activity and motor changes during DRL learning in cats. Physiology and Behavior 26:451–459, 1981.

Lee, H.K., Chai, C.Y., Chung, P.M., and Chen, C.C. Medullary unit responses to changes in local and hypothalamic temperatures in the cat. Brain Research Bulletin, 2: 375–380, 1977.

Legg, C.R. Effects of subcortical lesions on the pupillary light reflex in the rat. Neuropsychologia, 13: 373–376, 1975.

Lehmkuhle, S., Kratz, K.E., Manzel, S.C., and Sherman, S.M. An effect of early monocular lid suture upon the development of X-cells in the cat's lateral geniculate nucleus. Brain Research, 157: 346–350, 1978.

Lehrman, D.S. Ethology and psychology. In J. Wortis (Ed.), Recent advances in biological psychiatry (Vol. IV). New York: Plenum Press, 1962.

LeVay, S., Stryker, M.P., and Shatz, C.J. Ocular dominance columns and their development in layer IV of the cat's visual cortex: A quantitative study.

Journal of Comparative Neurology, 179: 223–244, 1978.

Levine, M.S., Ferguson, N., Kreinick, C.J., Gustafson, J.W., and Schwartzbaum, J.S. Sensorimotor dysfunctions and aphagia and adipsia following pallidal lesions in rats. Journal of Comparative and Physiological Psychology, 77: 282–293, 1971.

Levine, M.S. and Schwartzbaum, J.S. Sensorimotor functions of the striatopallidal system and lateral hypothalamus and consummatory behavior in rats. Journal of Comparative and Physiological Psychology, 85: 615–635, 1973.

Levitt, D.R. and Teitelbaum, P. Somnolence, akinesia, and sensory activation of motivated behavior in the lateral hypothalamic syndrome. Proceedings of the National Academy of Sciences, 72: 2819–2823, 1975.

Lin, Y.C. Autonomic nervous control of cardiovascular response during diving in the rat. American Journal of Physiology, 27: 601–605, 1974.

Lin, Y.C. and Baker, D.G. Cardiac output and its distribution during diving in the rat. American Journal of Physiology, 228: 733–737, 1975.

Lindholm, E., Shumway, G.S., Grijalva, C.V., Schallert, T., and Ruppel, M. Gastric pathology produced by hypothalamic lesions in rats. Physiology and Behavior, 14: 165–169, 1975.

Lindsley, D.B. Emotion. In S.S. Stevens (Ed.), Handbook of experimental psychology. New York: Wiley, 1951, pp. 473–516.

Lippa, A.S., Nash, R., and Greenblatt, E. Pre-clinical neuropsychopharmacological testing procedures for anxiolytic drugs. In S. Fielding and H. Lal (Eds.), Anxiolytics. New York: Futura, 1979.

Livingston, M.S. and Hubel, D.H. Effects of sleep and arousal on the processing of visual information in the cat. Nature, 291: 554–561, 1981.

Ljungberg, T. and Ungerstedt, U. Sensory inattention produced by 6-hydroxydopamine-induced degeneration of ascending dopamine neurons in the brain. Experimental Neurology, 53: 585–600, 1976.

Lockhard, R.B. The albino rat: A defensible choice or bad habit. American Psychologist, 23: 734–742, 1968.

Lorden, J.F. Effects of lesions of the gustatory neocortex on taste aversion learning in the rat. Journal of Comparative and Physiological Psychology, 90: 665–679, 1976.

Lore, R., Flannelly, K., and Farina, P. Ultrasounds produced by rats accompany decreases in intraspecific fighting. Aggressive Behavior, 2: 175–181, 1976.

Lore, R., Nikoletseas, M., and Flannelly, K. Aggression in rats: Does the colony-intruder model require a colony? Behavioral Biology, 28: 243–245, 1980.

Lorenz, K.Z. The comparative method in studying innate behaviour patterns. Symposia of the Society for Experimental Biology, 4: 221–268, 1950.

Lorenz, K.Z. The evolution of behavior. Scientific American, 199: 67–78, 1958.

Lorenz, K.Z. On aggression. London: Methuen, 1966.

Lown, B.A. Comparative psychology 25 years after. American Psychologist, 30: 858–859, 1975.

Lubar, J.F., Herrmann, T.F., Moore, D.R., and Shouse, M.N. Effect of septal and frontal ablations on species-typical behavior in the rat. Journal of Comparative and Physiological Psychology, 83: 260–270, 1973.

Lucas, E.A., Foutz, A.S., Dement, W.C., and Mitler, M.M. Sleep cycle organization in narcoleptic and normal dogs. Physiology and Behavior, 23: 737–743, 1979.

Luria, A.R. The Working Brain. Harmondsworth: Penguin, 1973.

Luschei, E.S. and Fuchs, A.F. Activity of brain stem neurons during eye movements of alert monkeys. Journal of Neurophysiology, 35: 445–461, 1972.

Lynch, J.C., Mountcastle, V.B., Talbot, W.H., and Yin, T.C.T. Parietal lobe mechanisms for directed visual attention. Journal of Neurophysiology, 40: 362–389, 1977.

Machne, X., Calma, I., and Magoun, W.H. Unit activity of central cephalic brain stem in EEG arousal. Journal of Neurophysiology, 18: 547–558, 1955.

Mackintosh, N.J. The psychology of animal learning. London: Academic Press, 1974.

Maffei, L. and Fiorentini, A. Monocular deprivation in kittens impairs the spatial resolution of geniculate neurones. Nature, 264: 754–755, 1976.

Maher, B.A. and McIntire, R.W. The extinction of the CER following frontal ablation. Journal of Comparative and Physiological Psychology, 53: 549–552, 1960.

Maier, N.R.F. The cortical area concerned with coordinated walking in the rat. Journal of Comparative Neurology, 61: 395–405, 1935.

Maire, F.W. and Patton, H.D. Hyperactivity and pulmonary edema from rostral hypothalamic lesions in rats. American Journal of Physiology, 178: 315–320, 1954.

Maire, F.W. and Patton, H.D. Neural structures involved in the genesis of "preoptic pulmonary edema," gastric erosions and behavioral change. American Journal of Physiology, 184: 345–350, 1965.

Malmo, R.B. and Bélanger, D. Related physiological and behavioral changes: What are their determinants? In S.S. Kety, E.V. Evarts, and H.L. Williams (Eds.), Sleep and altered states of consciousness. Research Publications of the Association for Research in Nervous and Mental Disease, Baltimore: Williams & Wilkins, 45: 288–313, 1967.

Margules, D.L., Lewis, M.J., Dragovich, J., and Margules, A. Hypothalamic norepinephrine: Circadian rhythms and the control of feeding behavior. Science, 178: 640–642, 1972.

Marler, P. and Hamilton, W.J. Mechanisms of animal behaviour. New York: Wiley, 1966.

Marr, D. Analysing natural images: A computational theory of texture vision. M.I.T. AI Memo, 33, 4, 1975.

Marr, D. Early processing of visual information. Philosophical Transactions of the Royal Society of London (Series B), 275: 483–519, 1976.

Marshall, J.F. Increased orientation to sensory stimuli following medial hypothalamic damage in rats. Brain Research, 86: 373–387, 1975.

Marshall, J.F. Comparison of the sensorimotor dysfunctions produced by damage to lateral hypothalamus or superior colliculus in the rat. Experimental Neurology, 58: 203–217, 1978.

Marshall, J.F. Somatosensory inattention after dopamine-depleting intracerebral 6-OHDA injections: Spontaneous recovery and pharamcological control. Brain Research, 177: 311–324, 1979.

Marshall, J.F. and Berrios, N. Movement disorders of aged rats: Reversal by dopamine receptor stimulation. Science, 206: 477–479, 1979.

Marshall, J.F., Berrios, N., and Sawyer, S. Neostriatal dopamine and sensory inattention. Journal of Comparative and Physiological Psychology, 94: 833–846, 1980.

Marshall, J.F. and Gotthelf, T. Sensory inattention in rats with 6-hydroxydopamine-induced degeneration of ascending dopaminergic neurons: Apomorphine-induced reversal of deficits. Experimental Neurology, 65: 398–411, 1979.

Marshall, F.J., Levitan, D., and Stricker, E.M. Activation-induced restoration of sensorimotor function in rats with dopamine-depleting brain lesions. Journal of Comparative and Physiological Psychology, 90: 536–546, 1976.

Marshall, J.F., Richardson, J.S., and Teitelbaum, P. Nigrostriatal bundle damage and the lateral hypothalamic syndrome. Journal of Comparative and Physiological Psychology, 87: 808–830, 1974.

Marshall, J.F. and Teitelbaum, P. Further analysis of sensory inattention following lateral hypothalamic damage in rats. Journal of Comparative and Physiological Psychology, 86: 375–395, 1974.

Marshall, J.F., Turner, B.H., and Teitelbaum, P. Sensory neglect produced by lateral hyopohalamic damage. Science, 174: 523–525, 1971.

Martin, J.P. The basal ganglia and posture. Philadelphia: J.B. Lippincott, 1967.

Mason, S.T. and Iversen, S.D. Theories of the dorsal bundle extinction effect. Brain Research Reviews, 1: 107–137, 1979.

Masterton, R.B., Heffner, H.E., and Ravizza, R.J. Evolution of human hearing. Journal of the Acoustical Society of America, 45: 966–985, 1969.

Mateer, C. and Kimura, D. Impairment of nonverbal oral movements in aphasia. Brain and Language, 4: 262–276, 1977.

McCarley, R.W. and Hobson, J.A. Single neuron activity in cat gigantocellular tegmental field: Selectivity of discharge in desynchronized sleep. Science, 174: 1250–1252, 1971.

McCarley, R.W. and Hobson, J.A. Discharge patterns of cat pontine brainstem neurons during desynchronized sleep. Journal of Neurophysiology, 38: 751–766, 1975a.

McCarley, R.W. and Hobson, J.A. Neuronal excitability modulation over the sleep cycle: A structural and mathematical model. Science, 189: 58–60, 1975b.

McCleary, R.A. Response specificity in the behavioral effects of limbic system lesions in the cat. Journal of Comparative and Physiological Psychology, 54: 605–613, 1961.

Maser, J. and Gallup, G.G., Jr. Tonic immobility and related phenomena: A partially annotated, tricentennial bibliography, 1636–1976. Psychological Record, 27: 177–216, 1977.

McGinty, D.J. Somnolence, recovery and hyposomnia following ventromedial diencephalic lesions in the rat. Electroencephalography and Clinical Neurophysiology, 26: 70–79, 1969.

McGowan, B.K., Garcia, J., Ervin, F.R., and Schwartz, J. Effects of septal lesions on baitshyness in the rat. Physiology and Behavior, 4: 907–909, 1969.

McGraw, C.P. and Klemm, W.R. Mechanisms of the immobility reflex ("animal hypnosis"): III. Neocortical inhibition in rats. Communications in Behavioral Biology, 3: 53–59, 1969.

McGraw, C.P. and Klemm, W.R. Genetic differences in susceptibility of rats to the immobility reflex ("animal hypnosis"). Behavior Genetics, 3: 155–162, 1973.

McKim, W.A. and Lett, B.T. Spontaneous and shock-induced burying in two strains of rats. Behavioral and Neural Biology, 26: 76–80, 1979.

McMullen, N.T. and Almli, R.C. Serial lateral hypothalamic destruction with various interlesion intervals. Experimental Neurology, 67: 459–471, 1980.

McNaughton, B.L., Barnes, C.A., and Andersen, P. Synaptic efficacy and EPSP summation in granule cells of rat fascia dentata studies *in vitro*. Journal of Neurophysiology, 46: 952–966, 1981.

Meaney, M.J. and Stewart, J. Environmental factors influencing the affiliative behavior of male and female rats (*Rattus norvegicus*). Animal Learning and Beahvior, 7: 397–405, 1979.

Meaney, M.J. and Stewart, J. A descriptive study of social development in the rat (*Rattus norvegicus*). Animal Behavior, 29: 34–35, 1981.

Michal, E.K. Effects of limbic lesions on behavior sequences and courtship behavior of male rats (*Rattus norvegicus*). Animal Behavior, 44: 264–285, 1973.

Miller, N.E. Learnable drives and rewards. In S.S. Stevens (Ed.), Handbook of experimental psychology. New York: Wiley, 1951, pp. 435–472.

Miller, N.E. Effects of drugs on motivation: The value of using a variety of measures. Annals of the New York Academy of Sciences, 65: 318–333, 1956.

Milner, A.D., Goodale, M.A., and Morton, M.C. Visual sampling after lesions of the superior colliculus in rats. Journal of Comparative and Physiological Psychology, 93: 1015–1023, 1979.

Milner, B. Some effects of frontal lobectomy in man. In J.M. Warren and K. Akert (Eds.), The frontal granular cortex and behavior. New York: McGraw-Hill, 1964.

Milner, P.M. Physiological psychology. New York: Holt, Rinehart and Winston, 1970.

Mishkin, M. Visual discrimination performance following partial ablations of the temporal lobe: II. Ventral surface vs. hippocampus. Journal of Comparative and Physiological Psychology, 47: 187–193, 1954.

Mishkin, M. Visual mechanisms beyond the striate cortex. In R.W. Russell, (Ed.), Frontiers in physiological psychology. New York: Academic Press, 1966, pp. 93–119.

Mitchell, D.E., Cynader, M., and Movshon, J.A. Recovery from the effects of monocular deprivation in kittens. Journal of Comparative Neurology, 176: 53–64, 1977.

Mitchell, D.E., Giffin, F., Wilkinson, F.E., Anderson, P., and Smith, M.L. Visual resolution in young kittens. Vision Research, 16: 363–369, 1976.

Mitchell, S.J. and Ranck, J.B., Jr. Generation of theta rhythm in medial entorhinal cortex of freely moving rats. Brain Research, 189: 49–66, 1980.

Montoya, C.P., Sutherland, R.J., and Whishaw, I.Q. Cadaverine and burying in the laboratory rat. Bulletin of the Psychonomic Society, 18: 118–120, 1981.

Moore, C.L., Kalil, R., and Richards, W. Development of myelination in optic tract of the cat. Journal of Comparative Neurology, 165: 125–136, 1976.

Morgan, C.T., Stellar, E., and Johnson, A. Food deprivation and hoarding in rats. Journal of Comparative Psychology, 35: 275–295, 1943.

Morgan, C.T. and Wood, W.M. Cortical localization of symbolic processes in the rat: II. The effect of cortical lesions upon delayed alternation. Journal of Neurophysiology, 6: 173–180, 1943.

Morris, D. The naked ape. New York: McGraw-Hill, 1967.

Morrison, S.D. The constancy of the energy expended by rats on spontaneous activity, and the distribution of activity between feeding and non-feeding. Journal of Physiology, 197: 305–323, 1968a.

Morrison, S.D. The relationship of energy expenditure and spontaneous activity to the aphagia of rats with lesions in the lateral hypothalamus. Journal of Physiology, 197: 325–343, 1968b.

Moruzzi, G. and Magoun, H.W. Brain stem reticular formation and activation of the EEG. Electroencephalography and Clinical Neurophysiology, 1: 455–473, 1949.

Moser, C.G., Tait, R.W., and Kirby, K.G. An examination of multiple defensive responses in a conditioned burying paradigm. Paper read at a meeting of the Canadian Psychological Association, Calgary, June, 1980.

Motokizawa, F. Electrophysiological studies of olfactory projection to the mesencephalic reticular formation. Experimental Neurology, 44: 135–144, 1974.

Mountcastle, V.B. Some neural mechanisms for directed attention. In P. Buser and A. Buser-Rougeul (Eds.), Cerebral correlates of conscious experience. Amsterdam: North Holland, 1978, pp. 37–51.

Movshon, J.A. Reversal of the behavioural effects of monocular deprivation in the kitten. Journal of Physiology, 261: 175–187, 1976a.

Movshon, J.A. Reversal of the physiological effects of monocular deprivation in the kitten's visual cortex. Journal of Physiology, 261: 125–174, 1976b.

Movshon, J.A. and Dursteler, M.R. Effects of brief periods of unilateral eye closure on the kitten's visual system. Journal of Neurophysiology, 40: 1255–1265, 1977.

Movshon, J.A. and Van Sluyters, R.C. Visual neural development. Annual Review of Psychology, 32: 477–522, 1981.

Moyer, K.E. Kinds of aggression and their physiological basis. Communications in Behavioral Biology, 2: 65–87, 1968.

Mullenix, P., Norton, S., and Culver, B. Locomotor damage in rats after X-irradiation in utero. Experimental Neurology, 48: 310–324, 1975.

Munk, H. Of the visual area of the cerebral cortex, and its relation to eye movements. Brain, 13: 45–70, 1890.

Munk, H. Uber die Funktionen der Grosshirnrinde. (3te Mitteilung). Berlin: A. Hirschwald, 1881. Reprinted in translation. Von Bonin, G. Some papers on the cerebral cortex. Springfield, IL: Charles C. Thomas, 1960, pp. 97–117.

Murphy, L.K. and Brown, T.S. Hippocampal lesions and learned taste aversion. Physiological Psychology, 2: 60–64, 1974.

Mussen, P.H. Developmental psychology. In P.R. Farnsworth and Q. McNemar, (Eds.), Annual review of psychology. Palo Alto: Annual Reviews, 1960.

Myers, R.D. (Ed.). Methods in psychobiology. New York: Academic Press, 1972.

Myers, R.E. Visual deficits after lesions of brainstem tegmentum in cats. Archives of Neurology, 11: 73–90, 1964.

Myers, R.E. Role of prefrontal and anterior temporal cortex in social behavior and affect in monkeys. Acta Neurobiologiae Experimentalis, 32: 567–580, 1972.

Myers, R.E. Neurology of social behavior and affect in primates: A study of prefrontal and anterior temporal cortex. In K.J. Zulch, O. Creutzfeldt, and G.C. Galbraith (Eds.), Cerebral localization. New York: Springer-Verlag, 1975.

Myers, R.E., Swett, C., and Miller, M. Loss of social group affinity following prefrontal lesions in free-ranging macaques. Brain Research, 64: 257–269, 1973.

Myhrer, T. Normal jump avoidance performance in rats with the hippocampal theta rhythm selectively disrupted. Behavioral Biology, 14: 489–498, 1975a.

Myhrer, T. Locomotor, avoidance, and maze behaviour in rats with selective disruption of hippocampal output. Journal of Comparative and Physiological Psychology, 89: 759–777, 1975b.

Nachman, M. and Ashe, J.H. Effects of basolateral amygdala lesions on neophobia, learned taste aversion, and sodium appetite in rats. Journal of Comparative and Physiological Psychology, 87: 622–643, 1974.

Nagel, J.A. and Satinoff, E. Mild cold exposure increases survival in rats with medial preoptic lesions. Science, 208: 301–303, 1980.

Nau, P.A. A descriptive study of exploration in rats. Unpublished Doctoral Thesis, Dalhousie University, Halifax, Nova Scotia, 1980.

Nauta, W.J.H. Hypothalamic regulation of sleep in rats: An experimental study. Journal of Neurophysiology, 9: 285–316, 1946.

Neimegeers, C.J.E., Vanbruggen, F.J., and Janssen, P.A.J. The influence of various neuroleptic drugs on shock avoidance responding in rats. Psychopharmacologia, 16: 161–174, 1969.

Neisser, U. The processes of vision. Scientific American, 219: 204–214, 1968.

Nelson, G.N., Masada, M., and Holmes, T.H. Correlation of behaviour and catecholamine metabolite extraction. Psychosomatic Medicine, 28: 216–226, 1966.

Newell, A. You can't play 20 questions with nature and win: Projective comments on the papers of this symposium. In W.G. Chase (Ed.), Visual information processing. New York: Academic Press, 1973, pp. 283–308.

Nielson, H.C., McIver, A.H., and Boswell, R.S. Effect of septal lesions on learning, emotionality, activity and exploratory behavior in rats. Experimental Neurology, 11: 147–157, 1965.

Nobrega, J.N., Wiener, N.I., and Ossenkopp, K.P. Development of acute feeding disorders, hyperactivity, and stomach pathology after medial and lateral hypothalamic lesions in rats. Physiological Psychology, 8: 77–87, 1980.

Nonneman, A.J. and Kolb, B. Lesions of hippocampus or prefrontal cortex alters species-typical behavior in the cat. Behavioral Biology, 12: 41–54, 1974.

Nonneman, A.J. and Kolb, B. Functional recovery after serial ablation of prefrontal cortex in the rat. Physiology and Behavior, 22: 895–901, 1979.

Norman, R.J., Villablanca, J.R., Brown, K.A., Schwafel, J.A., and Buchwald, J.S. Classical eyeblink conditioning in the bilaterally hemispherectomized cat. Experimental Neurology, 44: 363–380, 1974.

Norton, T.T. Receptive-field properties of superior colliculus cells and development of visual behavior in kittens. Journal of Neurophysiology, 37: 674–690, 1974.

Norton, T.T. and Lindsley, D.B. Visual behavior after bilateral superior colliculus lesions in kittens and cats. Federation Proceedings, 30: 615, 1971.

Novin, D., Wyrwicka, W., and Bray, G.A. Hunger: Basic mechanisms and clinical implications. New York: Raven Press, 1976.

Nowlis, V. Methods for the objective study of drug effects on group functioning. In L. Uhr and J.G. Miller (Eds.), Drugs and behaviour. New York: Basic Books, 1960.

Oakley, D.A. Cerebral cortex and adaptive behavior. In D.A. Oakley and H.C. Plotkin (Eds.), Brain behaviour and evolution. London: Methuen 1979, pp. 154–188.

Oatley, K. Perceptions and representations: The theoretical bases of brain research and psychology. London: Methuen, 1978.

Oke, A., Lewis, R., and Adams, R.N. Hemispheric asymmetry of norepinephrine distribution in rat thalamus. Brain Research, 188: 269–272, 1980.

O'Keefe, J. A review of the hippocampal place cells. Progress in Neurobiology, 13: 419–439, 1979.

O'Keefe, J. and Dostrovsky, J. The hippocampus as a spatial map. Preliminary evidence from unit activity in the freely moving rat. Brain Research, 34: 171–175, 1971.

O'Keefe, J. and Nadel, L. The hippocampus as a cognitive map. New York: Oxford University Press, 1978.

Olds, J. The central nervous system and the enforcement of behavior. American Psychologist, 24: 114–132, 1969.

Olds, J., Mink, W.D., and Best, P.J. Single unit patterns during anticipatory behavior. Electroencephalography and Clinical Neurophysiology, 26: 144–158, 1969.

Olioff, M. and Stewart, J. Sex differences in the play behavior of prepubescent rats. Physiology and Behavior, 20: 113–115, 1978.

Olson, C.R. and Freeman, R.D. Monocular deprivation and recovery during sensitive period in kittens. Journal of Neurophysiology, 41: 65–74, 1978.

Olton, D.S., Becker, J.T., and Handelmann, G.E. Hippocampus, space, and memory. Behavioral and Brain Sciences, 2: 313–365, 1979.

Olton, D.S., Branch, M., and Best, P.J. Spatial correlates of hippocampal unit activity. Experimental Neurology, 58: 387–409, 1978.

Orbach, J. Spontaneous ejaculation in rat. Science, 134: 1072–1073, 1961.

Orbach, J., Miller, M., Billimoria, A., and Solhkah, N. Spontaneous seminal ejaculation and genital grooming in rats. Brain Research, 5: 520–523, 1967.

Orlovsky, G.N. Work of the reticulo-spinal neurones during locomotion. Biophysics, 15: 761–771, 1970.

Orlovsky, G.N. Activity of vestibulospinal neurons during locomotion. Brain Research, 46: 85–98, 1972.

Ossenkopp, K.P., Wiener, N.I., and Norbrega, J.N. Ventromedial hypothalamic lesions and stomach ulcers: Reduction by non-nitrituve bulk ingested in the post lesion period. Physiology and Behavior, 24: 1125–1131, 1980.

Owings, D.H. and Coss, R.G. Snake mobbing by California ground squirrels: Adaptive variation and ontogeny. Behavior, 62: 50–69, 1977.

Passingham, R.E. Anatomical differences between the neocortex of man and other primates. Brain, Behavior and Evolution, 7: 337–359, 1973.

Passingham, R.E. Information about movements in monkeys (Macaca mulatta) with lesions of dorsal prefrontal cortex. Brain Research, 152: 313–328, 1978.

Passingham, R.E. and Ettlinger, G. A comparison of cortical functions in man and other primates. International Review of Neurobiology, 16: 233–299, 1974.

Pavlov, I.P. Conditioned reflexes. Oxford: Oxford University Press, 1927, Reprinted: New York: Dover, 1960.

Paxinos, G. and Bindra, D. Hypothalamic knife cuts: Effects on eating, drinking, irritability, aggression and copulation in the male rat. Journal of Comparative and Physiological Psychology, 79: 219–229, 1972.

Paxinos, G. and Bindra, D. Hypothalamic and midbrain neural pathways involved in eating, drinking, irritability, aggression and copulation in rats.

Journal of Comparative and Physiological Psychology, 82: 1–14, 1973.

Pearl, G.S. and Anderson, K.V. Effect of high-frequency peripheral nerve and dorsal column stimulation on neuronal responses in feline nucleus reticularis gigantocellularis after nociceptive electrical stimulation. Experimental Neurology, 57: 307–321, 1977.

Pelham, R.W., Lippa, A.S., and Sano, M.C. Effects of 6-hydroxydopamine on body weight: Feeding deficits or sensorimotor impairment. Communications in Psychopharmacology, 23: 553–563, 1977.

Pellegrino, L.J. and Altman, J. Effects of differential interference with postnatal cerebellar neurogenesis on motor performance, activity level, and maze learning in rats. Journal of Comparative and Physiological Psychology, 93: 1–33, 1979.

Pellionisz, A. and Llinas, R. Brain modeling by tensor network theory and computer simulation. The cerebellum: Distributed processor for predictive coordination. Neuroscience, 4: 323–348, 1979.

Penfield, W. The cerebral cortex in man. I. The cerebral cortex and consciousness. Archives of Neurology and Psychiatry, 40: 417–442, 1938.

Penfield, W. and Jasper, H.H. Epilepsy and the functional anatomy of the human brain. Boston: Little Brown, 1954.

Perenin, M.T. and Jeannerod, M. Residual vision in cortically blind hemifields. Neuropsychologia, 13: 1–7, 1975.

Perkel, D.H. and Bullock, T.H. Neural coding: A report based on an NRP work session. Neurosciences Research Program Bulletin, 6: 221–348, 1968.

Petersen, M.R., Beecher, M.D., Zoloth, S.R., Moody, D.B., and Stebbins, W.C. Neural lateralization: Evidence from studies of the perception of species-specific vocalizations by Japanese Macaques (Macaca fuscata). Science, 202: 324–326, 1978.

Peterson, B.W. Reticulo-motor pathways: Their connections and possible roles in motor behavior. In H. Asanuma and V.J. Wilson (Eds.), Integration in the nervous system. Tokyo: Igaku-shoin, 1979.

Peterson, B.W., Fillion, M., Felpel, L.P., and Abzug, C. Responses of medial reticular neurons to stimulation of the vestibular nerve. Experimental Brain Research, 22: 335–350, 1975.

Peterson, B.W., Franck, J.I., Pitts, N.G., and Daunton, N.G. Changes in responses of medial pontomedullary reticular neurons during repetitive cutaneous, vestibular, cortical, and tectal stimulation. Journal of Neurophysiology, 39: 564–581, 1976.

Pettigrew, J.D. The effect of visual experience on the development of stimulus specificity by kitten cortical neurons. Journal of Physiology, 237: 49–74, 1974.

Phillips, A.G. Object-carrying by rats: Disruption by mesencephalic lesions. Canadian Journal of Psychology, 29: 250–262, 1975.

Pierce, C.S. Illustrations of the logic of science. II. How to make our ideas clear. Popular Science Monthly, 12: 286–302, 1978.

Pinel, J.P.J. Evaluation of the one-trial passive avoidance task as a tool for studying ECS-produced amnesia. Psychonomic Science, 13: 131–132, 1968.

Pinel, J.P.J., Gorzalka, B.B., and Ladak, F. Cadaverine and putrescine initiate the burial of dead conspecifics by rats. Physiology and Behavior, 27: 819–824, 1981.

Pinel, J.P.J., Hoyer, E., and Terlecki, L.J. Defensive burying and approach-avoidance behavior in the rat. Bulletin of the Psychonomic Society, 16: 349–352, 1980.

Pinel, J.P.J. and Treit, D. Burying as a defensive response in rats. Journal of Comparative and Physiological Psychology, 92: 708–712, 1978.

Pinel, J.P.J. and Treit, D. Conditioned defensive burying in rats: Availability of burying materials. Animal Learning and Behavior, 7: 392–396, 1979.

Pinel, J.P.J., Treit, D., Ladak, F., and MacLennan, A.J. Conditioned defensive burying in rats free to escape. Animal Learning and Behavior, 8: 447–451, 1980.

Pinel, J.P.J., Treit, D., and Wilkie, D.M. Stimulus control of defensive burying in the rat. Learning and Motivation, 11: 150–163, 1980.

Pinto-Hamuy, T. Role of the cerebral cortex in the learning of an instrumental conditional response. In A. Fessard, R.W. Gerard, and J. Konorski (Eds.), Brain mechanisms and learning. Springfield, IL: Charles C. Thomas, 1961, pp. 589–601.

Pirchio, M., Spinelli, D., Fiorentini, A., and Maffei, L. Infant contrast sensitivity evaluated by evoked potentials. Brain Research, 141: 179–184, 1978.

Pitts, W. and McCulloch, W.S. How we know universals. The perception of auditory and visual forms. Bulletin of Mathematics and Biophysics, 9: 127–147, 1947.

Plotkin, H.C. Brain-behaviour studies and evolutionary biology. In D.A. Oakley and H.C. Plotkin (Eds.), Brain behaviour and evolution. London: Methuen, 1979.

Podvoll, E.M. and Goodman, S.J. Averaged neural electrical activity and arousal. Science, 155: 223–225, 1967.

Poggio, G.F. and Fisher, B. Binocular interaction and depth sensitivity in striate and prestriate cortex of behaving rhesus monkey. Journal of Neurophysiology, 40: 1392–1405, 1977.

Pohl, W. Dissociation of spatial discrimination deficits following frontal and parietal lesions in monkeys. Journal of Comparative and Physiological Psychology, 82: 227–239, 1973.

Poling, A., Cleary, J., and Monaghan, M. Burying by rats in response to aversive and nonaversive stimuli. Journal of the Experimental Analysis of Behavior, 35: 31–44, 1981.

Pompeiano, O. The neurophysiological mechanisms of the postural and motor events during desynchronized sleep. In Sleep and altered states of consciousness. Research Publications of the Association for Research on Nervous and Mental Diseases (Vol. 45), 1967, pp. 351–423.

Pompeiano, O. Mechanisms of sensorimotor integration during sleep. In E. Stellar and J.M. Sprague (Eds.), Progress in physiological psychology (Vol. 3). New York: Academic Press, 1970, pp. 3–152.

Pond, F.J. and Schwartzbaum, J.S. Interrelationships of hippocampal EEG and visual evoked responses during appetitive behavior in rats. Brain Research, 43: 119–137, 1972.

Pooe, T.B. and Fish, J. An investigation of individual, age, and sexual differences in the play of Rattus norvegicus (Mammalia: Rodentia). Journal of Zoology, 179: 249–260, 1976.

Pöppel, E., Held, R., and Frost, D. Residual visual function after brain wounds involving the central visual pathways in man. Nature (London), 243: 295–296, 1973.

Popper, K.R. and Eccles, J.C. The self and its brain. Berlin: Springer-Verlgag, 1977.

Prestrude, A.M. Some phylogenetic comparisons of tonic immobility with special reference to habituation and fear. Psychological Record, 1: 21–39, 1977.

Pribram, K.H., Ahumada, A., Hartog, J., and Roos, L. A progress report on the neurological processes disturbed by frontal lesions in primates. In J.M. Warren and K. Akert (Eds.), The frontal granular cortex and behavior. New York: McGraw-Hill, 1964, pp. 28–55.

Price, E.O. Domestication and early experience effects on escape conditioning in the Norway rat. Journal of Comparative and Physiological Psychology, 79: 51–55, 1972.

Pylyshyn, Z. The imagery debate: Analogue media versus tacit knowledge. Psychological Review, 88: 16–45, 1981.

Ranck, J.B., Jr. Studies on single neurons in dorsal hippocampal formation and septum in unrestrained rats. I. Behavioral correlates and firing repertoires. Experimental Neurology, 41: 461–555, 1973.

Ranck, J.B., Jr. Behavioral correlates and firing repertoires of neurons in septal nuclei in unrestrained rats. In J.F. De France (Ed.), The septal nuclei. New York: Plenum Press, 1976, pp. 423–462.

Ranje, L. and Ungerstedt, U. Discriminative and motor performance in rats after interference with dopamine neurotransmission with spiroperidol. European Journal of Pharmacology, 43: 39–46, 1977.

Ratliff, F. Some interrelations among physics, physiology and psychology in the study of vision. In S. Koch (Ed.), Psychology: A study of a science. Study II. Empirical substructure and relations with other sciences (Vol. 4), Biologically oriented fields: Their place in psychology and biological science. New York: McGraw-Hill, 1962, pp. 417–482.

Ravizza, R.J. and Belmore, S. Auditory forebrain: Evidence from anatomical and behavioral experiments involving human and animal subjects. In R.B. Masterson (Ed.), Handbook of behavioral neurobiology. New York: Plenum Press, 1978.

Rebec, G.V. and Groves, P.M. Differential effects of the optical isomers of amphetamine on neuronal activity in the reticular formation and caudate nucleus. Brain Research, 83: 301–318, 1975.

Reinberg, A. and Halberg, F. Circadian chronopharmacology. Annual Review of Pharmacology, 11: 455–492, 1971.

Rescorla, R.A. and Wagner, A.R. A theory of Pavlovian conditioning: Variations in the effectiveness of reinforcement and nonreinforcement. In A.H. Black and W.F. Prokasy (Eds.), Classical conditioning II: Current research and theory. New York: Appleton-Century-Crofts, 1972, pp. 64–99.

Reynolds, R.W. and Kimm, J. Chronic gnawing induced by electrolytic lesions dorsolateral and lateral to the lateral hypothalamus. Physiology and Behavior, 8: 1179–1181, 1972.

Ricci, G., Doane, B., and Jasper, H. Microelectrode studies of conditioning: Technique and preliminary results. Premier congres international des sciences neurologiques. Reunions plenieres, 1957, pp. 401–415.

Richter, C. A behavioristic study of the activity of the rat. Comparative Psychology Monographs, 1: 1–55, 1922.

Richter, C. Animal behavior and internal drives. Quarterly Review of Biology, 2: 307–343, 1927.

Richter, C. On the phenomenon of sudden death in animals and man. Psychosomatic Medicine, 19: 191–198, 1957.

Richter, C. Biological clocks in medicine and psychiatry. Springfield, IL: Charles C. Thomas, 1965.

Richter, C. Sleep and activity: Their relation to the 24-hour clock. Proceedings of the Association for Research on Nervous and Mental Diseases, 45: 8–29, 1967.

Richter, C. Experiences of a reluctant rat catcher. The common Norway rat—friend or enemy? Proceedings of the American Philosophical Society, 112: 403–415, 1968.

Richter, C., Holt, L.E., Jr., and Barelare, B., Jr. Nutritional requirements for normal growth and reproduction in rats studied by the self-selection method. American Journal of Physiology, 124: 596–602, 1938.

Rickard, H.C., Dignam, P.J., and Horner, R.F. Verbal manipulations in a psychotherapeutic relationship. Journal of Clinical Psychology, 16: 364–367, 1960.

Riess, B.F. The effect of altered environment and of age on the mother-young relationships among animals. Annals of the New York Academy of Sciences, 57: 606–610, 1954.

Rizzolatti, G. and Tradardi, V. Pattern discrimination in monocularly reared cats. Experimental Neurology, 33: 181–194, 1971.

Roberts, L.G. Machine perception of three-dimensional solids. In I.J.T. Tippett et al. (Eds.), Optical and electro-optical information processing. Cambridge, MA: The MIT Press, 1965.

Roberts, W.W., Mooney, R.D., and Martin, J.R. Thermoregulatory behavior in rodents. Journal of Comparative and Physiological Psychology, 84: 693–699, 1974.

Robinson, R.G. Differential behavior and biochemical effects of right and left cerebral infarction in the rat. Science, 205: 707–710, 1979.

Robinson, R.G. and Coyle, J.T. The differential effect of right versus left hemispheric cerebral infarction on catecholamines and behavior in the rat. Brain Research, 188: 63–78, 1980.

Robinson, T.E. Electrical stimulation of the brain stem in freely moving rats: I. Effects on behavior. Physiology and Behavior, 21: 223–231, 1978.

Robinson, T.E., Kramis, R.C., and Vanderwolf, C.H. Two types of cerebral activation during sleep: Relations to behavior. Brain Research, 124: 544–549, 1977.

Robinson, T.E. and Whishaw, I.Q. Effects of posterior hypothalamic lesions on voluntary behavior and hippocampal electroencephalograms in the rat. Journal of Comparative and Physiological Psychology, 86: 768–786, 1974.

Robinson, T.E., Whishaw, I.Q., and Wishart, T.B. Effects of posterior hypothalamic lesions on swimming movements in different water temperatures by the rat. Canadian Journal of Psychology, 28: 102–113, 1974.

Rolls, B. Drinking by rats after irritative lesions in the hypothalamus. Physiology and Behavior, 5: 1385–1393, 1970.

Rolls, E.T., Burton, M.J., and Mora, F. Hypothalamic neuronal responses associated with the sight of food. Brain Research, 111: 53–66, 1976.

Rolls, E.T. and Rolls, B.J. Altered food preferences after lesions in the basolateral region of the amygdala in the rat. Journal of Comparative and Physiological Psychology, 83: 248–259, 1973.

Rose, D. Midbrain and pontine unit responses to lordosis-controlling forms of somatosensory stimuli in the female golden hamster. Experimental Neurology, 60: 499–508, 1978.

Rosellini, R.A., Binik, Y.M., and Seligman, E.P. Sudden death in the laboratory rat. Psychosomatic Medicine, 38: 55–58, 1976.

Rosenblatt, J.S. Views on the onset and maintenance of maternal behavior in the rat. In L.R. Aronson, E. Tobach, D.S. Lehrman, and J.S. Rosenblatt (Eds.), Development and evolution of behavior: Essays in memory of T.C. Schneirla. San Francisco: W.H. Freeman, 1970, pp. 489–515.

Rosenblatt, J.S. and Lehrman, D.S. Maternal behavior of the laboratory rat. In H. Rheingold (Ed.), Maternal behavior in mammals. New York: Wiley, 1963.

Rosenblatt, J.S., Siegel, H.E., and Mayer, A.D. Progress in the study of maternal behavior in the rat: Hormonal, nonhormonal, sensory and developmental aspects. In J.S. Rosenblatt, R.A. Hinde, C. Beer, and M.-C. Busnel (Eds.), Advances in the study of behavior (Vol. 10), New York: Academic Press, 1979, pp. 225–311.

Rosensweig, S. Investigating and appraising personality. In T.G. Andrews (Ed.), Methods of psychology. New York: Wiley, 1948.

Ross, E.L., Komisaruk, B.R., and O'Donnell, D. Evidence that probing the vaginal cervix is analgesic in rats, using an operant paradigm. Journal of Comparative and Physiological Psychology, 93: 330–336, 1979.

Rosvold, H.E. and Mishkin, M. Non-sensory effects of frontal lesions on discrimination learning and performance. In A. Fessard, R.W. Gerard, and J. Konorski (Eds.), Brain mechanisms and learning. Springfield, IL: Charles C. Thomas, 1961, pp. 555–576.

Rosvold, H.E., Mishkin, M., and Szwarzbart, M.K. Effects of subcortical lesions in monkeys on visual discrimination and single alternation performance. Journal of Comparative and Physiological Psychology, 51: 437–444, 1958.

Roth, S.R., Schwartz, M., and Teitelbaum, P. Failure of recovered lateral hypothalamic rats to learn specific food aversion. Journal of Comparative and Physiological Psychology, 83: 184–197, 1973.

Rozin, P. and Kalat, J.W. Specific hungers and poison avoidance as adaptive specializations of learning. Psychological Review, 78: 459–486, 1971.

Rudell, A.P. The television camera used to measure movement. Behavior Research Methods and Instrumentation, 11: 339–341, 1979.

Rudell, A.P., Fox, S.E., and Ranck, J.B., Jr. Hippocampal excitability phase-locked to the theta rhythm in walking rats. Experimental Neurology, 68: 87–96, 1980.

Rusak, B. and Zucker, I. Biological rhythms and animal behavior. Annual Review of Psychology, 26: 137–171, 1975.

Rusoff, A.C. Development of ganglion cells in the retina of the cat. In R. Freeman (Ed.), Developmental neurobiology of vision. New York: Plenum Press, 1979, pp. 19–30.

Rusoff, A.C. and Dubin, M.W. Development of receptive-field properties of retinal ganglion cells in kittens. Journal of Neurophysiology, 40: 1188–1198, 1977.

Russell, W.M.S. and Russell, C. Violence: Monkeys and man. New York: Macmillan, 1968.

Sacks, O. Awakenings. New York: Random House, 1976.

Sakai, H. and Woody, C.D. Identification of auditory responsive cells in coronal-pericruciate cortex of awake cats. Journal of Neurophysiology, 44: 223–231, 1980.

Salas, G.D. Ultrasound and mating behavior in rodents with some observations on other behavioural situations. Journal of Zoology (London), 168: 149–164, 1972.

Salas, M. Effects of early malnutrition on the development of swimming ability in the rat. Physiology and Behavior, 8: 119–122, 1972.

Satinoff, E. and Henderson, R. Thermoregulatory behavior. In W.K. Honig and J.E.R. Staddon (Eds.), Handbook of operant behavior. Englewood Cliffs, NJ: Prentice-Hall, 1977.

Satinoff, E. and Shan, S.Y.Y. Loss of behavioral thermoregulation after lateral hypothalamic lesions in rats. Journal of Comparative and Physiological Psychology, 77: 302–312, 1971.

Satinoff, E., Valentino, D., and Teitelbaum, P. Thermoregulatory cold-defense deficits in rats with preoptic/anterior hypothalamic lesions. Brain Research Bulletin, 1: 553–565, 1976.

Schafer, E.A. On the functions of the temporal and occipital lobes: A reply to Dr. Ferrier. Brain, 11: 145–165, 1888.

Schallert, T., DeRyck, M., and Teitelbaum, P. Atropine stereotypy as a behavioral trap: A movement subsystem and electroencephalographic analysis. Journal of Comparative and Physiological Psychology, 94: 1–24, 1980.

Schallert, T., DeRyck, M., Whishaw, I.Q., Ramirez, V.D., and Teitelbaum, P. Excessive bracing reactions and their control by atropine and L-dopa in an animal analog of Parkinsonism. Experimental Neurology, 64: 33–43, 1979.

Schallert, T., Leach, L.R. and Braun, J.J. Saliva hypersecretion during aphagia following lateral hypothalamic lesions. Physiology and Behavior, 21: 461–463, 1978.

Schallert, T., Upchurch, M., Lobaugh, N., Farrar, S.B., Spirduso, W.W., Gilliam, P., Vaughn, D., and Wilcox, R.E. Tactile extinction: Distinguishing between sensorimotor and motor asymmetries in rats with unilateral nigro-striatal damage. Pharmacology, Biochemistry, and Behavior, 16: 455–462, 1982.

Schallert, T. and Whishaw, I.Q. Two types of aphagia and two types of sensorimotor impairment after lateral hypothalamic lesions: Observations in normal weight, dieted, and fattened rats. Journal of Comparative and Physiological Psychology, 92: 720–741, 1978.

Schallert, T., Whishaw, I.Q., DeRyck, M., and Teitelbaum, P. The postures of catecholamine-depletion catalepsy: Their possible adaptive value in thermoregulation. Physiology and Behavior, 21: 817–820, 1978.

Schallert, T., Whishaw, I.Q., and Flannigan, K.P. Gastric pathology and feeding deficits induced by hypothalamic damage in rats: Effects of lesion type, size, and placement. Journal of Comparative and Physiological Psychology, 91: 598–610, 1977.

Schallert, T., Whishaw, I.Q., Ramirez, V.D., and Teitelbaum, P. Compulsive abnormal walking caused by anticholinergics in akinetic 6-hydroxydopamine-treated rats. Science, 199: 1461–1463, 1978a.

Schallert, T., Whishaw, I.Q. Ramirez, V.D., and Teitelbaum, P. 6-Hydroxydopamine and anticholinergic drugs. Science, 202: 1215–1217, 1978b. 1978b.

Shapiro, S., Salas, M., and Vukovich, K. Hormonal effects upon the ontogeny of swimming ability in the rat: Assessment of central nervous sytem development. Science, 168: 147–151, 1970.

Scheibel, M.E. and Scheibel, A.B. The response of reticular units to repetitive stimuli. Archives Italiannes Biologie, 103: 279–299, 1965.

Scheibel, M.E., Scheibel, A.B., Mollica, A., and Moruzzi, G. Convergence and interaction of afferent impulses on single units of reticular formation. Journal of Neurophysiology, 18: 309–331, 1955.

Schlechter, J.M. and Butcher, L.L. Blockage by pimozide of (+) amphetamine-induced hyperkinesia in mice. Journal of Pharmaceutics and Pharmacology, 24: 407–409, 1972.

Schneider, G.E. Contrasting visumotor functions of tectum and cortex in the golden hamster. Psychologische Forschung 31:52–62, 1967.

Schneider, G.E. Two visual systems. Science, 1634: 895–902, 1969.

Schneirla, T.C. Contemporarary American animal psychology in perspective. In P.L. Harriman, L. Freeman, G.W. Hartmann, K. Lewin, A.H. Maslow and C.E. Skinner (Eds.), Twentieth century psychology. New York Philosophical Library, 1946.

Schwartz, N.B. and Kling, A. The effect of amygdaloid lesions on feeding, grooming and reproduction in rats. Acta Neurosurgica, 11: 64–66, 1964.

Schwartzbaum, J.S. Interrelationships among multiunit activity of the midbrain reticular formation and lateral geniculate nucleus, thalamocortical arousal, and behavior in rats. Journal of Comparative and Physiological Psychology, 89: 131–157, 1975.

Schwartzbaum, J.S. and Kreinick, C.J. Interrelationships of hippocampal electroencephalogram, visually evoked response, and behavioral reactivity to photic stimuli in rats. Journal of Comparative and Physiological Psychology, 85: 479–490, 1973.

Schwartzkroin, P.A. and Mathers, L.H. Physiological and morphological identification of a nonpyramidal hippocampal cell type. Brain Research, 157: 1–10, 1978.

Scott, J.P. The organization of comparative psychology. Annals of the New York Academy of Sciences, 223: 7–40, 1973.

Sechenov, I.M. Reflexes of the brain. Cambridge, MA: The MIT Press, 1965.

Sechzer, J.A., Ervin, G.N., and Smith, G.P. Loss of visual placing in rats after lateral hypothalamic microinjection of 6-hydroxydopamine. Experimental Neurology, 41: 723–737, 1973.

Segundo, J.P., Takenaka, T., and Encabo, H. Somatic sensory properties of bulbar reticular neurons. Journal of Neurophysiology, 30: 1221–1238, 1967.

Seligman, M.E.P. On the generality of the laws of learning. Psychological Review, 77: 406–416, 1970.

Sembello, W.J. and Gladfelter, W.E. Effect of hypothalamic lesions on the treadmill performance of rats. Physiology and Behavior, 13: 603–607, 1974.

Semmes, J.S., Weinstein, S., Ghent, L., and Teuber, H.-L. Correlates of impaired orientation in personal and extra-personal space. Brain, 86: 747–772, 1963.

Sherman, G.F., Garbanati, J.A., Rosen, G.D., Yutzey, D.A., and Denenberg, V.H. Brain and behavioral asymmetries for spatial preference in rats. Brain Research, 192: 61–67, 1980.

Sherman, S.M. Visual field defects in monocularly and binocularly deprived cats. Brain Research, 49: 25–45, 1973.

Sherman, S.M. Permanence of visual perimetry deficits in monocularly and binocularly deprived cats. Brain Research, 73: 491–501, 1974.

Sherman, S.M., Guillery, R.W., Kaas, J.H., and Sanderson, K.J. Behavioral, electrophysiological and morphological studies of binocular competition in the development of the geniculo-cortical pathways of cats. Journal of Comparative Neurology, 158: 1–18, 1974.

Sherrington, C.S. The brain and its mechanism. Cambridge: Cambridge University Press, 1933.

Shipley, J. and Kolb, B. Neural correlates of species-typical behavior in the Syrian golden hamster. Journal of Comparative and Physiological Psychology, 91: 1056–1073, 1977.

Shirai, Y. Analyzing intensity arrays using knowledge about scenes. In P. Winston (Ed.), The psychology of computer vision. New York: McGraw-Hill, 1975.

Siegel, J.M. Behavioral functions of the reticular formation. Brain Research Reviews, 1: 69–105, 1979a.

Siegel, J.M. Behavioral relations of medullary reticular formation cells. Experimental Neurology, 65: 691–698, 1979b.

Siegel, J.M., Breedlove, S.M., and McGinty, D.J. Photographic analysis of relation between unit activity and movement. Journal of Neuroscience Methods, 1: 159–164, 1979.

Siegel, J.M. and McGinty, D.J. Brainstem neurons without spontaneous unit discharge. Science, 193: 240–242, 1976.

Siegel, J.M. and McGinty, D.J. Pontine reticular formation neurons: Relationship of discharge to motor activity. Science, 196: 678–680, 1977.

Siegel, J.M., McGinty, D.J., and Breedlove, S.M. Sleep and waking activity of pontine gigantocellular field neurons. Experimental Neurology, 56: 553–573, 1977.

Siegel, J.M., Wheeler, R.L., Breedlove, S.M., and McGinty, D.J. Brainstem units related to movements of the pinna. Brain Research, 202: 183–188, 1980.

Siegel, J.M., Wheeler, R.L., and McGinty, D.J. Activity of medullary reticular formation neurons in the unrestrained cat during waking and sleep. Brain Research, 179: 49–60, 1979.

Siegfried, B. and Bureš, J. Handedness in rats: Blockage of reaching behavior by unilateral 6-OHDA injections into substantia nigra and caudate nucleus. Physiological Psychology, 8: 360–368, 1980.

Siegfried, B., Fischer, J., and Bureš, J. Intracranial colchicine impairs lateralized reaching in rats. Neuroscience, 5: 529–541, 1980.

Silverman, A.P. Rodent's defense against cigarette smoke. Animal Behavior, 26: 1279–1281, 1978.

Simons, B.J. Causes of excessive drinking in diabetes insipidus. Nature, 219: 1061–1062, 1968.

Simpson, G.G. Principles of animal taxonomy. New York: Columbia University Press, 1961.

Skinner, B.F. The behavior of organisms. New York: Appleton-Century-Crofts, 1938.

Skinner, B.F. Are theories of learning necessary? Psychological Review, 57: 193–216, 1950.

Skinner, B.F. What is the experimental analysis of behavior? Journal of the Experimental Analysis of Behavior, 9: 213–218, 1966.

Skinner, B.F. About behaviorism. New York: Knopf, 1974.

Slonaker, J.R. The normal activity of the albino rat from birth to natural death, its rate of growth and the duration of life. Journal of Animal Behavior, 2: 20–42, 1912.

Slotnick, B.V. Disturbances of maternal behavior in the rat following lesions of the cingulate cortex. Behaviour, 29: 204–236, 1967.

Smith, D.C. Developmental alterations in binocular competitive interactions and visual acuity in visually deprived cats. Journal of Comparative Neurology, 198: 667–676, 1981a.

Smith, D.C. Functional restoration of vision in the cat after long-term monocular deprivation. Science, 213: 1137–1139, 1981b.

Smith, D.C., Holdefer, R.N., and Reeves, T.M. The visual field in monocularly deprived cats and its permanence. Behavioral Brain Research, 5: 245–259, 1982a.

Smith, D.C. Holdefer, R.N., and Reeves, T.M. Visual acuity following unequal alternating monocular deprivation in the cat. Investigative Opthalmology and Visual Science (Suppl.), 22: 90, 1982b.

Smith, D.C., Spear, P.D., and Kratz, K.E. Role of visual experience in postcritical-period reversal of effects of monocular deprivation in cat striate cortex. Journal of Comparative Neurology, 178: 313–328, 1978.

Soso, M.J. and Fetz, E.E. Responses of identified cells in postcentral cortex of awake monkeys during comparable activity and passive joint movements. Journal of Neurophysiology, 43: 1090–1110, 1980.

Spear, P.D., Langsetmo, A., and Smith, D.C. Age-related changes in effects of monocular deprivation on cat striate cortex neurons. Journal of Neurophysiology, 43, 559–580, 1980.

Sperry, R.W. Restoration of vision after crossing of optic nerves and after contralateral transplantation of eye. Journal of Neurophysiology, 8: 15–28, 1945.

Sperry, R.W. Cerebral regulation of motor coordination in monkeys following multiple transection of sensorimotor cortex. Journal of Neurophysiology 10: 275–294, 1947.

Sperry, R.W. Mechanisms of neural maturation. In S. Stevens (Ed.), Handbook of experimental psychology. New York: Wiley, 1951.

Sperry, R.W. Neurology and the mind-brain problem. American Scientist, 40: 291–312, 1952.

Spiliotis, P.H. and Thompson, R. The "manipulative response memory system" in the white rat. Physiological Psychology, 1: 101–114, 1973.

Sprague, J.M., Levy, J., DiBerardino, A., and Berlucchi, G. Visual cortical areas mediating form discrimination in the cat. Journal of Comparative Neurology, 172: 441–488, 1977.

Sprague, J.M. and Meikle, T.H., Jr. The role of the superior colliculus in visually guided behavior. Experimental Neurology, 11: 115–146, 1965.

Stamm, J.S. Effects of cortical lesions on established hoarding activity in rats. Journal of Comparative and Physiological Psychology, 46: 299–304, 1953.

Stamm, J.S. The function of the median cerebral cortex in maternal behavior in rats. Journal of Comparative and Physiological Psychology, 48: 347–356, 1955.

Steele, M.K., Rowland, D., and Moltz, H. Initiation of maternal behavior in the rat: Possible involvement of limbic norepinephrine. Pharmacology, Biochemistry, and Behavior, 11: 123–130, 1979.

Stein, B.E., Clamann, H.P., and Goldberg, S.J. Superior colliculus: Control of eye movements in neonatal kittens. Science, 210: 78–80, 1980.

Stein, B.E., Labos, E., and Kruger, L. Sequence of changes in properties of neurons of superior colliculus of the kitten during maturation. Journal of Neurophysiology, 36: 667–679, 1973.

Stellar, J.R., Brooks, F.H., and Mills, L.E. Approach and withdrawal analysis of the effects of hypothalamic stimulation and lesions in rats. Journal of Comparative and Physiological Psychology, 93: 446–466, 1979.

Stephan, H. and Andy, O.J. Quantitative comparative neuroanatomy of primates: An attempt at a phylogenetic interpretation. Annals of the New York Academy of Sciences, 167: 370–387, 1969.

Steriade, M. Cortical long-axoned cells and putative interneurons during the sleep-waking cycle. Behavioral and Brain Sciences, 3: 465–514, 1978.

Striade, M. and Hobson, J.A. Neuronal activity during the sleep-waking cycle. Progress in Neurobiology, 6: 155–376, 1976.

Sterman, M.B. and Fairchild, M.D. Modification of locomotor performance by reticular formation and basal forebrain stimulation in the cat: Evidence for reciprocal systems. Brain Research, 2: 205–217, 1966.

Stone, A.A. Consciousness: Altered levels in blind retarded children. Psychosomatic Medicine, 24: 14–19, 1964.

Storr, A. Human aggression. London: Allen Lane, 1968.

Strauss, A.A. and Kephart, N.C. Psychopathology and education of the brain injured child. New York: Grune, 1955.

Stricker, E.M., Cooper, P.H., Marshall, J.F., and Zigmond, M.J. Acute homeostatic imbalances reinstate sensorimotor dysfunctions in rats with lateral hypothalamic lesions. Journal of Comparative and Physiological Psychology, 93: 512–521, 1979.

Strumwasser, F. Long-term recording from single neurons in brain of unrestrained mammals. Science, 127: 469–470, 1958.

Sun, C.L. and Gatipon, G.B. Effects of morphine sulfate on medial bulbo-reticular response to peripherally applied noxious stimuli. Experimental Neurology, 52: 1–12, 1976.

Sutherland, R.J. The effects of amygdala lesions upon neophobia, exploration, and autosexual behavior in the rat. Unpublished Honours Thesis, University of Toronto, 1974.

Sutherland, R.J. The dorsal diencephalic conduction system. A review of the anatomy and function of the habenular complex. Neuroscience and Biobehavioral Reviews, 6: 1–13, 1982.

Sutherland, R.J. and Nakajima, S. Taste preferences induced by trains of rewarding lateral hypothalamic stimulation of differing durations. Physiology and Behavior, 24: 633–636, 1980.

Sutherland, R.J. and Nakajima, S. Self-stimulation of the habenular complex in the rat. Journal of Comparative and Physiological Psychology, 95:781–791, 1981.

Svorad, D. "Animal hypnosis": (Totstell reflex) as an experimental model for psychiatry: Electroencephalographic and evolutionary aspect. AMA Archives of Neurology and Psychiatry, 77: 533–539, 1957.

Takahashi, L.K. and Lore, R.K. Foraging and food hoarding of wild *Rattus norvegicus* in an urban enviornment. Behavioral and Neural Biology, 29: 527–531, 1980.

Taylor, J. Selected writings of John Hughlings Jackson. London: Staples Press, 1958.

Teitelbaum, P., Schallert, T., DeRyck, M., Whishaw, I.Q., and Golani, I. Motor subsystems in motivated behavior. In R.F. Thompson (Ed.), Neuropsychological mechanisms of goal-directed behavior and learning. New York: Academic Press, 1980, pp. 127–143.

Teitelbaum, P., Wolgin, D.L., DeRyck, M., and Marin, O.S.M. Bandage-backfall reaction: Occurs in infancy, hypothalamic damage, and catalepsy. Proceedings of the National Academy of Sciences, 73: 3311–3314, 1976.

Terlecki, L.J., Pinel, J.P.J., and Treit, D. Conditioned and unconditioned defensive burying in the rat. Learning and Motivation, 10: 337–350, 1979.

Terlecki, L.J. and Sainsbury, R.S. Effects of fimbria lesions on maternal behavior in the rat. Physiology and Behavior, 21: 89–97, 1978.

Teschke, E.J., Maser, J.D., and Gallup, G.G. Cortical involvement in tonic immobility ("animal hypnosis"): Effect of spreading cortical depression. Behavioral Biology, 13: 139–143, 1975.

Teuber, H.-L. Physiological psychology. Annual Review of Psychology, 6: 267–296, 1955.

Teuber, H.-L., Battersby, W.S., and Bender, M.B. Visual field defects after penetrating missile wounds of the brain. Cambridge, MA: Harvard University Press, 1960.

Thomae, H. Die Periodek in Kindlichen Verhalten. Gottingen, Verlag, fuer Psychologie, 1957.

Thompson, R. Localization of the "visual memory system" in the white rat. Journal of Comparative and Physiological Psychology, 69: 4(pt. 2), 1969.

Thompson, R.F. Introduction to physiological psychology. New York: Harper & Row, 1975.

Thompson, R. A behavioral atlas of the rat brain. New York: Oxford University Press, 1978.

Thompson, R., Gates, C.E., and Gross, S.A. Thalamic regions critical for retention of skilled movements in the rat. Physiological Psychology, 7: 7–21, 1979.

Thorn, F., Gollender, M., and Erickson, P. The development of the kitten's visual optics. Vision Research, 16: 1145–1149, 1976.

Tilney, F. Behavior in its relation to the development of the brain. Bulletin of the Neurological Institute of New York, 3: 252–358, 1933.

Timney, B. Development of binocular depth perception in kittens. Investigative Opthalmology and Visual Science, 21: 493–496, 1981.

Tinbergen, N. The study of instinct. London: Oxford University Press, 1951.

Tinbergen, N. On the aims and methods of ethology. Zeitschrift für Tierpsychologie, 20: 410–433, 1963.

Tinbergen, N. Animal behavior. New York: Time-Life Books, 1965.

Tinbergen, N. The animal in its world: Explorations of an ethologist (Vol. 1). London: Allen & Unwin, 1972.

Tinbergen, N. The animal in its world: Explorations of an ethologist (Vol. 2). London: Allen & Unwin, 1973.

Toth, D.M. Temperature regulation and salivation following preoptic lesions in the rat. Journal of Comparative and Physiological Psychology, 82: 480–488, 1973.

Treit, D., Pinel, J.P.J., and Terlecki, L.J. Shock intensity and conditioned defensive burying in rats. Bulletin of the Psychonomic Society, 16: 5–7, 1980.

Treit, D., Pinel, J.P.J., and Fibiger, H.C. Conditioned defensive burying: A new paradigm for the study of anxiolytic agents. Pharmacology, Biochemistry, and Behavior, 619–626, 1981.

Treit, D., Terlecki, L.J., and Pinel, J.P.J. Conditioned defensive burying: Organismic variables. Bulletin of the Psychonomic Society, 16: 451–454, 1980.

Turner, B.H. Neural structures involved in the rage syndrome of the rat. Journal of Comparative and Physiological Psychology, 71: 103–113, 1970.

Turner, B.H. Sensorimotor syndrome produced by lesions of the amygdala and lateral hypothalamus. Journal of Comparative and Physiological Psychology, 82: 37–47, 1973.

Twitchell, T.E. The restoration of motor function following hemiplegia in man. Brain, 74: 443–480, 1951.

Twitchell, T.E. The automatic grasping response of infants. Neuropsychologia, 3: 247–259, 1965.

Umemoto, M., Murai, Y., Kodama, M., and Kido, R. Neuronal discharge patterns in conditioned emotional response. Brain Research, 24: 347–351, 1970.

Ungerstedt, U. and Arbuthnott, G.W. Quantitative recording of rotational behavior in rats after 6-hydroxydopamine lesions of the nigrostriatal dopamine system. Brain Research, 24: 485–493, 1970.

Urbaitis, J.C. and Meikle, T.H., Jr. Relearning a dark-light discrimination by cats after cortical and collicular lesions. Experimental Neurology, 20: 295–311, 1968.

Uttal, W.R. The psychobiology of mind. Hillsdale, NJ: Lawrence Erlbaum Assoc., 1978.

Vanderwolf, C.H. Medial thalamic functions in voluntary behavior. Canadian Journal of Psychology, 16: 318–330, 1962.

Vanderwolf, C.H. The effect of medial thalamic lesions on previously established fear-motivated behavior. Canadian Journal of Psychology, 17: 183–187, 1963.

Vanderwolf, C.H. Effects of experimental diencephalic damage on food hoarding and shock avoidance behavior in the rat. Physiology and Behavior, 2: 399–402, 1967.

Vanderwolf, C.H. Hippocampal electrical activity and voluntary movement in the rat. Electroencephalography and Clinical Neurophysiology, 26: 407–418, 1969.

Vanderwolf, C.H. Limbic-diencephalic mechanisms of voluntary movement. Psychological Review, 78: 83–113, 1971.

Vanderwolf, C.H. The role of the cerebral cortex and ascending activating systems in the control of behavior. In E. Satinoff and P. Teitelbaum (Eds.), Handbook of behavioral neurobiology: Motivation. New York: Plenum Press, in press.

Vanderwolf, C.H., Kolb, B., and Cooley, R.K. Behavior of the rat after removal of the neocortex and hippocampal formation. Journal of Comparative and Physiological Psychology, 92: 156–175, 1978.

Vanderwolf, C.H. and Robinson, T.E. Reticulo-cortical activity and behavior: A critique of the arousal theory and a new synthesis. Behavioral and Brain Sciences, 4: 459–514, 1981.

van Hof-Van Duin, J. Visual field measurements in monocularly deprived and normal cats. Experimental Brain Research, 30: 353–368, 1977.

Van Sluyters, R.C. Reversal of the physiological effects of brief periods of monocular deprivation in the kitten. Journal of Physiology, 284: 1–17, 1978.

Van Sluyters, R.C. and Freeman, R.D. The physiological effects of brief periods of monocular deprivation in very young kittens. Neuroscience Abstracts, 3: 433, 1977.

Vertes, R.P. Selective firing of rat pontine gigantocellular neurons during movement and REM sleep. Brain Research, 128: 146–152, 1977.

Vertes, R.P. Brain stem gigantocellular neurons: Patterns of activity during behavior and sleep in the freely moving rat. Journal of Neurophysiology, 42: 214–228, 1979.

Vertes, R.P. and Miller, N.E. Brain stem neurons that fire selectively to a conditioned stimulus for shock. Brain Research, 103: 229–242, 1976.

Villablanca, J.R. and Olmstead, C.E. Neurological development of kittens. Developmental Psychobiology, 12: 101–127, 1979.

Vincent, S.B. The function of the vibrissae in the behavior of the white rat. Behavior Monographs, 1: 7–85, 1912.

Vincent, S.B. The tactile hair of the white rat. Journal of Comparative Neurology, 23: 1–36, 1913.

Wagner, H.N. and Woods, J.W. Interruption of bulbocapnine catalepsy in rats by environmental stress. Archives of Neurology and Psychiatry, 64: 720–725, 1950.

Walker, A.E. and Fulton, J.F. Hemidecortication in chimpanzee, baboon, macaque, potto, cat and coati mundi. A study of encephalization. Journal of Nervous and Mental Diseases, 87: 677–700, 1938.

Wallace, R.J. and Tigner, J.C. Effect of cortical and hippocampal lesions on hoarding behavior in the albino rat. Physiology and Behavior, 8: 937–942, 1972.

Wan, Y.K. and Cragg, B. Cell growth in the lateral geniculate nucleus of kittens following the opening or closing of one eye. Journal of Comparative Neurology, 166: 365–372, 1976.

Warren, J.M. Learning in vertebrates. In D.A. Dewsbury and D.A. Rethlingshafer (Eds.), Comparative psychology. New York: McGraw-Hill, 1973.

Warren, J.M. A phylogenetic approach to learning and intelligence. In A. Oliverio (Ed.), Genetics, environment and intelligence. Amsterdam: Elsevier, 1977, pp. 37–56.

Warren, J.M., Cornwell, P.B., and Warren, H.B. Unilateral frontal lesions and learning by rhesus monkeys. Journal of Comparative and Physiological Psychology, 69: 498–505, 1969.

Warren, J.M. and Kolb, B. Generalization in neuropsychology. In S. Finger (Ed.), Recovery from brain damage. New York: Plenum Press, 1978.

Watson, J.B. Psychology as the behaviorist views it. Psychology Review, 20: 158–177, 1913.

Webster, W.G. Functional asymmetry between the cerebral hemispheres of the cat. Neuropsychologia, 10: 75–87, 1972.

Webster, W.G. Functional asymmetry between the cerebral hemispheres of the cat brain. Physiology and Behavior, 14: 867–868, 1975.

Weiskrantz, L., Warrington, E., Sanders, M.D., and Marshall, J. Visual capacity in the hemianopic field following a restricted occipital ablation. Brain, 97: 709–728, 1974.

Weisman, R.M., Hamilton, L.W., and Carlton, P.L. Increased gustatory aversion following VMH lesions in rats. Physiology and Behavior, 9: 801–804, 1972.

Weiss, P.A. Genetic neurology. Chicago: University of Chicago Press, 1950.

Welker, W.I. Analysis of sniffing of the albino rat. Behaviour, 22: 233–244, 1964.

Whalen, R.E., In Whalen, R.E., Thompson, R.F., Verzeano, M., and Weinberger, N.M. (Eds.), The neural control of behavior. New York: Academic Press, 1970.

Whalen, R.E. Brain mechanisms controlling sexual behavior. In F.A. Beach, (Ed.), Human sexuality. Baltimore: Johns Hopkins University Press, 1977, pp. 215–246.

Whillans, K.V. and Shettleworth, S.J. Defensive burying in rats and hamsters. Animal Learning and Behavior, 9: 357–362, 1981.

Whishaw, I.Q. Light avoidance in normal rats and rats with primary visual system lesions. Physiological Psychology, 2: 143–147, 1974.

Whishaw, I.Q. The Parkinsonian model rat: A color film. University of Lethbridge, 1979.

Whishaw, I.Q. and Cooper, R.M. Strychnine and suppression of exploration. Physiology and Behavior, 5: 647–649, 1970.

Whishaw, I.Q. and Kolb, B. Neocortical and hippocampal EEG in rats during lateral hypothalamic lesion-induced hyperkinesia: Relations to behavior and effects of atropine. Physiology and Behavior, 22: 1107–1113, 1979.

Whishaw, I.Q. and Kolb, B. Can male decorticate rats copulate? Behavioral Neuroscience, 1983, in press.

Whishaw, I.Q., Kolb, B., Sutherland, R.J., and Becker, J.B. Cortical control of claw cutting in the rat. Behavioral Neuroscience, 1983, in press.

Whishaw, I.Q., Nonneman, A.J. and Kolb, B. Environmental constraints on motor abilities used in grooming, swimming, and eating by decorticate rats. Journal of Comparative and Physiological Psychlogy, 95: 792–804, 1981.

Whishaw, I.Q. and Robinson, T.E. Comparison of anodal and cathodal lesions and metal deposition in eliciting postoperative locomotion in the rat. Physiology and Behavior, 13: 539–551, 1974.

Whishaw, I.Q., Robinson, T.E., Schallert, T., DeRyck, M., and Ramirez, V.D. Electrical activity of the hippocampus and neocortex in rats depleted of brain dopamine and norepinephrine: Relations to behavior and effects of atropine. Experimental Neurology, 62: 748–767, 1978.

Whishaw, I.Q. and Schallert, T. Hippocampal RSA (theta), apnea, bradycardia and effects of atropine during underwater swimming in the rat. Electroencephalography and Clinical Neurophysiology, 42: 389–396, 1977.

Whishaw, I.Q., Schallert, T., and Kolb, B. The thermal control of immobility in developing infant rats: Is the neocortex involved? Physiology and Behavior, 23: 757–762, 1979.

Whishaw, I.Q., Schallert, T., and Kolb, B. An analysis of feeding and sensorimotor abilities of rats after decortication. Journal of Comparative and Physiological Psychology, 95: 85–103, 1981.

Whishaw, I.Q. and Vanderwolf, C.H. Hippocampal EEG and behavior: Changes in amplitude and frequency of RSA (theta rhythm) associated with spontaneous and learned movement patterns in rats and cats. Behavioral Biology, 8: 461–484, 1973.

Wiener, N.I., Nobrega, J.N., Ossenkopp, K.P., and Shilman, D.M. Acute hyperkinesia after hypothalamic lesions: A comparison of the time course, level, and type of hyperkinesia induced by ventromedial and lateral hypothalmic lesions in rats. Experimental Neurology, 67: 346–362, 1980.

Wiesel, T.N. and Hubel, D.H. Single-cell responses in striate cortex of kittens deprived of vision in one eye. Journal of Neurophysiology, 26: 1003–1017, 1963.

Wiesel, T.N. and Hubel, D.H. Comparison of the effects of unilateral and bilateral eye closure on cortical unit responses in kittens. Journal of Neurophysiology, 28: 1029–1040, 1965.

Wiesner, B.P. and Sheard, N.M. Maternal behaviour in the rat. London: Oliver and Boyd, 1933.

Wilkie, D.M., MacLennan, A.J., and Pinel, J.P.J. Rat defensive behavior: Burying noxious food. Journal of the Experimental Analysis of Behavior, 31: 299–306, 1979.

Wilkinson, F.E. Reversal of the behavioral effects of monocular deprivation as a function of age in the kitten. Behavioral Brain Research, 1: 101–123, 1980.

Wilson, J.R. and Sherman, S.M. Differential effects of early monocular deprivation on binocular and monocular segments of cat striate cortex. Journal of Neurophysiology, 40: 891–903, 1977.

Wilsoncroft, W.E. Effects of medial cortex lesions on maternal behavior of the rat. Psychological Reports, 13: 835–838, 1963.

Winson, J. and Abzug, C. Neuronal transmission through hippocampal pathways dependent on behavior. Journal of Neurophysiology, 41: 716–732, 1978.

Wishart, T., Brohman, L., and Mogenson, G. Effects of lesions of the hippocampus and septum on hoarding behavior. Animal Behaviour, 17: 781–784, 1969.

Wishart, T.B. and Walls, E.K. Water intoxication and death following hypothalamic lesions in the rat. Physiology and Behavior, 15: 377–379, 1975.

Wolman, B.B. and Nagel, E. Scientific psychology. New York: Basic Books, 1965.

Woodruff, M.L. and Bailey, S.D. Hippocampal lesions and immobility responses in the rat. Physiological Psychology, 7: 254–258, 1979.

Woods, J.W. Behavior of chronic decerebrate rats. Journal of Neurophysiology, 27: 635–644, 1964.

Woods, J.W. "Taming" of the wild Norway rat by rhinencephalic lesions. Nature, 178: 869, 1956.

Woodworth, R.S. and Schlosberg, H. Experimental psychology. New York: Holt, 1960.

Wooldridge, M.W. A quantitative analysis of short-term rhythmical behavior in rodents, Unpublished Ph.D. thesis, Oxford University, 1975.

Wright, H.F. Observational child study. In P.H. Mussen (Ed.), Handbook of research methods in child development. New York: Wiley, 1960.

Wurtz, R.H., Goldberg, M.E., and Robinson, D.L. Behavioral modulation of visual responses in the monkey: Stimulus selection for attention and movement. Progress in Psychobiology and Physiological Psychology, 9: 43–83, 1980.

Yokota, T. and Hashimoto, S. Periaqueductal gray and tooth pulp afferent interaction on units in caudal medulla oblongata. Brain Research, 117: 508–512, 1976.

Young, D.W. and Gottschaldt, K.M. Neurons in the rostral mesencephalic reticular formation of the cat responding specifically to noxious mechanical stimulation. Experimental Neurology, 51: 628–636, 1976.

Young, P.T. Emotion in man and animal. New York: Wiley, 1943.

Yutzey, D.A., Meyer, P.M., and Meyer, D.R. Emotionality changes following septal and neocortical ablations in rats. Journal of Comparative and Physiological Psychology, 58: 463–465, 1964.

Zeigler, H.P. and Karten, H.J. Central trigeminal structures and the lateral hypothalamic syndrome in the rat. Science, 186: 636–637, 1974.

Zimbardo, P.G. and Montgomery, K.C. Effects of "free-environment" rearing upon exploratory behavior. Psychological Reports, 3: 589–594, 1957.

Zinsser, H. Rats, lice and history. New York: Bantam Books, 1934.

Author Index

Subject Index